MOZART I

MW00809933

The vibrant intellectual, social and political climate of mid eighteenth-century Europe presented opportunities and challenges for
artists and musicians alike. This book focusses on Mozart the man
and musician as he responds to different aspects of that world.
It reveals his views on music, aesthetics and other matters; on places
in Austria and across Europe that shaped his life; on career contexts
and environments, including patronage, activities as an impresario,
publishing, theatrical culture and financial matters; on engagement
with performers and performance, focussing on Mozart's experiences
as a practising musician; and on reception and legacy from his own
time through to the present day. Probing diverse Mozartian contexts
in a variety of ways, the contributors reflect the vitality of existing
scholarship and point towards areas primed for further study. This
volume is essential reading for students and scholars of late eighteenth-century music and for Mozart aficionados and music-lovers in
general.

SIMON P. KEEFE is James Rossiter Hoyle Chair of Music at the
University of Sheffield. He is the author of four books on Mozart,
including *Mozart in Vienna: The Final Decade* (Cambridge University
Press, 2017) and *Mozart's Requiem: Reception, Work, Completion*
(Cambridge University Press, 2012), which won the Marjorie
Weston Emerson Award from the Mozart Society of America. He is
also the editor of six volumes for Cambridge University Press, includ-
ing *Mozart Studies* and *Mozart Studies 2*. In 2005 he was elected a life
member of the Academy for Mozart Research at the International
Mozart Foundation in Salzburg.

Understanding and appreciation of musical works is greatly enhanced by knowledge of the context within which their composers lived and worked. Each of these volumes focusses on an individual composer, offering lively, accessible and concise essays by leading scholars on the many contexts – professional, political, intellectual, social and cultural – that have a bearing on his or her work. Biographical and musical influences, performance and publishing history and the creative afterlife of each composer's work are also addressed, providing readers with a multi-faceted view of how the composers' output and careers were shaped by the world around them.

Titles forthcoming in the series

Brahms in Context edited by Natasha Loges and Katy Hamilton
The Beatles in Context edited by Kenneth Womack
Beethoven in Context edited by Glenn Stanley and John D. Wilson
Richard Strauss in Context edited by Morten Kristiansen and Joseph E. Jones

MOZART IN CONTEXT

EDITED BY

SIMON P. KEEFE

University of Sheffield

CAMBRIDGE
UNIVERSITY PRESS

CAMBRIDGE
UNIVERSITY PRESS

University Printing House, Cambridge CB2 8BS, United Kingdom

One Liberty Plaza, 20th Floor, New York, NY 10006, USA

477 Williamstown Road, Port Melbourne, VIC 3207, Australia

314-321, 3rd Floor, Plot 3, Splendor Forum, Jasola District Centre, New Delhi - 110025, India

79 Anson Road, #06-04/06, Singapore 079906

Cambridge University Press is part of the University of Cambridge.

It furthers the University's mission by disseminating knowledge in the pursuit of education, learning and research at the highest international levels of excellence.

www.cambridge.org
Information on this title: www.cambridge.org/9781316632444
DOI: 10.1017/9781316848487

First published 2019
First paperback edition 2019

A catalogue record for this publication is available from the British Library

Library of Congress Cataloging in Publication data
NAMES: Keefe, Simon P., 1968–
TITLE: Mozart in Context / edited by Simon P. Keefe.
DESCRIPTION: Cambridge, United Kingdom ; New York, NY : Cambridge University Press,
[2018] | Includes bibliographical references and index.
IDENTIFIERS: LCCN 2018042045 | ISBN 9781107181052 (alk. paper)
SUBJECTS: LCSH: Mozart, Wolfgang Amadeus, 1756–1791. | Composers – Austria – Biography.
CLASSIFICATION: LCC ML410.M9 M7125 2018 | DDC 780.92–dc23
LC record available at https://lccn.loc.gov/2018042045

ISBN 978-1-107-18105-2 Hardback
ISBN 978-1-316-63244-4 Paperback

Contents

Illustrations

Tables

Musical Examples

Preface

Mozart in Context provides musical, cultural and historical background for approaching and appreciating the output of one of Western music's most famous sons. Careful contextualization of Mozart's achievements through the refinement and broadening of scholarly content and methodology has been an important thrust of Mozart studies over the last half-century or so, in tandem with – and building on – philological and documentary discoveries. The time is right for a single volume from late eighteenth-century specialists capturing recent developments and simultaneously offering new perspectives on Mozart interpretation.

This volume is organized into five parts, each one representative of a different constellation of contextual themes. 'Personality, Work, Worldview' homes in on Mozart the man and musician, interacting with others, working and revealing views on music, aesthetics and other matters. 'Towns, Cities, Countries' looks at places in Austria and across Europe that shaped the life of a much-travelled musician, setting Mozart's activities in these specific locations into musical, cultural and historical relief. 'Career Contexts and Environments' puts the constituent parts of Mozart's livelihood into perspective, examining patronage, activities as an impresario, publishing, theatrical culture and financial matters. 'Performers and Performance' evaluates Mozart's engagement with individual musicians as well as his own experiences as a practising musician. And 'Reception and Legacy' surveys understandings of Mozart's music from his own time through to the present day, focussing on the cataloguing of works, his influence on nineteenth-century composers and the recording of his music in addition to more standard reception-related topics such as critical and biographical trends and impact on theoretical and analytical modes of inquiry. By probing diverse Mozartian contexts in a variety of ways, the contributors collectively hope to reflect the vitality of existing scholarship and to stimulate further study.

The nineteenth-century philosopher and Mozart devotee Søren Kierkegaard famously stated in *Either/Or* (1843) that 'if ever Mozart became wholly comprehensible to me, he would then become fully incomprehensible to me'. There is no limit to our investigation of the contexts surrounding and informing Mozart's oeuvre and consequently no restriction on how we try to process and understand his own world and, indeed, the worlds we have created for him and in reaction to him. If the results of studying Mozart in multifarious contexts sometimes make him seem more distant from us than closer to us, we need be neither disappointed nor frustrated. Our large and small philological, documentary, critical and hermeneutic findings, however we interpret and process them relative to past work and aspirations for future understandings, invariably enhance – rather than give cause to challenge – Mozart's extraordinary status in western culture.

I am grateful to the Stiftung Mozarteum/Mozart-Museen und Archiv in Salzburg and Sotherby's in London for permission to reproduce the images in Chapter 8.

Contributors

LISA DE ALWIS, University of Colorado, Boulder, USA

PAUL CORNEILSON, The Packard Humanities Institute, Los Altos and Cambridge, USA

SERGIO DURANTE, University of Padua, Italy

EDMUND J. GOEHRING, University of Western Ontario, London, Canada

CHRISTOPH GROßPIETSCH, Stiftung Mozarteum Salzburg, Austria

MARTIN HARLOW, Royal Northern College of Music, Manchester, UK

JOHN IRVING, Trinity College of Music, London, UK

DAVID WYN JONES, Cardiff University, UK

SIMON P. KEEFE, University of Sheffield, UK

EDWARD KLORMAN, McGill University, Montreal, Canada

ULRICH LEISINGER, Stiftung Mozarteum Salzburg, Austria

KATHRYN LIBIN, Vassar College, Poughkeepsie, USA

DOROTHEA LINK, University of Georgia, Athens, USA

JEAN-PAUL C. MONTAGNIER, University of Lorraine, Nancy, France

ADELINE MUELLER, Mount Holyoke College, South Hadley, USA

SARAH POTTER, University of Leeds, UK

RUPERT RIDGEWELL, British Library, London, UK

STEPHEN RUMPH, University of Washington, Seattle, USA

HANNAH TEMPLETON, King's College London, UK

VIKTOR TÖPELMANN, Independent scholar, Germany

BERTIL VAN BOER, Western Washington University, Bellingham, USA

JESSICA WALDOFF, College of the Holy Cross, Worcester, USA

IAN WOODFIELD, Queen's University Belfast, UK

Abbreviations

LMF   Emily Anderson (trans. and ed.), *The Letters of Mozart and his Family*. 3rd edn. London: Macmillan, 1985.

MBA   Wilhelm A. Bauer, Otto Erich Deutsch and Joseph Heinz Eibl (eds.), *Mozart: Briefe und Aufzeichnungen, Gesamtausgabe*. 8 vols. Kassel: Bärenreiter, 1962–2005.

MDB   Otto Erich Deutsch, *Mozart: A Documentary Biography*. Translated by Eric Blom, Peter Branscombe and Jeremy Noble. 3rd edn. London: Simon & Schuster, 1990.

MDL   Otto Erich Deutsch, *Mozart: Die Dokumente seines Leben*. Kassel: Bärenreiter, 1961.

NMA   Wolfgang Amadeus Mozart, *Neue Ausgabe sämtlicher Werke*. Kassel: Bärenreiter, 1955–2007.

NMD   Cliff Eisen (ed.), *New Mozart Documents: A Supplement to O. E. Deutsch's Documentary Biography*. London and Palo Alto, CA: Stanford University Press, 1991.

PART I

Personality, Work, Worldview

CHAPTER I

Personal Relationships

Simon P. Keefe

As a cosmopolitan man who travelled extensively from his early childhood years onwards, Mozart had opportunities to meet and get to know a broader range of people across Europe than almost any other musician of his generation. Sociable and with a lively sense of humour, Mozart enjoyed the company of family and friends at home in Salzburg and Vienna as well as abroad, a fact amply revealed in his correspondence.

At every stage of life, Mozart maintained a range of friendships – some close, others ostensibly more functional – with individuals from different echelons of society, the lion's share connected in one way or another with music. Probably the best-known friendship grounded in mutual musical respect was with Joseph Haydn. The composers may have first met in December 1783 at concerts put on by the Tonkünstler-Societät in Vienna (an organization that came to the aid of families of deceased musicians). They certainly became well acquainted in early 1785 when reading through together Mozart's first six Viennese string quartets. At one such occasion, on 12 February 1785, Haydn famously commented to Mozart's father Leopold, who was visiting the imperial capital: 'I say to you before God and as an honest man that your son is the greatest composer I know in person or by name. He has taste and more than that the greatest compositional knowledge.'[1] Mozart dedicated the quartets to Haydn a few months later, referring to him six times in a single paragraph of Italian text printed at the beginning of the first edition as a dear friend or best friend ('mio caro amico', 'migliore amico' and 'amico carissimo').[2] Meetings were apparently a regular occurrence in late 1790, including for renditions of Mozart's string quintets (according to theologian, musician and Mozart associate Maximilian Stadler). Haydn's early biographer

---

[1] See MBA, vol. 3, p. 373; LMF, p. 886 (16 February 1785). All translations from MBA are my own, unless otherwise indicated.

[2] For the complete dedication from the edition published by Vienna-based Artaria, see MDL, p. 220 and MDB, p. 250; MBA, vol. 3, p. 404 and LMF, pp. 891–92 (1 September 1785).

Albert Christoph Dies, who interviewed him repeatedly between 1805 and 1808, reports a poignant farewell to coincide with Haydn setting off for London on 15 December 1790: 'Mozart on this day never left his friend Haydn. He dined with him, and said at the moment of parting, "We are probably saying our last farewell in this life." Tears welled from the eyes of both.'[3]

When resident in Vienna during his last decade (1781–91), Mozart was on friendly terms with members of the nobility and with other influential people. They included Countess Thun, one of his main Viennese patrons and, as of spring 1781, 'the most charming, dearest lady I have met in my life';[4] Johann Michael Puchberg, a textile merchant and fellow mason to whom Mozart directed at least nineteen requests for loans between 1788 and 1791 and with whom music was played and discussed; Baron Raimund Wetzlar von Plankenstern, a supporter, one-time landlord and godfather to the Mozarts' first child (who bore his Christian name); and Baron Gottfried van Swieten, a diplomat, civil servant and longstanding admirer of Mozart, who integrated him into a Sunday-afternoon music circle in 1782 and a few years later commissioned from him reorchestrations of four of Handel's major works. It would have been in Mozart's financial and reputational interests to cultivate relationships of these kinds. He freely attributed friendliness with Johann Kilian Strack, a court official closely connected to Emperor Joseph II, to Strack's perceived influence and explained carefulness not to visit too often as a fear of revealing his true motives.[5] But vested interests did not preclude genuine affection for those of high rank. Baroness Waldstätten – a patron who lent him money, temporarily housed Constanze several times in 1781–82 and put on a lavish banquet to celebrate the Mozarts' wedding – received sociable letters from him, including a humorously flirtatious one.[6] Although Mozart may have benefitted from writing the aria 'Mentre ti lascio, o figlia' K. 513 for Gottfried von Jacquin and the 'Kegelstatt' trio K. 498 and the four-hand Piano Sonata K. 521 for pianist sister Franziska, not least by associating himself with a distinguished Viennese family, he also enjoyed a relaxed friendship with Gottfried: from Prague shortly before and after the premiere of *Don Giovanni*, Mozart joked about eventually

---

[3] Vernon Gotwals (ed. and trans.), *Haydn: Two Contemporary Portraits* (Madison, WI and London: University of Wisconsin Press, 1968), p. 121.

[4] MBA, vol. 1, p. 98; LMF, p. 717 (24 March 1781).

[5] MBA, vol. 3, pp. 194, 201; LMF, pp. 794, 799 (23 January 1782, 10 April 1782).

[6] For the flirtatious letter in question, see MBA, vol. 3, pp. 232–33; LMF, pp. 824–25 (2 October 1782).

receiving a letter from him, then gently and jovially advised him about the virtues of true love rather than transient obsession.[7]

The humour in letters to Jacquin and Waldstätten was a feature of Mozart's close friendships with a number of individuals. He teased virtuoso horn-player Joseph Leutgeb in works written for him: jocular annotations on the autograph score of the Horn Concerto K. 417 in E♭ (1783) express pity for a 'donkey, ox and fool'; similar notes on the autograph of K. 412 in D (1791) invite him to 'rest a little! ... rest! ... ah, the end please! ... the finish? thank heaven! stop, stop! ... You beast – what a noise [coinciding with f#″ that is difficult to hand stop]. Ouch! Alas!' He also subjected the hapless Leutgeb to a ruse in 1791: sending a message to say that an old friend from Rome had come to visit, Mozart was greatly amused at subsequently encountering Leutgeb dressed to the nines with hair elegantly coiffured.[8] Franz Xaver Süssmayr, Mozart's assistant in 1791 and completer of the Requiem in 1791–92, repeatedly had his leg pulled as an 'idiot', an ox, 'Sauermayr' (a play on 'süss'/sweet and 'sauer'/sour), a 'real ass', and a 'shitter'.[9] Anton Stoll, the choirmaster at Baden befriended by Mozart during visits to Constanze on her recuperative stays in the town, was also teased in rhyme, verse and scatology.[10] And banter formed part of the friendship between Mozart and Emanuel Schikaneder, librettist of *Die Zauberflöte* (1791), creator of the role of Papageno, and director of the Wiednertheater where the opera premiered: Mozart even caught him out in one live performance by cheerily messing about with the placement of glockenspiel chords accompanying Papageno in an aria.[11] Mozart's letters to his cousin Maria Thekla Mozart, with whom he clearly enjoyed a rambunctious relationship in the mid to late 1770s, are virtuoso essays in clever and humorous nonsense. For one critic: 'Mozart sets up the stage of the jester and verbal acrobat, adopting principally the role of uninhibitedly bragging jokester. What had no doubt been produced, quasi improvisationally, in front of his cousin in direct interaction and had been tested for immediate effect, now continues in letters'.[12] We can only speculate whether the fourteen-year-old Mozart's short,

---

[7] MBA, vol. 4, pp. 54–6, 58–9; LMF, pp. 911–14 (15–25 October, 4 November 1787).

[8] MBA, vol. 4, p. 141; LMF, p. 956 (25 June 1791).

[9] MBA, vol. 4, pp. 144, 147, 150, 158, 153; LMF, pp. 958, 961, 963, 967, 966 (2 July, 5 July, 7 July, 7–8 October, 12 July 1791).

[10] MBA, vol. 4, pp. 132, 152–53; LMF, pp. 950, 965–66 (end of May, 12 July 1791).

[11] For the description of this practical joke to Constanze, see MBA, vol. 4, p. 160; LMF, p. 969 (8–9 October 1791).

[12] Ulrich Konrad, 'Mozart the Letter Writer and His Language' (trans. William Buchanan), in Simon P. Keefe (ed.), *Mozart Studies 2* (Cambridge: Cambridge University Press, 2015), pp. 1–22, at 2.

heartfelt relationship with a prodigious violinist contemporary Thomas Linley had a jocular dimension. They met in Rome in spring 1770 and became fast friends; Mozart wrote warmly to Linley a few months later.[13]

For a composer who could claim to be 'stuck in music' less than a month after one of the most traumatic events to affect him in young adulthood, the death of his mother Maria Anna on 3 July 1778 in Paris, it is no surprise that personal and musical relationships were sometimes cut from the same cloth.[14] The aforementioned teasing of Leutgeb is reflected in music written for him, including a hesitant main theme at the end of the finale of the Horn Concerto K. 417 and a comically unpromising one, combined with playful solo material, in the corresponding movement of the Horn Quintet K. 407. Lighthearted references to the need for rest and for the end of the work on Leutgeb's part poignantly mirror a series of increasingly less demanding horn concertos for him between 1783 and 1791, as age took its toll.[15] (Leutgeb was fifty-nine in October 1791.) Converging biographical circumstances and musical experiences also brought together the personal and musical elements of relationships. Mozart became fond of the Mannheim-based Cannabich family in 1777–78, depicting daughter Rosa in the slow movement of a piano sonata (most likely K. 309 in C). When it became clear an appointment would not be forthcoming for him in Mannheim making departure inevitable, '[Rosa] played my sonata entirely seriously . . . I tell you, I could not contain my weeping. In the end, the mother, the daughter and the treasurer also had tears in their eyes. . . . [It] is the favourite [sonata] of the whole house.'[16] Mozart fell in love with Aloysia Weber at around the same time, primarily discussing her musical qualities when writing to his father.[17] Also, half of the text of Mozart's one extant letter to Aloysia is devoted to musical matters, including advice on how to interpret several arias (with a promise of more advice in

---

[13] For a description of their encounters and Mozart's extant letter to Linley, see MBA, vol. 1, pp. 338, 388–89; LMF, pp. 129–30, 160–61 (21 April 1770, 10 September 1770). Linley died in a boating accident in 1778, aged 22.

[14] For more on Mozart's responses to his mother's death, including detailed attention to musical experiences even at such a troubled time, see Simon P. Keefe, 'Mozart "Stuck in Music" in Paris (1778): Towards a New Biographical Paradigm', in Keefe (ed.), *Mozart Studies 2*, pp. 23–54, especially 25–35.

[15] For discussion of Mozart's works for Leutgeb, see Simon P. Keefe, *Mozart in Vienna: The Final Decade* (Cambridge: Cambridge University Press, 2017), chapters 3, 11 and 12. See also Konrad Küster, *Mozart: A Musical Biography*, trans. Mary Whittall (Cambridge: Cambridge University Press, 1996), pp. 227–33.

[16] MBA, vol. 2, p. 178; LMF, p. 414 (10 December 1777).

[17] See MBA, vol. 2, pp. 226–27, 253, 286–87; LMF pp. 447–48, 462, 485–86 (17 January, 4 February, 19 February 1778).

a subsequent letter).[18] Mozart's imagined future musical encounters with Aloysia are symbiotically linked to his love for her. And associations between the musical and the personal could work in negative as well as positive ways. It is reasonable to assume, for example, that Mozart's low opinion of composer Georg Joseph Vogler's music, performance and personality are not entirely unrelated.[19]

Mozart's deepest relationships were with family members. He and older sister Nannerl were close in childhood, sharing performing experiences among the great and the good across Europe as well as in more modest surroundings at home. In all probability the Concerto for two pianos in E♭, K. 365 (1779–80), was also written for the two of them to play together. While their relationship cooled somewhat after Mozart's move to Vienna in 1781, and was strained during the settlement of Leopold's estate in 1787, they seem to have enjoyed their three months together in 1783 when Mozart visited Salzburg with Constanze: Nannerl's diary from this period lists participation in a range of leisure activities and pastimes, including eating ices, drinking punch, shooting, bathing, talking walks, visiting friends and (of course) making music.[20] Constanze, younger sister of Aloysia and wife of Mozart from 4 August 1782 onwards, was apparently a good partner for him. Letters from husband to wife during trips to Leipzig, Dresden, Potsdam and Berlin in 1789 and central and southern Germany in 1790, and while Constanze was taking the waters in Baden in 1791, testify to a caring, affectionate and loving bond.

The best-documented family relationship is between Mozart and Leopold.[21] When Mozart travelled to Germany and France in 1777–79, accompanied by his mother, father and son initially wrote to each other every few days (with contributions from Maria Anna until her death); letters from Mozart decreased to one every two weeks or so in the final months of the trip. In Munich from November 1780 to January 1781 to prepare for the premiere of *Idomeneo*, Mozart wrote sixteen times to Leopold in an eleven-week period and father to son on twenty occasions.

---

[18] MBA, vol. 2, pp. 420–21; LMF, pp. 581–83 (30 July 1778).

[19] For representative criticism of Vogler from Mozart, see MBA, vol. 2, pp. 101–02, 119–20, 135, 197, 227–28, and vol. 3, p. 187; LMF, pp. 356, 369–70, 378, 428, 448–49, 789 (4 November, 13 November, 20 November, 18 December 1777, 17 January 1778, 22 December 1781).

[20] See MBA, vol. 3, pp. 282–91, and (given in tabular form), in Ruth Halliwell, *The Mozart Family: Four Lives in a Social Context* (Oxford: Clarendon Press, 1998), pp. 408–23.

[21] For differing critical perspectives on the relationship between Mozart and Leopold, see, for example, Halliwell, *The Mozart Family*; Maynard Solomon, *Mozart: A Life* (New York: HarperCollins, 1995); David P. Schroeder, *Mozart in Revolt: Strategies of Resistance, Mischief and Deception* (New Haven, CT: Yale University Press, 1999).

Once in Vienna, Mozart corresponded regularly between spring 1781 and mid 1784, but less frequently in the ensuing three years up to Leopold's death on 28 May 1787. (While letters from Leopold to Mozart in the Viennese years have not survived, some of their content can be surmised from Mozart's.)

Here and there, disputes between father and son are a feature of the correspondence. During the 1777–79 trip, Leopold worried about distraction from practical responsibilities by Mozart's 'head full of notes',[22] and doubted his judgment on (for example) musical opportunities, friends, and travel plans and timeframes. On one occasion, reading a Mozart letter from Mannheim (4 February 1778) with 'astonishment and horror' and unable to sleep from anxiety and frustration, Leopold responded apoplectically to his son's ambitious idea of accompanying Aloysia to Italy to help further her operatic career: 'Your proposal – I can hardly write when I think of it – the proposal to travel around with Herr [Weber] and, NB, his two daughters almost tested my sanity. My dearest son! How can you have let yourself be taken even for an hour by such abominable thoughts. Your letter is not unlike a novel. And could you really decide to move around the world with strangers?'[23] Shattered by his wife's death in Paris a few months later and by having to process it six hundred miles away in Salzburg, Leopold accused Mozart of paying insufficient attention to her wellbeing, also expressing frustration at the belated communication of full details of her demise. Leopold opposed Mozart's move to Vienna in 1781 and marriage to Constanze in 1782; judging by Mozart's responses to his father's letters, Leopold was fiercely critical of both.

But Mozart and Leopold's relationship was also a productive and positive one. While Leopold continued to teach and carry out court duties after coming to terms with the son he described as a 'miracle that God let be born in Salzburg', he also devoted considerable amounts of time and energy to planning and partaking in the lengthy European trips that were designed to promote Mozart's skills far afield. And the child Mozart responded affectionately, such as last thing at night by singing lullabies, kissing him repeatedly and promising protection in old age by putting him in a glass case.[24] In later years, father and son were at their best discussing specific musical and dramatic matters, including many about *Idomeneo* (1780–81): Leopold acted as intermediary between Mozart in Munich and

---

[22] MBA, vol. 2, p. 194; LMF, p. 425 (18 December 1777).
[23] MBA, vol. 2, pp. 272, 276; LMF, pp. 474, 477 (11–12 February 1778).
[24] As remembered by Leopold in MBA, vol. 2, p. 273; LMF, p. 475 (11–12 February 1778).

librettist Giambattista Varesco in Salzburg, advancing his own arguments about the plot, text and music of the opera as well. And, irrespective of cracks and fissures in their relationship, personal contact and correspondence continued until Leopold's death: Leopold was delighted to witness first hand Mozart's popularity in Vienna in spring 1785; and Mozart wrote sensitively and sympathetically of death as the 'true goal of our life' and the 'truest, best friend of mankind' on learning of a serious illness for his father about eight weeks before he died.[25]

By his own admission, Mozart was happiest expressing himself to Leopold in music: 'I cannot write in verse; I am no poet. I cannot arrange idioms so artistically that they provide light and shade; I am no painter. I cannot even express my views and thoughts through signs and through mime; I am no dancer. But I can do it through sounds; I am a musician. So tomorrow at Cannabich's I will play a whole congratulations for your name-day and your birthday'.[26] As so often in relationships, and interactions with the world in general, Mozart the man and musician merge seamlessly.

[25] MBA, vol. 4, p. 41; LMF, p. 907 (4 April 1787).
[26] MBA, vol. 2, pp. 110–11; LMF, p. 363 (8 November 1777).

CHAPTER 2

Learning and Teaching

Adeline Mueller

An Austrian Telemachus

In a postscript to a letter home from Bologna dated 8 September 1770, Mozart reported to his sister Nannerl that he was reading François de la Mothe-Fénelon's didactic novel *Les aventures de Télémaque* (1699, republished 1717) and 'had already reached part two'.[1] The overall tone of the postscript is more than a little perfunctory, unusually neutral for the siblings. We hear nothing further from him about his progress with the book, but we can be fairly sure it was a gift from his father.[2] Leopold was a great admirer of Fénelon, and had even made a trip to Cambrai to visit the author's tomb four years earlier, during the family's first European tour.[3] In 1770, when Mozart wrote the postscript to Nannerl, father and son were on the first of three Italian tours, and Leopold's schedule for Wolfgang was relentless. One can almost feel his father's breath on Wolfgang's neck as he reports his progress to his sister 'in order not to fail in my duty'.[4]

At a time when contemporaries were already describing the eighteenth century as a 'pädagogisches Jahrhundert' and in an age exploding with didactic children's literature, it is not surprising that Leopold Mozart turned to Fénelon as a key text in his son's tutelage. The neoclassical novel, which imagines the moral education of Ulysses' son under the guidance of his tutor Mentor (Minerva in disguise), was so popular around

---

[1] MBA, vol. 1, p. 388; LMF, p. 160 (8 September 1770). (Translation slightly amended.)

[2] It could have been the German edition of 1727–39, an Italian translation dated 1747 or a bilingual French-German edition of 1766. The editors of MBA suggest that Mozart was probably reading the Italian translation. See MBA, vol. 5 (Kommentar I/II), p. 277.

[3] There, Leopold wrote reverently, 'I saw the tomb of the great Fénelon and his marble bust. He has made himself immortal by his *Télémaque*, his book on the education of girls, his dialogues of the dead, his fables, and other sacred and secular works'. MBA, vol. 1, p. 220; LMF, p. 65 (16 May 1766), quoted in Jean Starobinski, 'The Promise of *Idomeneo*', *The Hudson Review*, 55/1 (2002), pp. 21–22.

[4] MBA, vol. 1, p. 388; LMF, p. 160 (8 September 1770).

Europe that it went through countless editions and was cited, adapted and even satirized throughout the century; it was also one of only two novels Rousseau's eponymous *Emile* (1762) is allowed to read.[5] Jean Starobinski identifies both *Télémaque* and *Emile* as belonging to a literary genre he calls 'princely pedagogy', which sought to inspire a double emulation in its (inevitably male) readers: that of the prince and of the standard to which the prince himself aspires.[6]

Music is an important agent of both Telemachus' own *Bildung* (cultivation), and the *Bildung* he offers his subjects.[7] In Book 2, Telemachus, enslaved in Egypt, is encouraged by the musician Termosiris, another father figure, to civilize his fellow shepherd-slaves with music. 'My voice had a divine harmony', Telemachus relates, and his playing causes the shepherds to '[forget] their cottages and their flocks [. . .]; it appeared that these deserts were no longer wild, and all was sweet and laughing'.[8] Telemachus' playing, and its transformative effect on the shepherds, eventually leads to his own liberation from slavery.

Whatever Mozart's private thoughts about *Télémaque* as a didactic novel, it would end up casting a long shadow over his later works. It indirectly inspired his opera *Idomeneo* (K. 366), via the 1712 *tragédie en musique Idoménée* by Antoine Danchet and André Campra.[9] Its echoes can also be heard in his incidental music to *Thamos, König in Ägypten* (K. 345) and his Singpiel *Die Zauberflöte* (K. 620), both of which were based – at least in part – on a derivative of *Télémaque*, the Abbé Terrasson's *Life of Sethos* (1731). And while Mozart does not appear to have kept his copy of *Télémaque*, another work of utopian 'princely pedagogy' did appear in his library at the time of his death: John Kirkby's *The Capacity and Extent of*

[5] Katharina Clausius, 'Imagi(ni)ng Tragedy', paper presented at *Opera's Canonic Entanglements* conference, Český Krumlov, Czech Republic, 21 June 2017. See also Christoph Schmitt-Maaß, Stefanie Stockhorst and Doohwan Ahn (eds.), *Fénelon in the Enlightenment: Traditions, Adaptations, and Variations* (Amsterdam: Rodopi, 2014).

[6] Starobinski, 'The Promise of *Idomeneo*', pp. 20–21. See also Ruth B. Bottigheimer, 'Fairy Tales, *Telemachus*, and *Young Misses Magazine*: Moderns, Ancients, Gender, and Eighteenth-Century Children's Book Publishing', *Childrens' Literature Association Quarterly*, 28/3 (2003), pp. 171–75.

[7] For more on music as an agent of *Bildung*, see David Gramit, *Cultivating Music: The Aspirations, Interests, and Limits of German Musical Culture, 1770–1848* (Berkeley: University of California Press, 2002).

[8] François de Salignac de la Mothe-Fénelon, *Les avantures [sic] de Télémaque, fils d'Ulysse* (Paris: Jacques Estienne, 1717), vol. I, p. 33.

[9] See Tim Carter, 'In the Operatic Workshop: The Case of Varesco's and Mozart's *Idomeneo*', in Sabine Lichtenstein (ed.), *'Music's Obedient Daughter': The Opera Libretto from Source to Score* (Amsterdam: Rodopi, 2014), p. 76; Don Neville, 'From *tragédie lyrique* to Moral Drama', in Julian Rushton, *W. A. Mozart: 'Idomeneo'* (Cambridge: Cambridge University Press, 1993), p. 73; and Starobinski, 'The Promise of *Idomeneo*'.

the Human Understanding; exemplified in the Extraordinary Case of Automathes (1747).[10] The little-known Robinsonade tells of a shipwrecked boy who raises himself from infancy to an ideal state of adulthood.

Natural, moral, pragmatic and autonomous: these were the Enlightenment ideologies of learning and teaching (in the broadest senses of the words) when Mozart was growing up in the 1760s and 1770s. It seems clear that Leopold thought of Wolfgang as his Telemachus, his Emile, and that he saw himself as the Mentor: learned, ambitious and utterly devoted to the care of his son and protégé. Leopold was already a renowned pedagogue, his *Violinschule* (published six months after Wolfgang's birth) earning him accolades.[11] If Leopold read *Emile*, he certainly would have recognized himself in Rousseau's flattering self-portrait of the hypothetical father-tutor:

> I have hence chosen to give myself an imaginary pupil, to hypothesize that I have the age, health, kinds of knowledge, and all the talent suitable for working at his education, for conducting him from the moment of his birth up to the one when, become a grown man, he will no longer have need of any guide other than himself.[12]

For his part, Mozart appears to have internalized this paternal model of pedagogy – or at least was able to successfully summon it as a rhetorical strategy when coming to his father's aid.[13] In the summer of 1777, Mozart wrote a petition to Archbishop Colloredo, in an effort to revive his father's failed request for permission to travel. In his description of his father's efforts, Mozart summarized all of the obligations his upbringing had encouraged him to value:

> Most Gracious Prince and Lord! Parents endeavour to place their children in a position to earn their own bread; and in this they follow alike their own interest and that of the State. [...] My conscience tells me that I owe it to God to be grateful to my father, who has spent his time unwearyingly upon my education, so that I may lighten his burden, look after myself and later on be able to support my sister.[14]

Here, the philosophical aims of reform pedagogy were elided with Austrian Enlightenment mercantilism. Mozart signalled his allegiance

---

[10] This is one of just three books in English listed in Mozart's estate, out of some forty texted works.

[11] Ruth Halliwell, *The Mozart Family: Four Lives in a Social Context* (Oxford: Clarendon Press, 1998), p. 26.

[12] Jean-Jacques Rousseau, *Emile, Or On Education*, trans. Christopher Kelly and Allan Bloom (Hanover: Dartmouth College Press, 2010), p. 177.

[13] On Rousseau's model of fatherhood in *Emile*, see for instance Penny A. Weiss, *Gendered Community: Rousseau, Sex, and Politics* (New York: New York University Press, 1993), p. 65.

[14] MBA, vol. 2, p. 5; LMF, p. 267 (1 August 1777).

to the ideology of the productive family – in an age before the rise of the 'economically "worthless" but emotionally "priceless" child', Mozart showed his awareness that his education was a means to an end, namely, his adult potential to contribute to the household economy.[15]

The humiliating rejection of this second petition – with which Colloredo sought in no uncertain terms to put the Mozarts back in their place – shows how, as Ruth Halliwell observes, Wolfgang's 'upbringing and education had to some extent spoilt him for earning his living in the tough world of court musical establishments'.[16] He was raised to think he deserved to associate with kings, which made him unable to accept the everyday indignities of a court appointment. The letters leading up to Mozart's break with Archbishop Colloredo in spring 1781 build from complaints about having to share meals with the cooks and chandlers, to the final insult of being expected to 'have idled away a couple of hours every morning in the antechamber'.[17] Leopold wanted Wolfgang to be a *Kammerdiener*, but had raised him to be an Emile, a Telemachus, a prince. Perhaps the Mozarts even hoped that, as it had for Telemachus, Mozart's otherworldly music might earn him freedom from his own form of servitude.

For Mozart, whose father was his first and arguably only teacher, parenting and instruction inevitably elided with all manner of other roles and relationships. He identified himself as 'the child' of Johann Christian Bach and Joseph Haydn, and later positioned himself in a tradition of master composers including J. S. Bach and George Frideric Handel. He seems to have seen himself as a second teacher to his sister and was said to have treated some of his students (such as Johann Nepomuk Hummel) like his own children, while others (such as Aloysia Lange) became the object of his affections and still others (such as Josepha von Auernhammer) performing and publishing partners. Finally, as we shall see, he could purposefully blur the roles of parent and creator for rhetorical purposes. For Mozart, learning and teaching lay at the crossroads of public and private life, economy, labour and intimacy.

---

[15] Viviana A. Zelizer, *Pricing the Priceless Child: The Changing Social Value of Children* (Princeton: Princeton University Press, 1994), p. 3.
[16] Halliwell, *The Mozart Family*, p. 236.
[17] MBA, vol. 3, pp. 97–98; LMF, pp. 716–17 (24 March 1781), and MBA, vol. 3, p. 113; LMF, p. 730 (12 May 1781).

Learning

Wolfgang and Nannerl's home-based general education was typical of upper-class and upwardly mobile families.[18] Similarly, Mozart's youthful tours abroad (the European tour of 1763–66 with the whole family and the trips to Italy in 1770–73 with just Leopold) resembled the traditional Grand Tour, serving as 'social rituals' for 'round[ing] out the education' of the Mozart children through encounters with great art and historic sites.[19] Leopold acted as chaperone, and the Mozart family's destinations mirrored many Grand Tour itineraries, as did the sightseeing stops along the way: Versailles, Pompeii, the Vatican.[20] The education of the children was always, of course, paired with the promotion of their performances, and later, Wolfgang's compositions, the ultimate goal being a court appointment. Nevertheless, Leopold's approach to Mozart's musical training was cosmopolitan, opportunistic and experiential. A musical Grand Tour was the only option for a precocious son and his father who had already outgrown Salzburg, and for whom, as Halliwell notes, the traditional *Kapellhaus* apprenticeship would have been stifling and inadequate.[21]

We know little about the specifics of Leopold's approach to instructing Mozart once he was in his teens, but by that point he was composing at such an advanced level that his commissions were providing the bulk of his training. Mozart's wider circle of teachers, then, were the singers, musicians and composers he encountered in his travels. This might help explain his often idiosyncratic and yet highly idiomatic approach to composing. Alongside the composers and institutions to whom he and Leopold paid their respects (for example Padre Martini and the Accademia Filarmonica), from early on he was plunged into the rough-and-tumble world of performers. His famous remark to the tenor Anton Raaff in 1778, 'I like an aria to fit a singer as perfectly as a well-made suit of clothes', was on one level a strategic statement to flatter both Raaff and his father, to whom he reported it.[22] But, on another level, it reflects the indelible impressions made by the encounters Mozart had with singers and performers from childhood onwards, and their importance in his creative process.

---

[18] Halliwell, *The Mozart Family*, pp. 31–2.
[19] James Buzard, 'The Grand Tour and After (1660–1840)', in Peter Hulme and Tim Youngs (eds.), *The Cambridge Companion to Travel Writing* (Cambridge: Cambridge University Press, 2002), p. 38.
[20] On the educational dimension of these tours, see Halliwell, *The Mozart Family*, p. 57 and p. 143.
[21] Halliwell, *The Mozart Family*, p. 32.   [22] MBA, vol. 2, p. 304; LMF, p. 497 (28 February 1778).

Mozart also embodied the auto-didacticism that would soon find expression in Christian Friedrich Daniel Schubart's 1806 assertion: 'All great musical geniuses are self-taught'.[23] In the 1780s, after Mozart had established himself in Vienna, he would cultivate the persona of a student and devotee, eagerly performing and studying the music of Handel and the Bach family at Gottfried van Swieten's Sunday-morning salons and re-orchestrating Handel for van Swieten's *Gesellschaft der Associierten* concerts. In a visit to the Leipzig Thomaskirche in April 1789, Mozart heard the choir perform Bach's motet *Singet dem Herrn ein neues Lied*, after which he was reported to have cried, 'Now there is something one can learn from!'[24] The remark may be apocryphal, but it established Mozart in a historicist line connecting 'ancients' with 'moderns' through assiduous, lifelong study.

Teaching

Mozart's first experiences as a teacher took place during his journey to Munich, Mannheim and Paris in 1777–79. His first student was Rosa Cannabich, whom he began teaching gratis when he boarded with the Cannabichs in Mannheim in 1777; by the end of the year, he had established a teaching routine with three more students.[25] At the same time, however, Mozart had become infatuated with Aloysia Weber, and in an effort to avoid continuing on to Paris in order to remain with her, he professed an antipathy to teaching. As he claimed in a letter to his father:

> I wasn't born for that work. [. . .] I'll gladly give lessons as a favour, especially when I see that someone has talent, pleasure, and zest for learning. But to have to go to a house at a given time, or to have to wait for someone at a house, I can't do that, however much it might bring me. That's impossible for me. I leave that to people who can't do anything else except play the keyboard. I am a composer, and was born to be a Kapellmeister.[26]

Coming in the midst of a tense battle of wills between father and son, these sentences seem at best callous, at worst calculated to insult Leopold, who reminded Wolfgang that he himself was obliged to teach regularly in order

[23] Schubart, *Ideen zu einer Ästhetik der Tonkunst* (Vienna: J. V. Degen, 1806), p. 368. See Stephen Rose, *The Musician in Literature in the Age of Bach* (Cambridge: Cambridge University Press, 2011), p. 210.

[24] Friedrich Rochlitz, 'Anekdoten aus Mozarts Leben', *Allgemeine musikalische Zeitung*, 1 (1798–99), col. 117 (21 November 1798).

[25] Halliwell, *The Mozart Family*, pp. 261 and 271. Nannerl had begun teaching much earlier, in 1772.

[26] MBA, vol. 2, p. 264; LMF, p. 468 (7 February 1778); as given in Halliwell, *The Mozart Family*, p. 283.

to support the family and had done so nearly all his professional life.[27] The generational conflicts were multiple: in addition to Mozart's ulterior motive with respect to Aloysia, his chafing against teaching appears to have had many of the same roots as his resistance to the old system of courtly servitude. At this point, Mozart was more inclined to make his living through subscriptions and private commissions for talented friends and acquaintances among the upper classes.[28]

Once Mozart settled in Vienna in 1781, however, teaching was a major source of income, more ready and reliable than concerts and commissions. In a rare display of his father's shrewdness, Mozart proudly reported his strategy of charging his three students by the month rather than by the lesson, so as to avoid being out of pocket for skipped lessons.[29] At his peak, he taught for four hours a day, but he found ways to make his teaching do double duty, performing and publishing music he had composed for his students, such as the concertos and sonatas for two keyboards he prepared with Josepha von Auernhammer.[30] Teaching could also be as convivial, as when he praised his 'diligent' student Franziska von Jacquin, nicknaming her 'Signora Dinimininimi', or when he wrote in English, 'you are an ass', in a correction to a composition exercise by his English pupil Thomas Attwood.[31] Ultimately, teaching had its advantages: whatever the inconveniences, a private lesson with a wealthy dilettante was still a transaction between equals, a welcome improvement over waiting in the antechamber for the Archbishop's summons.

Although stories exist of Mozart's preference for billiards over lessons, he could also show great diligence and invention in approaching a teaching challenge. In a 1778 letter, Mozart gives his father an extended account of his composition lessons for the Mademoiselle de Guines, the daughter of the Duc de Guines, for whom he had composed the Concerto for flute and harp (K. 299). Mozart described his efforts to encourage his student to compose, despite her resistance and apparent lack of ideas. She seemed

---

[27] MBA, vol. 2, pp. 293–94; LMF, p. 490 (23 February 1778); summarized in Halliwell, *The Mozart Family*, p. 285.

[28] Halliwell, *The Mozart Family*, p. 218.   [29] MBA, vol. 3, p. 195; LMF, p. 795 (23 January 1782).

[30] For an account of Mozart's typical daily schedule in 1782, see MBA, vol. 3, pp. 197–98; LMF, p. 797 (13 February 1782).

[31] NMA, X/30/1, p. 44. See also Daniel Heartz, 'Thomas Attwood's Lessons in Composition with Mozart', *Proceedings of the Royal Musical Association*, 100 (1973–74), p. 179; Erich Hertzmann, 'Mozart and Attwood', *Journal of the American Musicological Society*, 12/2–3 (1959), p. 182; and Edward Klorman, *Mozart's Music of Friends: Social Interplay in the Chamber Works* (Cambridge: Cambridge University Press, 2016), pp. 269–71, on the Jacquins.

capable of mastering the rules of harmony and counterpoint, but struggled to begin a composition from scratch. So Mozart tried another approach:

> I wrote down four bars of a minuet and said to her: 'See what an ass I am! I have begun a minuet and cannot even finish the melody. Please be so kind as to finish it for me.' She was positive she couldn't, but at last with great difficulty—something came, and indeed I was only too glad to see something for once.[32]

This anecdote, and the extended account of which it forms a part, may again have been intended strategically, to demonstrate his perseverance to his father. But it is also candid in its detail, suggesting Mozart may genuinely have been seeking advice from his mentor in pedagogy. Leopold's reply blends the lecturing tone of a father or tutor with the conspiratorial sympathy of a colleague – teaching may have been one endeavour in which father and son could find genuine common ground.[33]

The Child and the Father

As Mozart completed the awkward and protracted transition from child prodigy to adult professional, from court servant to freelancer, he had to walk a fine line, setting himself apart from his peers without completely abandoning his forbears. There is perhaps no better example of his clever approach to this endeavour than the preface to his 'Haydn quartets' (Op. 10, 1785). It begins with something of a riddle:

> To my dear friend Haydn,
> A father who had resolved to send his children out into the great world took it to be his duty to confide them to the protection and guidance of a very celebrated Man, especially when the latter by good fortune was at the same time his best Friend.

One might assume Mozart is referring here to his own father Leopold, who had accompanied his own children into 'the great world'. But the twist comes when Mozart reveals that he, in fact, is the father, and his 'children' are his string quartets:

> Here they are then, O great Man and my dearest Friend, these six children of mine. They are, it is true, the fruit of a long and laborious endeavour, yet the hope inspired in me by several Friends that it may be at least partly compensated encourages me, and I flatter myself that this offspring will

---

[32] MBA, vol. 2, p. 357; LMF, p. 539 (14 May 1778).
[33] MBA, vol. 2, pp. 364–65; LMF, p. 541 (28 May 1778).

serve to afford me solace one day. [. . .] May it therefore please you to receive them kindly and to be their Father, Guide and Friend![34]

This was not the first time Mozart had referred to his compositions as his children: in 1782, he wrote to his father about conducting a performance of *Die Entführung aus dem Serail* in part 'to appear before the royal guests as the father of my child'.[35] But in the remarkable dedication of the Opus 10 string quartets, Mozart publicly and permanently claimed his tangle of identities as son, father, student, teacher and heir. There are echoes here of the web of fathers and teachers in *Télémaque*: Termosiris, Mentor and, behind them, Termosiris' mentor Apollo and Telemachus' long-lost father Odysseus. A few years later, in *Die Zauberflöte*, Mozart would send yet another of his 'children out into the great world': Tamino (wielding a magical flute not unlike the one played by Telemachus) would act as both student and teacher, charming beast and captor alike as he completed his own journey through wisdom to power.

---

[34] MDL, p. 220; MDB, p. 250.   [35] MBA, vol. 3, p. 239; LMF, p. 828 (19 October 1782).

CHAPTER 3

Compositional Methods

Ulrich Leisinger

Mozart is known to have composed with astonishing ease and velocity, and under circumstances that were not always favorable.[1] He was, without doubt, a remarkable improviser, gifted with creative exuberance, and possessed an exceptional memory that facilitated the production of more than 20,000 pages of music within a short lifetime. Even the earliest accounts of Mozart were full of anecdotal reports about his abilities. It is sufficient here to quote Daines Barrington who, before reporting to the Royal Society about his experiences with young Mozart during his stay in London, had collected information about the further progress of the prodigious child:

> I have made frequent inquiries with regard to this very extraordinary genius since he has left England [in July 1765], and was told last summer, that he was then at Salzbourg, where he had composed several oratorios, which were much admired. I am also informed, that the prince of Salzbourg, not crediting that such masterly compositions were really those of a child, shut him up for a week, during which he was not permitted to see any one, and was left only with music paper, and the words of an oratorio. During this short time he composed a very capital oratorio, which was most highly approved of upon being performed.[2]

The test piece is likely to have been the so-called *Grabmusik* K. 42, first heard on Good Friday 1767, even though it was an exaggeration to call this cantata 'a very capital' oratorio. Many of the anecdotes that Constanze Mozart had published in the earliest volumes of the *Allgemeine musikalische Zeitung* are of a similar ilk, including the famous story that Mozart composed the overture to *Don Giovanni* only during the night before the dress rehearsal and that he was once caught by the Emperor playing the

---

[1] On this topic in general see Ulrich Konrad, *Mozarts Schaffensweise. Studien zu den Werkautographen, Skizzen und Entwürfen* (Göttingen: Vandenhoeck & Ruprecht, 1992).

[2] MDL, p. 90; MDB, p. 99.

keyboard part of a violin sonata from an empty sheet of music paper having had insufficient time to write his own part.[3] Similarly, Franz Xaver Niemetschek in the first book-length biography of Mozart contributed to the impression that the master had fully worked out every new composition before notating it: 'The work was always finished in his head before he sat down at the writing desk.'[4]

A more differentiated picture could already be obtained in the 1820s and 1830s. In the *Harmonicon* of 15 March 1824, Johann Reinhold Scholz, a German-born merchant who had settled in London, reported a visit to Johann Anton André in Offenbach where he saw many autograph manuscripts by Mozart: 'The notes in the earliest manuscripts of Mozart are all very slovenly written, and the pages are full of frequent insertions and erasures; but his later works, I mean all those to which he owes his great celebrity, are beautifully and clearly written in small notes.' In 1833, Johann Anton André described in similar terms the appearance of the Mozart autographs in the 'Bemerkungen' that accompanied the handwritten catalogue of manuscripts still in his possession.[5] He reported that some manuscripts showed obvious traces that Mozart had left them in a 'Partitur-Entwurf', which he only later orchestrated and to which he was still adding material while orchestrating. He also pointed out that Mozart had notated some 'sections of multi-part works' on separate sheets before entering them into the manuscript score. Indeed, almost a hundred so-called sketch leaves by Mozart have come down to us.[6] On these sketch leaves (other sketches were written on empty spots of music paper no longer needed) Mozart notated excerpts that proved to be difficult, as for example with the skilful overlay of the three on-stage orchestras in Act 1 of *Don Giovanni* and the operatic canon 'E nel tuo, nel mio bicchiero' from the Act 2 finale of *Così fan tutte*, often with minute note heads and without key signatures, clefs or text underlay. Most, but not all of the surviving sketches can be related to works that he completed.

---

[3] For both anecdotes see [Friedrich Rochlitz], 'Einige Anekdoten aus Mozarts Leben, von seiner hinterlassenen Witwe uns mitgetheilt', *Allgemeine musikalische Zeitung*, 1 (1798–99), col. 290 (6 February 1799).

[4] Niemetschek, *Leben des K. K. Kapellmeisters Wolfgang Gottlieb Mozart* (1798), ed. E. Rychnovsky (Prag: Taussig, 1905), p. 54 (my translation): 'In seinem Kopfe lag das Werk immer schon vollendet, ehe er sich zum Schreibpulte setzte'.

[5] Johann Anton André, 'Bemerkungen' (1833), apparently first published in the preface to the third edition of the Köchel catalogue, edited by Alfred Einstein (Leipzig: Breitkopf & Härtel, 1937), pp. xxxi–xxxiii.

[6] NMA, X/31/4, edited by Ulrich Konrad.

A neglected repertoire, Mozart's fragments, helps us to reconstruct his compositional method.[7] Mozart left more than 150 fragments, some consisting of a few notes only, such as the one-bar initial idea of a slow movement for the String Quartet in D minor K. 421, and others combining complete and drafted movements such as the Mass in C minor K. 427 and the Requiem K. 626. We tend to regard fragments as unfinished compositions. But for a better understanding of their existence it may help to see a completed work as a 'finished fragment'. This change in perspective is not merely a witty play with words; it rather reminds us that the realization of every known composition started with an empty sheet of manuscript paper that was gradually filled with ink-blots in a mechanical procedure.

No piece, not even the tiniest one, was finished right away. Rather the clefs, key signatures, the notes and rests, slurs and ties, dots and strokes, the tempo indications and dynamic markings and so on were written on to the paper one after the other. When everything went well Mozart left a complete work that lacked only a performance for it to come 'alive'. The compositional process was, however, interrupted from time to time, most often involuntarily, including when Mozart had reached the end of a page and had to wait until the ink had dried before he could turn over and continue his musical notation. This can often be observed in fragments from his early years, where the music is written in all parts until it breaks off at the end of a page. These fragments lack, so to speak, nothing except an ending. If the cut-off point coincides with the verso of a sheet of music paper it is not always possible to distinguish between compositions that were never completed and those whose end was accidentally lost. Usually Mozart had little difficulty continuing the writing process after an interruption: changes in the colour of the ink, the size of note heads, the orientation of stems and the like often make it possible to identify the spots where Mozart resumed work after a break. But if too much time elapsed before the compositional procedure could be taken up again, it became difficult (even for Mozart) to bring a piece to an end.

Clearly, Mozart abandoned some pieces intentionally, because he wanted to replace the initial work with a new one. This is obvious where Mozart marked a fragment as invalid by striking through it or by just starting the piece that was meant to supersede the earlier one right after it and thus making it impossible to continue the writing process of the

---

[7] See NMA X/31/3 and Ulrich Leisinger, 'Die Fragmente Mozarts als kompositorisches und aufführungspraktisches Problem', in Joachim Brügge (ed.), *Sowohl Mozart als auch … Salzburger Jubiläumstagung der Rezeptions- und Interpretationsforschung (2016)* (Freiburg: Rombach, 2017), pp. 284–304.

abandoned fragment at a later point. Mozart did not shy away even from giving up pieces that were almost complete: for example, the handwriting and the paper type make it clear that the Rondo in A for string quartet K. 464a was intended as the final movement of the fifth of his 'Haydn' quartets. This piece had already amounted to 170 bars and it would have taken Mozart only a couple of hours to finish both movement and entire string quartet (K. 464). But he decided to put the movement aside, starting afresh with what is known today as the finale, K. 464/iv. Nothing is wrong with the original movement K. 464a, except that Mozart did not regard it as ideal in the context of this particular quartet.

Our knowledge about Mozart's motivations for composing specific works is incomplete, but it appears that – with few exceptions – he did not begin to write a piece without a concrete occasion for it to be performed or published. If an immediate incentive to compose a work no longer existed, Mozart often put it aside, certainly hoping (sometimes in vain) to finish it on a later occasion. It is typical for this special kind of fragment to consist of a mixture of complete and drafted movements with certain other movements – needed to create a whole – not being tackled at all. The most prominent example is the great Mass in C minor K. 427 where the Credo never got beyond the first two partial movements. In the 'Credo in unum Deum' and the 'Et incarnatus est' only the main parts were notated while the secondary parts were left empty. The main ones comprise the vocal parts and the instrumental bass, the remaining instrumental parts being indicated only where the vocal parts have rests or when indispensable in terms of musical substance, such as the entire string section in the opening ritornello and the soloistic woodwinds in the 'Et incarnatus est'.

The appearance of this autograph aligns with the compositional method taught by Heinrich Christoph Koch (1749–1816), Kapellmeister at the court of Sondershausen, as demonstrated in the *Versuch einer Anleitung zur Composition* issued in three volumes between 1782 and 1793 and further refined in the *Musikalisches Lexikon* of 1802.[8] It should be noted that Mozart was probably unaware of the *Versuch* and that his own approach predates Koch's writings by several years.

Koch distinguishes between the 'Anlage', the 'Ausführung' and the 'Vortrag'. Only the 'Vortrag', the performance, turns a 'dead musical text' into a composition, which becomes accessible to most people only

---

[8] Heinrich Christoph Koch, *Versuch einer Anleitung zur Composition*, 3 vols. (Rudolstadt and Leipzig: A.F. Böhme, 1782–1793), and Koch, *Musikalisches Lexikon* (Frankfurt: A. Hermann, 1802).

as a listening experience. The other terms – 'Anlage' ('layout') and 'Ausführung' ('execution') – relate to the compositional process as such. The result of the 'Ausführung' is the musical score as we know it, which may, however, be notated to varying degrees. Thus, a composition can be completely 'laid out' without being fully 'executed'. Obvious examples of this, at least at the level of individual movements, can be found in the Requiem K. 626 and the Mass in C minor K. 427. That the distinction between 'Anlage' and 'Ausführung' was regarded by many musicians and theorists as relevant and not mere sophistry becomes apparent in the so-called 'Requiem-Streit' which, in 1826, ignited around the question of to what extent the Requiem was to be regarded as genuine given that it was not completed by Mozart himself.

That for Mozart the act of composition was virtually finished once the 'Anlage' had been set up can be derived from some (at first glance puzzling) entries in the catalogue of his own works. Under the date 17 September 1789 he entered, for example, the aria 'Schon lacht der holde Frühling' K. 580. The surviving autograph is, however, incomplete in that it lacks most of the instrumental accompaniment and the entire concluding orchestral ritornello. Similarly, in the autographs of the two songs 'Die Alte' K. 517 and 'Die Verschweigung' K. 518, known to every Mozart enthusiast through completions that were published soon after the composer's death, the keyboard systems are largely left blank. While in these instances 'complete' drafts survive, many drafts are fragmentary in the sense that they are not fully scored and that furthermore they break off before the final cadence.

A conversation between Johann Christian Lobe, a German composer and theorist, and Johann Nepomuk Hummel, who had studied with Mozart as a child, might offer a clue to understanding the advantages of Mozart's notational and compositional habits.[9] Lobe as a young man and emerging composer was surprised to see that Hummel wrote down only the melody line of a composition, filling in the accompaniment afterwards. Hummel explained to his student that he indeed wrote down only the main part, which he had quite complete in his head and which he had often already drafted elsewhere in advance. According to Hummel, in every piece of music there is usually only one main part, which, however, is not always assigned to one and the same instrument throughout. This melodic thread will first need to be carried through from the beginning to the end of the

---

[9] Johann Christian Lobe, *Aus dem Leben eines Musikers* (Leipzig: J.J. Weber, 1859), chapter 5 ('Gespräch mit Hummel'), pp. 62–79.

score. Nevertheless, it may happen that even an experienced composer reaches a point where – at first – a continuation is not obvious, forcing an interruption in the work. Those who write down the score in its entirety one page after the other have the disadvantage, according to Hummel, of remaining fixed on the sequence of individual moments and thus risk losing track of the relationship among the musical events and of the big picture. Furthermore, good voice-leading is greatly facilitated by writing down the accompaniment as a melodic line (and not merely as a harmonic fill-in). In this respect, Hummel praises Mozart's middle voices specifically, making it clear that he must have given attention to his tutor's working habits during his two-year stay at Mozart's house as a young boy.

There is one major difference between Hummel's and Mozart's method: for Mozart, the 'Anlage' contained not only the main melody but all the main parts, usually melody and bass, and in dense textures such as chamber music for strings or choral works sometimes up to five voices at the initial stage. Mozart could put away this draft to fill in the gaps at a later sitting since the draft contained the entire substance of the piece. If he succeeded, the draft became a work; if not, it remained a fragment. As André already indicated in 1833, some of Mozart's large-scale compositions were left in a fragmentary state for a period of time; recent scholarship has shown that famous compositions from the Viennese period, such as the keyboard concertos in A, K. 488 and in C, K. 503, were completed years after having been originally conceived.[10] Mozart applied this compositional method only from c. 1778 onwards; the concerto movement for keyboard and violin K. 315f, begun in Mannheim in November 1778, is the earliest extended example of its kind. Also, the earlier habit of working in all parts from beginning to end can still be observed in the Mass in C, K. 337, dated March 1780, where Mozart briskly abandoned a Credo that had been carried out for no fewer than 136 bars.

Mozart's scores are clearly written (even though Leopold more than once criticized Wolfgang's bad handwriting). They show some traces of later revisions, such as refinements of melodic lines (for example in the violin and piano concertos); these revisions are not always carried out in all parts, thus leading to a problematic mixture of ante and post *correcturam* readings, as in the Piano Concerto in C minor K. 491. Mozart also had a strong sense for musical proportions, which stimulated him to prolong

---

[10] Alan Tyson, 'Proposed New Dates for Many Works and Fragments Written by Mozart from March 1781 to December 1791', in Cliff Eisen (ed.), *Mozart Studies* (Oxford: Clarendon Press, 1991), pp. 213–26.

pre-cadential areas and codas as in the third movement of the Piano Sonata in C minor K. 457. While in vocal music, most notably in *Die Entführung aus dem Serail*, Mozart sometimes shortened passages to accommodate individual singers, he did so much less frequently in instrumental pieces, exceptions including the Symphony in D ('Paris') K. 297 and the Horn Concerto in D, K. 412.[11] Time and again, we also encounter substantial revisions where Mozart crossed out entire drafted passages replacing them with something new.

Not only did Mozart's working habits change over time, but different methods apply to different genres. While in choral movements and chamber music for strings four or five independent parts are often given, soloistic vocal music and dance pieces are usually restricted to one single melodic line. These drafts have sometimes been mistaken as a simple melodic sketch, but there is a relevant distinction insofar as sketches are usually hastily notated in a private script while drafts ('Entwürfe') are legibly written and typically laid out as full scores. Keyboard music, on the other hand, usually shows few signs of a complex work history because most of it originated as improvisations. Here, the differences that can be observed between autographs and original editions have little to do with the substance of a work; typically, an additional layer of performance indications, such as embellishments or dynamic markings, was added by Mozart to suit an anonymous market of amateur musicians, who were unfamiliar with his manner of improvisation in performance.

A closer inspection of the autographs reveals that Mozart did not always compose pieces from beginning to end. For his later operas, he apparently started with the smaller ensemble pieces, duets and trios, while the arias were written only once the cast was fixed. And, from *L'oca del Cairo* (1783) onwards, the overture was no longer composed first; in this respect, the anecdote about the genesis of the overture to *Don Giovanni* referenced above is probably not exaggerated. Paper studies reveal that Mozart in his Viennese years did not always find the appropriate matching ideas to create a whole. Numerous abandoned drafts survive, particularly for final movements: the A major concerto K. 488 is just one example where Mozart had three false starts, K. 488a–c, before reaching the final version of the rondo theme.

---

[11] On the shortening of the first movement of K. 412 to accommodate ageing horn-player Joseph Leutgeb, see Simon P. Keefe, *Mozart in Vienna: The Final Decade* (Cambridge: Cambridge University Press, 2017), pp. 558–61.

Paper studies reveal that in some instances slow movements were created first and then expanded into multi-movement works. This can be observed for example in the Horn Concerto in E♭, K. 447 and most peculiarly in the Fantasy and Sonata in C minor K. 475 and K. 457; here, the slow movement was the seminal cell to which were added the two outer movements to form a keyboard sonata. Finally, the sonata was preceded (for publication) by a fantasy. The entire compositional process for a piece of just fourteen pages of music was thus spread over almost two years. This demonstrates that Mozart, contrary to popular belief, did not always compose with ease and somnambulatory self-certainty.

CHAPTER 4

Religious Views

David Wyn Jones

'I was so happy that as soon as the symphony was over, I went off to the Palais Royal, where I had a large ice, said the rosary as I have vowed to do – and went home ...'[1] Mozart's report to his father following the first performance of the 'Paris' symphony in June 1778 is one of the most frequently quoted extracts from the family correspondence, encapsulating many familiar traits of the composer's personality, good and bad: his delight at the success of the performance, the lack of diplomacy associated with the decision to leave the concert as soon as his contribution was over, his childlike enthusiasm for a large ice and, to please his father, the exaggerated sense of decorum implicit in the decision to go home immediately to his lodgings. Less frequently commented upon is the very particular reference to a standard religious practice, the reciting of the rosary. This act of meditation would have taken several minutes, as it moved chronologically through the life of Jesus and the central mysteries of the Christian faith, Annunciation, Visitation, Birth of our Lord, Presentation in the Temple, Agony in the Garden, Scourging, Crowning with Thorns, Carrying of the Cross, Crucifixion, Resurrection, Ascension, Descent of the Holy Ghost and the Assumption of the Blessed Virgin.[2] It raises a number of related questions. Was this religious observance regularly practised by Mozart? Did he use rosary beads to aid the memory and to mark out the rhythm of the contemplation? Above all, was it part of a wider religious personality that has been underplayed in comparison with more familiar aspects, such as the excitable energy and perceived immaturity evident in the same letter?

Particularly up to 1781, but not exclusively so, the Mozart family correspondence contains repeated evidence of daily life being conducted

---

[1] MBA, vol. 2, p. 389; LMF, p. 558 (3 July 1778).
[2] 'Rosary', in William E. Addis, Thomas Arnold (eds), *A Catholic Dictionary* (15th edition, London: Virtue & Co. Ltd., 1953), pp. 703–05.

according to the norms of Catholic society at the time. In a letter to his son
dated 25 September 1777, at the beginning of the trip that eventually took
Mozart to Paris, Leopold mentions that he had been reciting the
rosary daily.[3] More generally, the family correspondence habitually
refers to events, secular as well as sacred, as happening on, or close to, well-
known saint's days, St Andrew (30 November), St Anthony (17 January), St
Charles (4 November), St Francis (4 October), St Elizabeth (17 November)
and so on, hardly ever quoting the actual date or using broad indications
such as the middle of next month. As was common in Catholic territories,
name days (the saint's day after whom an individual was named) were the
cause of celebration, more so than birthdays. The Mozart family correspondence repeatedly refers to this practice, sometimes detailing an associated religious observance too: Mozart's mother, Maria Anna, and his
sister Nannerl celebrated their name day on 26 July, Wolfgang on
31 October and Leopold on 15 November. One year after Mozart's marriage
to Constanze, Leopold and Nannerl were uncertain about the date of her
name day. Mozart replied: 'My wife's name day is neither in March nor
in May, but on 16 February; and is not to be found in any calendar'.[4]
Standard phraseology in the family letters is often of a religious nature,
such as 'In God's name', 'Praise and thanks be to God' and 'Te Deum
Laudamus'; the text of the Te Deum also supplied Leopold with a phrase
he described as his motto ('Leib-spruch'): 'In te, Domine, speravi, non
confundar in aeternum' ('In Thee, O Lord, have I trusted, let me never be
confounded').[5]

Name day celebrations, feast days, occasional more detailed reference to
religious practice and standard components of daily speech were all the
entirely natural consequence of the all-encompassing Catholic environment
in which the Mozart family lived, the prince-archbishopric of Salzburg. In
1732, seven years before Leopold arrived in Salzburg, Archbishop Firmian
had forcibly expelled the last remaining Protestants in the principality, some
20,000 in number. With twenty or more churches, monasteries and convents, Salzburg embodied the might, power and influence of the Catholic
Church and was often referred to as the Rome of the north. As employees of
Archbishop Schrattenbach and then Archbishop Colloredo, Leopold and
Wolfgang Mozart's principal duty was to provide music for the liturgy, and
the annual rhythm of the church calendar both dominated their professional
lives and nurtured their religious outlooks.

---

[3] MBA, vol. 2, p. 9; LMF, p. 273.   [4] MBA, vol. 3, p. 271; LMF, p. 850 (7 June 1783).
[5] MBA, vol. 1, p. 246; LMF, p. 77 (10 November 1767).

Thanks to Leopold's ambition on behalf of his two gifted children, members of the family travelled much more widely than many residents in Salzburg. Sometimes the subsequent correspondence alludes to religious practice, whether similar or different. In April 1770, father and son visited St Peter's and the Sistine Chapel, where they heard Allegri's celebrated Miserere during the mass and the six-year-old Mozart had to be lifted up to kiss the foot of the statue of St Peter; Rome was also where Leopold acquired a relic of the cross.[6] London, on the other hand, was 'a dangerous place ... where the majority of the inhabitants have no religion and where one has only evil examples before one'.[7] Earlier on this journey, in Amsterdam, they had met a former native of Salzburg who had converted to Calvinism: 'My most urgent desire was to lead him back to the right path. I made every effort' wrote Leopold.[8] He did not succeed. Previously they had travelled through the Palatine region, where Catholics, Lutherans, Calvinists and Jews had complete freedom of worship; accordingly, Leopold noted the absence in travelling inns of water stoups, religious paintings and crucifixes.[9] When the Mozarts reached the Austrian Netherlands, Leopold was overwhelmed by the religious paintings of Rubens and other Dutch masters but a little disappointed that rosaries were not evident and that the practice of beating the breast during the elevation of the host was absent too.[10]

Three recurring tenets of belief and, from that, of normative behaviour are evident in Leopold's letters: a trust in God's will, the comforting rather than calamitous role of fate, and a consuming sense of obligation to nurture the God-given talents of his children. Wolfgang inherited these attitudes and they surface in his letters too. Biographers have long been fascinated by the increasing tension between father and son as Wolfgang reached adulthood, asserting his independence while the father continued to assert his sense of paternal duty. It would be a mistake, however, to characterize this relationship in terms of increasing secularization versus traditional religion. When, in the few weeks following Mozart's decision to resign from his position at the Salzburg court in favour of a more perilous future in Vienna and Leopold's worries spilled over into concern about his son's lifestyle in general, Mozart's reply was a reassuring one: 'I attend mass

[6] MBA, vol. 1, pp. 333–35, 336; LMF, pp. 126–27 (14 April 1770). And MBA, vol. 1, 370; LMF, p. 149 (21 July 1770).

[7] MBA, vol. 1, pp. 180–81; LMF, p. 56 (letter to Lorenz Hagenauer, 19 March 1765).

[8] MBA, vol. 1, p. 221; LMF, p. 65 (letter to Hagenauer, 16 May 1766).

[9] MBA, vol. 1, p. 80; LMF, p. 26 (letter to Hagenauer, 19 July 1763).

[10] MBA, vol. 1, pp. 106–07; LMF, pp. 30–31 (letter to Hagenauer, 17 October 1763).

every Sunday and every holy day and, if I can manage it, on weekdays also, and that you know, my father'.[11] A year later, following his marriage at St Stephen's to Constanze, Mozart once more reassures his father with a description of religious practice:

> for a considerable time before we were married we had always attended mass and gone to confession and taken communion together; and I found that I never prayed so fervently or confessed and took communion so devoutly as by her side; and she felt the same. In short, we are made for each other; and God who orders all things and consequently has ordained this also will not forsake us.[12]

The last observation, in particular, could have been written by Leopold rather than Wolfgang.

Although Wolfgang and Constanze were married in the cathedral of St Stephen's, it did not follow that this was their habitual place of worship in Vienna. Convenience rather than loyalty to a particular church was the rule, and Mozart, like others, would have performed his devotions at any number of churches in the inner city. His last address was in the Rauhensteingasse in the parish of St Stephen's and it was here that his death on 5 December 1791 was registered and where the body was blessed before its journey to St Marx cemetery in the outer suburbs. But two other churches figured in the narrative: on his deathbed a priest was summoned from St Peter's, at the other, western end of the Graben, and a memorial requiem mass was held in St Michael's, opposite the Hofburg, on 10 December. Since the latter church was adjacent to the Burgtheater, it was much favoured by the theatrical world, singers, composers, instrumentalists and managers, and it was this wider association that explains why it was chosen for Mozart's commemorative requiem service. Within a fortnight that link was underscored by a benefit concert for Constanze Mozart, held in the Burgtheater on 23 December.[13]

The extensive list of the composer's effects that formed part of his estate contained only one religious item, a copy of a Latin Bible printed in Cologne in 1769, valued at seventeen kreuzer, though it is possible that some of the sixty pieces of china, three porcelain figures and a casket that were listed without further detail were religious items.[14] Joseph II had ordered the closing down of private chapels in Vienna – including the one

---

[11] MBA, vol. 3, p. 129; LMF, p. 743 (13 June 1781).

[12] MBA, vol. 3, p. 220; LMF, p. 814 (17 August 1782).

[13] David Black, 'Mozart and the Practice of Sacred Music, 1781-91' (PhD thesis, Harvard University, 2007), pp. 376–80.

[14] MDL, pp. 495–96, 498; MDB, pp. 586, 589.

in the Trattnerhof where Mozart lived for a while – but there is no reason to doubt that private rooms were still commonly adorned with images of the Virgin Mary, crucifixes and stoops to hold holy water. In a post scriptum to a letter dated 10 December 1783, Wolfgang asks whether his father could send him a couple of 'Loretto-kindlein'. These were images of the infant Jesus derived from the pilgrimage church in Loreto, near the Adriatic coast, that housed the Santa Casa, the dwelling place of Mary, Joseph and the young Jesus, reputedly transported by angels from Nazareth to Italy in the thirteenth century. Mozart had visited Loreto in July 1770 with his father, but the reference in the letter of 1783 more likely refers to the Loreto statue in Salzburg that had acquired miraculous healing properties. While Advent was an appropriate time to ask for such an object, probably a wooden carving (possibly one of the china or porcelain items listed in the estate), the correspondence hints that it may also have served as a healing agent for a minor ailment.[15]

The Mozart correspondence of the 1780s is almost completely silent on the far-reaching reforms enacted by Joseph II that affected the role of the Catholic Church, even when those reforms had consequences for musical life and, indeed, for musical composition itself. Early in 1782, while he was working on *Die Entführung aus dem Serail*, Mozart excitedly reported a sensational rumour to his father: 'the Pope is supposed to be coming to Vienna. The whole town is talking about it. But I do not believe it, for Count Cobenzl told me that the Emperor will decline his visit.'[16] The proposed visit by Pius VI, the first time a Pope had travelled outside the papal state for two-and-a half centuries, was occasioned by the acute nature and the unseemly speed of Joseph's religious reforms. The emperor had already ordered the suppression of those monastic contemplative orders, such as the Carthusian, that did not serve the wider community as teachers or as carers for the sick, and had challenged the authority of the Pope to nominate bishops in Lombardy (a policy later enacted in the Austrian Monarchy too); even more fundamentally challenging, the emperor had weakened the centuries-old standing of the Catholic Church in the monarchy by advancing the toleration of Protestants, Jews and the Greek Orthodox church. As deputy state chancellor, Count Philipp Cobenzl was a reliable source about Joseph's intentions to ignore the Pope, but the emperor changed his mind and the visit duly took place

---

[15] MBA, vol. 3, p. 297; LMF, p. 864 (10 December 1783). This letter refers to the content of an earlier letter (6 December 1783), a prescription for ointment rash. MBA, vol. 3, p. 295; LMF, p. 862.

[16] MBA, vol. 3, p. 190; LMF, pp. 790–91 (9 January 1782).

between 22 March and 22 April. Although Pius VI was received with the utmost dignity and highest ceremony, the visit failed to dissuade Joseph from pursuing his reforms.[17]

As a member of the Salzburg court, Mozart had habitually played the organ in liturgical services. He had also frequently taken the opportunity to play the organ in church services during his travels in Italy and Germany. For Mozart, it was part of an indivisible personal and religious existence that was now directly threatened, as Joseph II's reforms moved on to cover the role of music in the liturgy. Duplication of daily mass services in Vienna's many churches was replaced with a uniform timetable of services in one church at a time. Orchestrally accompanied masses were restricted to Sundays and feast days, and the dedicated support of particular brotherhoods for liturgical music in some churches was abruptly discounted by the blanket suppression of all religious brotherhoods.[18] While Mozart was denied the previously numerous casual opportunities to play the organ in liturgical services in Vienna, many more musicians lost their entire livelihood as well as a way of life.

In the summer of 1791, Mozart made contact with the Piarists church in the southern suburb of Josephstadt, walking in the Corpus Christi procession that began and ended at the church.[19] Its associated seminary, like all church seminaries in the monarchy, had been closed earlier in the decade in favour of a policy that promoted newly established general seminaries. Mozart's eldest son, Karl Thomas, was educated at a private boarding school in the village of Perchtolsdorf, outside Vienna, but Mozart was unhappy with that provision and explored the possibility of having him educated in the newly re-established Piarist seminary in the city. These plans never came to fruition; following Mozart's death, Karl was instead educated in Prague.

In his comparatively short life, Mozart had direct experience of religious life in many European countries, his own upbringing was one of total immersion in the Catholic faith in thought and deed, and, in the last decade of his life in Vienna, he witnessed at first hand the consequences of Joseph II's modernization of the Catholic Church in the Austrian Monarchy. As mentioned earlier, Leopold's concern that Wolfgang should

---

[17] Derek Beales, *Prosperity and Plunder. European Catholic Monasteries in the Age of Revolution, 1650–1815* (Cambridge: Cambridge University Press, 2003), pp. 179–228; Beales, *Joseph II, Volume II: Against the World, 1780–1790* (Cambridge: Cambridge University Press, 2009), pp. 214–38.

[18] Beales, *Against the World*, pp. 316–22. Reinhard G. Pauly, 'The Reforms of Church Music under Joseph II', *Musical Quarterly*, 43 (1957), pp. 372–82. MDL, p. 348; MDB, p. 397.

[19] MDL, p. 348; MDB, p. 397.

continue to practise his faith has often been used as evidence of an increasingly difficult relationship between the two, but is better understood as the natural consequence of a shared religion, specifically the responsibility of the loving father, something that Wolfgang would have understood, as is evident from one genial response, 'Straight after God comes Papa'.[20] More generally, biographical tradition from the nineteenth century onwards has consistently pushed Mozart's religious nature to one side in order to promote the idea of a free spirit whose creativity rose above his immediate environment. Ironically, this Romantic view was considerably helped by the tale of the unfinished Requiem, a cruel denial of personal salvation; more generally, the marginalization of Mozart's religious belief has been helped by the fact that the biographical narrative of the 1780s was easily based on secular works, sonatas, concertos, quartets, symphonies and operas, with his grandest sacred work, the Mass in C minor, remaining, like the Requiem, incomplete. As to the question of whether Mozart's religious views changed, there is no evidence of fundamental revision in adulthood and considerable circumstantial evidence that they remained integral to his personality not something that was practised on occasions. As in the case of Emperor Joseph, Mozart's religious life changed but his religion did not.

If one accepts that religious belief remained a vital component of Mozart's being throughout his life, a greater sense of continuity in the biographical narrative between the Salzburg and Vienna periods arises. Composing, performing and imbibing musical Catholicism was a constant characteristic of the Salzburg period (including the journeys to Italy and Germany); it was only interrupted in the early Viennese years because of the effects of Joseph II's reforms, though its undimmed allure is evident in the ambition and reach of the Mass in C minor; and there were increasing signs in the last four years of Mozart's life, arising from his position in the imperial court, the petition to succeed Hofmann as Kapellmeister at St Stephen's and the composition of the Requiem, that the personal and the religious were once more to be united with the professional.

---

[20] As reported in Leopold's letter to Wolfgang, 23 February 1778, and reaffirmed in Mozart's letter to Leopold, 7 March 1778. MBA, vol. 2, pp. 296, 318; LMF, pp. 492, 506.

CHAPTER 5

Aesthetic Views

Edmund J. Goehring

For evidence of Mozart as champion of art as a cause – as an instrument of an idea, whether social or aesthetic – one could produce his letter of 5 February 1783. Here, he expresses an enthusiasm for helping along the German stage, whose establishment in Vienna was proceeding by fits and starts.[1] 'Every nation has its own opera', he reasons to his father, 'and why not Germany?'[2] At least for theatre reformers, who came from Vienna's highest echelons, the wish to offer the public a more convenient theatre accompanied the higher ambition of offering it a more instructive one. Once cleansed of the barbarisms of Austria's earlier Baroque, ceremonial culture, an Enlightened German theatre would school the nation by harnessing the stage's hitherto wayward sensuous powers – its sights and sounds – in such a way as to make virtue appear enticing.

The piece that Mozart selected to convey this patriotic ardour was Carlo Goldoni's *Il servitore di due padroni* (The Servant of Two Masters, 1746). Not only was this an Italian work, it also belonged to the very farcical tradition that proponents of an Enlightened German stage were trying to wean the populace off. Just over three months later, Mozart's earlier patriotism seems to have receded still further. Now, a different national drama draws his interest: 'I should dearly love to show what I can do in an Italian opera', he reports.[3] Mozart had not undergone a philosophical conversion in the interval. Instead, Joseph II had reinstated the Italian opera company in Vienna and with it Mozart's options. The creative opportunity – to compose *opera*, irrespective of attending creed or ideology – drove the thought, and not the other way around.

Such vacillations on Mozart's part, along with the testimony of his eclectic output, should sound cautions against regarding him as one who

---

[1] On the early history of Viennese theatre, see W. E. Yates, *Theatre in Vienna: A Critical History, 1776–1995* (New York: Cambridge University Press, 1996), chapter 1, 'The Establishment of the "City of Theatre"', pp. 1–24.

[2] MBA, vol. 3, p. 255; LMF, p. 839.   [3] MBA, vol. 3, p. 268; LMF, p. 848 (7 May 1783).

sought to apply aesthetic or other philosophical theories to his compositions. It is not that such aspirations for art were unavailable to him. They
were just not signal parts of his artistic temperament. A Milton epic tasked
itself with justifying the ways of God to man. A Bach Passion used musical
ritual to elucidate a central mystery of Christian faith. Christian
Fürchtegott Gellert, one of the more influential literati of Mozart's day,
wrote *Spiritual Odes and Songs*, which advanced a 'physico-theology':
a variant on the idea that the natural world revealed God's goodness.
Mozart knew Gellert's poems, but even though Mozart's contemporaries
set them to music, they had at best a marginal presence in his own
compositions, as was also the case with bourgeois drama, which occupied
some of the day's greatest playwrights, like Gotthold Lessing, but not
Mozart.[4]

Mozart was not even dogmatic about his own resistance to dogma.
When the occasion called for it, he knew how to preach. Near the middle
of the first-act finale of *The Magic Flute*, Pamina and Papageno, having
pacified a hostile army with a set of magic bells, pause to reflect on the
power of music:

Yes, Harmony gently eases	Ja, sanft mildert Harmonie
every trouble,	Jegliche Beschwerden,
melts the heart to sympathy,	Schmilzt das Herz zur Sympathie,
says to Joy, Arise!	Sagt zur Freude: Werde![5]

This is pure Boethianism. Music manifests the *harmonia* that governs the
universe, the social order and the inner self. By the end of the opera,
Mozart hymns an even higher ambition about music:

Through the power of tone we tread	Wir wandeln durch des Tones Macht
joyfully through the dark night of death.	Froh durch des Todes düstre Nacht.

Now, music has fulfilled one of philosophy's highest quests, which is
overcoming the fear of death.

Thus, to observe in Mozart a reticence about theorizing is not to deny
him book-learning or to describe his music as a stimulator of sensations but
not of thoughts or to assert that he composed with prelapsarian ease instead
of self-conscious labour.[6] Rather, Mozart's musical intellect manifested

---

[4] Charles Rosen, *The Classical Style: Haydn, Mozart, Beethoven* (expanded edition, New York:
W. W. Norton, 1997), p. 317.
[5] Text based on that given in the first full-score edition (1814).
[6] David Schroeder, 'Mozart and Late Eighteenth-Century Aesthetics', in Simon P. Keefe (ed.),
The Cambridge Companion to Mozart (Cambridge: Cambridge University Press, 2003), pp. 50–51.

itself through his use of tones. Viewed as a technical achievement, his dramaturgy makes the words, the poetry, 'the obedient daughter of the music', as he writes in a letter of 13 October 1781. Viewed more synoptically, Mozart's feeling for musical theatre invested the ethical interest of his tales not just in his character's utterances but in their comportment.[7]

In a dramaturgy where observation prevails over regulation and plenitude over rectitude,[8] interactions between composers and their librettists are likely to be conducted in a spirit of compromise. Mozart certainly had his difficulties with his librettists but mainly in settling the question of how to make a good effect for the audience. The Ghost in *Hamlet* goes on too long, Mozart thought, with the overall scene thereby losing its power to terrorize the imagination; likewise, using an aria instead of a recitative during a storm scene in *Idomeneo* would 'cut a poor figure' for the audience.[9]

Paradoxically, this more collaborative disposition makes Mozart the superior metaphysician. He tacitly recognizes that there can be no *perfect* union of text and music (whatever that would look like), because music and text subscribe to different norms. That is the gist of his earlier-cited remark about subordinating text to music: a libretto's rhyme and meter, he worried, might constrain melodic invention. But that admission does not thereby qualify Mozart as a disappointed idealist, who concludes that, absent a perfect union, there can be no union at all. According to this more recent critical approach, opera is by necessity an unsettled art, an irresolvable dispute among opposing forces of tone, word and staging.[10] Yet that modernist position overlooks how the unavoidable tension between text and music presents an opportunity: friction makes composing an opera a creative act (rather than a mechanical one).

To observe those priorities made audible in the act of composition itself, one can turn to the third-act sextet of *Figaro*. The text of the ensemble begins with verses that use eight-syllable lines (*ottonari*), and Mozart's melody traces out the text syllable for syllable (though notice that he flattens out some of the line's iambic rhythms, so already is shaping the poetry according to his musical interests, Example 5.1). When coming

---

[7] Wye Jamison Allanbrook, *Rhythmic Gesture in Mozart: 'Le nozze di Figaro' and 'Don Giovanni'* (Chicago: University of Chicago Press, 1983), p. 9.

[8] The plenitude/rectitude distinction comes from Jonas Barish, *The Antitheatrical Prejudice* (Berkeley: University of California Press, 1981), p. 117.

[9] See the letters of 29 and 15 November 1780, respectively (LMF, pp. 674, 664–65).

[10] See, for example, David J. Levin, *Unsettling Opera: Staging Mozart, Verdi, Wagner, and Zemlinsky* (Chicago: University of Chicago Press, 2007).

5.1 Mozart, 'Riconosci', from *Le nozze di Figaro*, bars 1–3.

Ri - co - no - sci in que - sto am - ples - so

upon the sextet's musical and dramatic resolution, however, Mozart finds himself in a bit of a bind. On the one hand, his affinity for balanced, quasi-independent musical forms (another expression of his belief that the text should serve the music) calls for the return of the main melody. On the other hand, the original melody will no longer fit, because the lines of the verses have changed from eight to six syllables.

Mozart solves the problem essentially by evading it. He transfers the original melody to the winds, which do not have to worry about aligning notes to syllables, and gives the voice a melody that conforms to the new line length (Example 5.2). Again, a practical spirit prevails. True, no creative act can wholly avoid ontological or metaphysical questions. Any new contribution to a genre, however slender, inflects that genre, however slightly.[11] But the main question that Mozart is putting before his audience is not, opera, what is that? but, how to make *this* opera compelling. Answering that challenge requires us to regard opera as a collaborative rather than antagonistic enterprise. What is more, such an orientation guides some of the finest works in the repertory, which are 'products not of theory but of exigencies opportunistically embraced', as one excellent critic reminds us.[12]

***

If it does not make much sense to think of Mozart as a systematizer, as a philosopher in tones, neither can he be said to have acted capriciously. He had reasons for what he did, and those reasons necessarily arose from and existed in relation to the culture available to him. Most broadly, they were grounded in a confidence in the vigour of convention and the authority of beauty. In this, Mozart continued and elaborated a poetical tradition, extending back to antiquity, about how Art should relate to Nature. In his time, two main paths were available: that of verisimilitude and that of mimesis.[13] Verisimilitude took the social world as its standard of

---

[11] Alastair Fowler, *Kinds of Literature: An Introduction to the Theory of Genres and Modes* (Cambridge, MA: Harvard University Press, 1982), p. 23.

[12] Gary Schmidgall, *Shakespeare and Opera* (New York: Oxford University Press, 1990), p. xx.

[13] Jane K. Brown, *The Persistence of Allegory: Drama and Neoclassicism from Shakespeare to Wagner* (Philadelphia: University of Pennsylvania Press, 2007), pp. 52–60.

5.2 Mozart, 'Riconosci', from *Le nozze di Figaro*, bars 74–6.

Lo sde - gno cal - ma - te, mia ca - ra   fi - gliuo - la, sua

probability. In its most pedantic forms, it forbade the dramatist from inventing a world of his own that would be judged by the coherence and liveliness of its internal rules. At times, Mozart inclined towards this view (although it runs much more strongly in Leopold). In a letter of 13 November 1780, for example, he argues that Idomeneo, a king, cannot appear in a ship by himself, because real kings do not travel alone.[14] Mostly, however, Mozart in practice passively ignores, if not actively contests, a stage governed by the rules of verisimilitude.

To see how, it is useful to turn to Goldoni, who is occasionally cited as a leading influence on Mozart. It hits nearer the mark to say that Mozart retained Goldoni's technique – especially his tighter control over the rhythms of comedy – but discarded his ethic. At least, that is what happens with their respective treatments of the Don Juan legend. Goldoni, for his part, tried to correct this most incorrect of tales by bending its situations to the standards of verisimilitude. When his Don Juan is shipwrecked, for example, Goldoni allows him time to dry off his clothes before the next misadventure befalls him. Likewise, Goldoni has the Commendatore's statue constructed early in the drama so that the audience will not have to wonder how it got built so quickly for the damnation scene later on.

Mozart rejects such 'improvements'. The contrast in ethos is at its most laconic in Goldoni's and Mozart's variations on the old theme of light and darkness. Contrary to just about every other Don Juan tale, Goldoni's damns his libertine in broad daylight. Indeed, Goldoni's demythologization is so extensive that matters of justice and retribution are determined not against the vague testimony of emissaries from the world beyond but through the documentary proceedings of courtrooms down here. For when it comes to the dispensation of justice, 'proofs need to be clear, as clear as the noon-day sun' ('Ove si tratta di giudicar, / le prove si

[14] MBA, vol. 3, pp. 17–18; LMF, p. 663.

richiedono / chiare, qual chiaro è nel meriggio il sole'; *Don Giovanni Tenorio*, 3.9). In radical contrast, Mozart envelops his whole Don Juan telling in darkness. When Don Juan finds himself in a graveyard in the dead of night, for example, he exclaims, 'che bella notte! / È più chiara del giorno'. If this apostrophe to the night resembles that of a Christian mystic like John of the Cross – 'O night more lovely than dawn' ('oh noche amable más que la alborada!') – the ecstasy of Mozart's Juan has a different object. He finds the night so enticing, he elaborates, because 'it seems made for going around and chasing girls' ('sembra fatta / Per gir a zonzo a caccia di ragazze'; 2.3).

Not all of Mozart's dramatic (or non-dramatic) works are shaded in crepuscular hues. His rejection of verisimilitude can also manifest itself as a renewal and extension of the more ancient and venerable category accessible to his day: mimesis. Of art, mimesis asked not simply that it copy nature; it asked that it beautify it (the reasoning was that art lost any claim to distinctiveness and utility if all it did was to reproduce what was already there). Even in those cases where music was to depict something unruly – tempests in the natural world, rage within the human psyche – it 'must never offend the ear, but must please the listener, or in other words must never cease to be music', as Mozart explained (letter of 26 September 1781).[15]

Mimesis lets the quotidian be imbued with the ideal. Art can depict not just what is but what might be, in a variant on Aristotle's argument for the superiority of poetry to history, because poetry deals in universals, history in particulars (*Poetics* 1451b). That more capacious sense of theatre and its possibilities is made luminous in *Figaro*, especially in the Count's 'Contessa, perdono', from the famous last-act reconciliation scene. There, Mozart creates, or discovers, an immanent idealism. The rituals that sustain and renew everyday social life, like weddings or, in this case, apologies, point to something larger than the individuals who participate in them and try to live up to them. They are not just testimonies to what is; they are promises and therefore hopes for what might be.[16]

Mozart's investment in art as a form of stylization calls into question a familiar way of thinking about his treatment of characters, which is that he abandoned stereotypes for the genuine article. It is one thing to say that

---

[15] MBA, vol. 3, p. 162; LMF, p. 769.

[16] For *Figaro*'s magnanimous vision of social life, see Edmund J. Goehring, 'Ironic Modes, Happy Endings: *Figaro* Criticism and the Enlightened Stage', *Il saggiatore musicale*, 18/1–2 (2011), pp. 27–72. For immanent idealism as a discovery in Shakespeare, see A. D. Nuttall, *Shakespeare the Thinker* (New Haven: Yale University Press, 2007), p. 253.

Mozart would sometimes elicit a feeling of interiority from his stage characters. In this, he is exploiting and furthering a broader eighteenth-century development. Earlier in the century, music was mostly public and ceremonial in nature. It still retains that function today, but the later eighteenth century gave it another one, which was as an expression of inwardness.[17] Even here, however, distinctions are necessary. The psychic darkness that veils Tamino as he stands before the gates of Sarastro's Temple comes from a lack of knowledge about who is good or evil and what is true or false. But Fiordiligi struggles in *Così fan tutte*'s second act because she does not know who *she* is: 'Come appena io medesma or mi ravviso' – 'I hardly recognize myself' (2.12). And yet her interior journey unfolds in an opera whose situations are far more artificial and contrived than almost anything found in a putatively realistic opera like *Figaro*.

For Mozart, then, convention was not something to be overcome in deference to realism. Convention was a source of creativity and insight into both the interior and public world. The minute realism occasionally ascribed to him is more characteristic of early Romantics like the young Wordsworth, who observed nature in its changing specificity (although always with a sense of loss).[18] Romantic critics confronting Mozart still judged his work by the behests of Nature but gave a different sense to that ill-defined, sometimes coercive, but inescapable term. In 1803, Ignaz Arnold, marginal as a Mozart biographer but enlightening as an apprecia-tor of his music, paused to reflect on the harmonic motion of the transi-tional passage in 'Ah taci ingiusto core', from *Don Giovanni*, as it works its way back from C major to the tonic, A major (Example 5.3). Arnold concludes by praising Mozart for a musical solution that forms the tonic (*Grundton*) in a way that is 'entirely natural' ('ganz natürlich').[19]

An earlier generation of critics, and many of Arnold's contemporaries, would have dissented. This sinuous, chromatic passage is precisely the kind of writing that they found anything but natural. It encapsulated all that was difficult and overly learned about Mozart. 'His melodic writing', as one critic a decade before Arnold complained, 'is overburdened with too frequent changes in harmony, with accompaniments and ungrateful inter-vals that are often very difficult for the singer to remember and produce'.[20] (And that is not even to address the ethos of this artful setting.

[17] Brown, *The Persistence of Allegory*, p. 159.
[18] Glenn Most, 'The Second Homeric Renaissance: Allegoresis and Genius in Early Modern Poetics', in Penelope Murray (ed.), *Genius: The History of an Idea* (New York: Blackwell, 1989), p. 71.
[19] Ignaz Ferdinand Arnold, *Mozarts Geist* (Erfurt: Hennings, 1803), p. 193.
[20] From 'Ueber die Mode in der Musik', *Journal des Luxus und der Moden*, 8 (July 1793), p. 401.

5.3 Mozart, 'Ah taci, ingiusto core', from *Don Giovanni*, bars 52–4.

52 Voice only

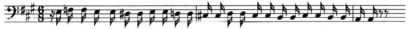

Se se-gui-ta-te,io ri- do, ri- do, ri- do, ri- do, ri- do, ri- do, ri- do, ri- do, ri- do, ri-do.

A Goldonian might have marvelled at Mozart's craft but would almost certainly have rebuked him all the more for squandering his invention on so trivial, so baroque, a scenario.) In a word, a passage like this marked Mozart as a genius, an epithet sometimes used as an antonym to what was tasteful and pleasing. Thus, it is misleading to think that Mozart's primary aim as a composer was to write melodies popular enough to win him a large income. Otherwise, we would be forced to conclude that Mozart lacked the talent to write in the manner of a rival like Martín y Soler, whose tuneful operas had, for a time, a noticeably bigger box-office draw than Mozart's.

Although Mozart did not bury Nature in Art, discerning the grace and ease about his invention would require training and experience. Proust's later remarks about genius are apropos here: 'What makes it difficult for a work of genius to be admired at once is the fact that its creator is out of the ordinary, that hardly anyone is like him. It is his work itself which, by fertilizing the rare spirits capable of appreciating it, will make them grow and multiply.'[21] It would take some time for Mozart to teach his audiences how to listen to him.

The more persisting challenge in reconciling Mozart's past with a changed present appeared slightly later, with modernity. Its shift in 'aesthetic appreciation from one founded on taste, beauty, and pleasure to one concerned with criticism, with meaning, and with a kind of self-education' would eventually lead to a practice and criticism of art that rejected nature in favour of self-consciousness.[22] In contrast, Mozart's creative world was sustained on a confidence in what Jacques Barzun calls 'the grand Renaissance conception of high art',[23] which looked on beauty and convention as vital, dynamic forces. Mozart's correspondence and, arguably, his own music give little sense that he thought he was living in

[21] Marcel Proust, *In Search of Lost Time* (New York: Penguin Books, 2003), book 2, chapter 9, p. 107.
[22] Robert B. Pippin, 'What Was Abstract Art? (From the Point of View of Hegel)', in *The Persistence of Subjectivity: On the Kantian Aftermath* (New York: Cambridge University Press, 2005), p. 290. See also Robert B. Pippin, *After the Beautiful: Hegel and the Philosophy of Pictorial Modernism* (Chicago: University of Chicago Press, 2013).
[23] Jacques Barzun, *The Use and Abuse of Art* (Princeton: Princeton University Press, 1974), p. 148.

a diminished or broken world, where the greatest artistic achievements had already passed him by and all that art could do was register the loss. Paradoxically, it might be Mozart's earliest detractors who can show us the way to thinking of his music as something more than a curio for the antiquarian. They can remind us of the strangeness, the irreducible otherness, of a Mozartean beauty, whose potency lingers even in a demythologized world.

CHAPTER 6

Mozart and Contemporary Composers

Bertil van Boer

Relationships between eighteenth-century composers were often complex; even though many composers had more or less permanent employment with various patrons and musical establishments, personal collegial interaction – sometimes as the result of a tour or other travel as well as correspondence – provided a means and opportunity for relationships. For example, a composer like Johann Stamitz could travel to Paris from his post in Mannheim, where he could develop and enhance his international reputation, and in the process come into contact with composers outside his normal collegial circle. Such travels and interactions were not uncommon and played an important part in Mozart's life. He lived and participated in a world that was far from isolated, and his own music both influenced and was influenced by that of his colleagues.

From the earliest biographies onwards, Mozart's interaction with his contemporaries has been approached mainly from his own point of view. As just one example, we find an old, annotated compilation by Friedrich Kerst and Henry Krehbiel (1926) in which an entire chapter is devoted to his opinions of a select number of his colleagues.[1] Though documentation and research has progressed immeasurably since then, remnants of this singular focus exist, as summed up by Silke Leopold:

> Among the constants in the Mozart literature belongs the reflection of Mozart's existence as an artist in a world that was distinguished by the radical changes in the political and societal nature ... [From] the standpoint of an observer, the fault for Mozart's failure with the extant relationships was caused partly by society that refused to recognize his genius, and partly can be attributed to Mozart himself.[2]

---

[1] See Friderich Kerst and Henry Krehbiel, *Mozart: The Man and the Artist Revealed in His Own Words* (London: Geoffrey Bles, 1926; reprint New York: Dover, 1965).

[2] Silke Leopold, 'Mozarts künstlerisches Selbstverständnis zwischen Anpassung und Autonomie', in Leopold (ed.), *Mozart Handbuch* (Kassel: Bärenreiter, and Stuttgart: Metzler, 2005), p. 16 (author's translation).

The background to this statement lies in Mozart's oft-quoted opinions of colleagues. From his correspondence and anecdotal evidence, he seems often to have held views diametrically opposed to the views of others, expressed in vociferous commentary and effusive praise with little in between. Those he esteemed (Johann Christian Bach, Joseph Haydn) were lauded, while those he found wanting personally or musically (including Abbé Vogler, Muzio Clementi, Leopold Koželuch, and that 'ass' Luigi Gatti) were often excoriated. These views of his contemporaries and their music seem to have been the starting point for the majority of discussions about his collegial relationships, which in turn either have been accepted wholesale or have provided subject matter for both demystification and deconstruction.[3] His reputation and relationships have often been treated subjectively, being viewed through the lens of a supposed inability to 'recognize his genius' or in terms of scheming rivals who saw Mozart as a superior competitor and sought to check his professional advancement at every opportunity.

Two concepts cropping up continually in reference to Mozart and his colleagues, 'genius' and 'rival', need to be situated in an eighteenth-century context. The former has been coloured by a nineteenth-century view of the genius as essentially someone with a distinctive intellect, a propensity for unique and progressive abstract thought or creativity and possession of complete 'originality'. If mass popularity is added into this mix, the term 'icon' or 'iconic' also applies. Mozart's reputation today is the epitome of this definition, yet in his time a 'genius' was less well defined. A good example is found in Carl von Dittersdorf's autobiography in which, speaking of the Viennese fad for elaborate cadenzas, he notes only enjoying the work of 'creative geniuses' such as Mozart and Clementi. Later, in a discussion with Joseph II, he states that both Haydn and Mozart are 'geniuses', even while criticizing them for musical foibles including in Mozart's case too many ideas and overbearing accompaniment in the operas.[4] A second example is Haydn's statement in 1800 that Mozart was

---

[3] The demystification of the icon has been a feature of general and specialized studies in recent decades, including in Daniel Heartz's *Haydn, Mozart and the Viennese School 1740–1780* (New York: Norton, 1995), H. C. Robbins Landon's *Mozart and Vienna* (London: Thames and Hudson, 1991), and Mary Hunter's *The Culture of Opera Buffa in Mozart's Vienna* (Princeton: Princeton University Press, 1999).

[4] Carl Ditters von Dittersdorf, *The Autobiography of Carl von Dittersdorf* (1801), trans. A. D. Coleridge (London: Richard Bentley and Son, 1896; reprint New York: Da Capo, 1970), pp. 44, 251–53. Writing the book in 1799, Dittersdorf makes a literary parallel in his discussion with Joseph II, noting that Mozart is equivalent to Friedrich Klopstock and Haydn to Johann Furchtegott Gellert.

one of two geniuses he knew.[5] In the critical literature of the period, the term implies special musical talent, a wealth of musical ideas and a fluid ability both to compose and perform at will. Some sort of divine inspiration or absolute originality is not implied, as Haydn himself noted to Charles Burney.[6] The definition of rivalry needs similarly to be refined. In the eighteenth century, rivalry was multifaceted, ranging from political intrigue and outright cabals to neglect or friendly competition. The former was often ubiquitous and petty, while the latter rarely rose beyond the level of a game or sporting event. In Mozart's life, suspicion may have played a more important role than reality. For example, when his Sinfonia concertante (K. 297b) was suppressed by Joseph Legros at the Concert Spirituel in Paris in 1778, Mozart made a point privately of accusing Giuseppe Cambini of being behind it; most biographers have taken Mozart's statement at face value, as an example of an inferior composer subverting the work of a superior one. The reality, though, was probably different. First, Cambini was a popular and frequently performed composer who regarded Mozart as an unestablished newcomer. Though Mozart and Legros were on relatively good terms, Mozart's works were not especially successful at Parisian public concerts (excepting the 'Paris' Symphony).[7] Mozart did write a number of pieces for Legros, but they were occasional one-off works. A better example is the later Viennese intrigues of Koželuch, who seems frequently to have spread base canards about his colleagues. Indeed, the Salzburg broadside *Pfeffer und Salz* noted in the issue dated 5 April 1785 that 'it is well known that Herr Leopold Koželuch competes with Mozart'.[8] That said, Koželuch and Mozart remained on speaking terms: Koželuch was often noted for his obstreperous nature in their recorded conversations, in fact, and was later branded a *miserabilis* by Beethoven. They may have been rivals in the profession, but the social protocols of the time decreed a standard of decorum

---

[5] See Carl Gustaf Stellan Mörner, *Johann Wikmanson und die Brüder Silverstolpe* (Stockholm: Ivar Hæggström, 1952), p. 310; Irmgard Leux-Henschen, *Joseph Martin Kraus in seinen Briefen* (Stockholm: Reimers, 1978), pp. 110–11. The other genius was Mozart's almost exact contemporary, Joseph Martin Kraus (1756–92).

[6] Burney overheard Haydn stating: 'He [Mozart] was a truly great musician. I have been often flattered by my friends of having some genius; but he was much my superior'. See Jens Peter Larsen and Georg Feder, *The New Grove Haydn* (New York: Norton, 1982), p. 80.

[7] For a recent revisionist discussion of Mozart's six-month stay in Paris, casting his achievements there in a more positive light, see Simon P. Keefe, 'Mozart "Stuck in Music" in Paris (1778): Towards a New Biographical Paradigm', in Keefe (ed.), *Mozart Studies 2* (Cambridge: Cambridge University Press, 2015), pp. 23–54.

[8] Quoted in Peter Clive, *Mozart and His Circle* (New Haven: Yale University Press, 1993), p. 84.

(irrespective of pointed language and asides). Indeed, it was Koželuch's own publishing firm, the *Musikalisches Magazin*, that published a set of Mozart's variations and intended to bring out his 'Prussian' quartets too, casting their interaction in a different light and perhaps making it less inimical than the anecdotal evidence suggests.

Of course, Antonio Salieri is the main colleague with whom history has postulated a problematic relationship; expanded out of context, it has become a crucial rivalry captured in prose, drama (Pushkin's *Mozart and Salieri*), and a motion picture (Peter Shaffer and Miloš Forman's *Amadeus*). Despite the fact that Mozart felt from time to time that Salieri was jealous of him and had instigated intrigues, their relationship was fundamentally a professional one. Salieri had attained the post of Imperial Kapellmeister in 1788 after almost two decades of service to the Viennese musical establishment, not to mention achieving a reputation in Paris as the successor to his mentor Christoph Willibald von Gluck with the opera *Les Danaïdes* in 1783. Gluck also served as a mentor of sorts to Mozart, even requesting a special performance in 1782 of *Die Entführung* and becoming a regular attendee at Mozart's concerts and academies. At Gluck's death, Mozart was appointed Imperial *Kammermusicus*, thus making him and Salieri the principal official musical figures at the Viennese court. Perhaps the best indication of collegiality between the two is witnessed in October 1791, when Salieri enthusiastically praised *Die Zauberflöte*.[9]

There can be no doubt that Mozart achieved a considerable reputation during his lifetime, in the Holy Roman Empire and further afield. Far from struggling to achieve stature after the heady years of being a child prodigy, he became a well-known personage in the musical world both as a performer and composer. His stature was acknowledged in the 1785 magazine *Dilletanterien* by Christian Gottlob Neefe, Beethoven's early teacher, who noted that while Haydn was regarded as the monumental figure of the time, 'Mozart, Koželuch, Kraus, Pleyel, Reicha, and Rosetti all stand alongside him or follow in his worthy footsteps'.[10] According to Neefe, then, Mozart was regarded as being among a septet of the most important composers of the era. Numerous mentions of Mozart in the foreign press during his Viennese decade also vouchsafe a widespread reputation.

As a child prodigy promoted mainly by his father Leopold, himself an important composer in Salzburg, the young Mozart encountered a plethora of significant musical figures both at home and during his travels;

---

[9] See MBA, vol. 4, pp. 161–62; LMF, p. 970 (14 October 1791).
[10] Christian Gottlob Neefe, *Dilletanterien* (Bonn: n.p., 1785), p. 131.

they were either drawn to the precocious child (Johann Christian Bach) or were sought out for the professional endorsements they could offer (Padre Martini). Local composers such as close family friend Anton Cajetan Adlgasser and Michael Haydn were all intimately involved with Salzburg musical life; the child Mozart composed a collaborative work with both, *Die Schuldigkeit des ersten Gebots*, and later in life was able to work alongside and help Michael Haydn. His high opinion of the latter is evidenced in his composition of a slow introduction to Haydn's Symphony in G major (K. 444), as well as a gloss on one of Haydn's horn concertos (K. 412). Among composers of the previous generation, Mozart admired the counterpoint of Johann Eberlin, though eventually noted that it was not up to the level of either Handel and Bach, whose music he became especially acquainted with in Vienna through his friend Baron Gottfried van Swieten.

During his youth Mozart was thrown into contact with older composers, particularly when completing a commission simultaneously with them: the opera *Mitridate* coincided with Josef Mysliveček's *La Nitetti* in Milan in 1770 and *Ascanio in Alba* with Johann Adolf Hasse's *Ruggiero* the following year. The interaction between the young Mozart and his compositional elders seems to have been both cordial and instructive, including when striking out on his own in the late 1770s and nurturing professional and social friendships in Mannheim with composers such as Christian Cannabich, Johann Baptist Wendling and Ignaz Fränzl. He also admired court Kapellmeister Ignaz Holzbauer, who introduced him to the social hierarchy there. But he found Abbé Vogler's music pretentious and overblown, supporting a reputation of the man as an opportunist and charlatan. Mozart was effusive about the music of older composer Franz Xaver Richter in Strasbourg, noting that it contained 'much fire'.

In Paris (1778), Mozart also had the opportunity to interact with other composers, though he was less adept politically at navigating the intricate social shoals of the French musical establishment. His renewed acquaintance with Johann Christian Bach seems to have been a highlight. But his opera project, embroiled in the contretemps between the partisans of Gluck and Piccini, did not get off the ground, and entry into the world of the opéra comique, dominated by resident composers such as Philidor, Monsigny, and Grétry, was not an attractive alternative. Mozart emerged as a well-regarded composer in Paris, despite his inability to make permanent inroads there; a few years later, Paris-based Franz Heina began to publish and distribute his music.

When Mozart moved to Vienna in 1781, he entered a vibrant professional environment for composers, almost all of whom he had opportunities to get to know personally. Anecdotal evidence exists for chamber music soirees at which he performed (on the viola) with Haydn, Dittersdorf and Jan Vanhal, adding Maximilian Stadler as second viola whenever quintets were played. His own composition students included Thomas Attwood, Franz Süssmayr, Johann Nepomuk Hummel, Joseph Eybler and Maria Theresia von Paradies. Attwood's notebook gives a good idea of Mozart's methodology as a teacher and guide, an overall portrait emerging of a patient and gentle, if thorough, mentor. Hummel, who apparently lived with the Mozarts for a couple of years from the age of eight onwards, was given an opportunity to debut his talent at one of Mozart's academies in 1787. Other young composers starting their career and helped by Mozart through having a slot on one of his programmes include Adalbert Gyrowetz, who premiered a symphony at a concert in 1785. Mozart also engaged in collegial collaboration when writing – as one of a stable of composers – for Emanuel Schikaneder's theatrical projects. Mozart and Schikaneder had become acquainted in Salzburg around the time of *Idomeneo*, and the director was one of the impresarios of the Kärntnertortheater when *Die Entführung* premiered in 1782. In 1789 Schikaneder had returned to Vienna as a partner in the suburban Theater auf der Wieden (Wiednertheater), where he both revived Singspiels and commissioned new ones, such as Paul Wranitzky's *Oberon*. Mozart's friendship with Schikaneder was apparently renewed around that time, as he collaborated with the in-house composers for the pasticcio *Der Stein der Weisen* in 1790.

In addition to standard collegial interaction, Mozart became aware of other composers with whom he had had little or no personal contact. Brief and distant conversations with Piccinni and Gossec took place in Paris in 1778, and in 1789 in Dresden he had an occasion to meet Johann Gottlieb Naumann, who arranged for a private concert with the Elector. Thanks to Baron van Swieten, Mozart was introduced to the counterpoint of Bach and Handel and commissioned to orchestrate four of Handel's works, as well as one by Bach's son, Carl Philipp Emanuel, for Tonkünstler-Societät concerts. Georg Anton Benda was another composer with whom Mozart was personally unacquainted but whose music he admired. On 12 November 1778, for example, Mozart wrote to his father: 'You know that Benda has always been my favourite among Lutheran Kapellmeisters'.[11] Another, closer to home, was Ignaz Pleyel, whose music he apparently

---

[11] MBA, vol. 2, p. 506; LMF, p. 631 (translation amended).

came across only in the 1780s in Vienna, noting: 'It would be a good and fortunate day for music, if someday Pleyel were able to be the new Haydn for us'.[12] There was no opportunity to meet Pleyel, but the same cannot be said for three other composers. The first is Henri-Joseph Rigel, who was renowned in Paris as a teacher and innovative composer at the time of Mozart's visit. The other two were Kraus and Johann Friedrich Reichardt, both of whom were in Vienna at the beginning of 1783. Mozart's name does not appear in the writings of either composer (nor do their names in Mozart's surviving letters prior to his visit to Salzburg in July 1783); but in the case of Kraus, an honoured visitor to the Holy Roman Empire as Royal Swedish Vice-Kapellmeister, the proximity of their living quarters – just around the corner from each other – invites speculation about an actual meeting.[13]

Finally, there is the matter of composers who were close personal friends of Mozart. Interactions in this respect are not always straightforward to evaluate, on account of the overlap between Mozart's personal and professional lives. And we must mention here his sometimes playful (even juvenile) nature, as manifest in the commentary on the manuscript of the Horn Rondo in D major K. 412 referring to horn-player and composer Joseph Leutgeb.[14] One true friend, albeit briefly, was Thomas Linley, Jr, who Mozart met in 1770 in Florence at the age of fourteen. More important was a personal connection with the Duschek family in Prague, with whom Mozart stayed during the composition of *Don Giovanni* and *La clemenza di Tito*, and also met in Dresden in April 1789. While there is no doubt that Mozart was closer to Madame Josefa Duschek, who perhaps served as a sort of surrogate mother to him, he was also close to her husband, composer František.

In short, Mozart, far from being a rather solitary and sometimes aloof composer, was often gregarious. Like many in the late eighteenth century, he had some harsh and contradictory opinions of colleagues, but his personal interactions were no different from those of the majority of his contemporaries. He met, knew or knew about many of them, as they knew about him. And, on the whole, they regarded him in a collegial manner rather than as a rival of superior talent whose existence could be deemed a threat.

---

[12] MBA, vol. 3, p. 311; LMF, p. 875 (24 April 1784; translation amended).
[13] See Bertil van Boer, 'The Case of the Circumstantial Meeting: Wolfgang Amadeus Mozart and Joseph Martin Kraus in Vienna', *Eighteenth-Century Music*, 1 (2004), pp. 85–90.
[14] NMA, V/14/5, p. xvii and pp. 127–34.

CHAPTER 7

Mozart and Freemasonry

Jessica Waldoff

Mozart's premature death remains an irreplaceable loss for Art ... half Europe revered him, the great called him their darling, and we— we called him our Brother. Just as fairness demands that we remember his abilities as an artist, let us not forget to offer a fitting sacrifice to his excellent heart. He was a diligent member of our Order: brotherly love, a peaceable disposition, advocacy of a good cause, beneficence, a true, sincere sense of pleasure whenever he could help one of his Brethren with his talents: these were the chief characteristics of his nature. He was a husband, a father, a friend to his friends, a Brother to his Brethren; he lacked only the riches that would have enabled him to make hundreds as happy as he would have wished.[1]

These words, taken from the 'Masonic Oration' given at the lodge 'Zur neugekrönten Hoffnung' (New Crowned Hope) shortly after Mozart's death, offer a unique portrait of the composer. His Masonic brethren valued his art, but they valued his humanity more. The comparison is reminiscent of the priests' meeting in *Die Zauberflöte* at the beginning of Act 2 to discuss Tamino's readiness to undergo the trials. When the Speaker says, 'He is a prince', Sarastro responds, 'More than that, he is a man' [*Mensch*]. Freemasonry was an important presence in Mozart's life. From the end of 1784 to his death in 1791, he regularly attended lodge meetings, dinners and special events; he composed Masonic music for a number of Viennese lodges and participated in concerts and other performances arranged by or for the benefit of his lodge brothers; and through his engagement with the Masons, he developed relationships and loyalties that had a profound effect on his personal and professional wellbeing.

Freemasonry flourished in Vienna, as it did elsewhere in Europe, because it promoted values important to the age: free speech, tolerance, benevolence and fraternity. Within the Temple all brothers met as equals:

---

[1] MDL, pp. 392–93; MDB, p. 448 (translation slightly amended).

identity was based on individual merit and achievement rather than birthright, and individual lodges were independently governed. As a cultural phenomenon, Masonry was international, reaching across nations and continents. Many of the century's leaders – Frederick the Great, Grand Duke Karl August of Weimar, George IV of England, George Washington and Benjamin Franklin – were Masons, as were writers of various nations – Pope, Sterne and Swift; Beaumarchais, Stendhal and Voltaire; Goethe, Lessing and Wieland. The vast majority of Masons, however, were ordinary men of education and means who encountered contemporary ideas and events as readers, consumers, observers and critics. The real 'work' of the lodges was ultimately rooted in their sociability; meetings provided opportunities for discourse, discovery and debate, allowing members to engage with the great questions of the age.

Mozart was certainly aware of the order of Freemasons long before he moved to Vienna. He had many close associates who were Freemasons and members of the Order of Illuminati (almost all of whom were Freemasons) in Salzburg and elsewhere. During his stays in Mannheim and Paris, for example, he was befriended by prominent Masons and Illuminists, including Baron Otto Heinrich von Gemmingen (diplomat and playwright), Christian Cannabich (conductor and composer) and Joseph Legros (director of the Concert Spirituel). He composed the song 'O heiliges Band' (K. 148) in the mid 1770s, which is explicitly marked 'Hymn of Praise for Festivities at the St. John Lodge' and takes its text from a Masonic songbook of 1772.[2] He also composed incidental music for Baron Tobias Philipp Gebler's quasi-Masonic play *Thamos, König in Ägypten* of 1773, although the version we know probably dates from 1779. It is easy to imagine how the ideals of Freemasonry would have appealed to the Mozart who had sent the following comment to Padre Martini in 1776: 'We live in this world in order to learn industriously and, by interchanging our ideas, to enlighten one another and thus endeavour to promote the sciences and the fine arts.'[3]

Many of Mozart's Viennese friends and acquaintances were Masons: his brother-in-law Joseph Lange, the tenor Valentin Adamberger, Joseph Haydn, Count August von Hatzfeld, the clarinettist and basset-horn player Anton Stadler, Emanuel Schikaneder, Paul Wranitzky and, of course, Michael Puchberg, whom he frequently addressed with the abbreviation 'O.B.' (*Ordensbruder*). Ignaz von Seyfried reported years later that Mozart enjoyed the camaraderie of fellow Masons at an 'eating' lodge, where

---

[2] Katharine Thomson, *The Masonic Thread in Mozart* (London: Lawrence and Wishart, 1977), p. 44.
[3] MBA, vol. 1, p. 532; LMF, p. 266 (letter of 4 September 1776).

brothers enjoyed good food, games and music.[4] Many important patrons of music in Vienna were Masons, including Count Franz Joseph Thun, Count Johann Baptist Esterházy, Count Anton Georg Apponyi, Prince Johann Baptist Carl Dietrichstein and Count Joseph Pálffy. Of the 174 subscribers to Mozart's Lenten concerts at the Trattnerhof in 1784, about a quarter were Masons. Several of Mozart's Viennese publishers were also Masons, including Pasquale Artaria, Christoph Torricella and Franz Anton Hoffmeister.

Mozart's official engagement with Freemasonry began on 5 December 1784 when he was proposed for membership in the lodge 'Zur Wohltätigkeit' (Beneficence), which, along with seven other lodges in Vienna, followed the English Ritual of St John. As a Seeker wishing to join the order, he would have signed a declaration stating that he was acting independently, was not motivated by personal gain and would not divulge any aspect of what was about to be revealed to him. Mozart was admitted as an Apprentice Mason on 14 December, was promoted to the Fellow Craft degree on 7 January 1785 and became a Master Mason soon thereafter. Founded on 2 February 1783, Beneficence was comparatively small, recording thirty-two members in 1784. True to its name, the lodge frequently engaged in charitable works and in the spring of 1784 had raised 4184 florins for flood victims.[5] We cannot be certain what drew Mozart to this particular lodge, but he knew its Master, Gemmingen, who had befriended the composer during his stay in Mannheim in 1777–78. (In a letter to his father, Mozart mentions working on a 'duodrama' based on Gemmingen's *Semiramis* in 1778, but no music for the collaboration survives.[6]) Only two members of Beneficence were nobles: Gemmingen and Count Karl Lichnowsky (with whom Mozart later travelled in the spring of 1789).

As did other members of his lodge, Mozart frequently attended meetings of the larger and more prominent lodge 'Zur wahren Eintracht' (True Concord), which gained pre-eminence for its devotion to learning and scientific advancement after the election of renowned scientist and scholar Ignaz von Born as Grand Master in 1782. When the German naturalist and writer Georg Foster visited several Viennese lodges in 1784, he reported that all were thriving but singled out True Concord for its leadership:

[4] MDB, p. 525.
[5] Volkmar Braunbehrens, *Mozart in Vienna: 1781–1791*, trans. Timothy Bell (New York: Grove Weidenfeld, 1986), p. 240.
[6] MBA, vol. 2, p. 516; LMF, p. 638 (3 December 1778).

The lodge Zur wahren Eintracht is the one working most actively for enlightenment. It publishes a Freemason's journal in which everything – faith, the oath and ceremonies, and even fanaticism – is more openly discussed than at home in Saxony. The best scholars and poets are members of this lodge. They make light of the whole idea of secrecy and have transformed the entire thing into a society of rational, unprejudiced men dedicated to enlightenment.[7]

The best minds in Vienna – men of science, letters, medicine, law and the arts – were members, including Joseph von Sonnenfels, perhaps the leading figure of the Austrian enlightenment. No lodge was more firmly committed to working on behalf of Josephine reforms and, by 1785, membership in True Concord had grown to about two hundred. Meetings were held as often as twice a week; they frequently featured scholarly lectures and presentations. The lodge library included 1,900 volumes as well as a collection of natural history specimens. The lodge sponsored publications, including the *Physikalische Arbeiten der Einträchtigen Freunde in Wien* (Physical Works of the Friends of Concord in Vienna) and the *Journal für Freymaurer*, which was launched in 1784 with a print run of a thousand. The first issue featured Born's essay 'Ueber die Mysterien der Aegyptier', which influenced Emanuel Schikaneder's and Mozart's conception of *Die Zauberflöte*.[8] Under Born's leadership, True Concord served as a meeting place for the intellectual elite and aspired to become a kind of 'Masonic Academy' for the arts and sciences.

Several lodges, including Beneficence and True Concord, met at the house of Baron Moser in the Landskrongasse on the second floor in a series of rooms that included the grand meeting hall preserved in the painting *Initiation Ceremony in a Viennese Masonic Lodge* (now housed in the Historisches Museum der Stadt Wien, in Vienna). The painting shows a ceremony at which a blindfolded initiate is about to but has not yet seen the light: Masonic imagery is visible on the walls and in the clothing of the members (red and blue aprons and insignia); and Mozart is thought to be the figure on the far right wearing his Masonic apron and square (the emblem of a Master Mason).[9] This image helps us to imagine Mozart as an active member of the Craft. Early in 1785, he arranged for his father, then visiting

---

[7] As given in Braunbehrens, *Mozart in Vienna*, p. 237.

[8] Peter Branscombe, *W. A. Mozart: Die Zauberflöte* (Cambridge: Cambridge University Press, 1991), pp. 20–25 and 41.

[9] For a discussion of this painting, which has been attributed to Ignaz Unterberger, see, among others, H. C. Robbins Landon, *Mozart and the Masons: New Light on the Lodge 'Crowned Hope'* (London: Thames and Hudson, 1982), pp. 30–52.

Vienna, to join Beneficence, and Leopold participated in an installation ceremony like the one pictured. He moved quickly from Entered Apprentice to the Fellow Craft Degree to Master Mason on 22 April. On 26 March, Mozart completed the 'Lied zur Gesellenreise' (K. 468), a song for the Fellow Craft journey, very likely written in connection with his father's participation in that installation ceremony on 16 April. The text is by poet Joseph Franz von Ratschky, a member of True Concord.

The 'Lied zur Gesellenreise' is the first of several explicitly Masonic works Mozart composed for special occasions in 1785. On 24 April, *Die Maurerfreude* (Masonic Joy, K. 471), a cantata for soloist and three-part chorus, premiered at a splendid dinner given by 'Zur gekrönten Hoffnung' (Crowned Hope) in Born's honor. Eighty-four brothers were present, including Mozart and his father, to celebrate a scientific discovery for which Born was ennobled; Joseph raised him to the degree of *Reichsritter*. Adamberger sang the solo part and the text by Franz Petran appropriately described how Born was crowned with laurels by 'Joseph the Wise'. Repeat performances were given at True Concord and other lodges later that year, and the score was published in August for the benefit of the poor. Over the summer, Mozart composed two Masonic songs (now lost), which were performed in August at True Concord. In November of the same year, Mozart's *Maurerische Trauermusik* (Masonic Funeral Music, K. 477) was performed at a lodge of sorrows given by Crowned Hope to honour two recently departed Masons, Duke Georg August Mecklenburg and Count Franz Esterházy von Galántha. This is the first known performance of this work, but Mozart entered it in his thematic catalogue, the *Verzeichnüß*, in July (months before either of these men died) and Philippe A. Autexier has suggested that it was originally conceived with chorus for a performance in August. If so, that version is lost.[10] During this period, Mozart provided music for and participated in a number of concerts and performances, serving as a kind of resident composer for his and other lodges.

This was an auspicious moment for Freemasonry in Vienna, with eight lodges following the English ritual of St. John, a few following other rites, and perhaps as many as 800 members in total. The founding of a National Grand Lodge of Austria in 1784 had created independence from the National Grand Lodge in Berlin and made possible the establishment of provincial lodges in Austria, supporting the rise of Freemasonry in Habsburg lands. But

---

[10] See Philippe A. Autexier, 'Wann wurde die Maurerische Trauermusik uraufgeführt?' *Mozart-Jahrbuch 1984–85*, pp. 6–8, and Neal Zaslaw, *Mozart's Symphonies: Context, Performance Practice, Reception* (New York: Oxford University Press, 1989), pp. 443–44.

despite this success, or perhaps on account of it, Joseph II soon took action to reverse course. The 'Freimaurerpatent' (Masonic Decree), issued on 11 December 1785 and effective 1 January 1786, challenged the secret nature of Masonic societies and established new rules for their organization and activities going forward. The reasons for this decree and its timing are not entirely clear, but its wording seems to privilege the rationalist, enlightened Freemasons (many of them members of the Order of Illuminati) over their more mystical and secretive counterparts, the Rosicrucians and Asiatic Brethren. The document describes societies 'whose secrets are unknown to me' and whose assemblies 'can have a corrupting effect on law and order'. At the same time, Masonic societies are offered the protection of the State 'as long as their good work continues'.[11] Whatever the reasons for the Masonic Decree, its overall effect was to diminish the role of Freemasonry in Habsburg realms altogether. The Viennese lodges were restructured and reduced to two; membership lists were now required to be submitted to the authorities; lodges in the provinces were limited to one per capital; and lodges in smaller towns were no longer allowed.

It is important to separate the notion of secrecy central to Freemasonry from the fear of secret societies and their assemblies found in this document. The secrecy associated with membership was probably not a real concern. While it is true that every Mason took a vow of secrecy, it was clear that this referred to the rituals associated with the Craft. In Vienna, however, it is not at all clear that this secrecy was preserved. *The Spy of Vienna*, a magazine published by Johann Thomas von Trattner (who was himself a Mason), reported on aspects of the rituals of initiation in 1784.[12] Members gave Masonic white gloves to ladies and wore tokens themselves in public. Masonic songs were widely published and shared. The real secret known only to the initiate was the *experience* of belonging derived from participation in Masonic meetings and rituals.[13] Be that as it may, it is clear that free speech and freedom of assembly were potential dangers to any autocratic state. After the outbreak of the French Revolution, the Masons were often blamed both as enemies of the *Ancien Régime* and as conspirators. A memorandum authored by Vienna's minister of police, Count Johann Anton Pergen, suggested that secret societies such as the Masons were responsible for both the loss of the English colonies in America and the fall of the French Monarchy.[14]

---

[11] Braunbehrens, *Mozart in Vienna*, p. 243.   [12] Braunbehrens, *Mozart in Vienna*, p. 235.

[13] Paul Nettl, *Mozart and Masonry* (New York: Dorset Press, 1957), p. 4.

[14] See Margaret C. Jacob, *Living the Enlightenment: Freemasonry and Politics in Eighteenth-Century Europe* (New York and Oxford: Oxford University Press, 1991), p. 10, and Braunbehrens, *Mozart in Vienna*, p. 254.

In the wake of the Masonic Decree, two new lodges were established under the supervision of the Grand Master of the Austrian National Lodge, Prince Johann Baptist Carl Dietrichstein; each was limited to 180 members. In this way, the reorganization reduced both the number of lodges and the total number of Masons in Vienna. The first new lodge, 'Zur Wahrheit' (Truth), which merged True Concord with two other lodges, was established with Born as Grand Master in January 1786 and a hundred members. But ill feeling and disputes grew, and membership dwindled over the next eighteen months. Born resigned in August 1787, and the lodge was disbanded in April 1789. The second new lodge, New Crowned Hope, which merged Crowned Hope, Beneficence and 'Zu den drei Feuren' (Three Fires), was established with Gebler (author of *Thamos*) as Master in January 1786 with 116 members. Mozart composed songs for the opening and closing of the first meeting: 'Zerfliesset heut', 'geliebte Brüder' (Flow this day, beloved brothers, K. 483), and 'Ihr unsre neuen Leiter' (You, our new leaders, K. 484). In the first verse of 'Zerfliesset heut', the poet cleverly references the three former lodges and trusts the future to Joseph's protection:

Zerfließet heut' geliebte Brüder,	Melt today, beloved brothers,
In Wonn- und Jubellieder,	in songs of bliss and rejoicing;
Josephs Wohltätigkeit	*Joseph's beneficence,*
Hat uns in deren Brust	in whose breast burns, for us,
Ein dreifach Feuer brennt,	*a threefold fire,*
Hat unsre *Hoffnung neu gekrönt.*	has *crowned our hope anew.*

Overall, New Crowned Hope fared better than Truth, emerging from the transition period with close to ninety members in 1790. Mozart was certainly among the most loyal: he was one of only two brothers to maintain membership from 1784 to 1791 (the other was a printer, Christian Friedrich Wappler).[15]

Mozart remained actively engaged after 1786, though he evidently had fewer opportunities to compose Masonic music. On 30 March 1787, he signed the souvenir album of fellow Mason Johann Georg Kronauer, 'Your true, sincere friend and Brother, Wolfgang Amadé Mozart, Member of the very hon. lodge of The New-crowned Hope in the Orient of Vienna'.[16] Mozart sought out and was welcomed by Masons when he travelled – at 'Zur Wahrheit und Einigkeit' (Truth and Union) in Prague, for example. He identifies himself as a Freemason when writing a dedication for 'Kleine

---

[15] Braunbehrens, *Mozart in Vienna*, p. 250.
[16] See MDB, p. 287, and Nettl, *Mozart and Masonry*, p. 24.

Gigue' (K. 574) in the guest book of the Saxon court organist Karl Immanuel Engel. While in Dresden, in 1789, he met with fellow Mason Johann Gottlieb Naumann, composer of the quasi-Masonic opera *Osiride* (1781) and a collection of Masonic songs *40 Freimaurer Lieder* (1782).[17] When Mozart needed financial assistance, he turned almost exclusively to his Masonic brothers for help: Franz Hofdemel, Count Lichnowsky and especially Michael Puchberg. Mozart even considered founding a secret society of his own, which he planned to call 'The Grotto'. After her husband's death, Constanze sent his essay on this topic (now lost) to the publisher Breitkopf & Härtel.[18]

Mozart began the composition of *Dir, Seele des Weltalls* (K. 429), a cantata based on a text by fellow Mason L. L. Haschka (author of the Emperor Hymn) that may have been intended for St John's Feast in 1786, but left it incomplete. In 1791, Mozart was commissioned by Franz Ziegenhagen, a Regensberg merchant and Mason, to compose a cantata, 'Die ihr des unermeßlichen Weltalls Schöpfer ehrt' (K. 619), to his own pantheistic and Masonic text. In writing *Die Zauberflöte*, Mozart and Schikaneder appear to have been influenced in a variety of ways by Masonic ritual and thinking, but these elements (the Egyptian setting, the role of the trials, the veiling of the initiates, the journey through darkness to light, the ritualized knocking represented in the music by the threefold chord first heard in the overture, and so on) are woven into their new fantastical setting without any direct affiliation to the Masons. Mozart's final Masonic composition, *Eine kleine Freymaurer-Kantate* (K. 623), was composed for the inaugural meeting in the new premises of New Crowned Hope and premiered on 17 November with the composer himself conducting. It was published by his Masonic brethren in 1792, after his death, 'in order to assist his distressed widow and orphans'.

In closing, it seems appropriate to turn to the habits and conventions that governed Mozart's Masonic music. All of these works were composed for a particular purpose, event or commission. Music was essential to Masonic meetings and dinners, which depended on the power of song and collective music-making to create a sense of spiritual elevation and unified purpose. Masonic songbooks included songs for the opening and closing of lodge meetings, for the Entered Apprentice, Fellow Craft and Master Mason ceremonies, for the Feast of St John (24 June) and for the celebration of Masonic values (wisdom, beauty, truth, and liberty, among

---

[17] Nettl, *Mozart and Masonry*, pp. 38–39.
[18] Maynard Solomon, *Mozart: A Life* (New York: HarperCollins, 1995), pp. 333–34.

them). Songs were written in a simple style for voice and clavier (or organ), and some were created by putting new words to familiar tunes (religious hymns or popular songs). Most Masonic music is participatory, including a role for a chorus, which either alternates verses with a soloist or repeats lines at the end. Even in the cantatas, this antiphonal quality of the music is central: in *Die Maurerfreude*, the soloist enjoins the chorus to 'sing, sing, sing'; in *Eine kleine Freimaurer-Kantate*, the chorus gladly responds to the instruments (opening) and to the soloists (closing) with a simultaneous statement of joy at the consecration of their Temple. The only exception in Mozart's Masonic oeuvre, perhaps significantly, is the most striking and memorable of his Masonic compositions – the *Maurerische Trauermusik* with its C minor mood, sighing figures, agitated accompaniment, unusual wind writing and passages of chromatic harmony. This instrumental work includes no participatory chorus (at least in the form we know), but perhaps it is the exception that proves the rule. Its middle section clearly quotes a prominent chant (from the Lamentations of Jeremiah) associated with Holy Week and appropriate to the mournful occasion that must have inspired sympathetic response and immediate engagement in contemporary audiences.[19] The presence of this work's associated (but unsung) text challenges us to imagine the emotional power unleashed at its first performance and reminds us that the function of this music was inextricably tied to circumstances and conventions now almost impossible to recreate. Mozart's Masonic music inspired a collective spirit of camaraderie, reverence and music-making that was essential to the bonds of brotherhood. In order to appreciate Mozart's engagement with the Masons we must go far beyond his music to appreciate not only his 'excellent heart' but what it meant to be a 'Brother to his Brethren'.

---

[19] See, among others, Konrad Küster, *Mozart: A Musical Biography*, trans. Mary Whittall (Oxford: Clarendon Press, 1996), pp. 202–203.

CHAPTER 8

Mozart Iconography

Christoph Großpietsch
Translated by Simon P. Keefe

Portraits were probably made of Mozart throughout his life – as a child in Salzburg, a musician in Vienna and especially on trips across Europe – including many that are now no doubt lost. The Mozarts had dealings with important artists, such as the German-born London painter Johann Zoffany (1733–1810), the Viennese court painter Johann Eusebius Alphen (1741–72) and Rosa Hagenauer-Barducci (1743–86), who came from Salzburg and, like Mozart, later settled in Vienna. But no Mozart portrait is attributed nowadays to these painters. Some of the authentic Mozart portraits, though, are among the most popular of any Western classical composer. There are also highly problematic representations, including the oil painting – supposedly by the painter 'Tischbein' – that had already been rejected by 1850 but which was rapidly disseminated in prints and paintings instigated by the 'discoverer' of the picture, Frankfurt music publisher Carl August André (1806–87) (see Figure 8.1). This is just one example among numerous speculative or manipulated images for which reliable or credible authentication does not exist. And such a situation explains why, in 1961, the musicologist Otto Erich Deutsch undertook the task of presenting all of the authenticated Mozart portraits in his study of Mozart iconography. Deutsch identified no more than twelve pictures, a figure that has hardly increased since then.

What did Mozart really look like? The musician, often idealized as an Apollo, was different from how he has come to be imagined – inconspicuous in appearance, in fact, not beautiful, small and with a large head and a pale face. Even as a child he had scars caused by serious illnesses. His face included a curved nose and two protruding large, blue, squinting eyes, below bushy eyebrows. When he performed, his gaze was scattered, even fiery. He was hasty by nature and, it seems, rarely remained silent. His small, feminine hands were elegant when improvising at the piano. During the Viennese years, Mozart must have gained weight. We do not know whether it was the round face or the scars that prompted him to want to be

W.A.MOZART.

Figure 8.1 Reproduction from the so called 'Tischbein-Mozart' portrait of
C. A. André. Copper engraving, c. 1851. Lazarus Gottlieb Sichling (1812–63)
© Salzburg, Stiftung Mozarteum/Mozart-Museen und Archiv

portrayed only in profile, as Constanze Mozart later confessed: 'He was not
at all happy to be depicted facing forward.' Indeed, there is only one
authentic portrait that does not show the adult Mozart in profile.

The child portrait (1762/63) by the Salzburg court painter Pietro
Antonio Lorenzoni (1721–82), with the assistance of others in his

Figure 8.2 Boyhood Portrait (W. A. Mozart in formal attire). Oil painting, 1762/63.
Pietro Antonio Lorenzoni (1721–82).
© Salzburg, Stiftung Mozarteum/Mozart-Museen und Archiv

workshop, is the earliest one of Mozart and shows the young composer, with his round face, in front of a small keyboard instrument in the magnificent clothes of the Viennese court, and in the 'lilac colour' described by his proud father (Figure 8.2). The painting was produced shortly before the Mozart family embarked on their three-year Grand Tour of northern and central Europe.

Soon after in Paris (1763), father Leopold, sister Maria Anna (Nannerl) and Mozart were depicted together as a musical trio on a watercolour by

Carrogis de Carmontelle (1716–1806), the so-called 'Kleinen Familienbild' ('Little' Family Picture). It was so much in demand by collectors that the artist created several almost identical versions. In 1764, Leopold Mozart came up with the idea of Jean-Baptiste Delafosse (1721–75) making a copper engraving for promotional purposes, perhaps also with the assistance of Christian von Mechel (1737–1817) (Figure 8.3). Particularly revealing is a Parisian social scene with the ten-year-old Mozart (1766), showing an afternoon tea concert with Prince Louis-François de Bourbon-Conti (1717–76) in the Palais Temple and also including Leopold and the singer Jelyotte (Figure 8.4). The original title of the group portrait by Michel-Barthélemy Ollivier (1712–84) is 'Le thé à l'anglaise dans le salon des Quatre-Glaces au Temple'. The host Louis François Prince de Bourbon-Conti, Great Prior of the Order of the Temple, was well known in Paris as a patron and music lover.

In 1782, Mozart expressed a desire for a 'roten Frok' (red smock), an English long coat. It was precisely this *bon mot* that inspired idealistic imagination of Mozart portrayed in a red robe. A red 'juste-au-corps', a standard jacket of French origin, is in fact found on three authenticated portraits: on the painting 'Mozart in Verona' (1770); on the 'Miniature for the Bäsle' (1777/78); and on the 'Large Family Portrait' (1780/81) from his hometown, Salzburg.

The unsigned painting 'Mozart in Verona' (Figure 8.5), now thought to be the work of Gianbettino Cignaroli (1706–70), is perhaps the most magnificent portrait of Mozart, with an opulent Rococo frame containing the original labelling. The blue-eyed young master sits in front of a Venetian harpsichord from 1583 by the instrument maker Giovanni Celestini, on which is given Mozart's harpsichord 'Molto allegro' (K. 72a) known only in fragmentary notation through this painting. A large violin (or perhaps a viola) on top of the keyboard instrument also suggests a young string virtuoso.

Violin and keyboard instruments also dominate the 'Großen Familienbild' ('Large' Family Picture, 1780/81), where the composer and his sister Maria Anna (1751–1829) sit at a keyboard (perhaps a harpsichord). Mozart was one of the first composers of four-hand keyboard music. While brother and sister are playing four-handed, they also exhibit the modern technique of hand-crossing. On the right, Leopold proudly holds a violin and presents his well-known treatise, the *Violinschule* (Figure 8.6). The work was produced in an anonymous Salzburg workshop (and the specific attribution to della Croce is probably incorrect). In addition to this grand picture, one of the most popular of the composer is the posthumous

LEOPOLD MOZART, *Pere de MARIANNE MOZART, Virtuose âgée de onze ans et de J.G.WOLFGANG MOZART, Compositeur et Maitre de Musique âgé de sept ans.*

Figure 8.3 Father Mozart with his two children. ('Little' family portrait of the Mozarts.) Copper engraving and etching, Paris 1764, based on Carmontelle, 1763. Jean-Baptiste Delafosse (1721–75)
© Salzburg, Stiftung Mozarteum/Mozart-Museen und Archiv

Figure 8.4 Tea at Prince Louis-François de Conti's, in the 'Temple'. Copy by
Sedlacek after Michel-Barthélemy Ollivier, 1766.
© Salzburg, Stiftung Mozarteum/Mozart-Museen und Archiv

oil portrait by the Salzburg painter Barbara Krafft (1764–1825) from 1818/
19. This painting was later used to complete the composer gallery of the
Gesellschaft der Musikfreunde in Vienna, founded by Joseph
Sonnleithner. Although inauthentic, this portrait, stimulated by the
work of musicologist Otto Erich Deutsch, has enjoyed enormous popularity since the Mozart bicentenary of 1956 and is frequently reproduced in
books and on-line.

Among the miniatures, the one for Mozart's younger cousin the Bäsle
(Figure 8.7) – handed down by the family of Mozart's cousin's son-in-law –
stands out. Although this portrait from the collection of Maria Anna
Thekla Mozart (1758–1841), nicknamed *Bäsle*, carried out around 1778, is
of mediocre quality, it is of particular importance as one of two reciprocal
images. Another miniature on ivory, which was attributed to the artist
Martin Knoller (1725–1804) and regarded by Deutsch as authentic, does
not in fact appear to be Mozart, according to the latest research, and is one
of many portraits that can be categorized as speculative (Figure 8.8).

Figure 8.5 Mozart in Verona. Oil painting. Copy by Ingrid Ramsauer (born 1953), after Gianbettino Cignaroli, 1770.
© Salzburg, Stiftung Mozarteum/Mozart-Museen und Archiv

This miniature and the portrait of Mozart as Knight of the Golden Spur (1777) (Figure 8.9) show Mozart attired not in red but in light blue as well as in a dark purple colours. The painting of 1777 was commissioned in Salzburg for Padre Martini (1706–84), resident of Bologna, a full four years after Mozart's last Italian tour. It was sent to Bologna from Salzburg by Leopold, when Mozart was on his way to Mannheim. Leopold calls it a 'Copia', but does not mean a copy as such, rather a 'likeness' of Wolfgang's face. Johann Nepomuk della Croce (1736–1819) from Burghausen appears to have been the artist.

Figure 8.6 'Large' family portrait of the Mozarts. Oil painting, 1780/81.
Anonymous, traditionally attributed to Johann Nepomuk della Croce (1736–1819).
© Salzburg, Stiftung Mozarteum/Mozart-Museen und Archiv

Once Mozart had settled in Vienna in 1781, another miniature was produced. Considered lost until 1956, the 'Portrait on a Box' (1783) by Joseph Grassi (1757–1838) (Figure 8.10), is not only the earliest Viennese portrait of Mozart but also an unflattering forward-facing portrait. Titled and dated 'Joh: Mozart 1783' it was subsequently inserted in a tobacco box left to Grassi's brother, the porcelain modeler Anton Grassi (1755–1807). Only after Anton's death in 1807 did it come back to Joseph, and the small, framed portrait was mounted on the box. In Dresden the Mozart minia-ture was known to the copper engraver Johann Christian Benjamin Gottschick (1776–1844), who used it as a model for a copper engraving (Figure 8.11). The portrait artist Joseph Grassi spent most of his life in the Residenzstadt Dresden, and Gottschick was his disciple there.

Of great importance are two images produced c. 1788/89 by Mozart's friend Leonhard or Leonard Posch (1750–1831), one of an antiquated and the other of a bourgeois appearance. Posch was a sculptor, wax-wizard and producer of medals who worked with a variety of materials such as marble,

Figure 8.7 W. A. Mozart, c. 1777/78. Miniature on ivory, gift for Mozart's cousin
'Baesle'. Anonymous artist
© 2014 Sotheby's London/Unknown private collection

wax, plaster, meerschaum (sepiolite), wood and often iron. While the
technique of applying wax over moulding was widespread until the nineteenth century (Figure 8.12), it is the half-reliefs of the bourgeois version
(Figure 8.13) that have become best known through graphic art, beginning
with the 1789 portrait by Mansfeld the Younger (1763–1817) (Figure 8.14).
This version in contemporary clothes is one of two of Constanze Mozart's
most admired portraits of her husband. She appreciated its embossing (lost

Figure 8.8 Young man in a blue habit (last decades of the eighteenth century).
Miniature on ivory, said to be 'MOZART's PORTRAIT'. Anonymous,
traditionally attributed to Martin Knoller (1725–1804).
© Salzburg, Stiftung Mozarteum/Mozart-Museen und Archiv

since 1945) with so-called meerschaum (sepiolite; a mixture of wax and
plaster), which reveals Mozart's less idealized face (Figure 8.15).

The two last-known portraits from Mozart's lifetime were fashioned
around 1789, when the imperial 'chamber composer' was already enjoying
great international prestige as an operatic composer. The oil painting by
Johann Joseph Lange (1751–1831), a teacher of Ferdinand Georg
Waldmüller (1793–1865), was later expanded to become 'Mozart at the
Piano' (Figure 8.16). But this version remained fragmentary, perhaps on
account of the awkward proportions of the instrument. This expressive
portrait is the other one particularly admired by Constanze and today is
one of the most frequently reproduced images of Mozart. There is a similar
portrait of Constanze currently in Glasgow, which was also expanded.

Figure 8.9 Mozart as Knight of the Golden Spur. Copy, 1926 by Antonio Maria
Nardi after the oil painting by della Croce (?), 1777.
© Salzburg, Stiftung Mozarteum/Mozart-Museen und Archiv

Lithographs adorn the famous Mozart biography by Constanze's second husband Georg Nissen, which was published in early 1829.

The delicate drawing of Dorothea Stock (1760–1832), produced in Dresden on Mozart's 1789 trip through Saxony, takes up the silver pencil technique developed by her teacher Anton Graff (1736–1813) (Figure 8.17). Hidden from the public for a long time, it was disseminated in 1863 as a copper engraving. Previously, its original was unknown to the Mozart family and to Mozart experts.

The two fashionable head silhouettes by Heinrich Philipp Carl Bossler (1744–1812; Figure 8.18) and Hieronymus Löschenkohl (1753–1807), simple copper engravings, comprise youthful idealized profiles. At present, it is

Figure 8.10 'Joh: Mozart, 1783'. Miniature on ivory, later fixed on a tobacco box.
Joseph Grassi (1757–1838).
© Salzburg, Stiftung Mozarteum/Mozart-Museen und Archiv

assumed that Löschenkohl was based on Bossler's rather than vice versa; for a long while, Bossler's work was wrongly dated eleven years too late and thus wrongly appeared to come after rather than before Löschenkohl. Only a few original specimens of both silhouettes of 1784 and 1785 are now extant.

Posthumous Mozart portraits either take Posch's in civilian costume as a model for their depictions or strongly orientate themselves towards antiquated representations. Later, entirely new portrayals come into play, without direct historical relevance to Mozart's era, including by Carl Mayer (1798–1868), Friedrich Bollinger (1777–1825) and Jean Urbain Guérin (1760–1836). Since the 1830s, in fact, freely designed, anecdotal illustrations have dominated scenic representations of Mozart's life.

WOLFGANG AMADEUS MOZART.

Nach einem Miniaturgemälde 1785. gestochen von Gottschick 1829.

Figure 8.11 'Wolfgang Amadeus Mozart'. Copper engraving, Dresden 1829, after J. Grassi. Johann Christian Benjamin Gottschick (1776–1844). © Salzburg, Stiftung Mozarteum/Mozart-Museen und Archiv

In the twentieth and twenty-first centuries, the mythologized Mozart has become central to pictorial representations. Artists such as Horst Janssen (1929–95), Steve Kaufman (1960–2010) and others rely in their own work on easily recognizable Mozart pictures, such as those by Posch, Lange and Krafft. Equally, the spectrum of Mozart representations has proved much richer than the few pictures still serving as models for modern interpretations might imply.

Figure 8.12 Medallion in red wax, framed, circle bas-relief, 1788. Photograph earlier than 1945. Leonhard Posch (1750–1831). Formerly Mozart-Museum, Salzburg (missing since 1945)
© Salzburg, Stiftung Mozarteum/Mozart-Museen und Archiv

Figure 8.13 W. A. Mozart. Bust portrait in semi profile, plaster bas-relief, framed, c. 1789 (end of eighteenth century). Leonhard Posch (1750–1831)
© Salzburg, Stiftung Mozarteum/Mozart-Museen und Archiv

Figure 8.14 'W. A. Mozart'. Copper Engraving and etching, Vienna, 1789 (part of
a printed music edition by 1791). Johann Georg Mansfeld d.J. (1763–1817)
© Salzburg, Stiftung Mozarteum/ Bibliotheca Mozartiana

Figure 8.15 'W. A. Mozart, 1788'. Photogravure of the sepiolite bas-relief medallion, as a brooch (missing since 1945). Hanfstaengl, München (last decades of the nineteenth century).

© Salzburg, Stiftung Mozarteum/Mozart-Museen und Archiv

Figure 8.16 'Mozart at the piano', the so called 'unfinished portrait'. Oil portrait, 1789, enlarged. Johann Joseph Lange (1751–1831).
© Salzburg, Stiftung Mozarteum/Mozart-Museen und Archiv

Figure 8.17 W. A. Mozart. Silverpoint drawing on carton, Dresden, April 1789.
Dorothea Stock (1760–1832).
© Salzburg, Stiftung Mozarteum/Bibliotheca Mozartiana

Figure 8.18 'Signor Mozart'. Copper engraving (as silhouette), Speyer 1784.
Heinrich Philipp Carl Bossler (1744–1812).
© Salzburg, Stiftung Mozarteum/Mozart-Museen und Archiv

PART II

Towns, Cities, Countries

CHAPTER 9

Salzburg

Viktor Töpelmann

Everything here breathes the spirit of pleasure and delight: one feasts, dances, makes music, loves and plays frantically.[1]

For Johann Kaspar Riesbeck, who came to Salzburg in 1777, the city was a carefree idyll. The Arcadian beauty of the area, sublime mountains trailing off into the green riverbanks of the Salzach, enhanced this impression. During his stay, Riesbeck encountered 'amongst the nobility [. . .] not just very good company, but also people who excel in their profound knowledge'.[2] Furthermore, he was greatly impressed by the erudition and the government skills of the ruling archbishop Hieronymus Joseph von Colloredo and stated that 'regarding his head, one cannot praise the present duke with enough good words'.[3]

Riesbeck's enthusiasm for the city, for its inhabitants and in particular for Archbishop Colloredo stands in striking contrast to Wolfgang Amadé Mozart's scathing comments about his home town in the late 1770s and his loathing of the ruler. For Mozart, Salzburg was 'no place for my talent',[4] a city with 'no inspiration for my genius' and his music was not appreciated there.[5] Furthermore, Colloredo represented the archetypical narrow-minded and evil sovereign, an 'arrogant, vain shaveling', who despised Mozart.[6]

Like Riesbeck's glorification of the town, Mozart's view of Salzburg in the 1770s was highly personal, tied up with his biography. Mozart and his father Leopold clearly were favoured employees at court during the reign of Archbishop Siegmund Christoph von Schrattenbach from 1753 to 1771:

---

[1] Johann Kaspar Riesbeck, *Briefe eines reisenden Franzosen über Deutschland an seinen Bruder zu Paris*, vol. 1 (Zurich, 1784), p. 209. (All translations in this chapter are the author's own unless otherwise indicated.)
[2] Riesbeck, *Briefe*, vol. 1, p. 203.   [3] Riesbeck, *Briefe*, vol. 1, p. 207.
[4] MBA, vol. 2, p. 439; LMF, p. 594 (7 August 1778).
[5] MBA, vol. 3, p. 121; LMF, p. 736 (26 May 1781).
[6] MBA, vol. 3, p. 123; LMF, p. 738 (26 May–2 June 1781).

having served as fourth violinist for more than ten years, Leopold Mozart advanced to the position of second violinist before 1758 and in 1763 was promoted to the post of vice Kapellmeister. Schrattenbach supported the family financially on their travels through Europe in the 1760s and 1770s, and he repeatedly granted extended leave of absence to Leopold and Wolfgang, who was appointed as an unpaid Konzertmeister in 1769, aged thirteen. In 1772 Colloredo succeeded as Archbishop of Salzburg and, to begin with, must have valued Mozart's talent: soon after taking office he granted an annual remuneration of 150 gulden for Mozart's post as concert master. It is difficult to track the exact course of the breakdown of the relationship between the archbishop and the Mozart family after that, but it obviously deteriorated quickly. Already in 1773, Leopold and Mozart travelled to Vienna in an unsuccessful attempt to obtain a post at the imperial court. In the eyes of the Mozart family and thus also in the eyes of many Mozartian biographers who relied uncritically on the family correspondence, Colloredo took the exclusive blame for their grievances in Salzburg. Yet the Mozarts were difficult employees, proud and haughty, used to and insisting on their habitual privileges that they enjoyed under Schrattenbach's system of nepotism.

Whether Mozart liked the city or not, whether it was 'good' or 'bad', fount of or hindrance to Mozart's genius,[7] Salzburg was his home for twenty-four years (although nearly nine of these were spent travelling). Thus the city, the cultural context, the working conditions and the musical institutions were formative in his worldview and his expectations elsewhere and later in life.

The area of Salzburg had been a Celtic settlement for several centuries before the Romans erected a fortification called Iuvavum around 15 BC. Yet, by the seventh century AD, the Roman municipality was in ruins again. It is the founding of the Archabbey St Peter by St Rupert of Worms in 696 that qualifies as the beginning of the modern city. In 1278 the archbishops of Salzburg were ennobled as imperial princes and the sacred state became a powerful entity within the Holy Roman Empire over the following centuries. At its peak, the archbishopric Salzburg covered a geographical area that included large parts of southern Bavaria and stretched as far east as Wiener Neustadt and as far south as Graz.

At the centre of the sacred princedom stood the archiepiscopal court, which incorporated the official court music. Founded in 1597, the Salzburg

---

[7] These questions loom large in many writings on Mozart in Salzburg: see for example Manfred Hermann Schmid, *Mozart in Salzburg: Ein Ort für sein Talent* (Salzburg: Anton Pustet, 2006).

court music united several independent institutions: the court music proper (encompassing solo singers and instrumentalists), the cathedral deacons (*Chorherren* and *Choralisten*), the choirboys (*Kapellknaben*) and the court and field trumpeters and timpanists. This structure remained unchanged until the late eighteenth century, as an account of the court music published by Leopold Mozart in 1757 documents.[8] Mozart lists thirty instrumentalists as members of the court music in addition to Kapellmeister Johann Ernst Eberlin and vice Kapellmeister Giuseppe Francesco Lolli. Six solo singers were part of the court music proper, and positions for three castrati were vacant at the time. The choir at the cathedral consisted of thirty *Chorherren* and *Choralisten* and fifteen choirboys. The stately court and field trumpeters were organized in two groups of five trumpeters and one timpanist each.

The main obligation of the entire court music was the provision of music at the cathedral on feast days. At other times, each group fulfilled independent duties. The instrumentalists and solo singers performed secular music ranging from small-scale chamber music to elaborate theatrical productions at court. The choral deacons and choirboys provided the music for the day-to-day services at the cathedral. The court trumpeters sounded fanfares at court and, in addition, all trumpeters played a string instrument and were required to support the court orchestra whenever needed. The direction of the music at court and at the cathedral was shared on a weekly rota between the Kapellmeister and his deputies, and whoever was in charge decided on the repertoire performed and the personnel required.

On high feast days the performing forces involved at the Salzburg cathedral were lavish: on Christmas Eve 1745 for instance, they comprised vocal soloists, twelve violins, two bassoons, three double basses, six trumpets, timpani, two organs and a full choir supported by three trombones, which were played by civic watchmen.[9] The soloists and instrumentalists were placed on the four balconies attached to the four corners of the central crossing of the cathedral; the musical director and the choir supported by a small chest organ and a double bass stood on the level floor before the sanctuary. On lesser feast days, the ensemble set-up basically stayed the

---

[8] Published in Friedrich Wilhelm Marpurg, *Historisch-Kritische Beyträge zur Aufnahme der Musik*, vol. 3 (Berlin, 1757), pp. 183–97.

[9] According to the diary notes of the student Heinrich Pichler: see Franz Martin, 'Vom Salzburger Fürstenhof um die Mitte des 18. Jahrhunderts', *Mitteilungen der Gesellschaft für Salzburger Landeskunde*, vol. 77 (1937), p. 10.

same minus trumpets and timpani. For ordinary weekday services the choir was only accompanied by the chest organ and double bass.

Aside from the cathedral, several other religious institutions in Salzburg also provided opportunities for large-scale church music. The Archabbey St Peter maintained a respectable musical life throughout the centuries. Being closely tied to the Benedictine University, the majority of the musicians at St Peter's were drawn from the students in town, though some brethren were professional musicians. Concerted church music, mostly written by local composers, was performed on religious feast days and also at important community events such as the election of an abbot. In 1769 a mass (K. 66) by the twelve-year-old Mozart was performed at the ordination of Cajetan Hagenauer, son of the Mozart family's landlord Johann Lorenz Hagenauer. In 1783, during Mozart's only visit to his native town after his departure to Vienna, his sister Nannerl noted in her diary on 26 October, the feast day of the second patron of the abbey St Amandus: 'to St Peter for mass, my brother's mass was produced [and] the entire court music was present'.[10] Music was also an important aspect of social life within the monastery; a varied repertoire of secular instrumental music from near and far can still be found in its music archive.

The origins of the Benedictine nunnery Stift Nonnberg also stretch back to the early days of the city; it was founded by St Rupert around 714 and richly endowed by the dukes of Bavaria. The statutes admitted only noble girls, but this rule could be eased for musically gifted applicants as music played an important part at the nunnery. Even the strict cloistering of the community was slackened to allow for the musical education of the girls: Franz Ignaz Lipp and Maximilian Raab, two contemporaries of the Mozart family, served there as music teacher and cantor. Generally, the nuns themselves provided the music during services at the church, but on special feasts the court music was drawn in to perform at the Nonnberg.

Large-scale performances of church music outside the cathedral were radically curtailed from the beginning of Archbishop Colloredo's reign onwards, as a central agenda of his reforms was to limit the excessive splendour of the church. This obviously played a part in the Mozarts' growing discontent with the musical environment in their hometown. Leopold as well as Wolfgang complained about this repeatedly,

---

[10] Geneviève Geffray (ed.), *Marie Anne Mozart 'meine tag ordnungen'* (Bad Honnef: K.H. Bock, 1998), p. 180. The work performed is traditionally identified as the Mass in C minor (K. 427).

sarcastically calling the litanies at court 'beer-litanies' as their shortness enabled the deacons to return quickly to the inn for more drinking.[11]

Colloredo's austerity policy also reduced the secular music-making at court. During Schrattenbach's reign, instrumental music flourished in Salzburg, and court musicians such as Leopold Mozart, Ferdinand Seidl and Caspar Cristelli composed numerous symphonies for the court.[12] This favourable environment had disappeared by the late 1770s: in September 1778 Leopold Mozart laments the infrequency and brevity of evening concerts at court, which lasted only an hour and a quarter and included just four pieces.[13]

Similarly, staged operas and other dramatic pieces with music were a common part of festivities under Schrattenbach but reduced to a minimum by Colloredo. Since its foundation in 1617, the Salzburg University regularly mounted large-scale theatrical productions in its university theatre. A fixture within the calendar was the annual *Finalkomödien*, Latin dramas for the end of the school year, but theatre performances were also given on religious feast days or in honour of visiting guests. The music for these dramas was mostly written by a member of the court music and instrumentalists from the court took part in the events. In 1767 Mozart composed his first dramatic work, *Apollo et Hyacinthus* (K. 38), for performance at the university.

These opulent baroque stage dramas must have been a particular nuisance to Colloredo, because he set out to reform the *Finalkomödien* immediately after his accession to the archbishop's see and then abolished the school plays permanently in 1778. Instead, a public theatre was opened on the other side of the river in 1775. Spoken theatre made up the lion's share of performances by travelling troupes at the new venue, but there were also music theatre productions. The Mozart family, living just opposite the new theatre, took great interest in the plays performed and often befriended visiting actors. Around the same time, Colloredo also instigated the refurbishment of the Redoutensaal in the town hall. This was primarily a custom-built hall for the carnival festivities encompassing masques and social dancing, but it also served as a public concert venue for travelling virtuosos.

Another musical genre associated with the end-of-year ceremonies at the Benedictine University was the orchestral serenade. These works consisted

[11] MBA, vol. 3, p. 547 (letter to Nannerl, 22 May 1786). Not in LMF.

[12] For a sample of orchestral works from that period, see Cliff Eisen (ed.), *Orchestral Music in Salzburg 1750–1780* (Madison, WI: A-R Editions, 1994).

[13] MBA, vol. 2, pp. 482, 485 (17 September and 24 September 1778). Not in LMF.

of a flexible number of dances and concerto-like movements for various
instruments, usually framed by an opening and closing march. While the
Finalkomödie was part of the official ceremonies and performed by court
musicians, the serenades were put on by the students. Leopold as well as his
son contributed significantly to the genre: Leopold composed more than
thirty serenades until 1757, and Wolfgang wrote the serenades for the
celebrations in 1774 (K. 203) and 1775 (K. 204) as well as the so-called
'Posthorn' serenade (K. 320) in 1779. Name days, weddings and birthdays
provided further opportunities for performances of serenades, diverti-
menti, cassations and notturni on Salzburg's streets.

The diary entries from summer 1776 by Joachim Schidenhofen, a close
friend of the Mozart family, give an idea of the frequency of such musical
celebrations in the city.[14] On 11 June Schidenhofen attended a musical
performance at the house of Giovanni Battista Gussetti, a local pharmacist
and amateur musician. A week later on 18 June, a divertimento by Mozart
(K. 247) was performed on the occasion of the Countess Maria Antonia
Lodron's name day. After dinner on 7 July, Schidenhofen listened to
a serenade in honour of Maria Anna Elisabeth Antretter (possibly
Mozart's Divertimento K. 251). On 21 July Mozart's march and serenade
K. 249 and K. 250 were performed at the garden house of the merchant
Sigmund Haffner as a wedding present for his sister Maria Elisabeth. In the
evening of 30 July, Countess Antonie von Lützow's departure from the city
merited a musical serenade. On 18 and 19 August Schidenhofen attended
the end-of-year serenades by the university students: on the first day the
students performed compositions by Josef Hafeneder, and on the second
day music by Michael and Joseph Haydn was played.

Schidenhofen's as well as Nannerl Mozart's diary also record plenty of
instances of private music-making indoors at the home of nobles and,
obviously, at the Mozarts' own home. After the Mozarts moved from
Getreidegasse in the centre of the old town to the larger lodgings on the
other side of the river in October 1773, they had the so-called
Tanzmeistersaal at their disposal, a large hall formerly used by the local
dancing master for instruction. This hall was ideally suited for the regular
musical and social gatherings, which involved music-making as well as
playing cards and shooting sessions. Many of Mozart's instrumental concertos and divertimentos from the 1770s were composed for performances
in such semi-public environments: for example, he wrote the Piano

---

[14] See Rudolph Angermüller (ed.), *Joachim Ferdinand von Schidenhofen – Ein Freund der Mozarts* (Bad
Honnef: K.H. Bock, 2006).

Concerto for three pianos K. 242 for the Countess Antonia Maria Felicitas Lodron and her two daughters Maria Aloisia and Maria Josepha, who later became piano pupils of Leopold; and the Piano Concerto in C major K. 246 was dedicated to the Countess Antonie Lützow.

A widespread culture of private domestic music-making in town can be inferred from the large amounts of music that were listed in sales catalogues of the local book shop Mayr and that were brought to the city by itinerant book traders at the spring and autumn fairs during the later eighteenth century. While the official church music and the orchestral repertoire at court and in town consisted mostly of home-grown, Viennese or Italian compositions, the printed sheet music sold in Salzburg for domestic music-making stemmed from all parts of Europe and included a considerable proportion of works by North German composers. The Salzburg public craved the same kinds of easy piano pieces, songs and chamber music as the North German *Liebhaber*, and many of the theoretical books on music and practical music treatises published in North Germany also circulated in Salzburg.

This rich musical context of the city was matched by an equally lively and enlightened intellectual environment in the 1770s. Riesbeck's travelogue cited at the opening of this chapter lists Leopold Maria Joseph Kuenburg and the brothers Vigilius Maria and Franz Laktanz von Firmian among the Salzburg 'people who excel in their profound knowledge'.[15] Close and amicable personal ties existed between the Mozart family and these people. Yet, it was not just the high nobility in town who wanted to participate in modern cultural and intellectual trends. In the traditional view, the Mozarts stood out from their Salzburg environment through intellectual interests and wide-ranging erudition, acquired to a large degree on their travels. Leopold knew the arts and the sciences, bought optical appliances in London, met some of the Paris *philosophes* personally, conversed by letter with the author Christian Fürchtegott Gellert and was stunned at seeing the expressive paintings of Rubens in the Low Countries; and, exceptionally, Wolfgang was given the opportunity to witness all of this as a child. Yet Voltaire's and Rousseau's writings were widely available and read in Salzburg, and Flemish art also hung in art galleries of their home town. Friends of the Mozarts were fascinated by modern technology and science, too; they owned state-of-the-art optical equipment and shared Leopold's admiration for Gottsched and Gellert. So, far from alienating the Mozarts from their environment, their

---

[15] Riesbeck, *Briefe*, vol. 1, p. 203.

intellectual interests and erudition provided points of contact and social exchange.

For a middle-sized town, Salzburg boasted an extremely rich and varied cultural and musical life, and the Mozart family actively partook of all aspects of it from the 1750s until the late 1770s. Regarding musical life, they even occupied a central role in town and at court until the rift between Wolfgang and Archbishop Colloredo in the late 1770s. Thus Mozart's second and final resignation from Salzburg court duties in 1781 terminated his short spell as Salzburg court organist, a well-remunerated post granted to him in 1779 upon his grudging return to his hometown after the trip to Paris. But Mozart's dismissal also severely damaged the social network of his father and sister in Salzburg. Apparently, Leopold Mozart mostly confined himself to his home thereafter and withdrew from society, as he describes in a letter from September 1782: 'For several months I have not appeared at court and only do so when I am obliged to. I live quietly with my daughter and have a few friends who come to see me. Reading, music and an occasional walk are our recreation.'[16]

---

[16] MBA, vol. 3, p. 229; LMF, pp. 820–21 (letter to Baroness von Waldstätten, 13 September 1782). (Translation from LMF.)

CHAPTER 10

Vienna

David Wyn Jones

Mozart lived permanently in Vienna from 1781 until his death ten years later in 1791. But he, together with his father Leopold, was well acquainted with the city before that, making three substantial visits: in 1762 (September to December), 1767–68 (briefly in October, permanently from January to December) and in 1773 (July to September). Vienna was the capital of the Holy Roman Empire, more properly the Holy Roman Empire of the German Nations; in Mozart's lifetime three successive members of the Habsburg family served as emperors, Franz Stephan (the husband of Maria Theresia) from 1745 to 1765, Joseph II from to 1765 to 1790, and Leopold II from 1790 to 1792. Salzburg was not part of the hereditary lands directly ruled by the Habsburgs – it did not become part of Austria until 1805 – but a principality loyal to the Habsburg dynasty, ruled by an archbishop who was also dignified, as the family letters of Mozart often indicate, by the title of Prince of the Holy Roman Empire. Much of that natural loyalty between the Salzburg principality and the imperial capital was founded on a shared religious identity, zealously Catholic, one that presented itself in a similar civic and rural landscape of churches, monasteries, convents and shrines. It was also a product of geography: Vienna was only two days' travel by coach from Salzburg, three if a boat was taken from Linz along the Danube to the imperial capital. Mozart's comments on the provincial nature of musical life in Salzburg are often quoted, usually understood in a European context of comparison with life in London, Mannheim, Paris and elsewhere, but it had a particular force when applied to Salzburg and Vienna: Salzburg was a city within a principality within an empire, whereas Vienna was the capital of the hereditary lands (the monarchy) as well as the empire. The lure of Vienna was a strong one, and it was entirely appropriate that Mozart should wish to make his mark there.

The particulars of that attraction changed during Mozart's lifetime as political, social and economic history impacted on the role of music in

Vienna. While the Mozart correspondence, mainly authored by Leopold up to 1781 and by Wolfgang from 1781 onwards, sometimes refers to wider events, as private exchanges they do not give a full account of them; usually there was a shared knowledge of the circumstances that did not need to be explained, allowing instead for comment on the personal successes and failures, the gossip and intrigue that animated those circumstances.

The excitable sense of experiencing Vienna, the imperial capital, for the first time in the autumn of 1762 is constantly evident from Leopold's letters back to Salzburg. Displaying the astonishing capabilities of the six-year-old Mozart was the focus of the visit, and entry into the highest society was facilitated by the imperial connection between the two cities. Within weeks the young Mozart, together with his father, his mother and his sister, had met the Empress, Maria Theresia; the Emperor, Franz Stephan; and many of their musically talented children, including Archduke Joseph (aged 21), Archduke Leopold (aged 15), Archduke Ferdinand (aged 8) and Archduke Maximilian (aged 6), all of whom were to feature in Mozart's later career. 'Their Majesties received us with such extraordinary graciousness' wrote Leopold 'that, when I shall tell of it, people will declare that I have made it up. Suffice it to say that Wolferl jumped up on the Empress's lap, put his arms round her neck and kissed her heartily.'[1] The Mozart family also had lunch with the imperial Kapellmeister, Georg Reutter (1708–72), the eighteenth to have served the musical court since its foundation at the end of the fifteenth century. Until the middle of the eighteenth century the musical history of the court had been one of continual expansion, but it was Reutter's fate to preside over a refocussing of its activities, prompted by wider musical fashion and by the financial constraints brought about by the Seven Years War. The long, and sometimes extremely lavish, tradition of private operatic performances at court to celebrate birthdays, name days and weddings of leading members of the imperial family had been discontinued; the former private theatre, the Burgtheater, was now a public theatre run at arm's length from the court; and Reutter's duties were restricted to providing church music, itself also the subject of increased financial stringency. Ironically, this period of retrenchment took place when the number of musically gifted members of the imperial family, the Empress Maria Theresia and her nine children, was at an all-time high, as singers, keyboard players, string players and directors, and it was this continuing wider interest in music rather than the consequences of financial stringency that caught the attention of the Mozart family.

[1] MBA, vol. 1, pp. 52–3; LMF, p. 6 (letter to Hagenauer, 19 October 1762).

Momentarily, Leopold thought he could work in this environment: 'If only I knew what the future will finally bring. For one thing is certain: I am now in circumstances that allow me to earn my living here too.'[2]

Although the second visit by the Mozart family (father, mother and the two children) in 1767–68 was a much longer one, over a year, it turned out to be a completely different experience; it left Leopold, in particular, with a very jaundiced view of musical life in the city, one that was to remain with him for the rest of his life, informing his nervousness about Wolfgang's decision to move there in 1781. It began well with an audience at court. But the court was no longer the musically engaged one of the earlier visit. Following the death of Emperor Franz Stephan in 1765, the Empress had become rather withdrawn; the new Holy Roman Emperor was her son, Joseph, and the recent death of his second wife, Princess Maria Josepha of Bavaria, also cast a shadow over the court, even though the marriage itself had been an unhappy one. In deference to the court, the Viennese aristocracy had also curtailed its musical activity.[3] Control of all the theatres in Vienna, in the suburbs as well as the court theatres in the inner city, had been handed over to Joseph d'Afflisio, an experienced, if rather duplicitous entrepreneur. Nominally, he had complete control but Joseph II and Prince Kaunitz wanted to exert their influence too.[4] The young Mozart became caught in this tangle of commercial expediency and imperial uncertainty. As a youth who had just celebrated his sixteenth birthday and as a German rather than an Italian, he was given the doubly risky opportunity to compose a comic Italian opera, *La finta semplice*, on an existing text by the celebrated Carlo Goldoni. Mozart completed the work, but rumour and opera-house intrigue ensured that it was never performed in Vienna, much to Leopold's disgust.

Five years elapsed before Leopold and Wolfgang were to return to the city for a shorter visit of ten weeks, from 14 July 1773 to 26 September 1773. Once again, they were received at court by Maria Theresia, but nothing eventuated from that meeting. The visit did, however, coincide with momentous changes in the long-standing role of the Jesuits in society, in education as well as in religious orthodoxy. A papal bull had been issued, dissolving the order. For Joseph II, who like many generations of the imperial family had been educated by the Jesuits, this conveniently played

---

[2] MBA, vol. 1, p. 57; LMF, p. 10 (letter to Hagenauer, 30 October 1762).

[3] MBA, vol. 1, pp. 255–56; LMF, pp. 80–1 (letter to Hagenauer, 30 January–3 February 1768).

[4] Derek Beales, *Joseph II, Volume I: In the Shadow of Maria Theresa, 1741–1780* (Cambridge: Cambridge University Press, 1987), pp. 159–60. Franz Hadamowsky, *Wien, Theatergeschichte: Von den Anfängen bis zum Ende des Ersten Weltkriegs* (Vienna: Jugend und Volk, 1988), pp. 221–25.

into a wider political agenda, the desire to reform education and to make religious institutions more beholden to the Austrian Monarchy than to Rome. In a rather chaotic manner, over a period of a few months, the Jesuit order was not only formally dissolved but its property was transferred to the state and ex-Jesuits redeployed as teachers and lay priests.[5]

The Vienna that Mozart grew to know in his adult years was a city of some 210,000 citizens, one third of whom lived in the inner city,[6] an area traversed by foot in fifteen minutes or so. A walled city, it was separated from the suburbs by heavy fortifications and, to the south and east, by an area of open land (broadly the route of the present Ringstrasse), all originally designed to give protection from the traditional enemy, the Ottoman Empire. Except for some main thoroughfares, such as the Graben, and some squares, such as Am Hof and the Mehlmarkt, it was a crowded area with many high buildings. The spires of two churches dominated the skyline, St Stephen's, close to the centre of the city, and the Augustinerkirche, adjacent to the imperial palace, the Hofburg. For centuries, this sense of a protected enclosure had been emphasized by the night-time closure of the city gates; in Joseph's time, as a clear signal of a new confidence and openness that characterized much of his reign, they were open at all times.

Making the suburbs more accessible to the inner city was also facilitated, with the opening of two areas of imperial parkland to the north of the city for the use of the general public, the Augarten and the Prater, both frequently visited by Mozart and his young family. In order to remain close to the Hofburg, to the many aristocratic palaces and to key musical businesses such as those of Johann Traeg, the music dealer and copyist, and Artaria, the music publisher, Mozart lived for most of the time in the inner city, at twelve different addresses. Rented accommodation was generally more expensive there than in the suburbs and Mozart twice moved outside the inner city, to the Alsergrund to the west and to the Landstrasse to the east. Even though they were only some ten minutes away from the city walls, Mozart would have missed the convenience of being in the inner city and, on both occasions, his next move was back there.

A recurring topic in Mozart's correspondence with his father during the early 1780s is the young composer's very traditional ambition to serve at the imperial court. He was acquainted with Joseph II, knew many of the

---

[5] Beales, *In the Shadow of Maria Theresa*, pp. 462–64.
[6] Statistics from Ignaz de Luca, *Topographie von Wien* (Vienna, 1794; facsimile edition, Vienna: Promedia, 2003), pp. 12–15.

influential courtiers and it was a genuine aspiration: 'There is no monarch in the world whom I should be more glad to serve than the Emperor.'[7] When the false rumour spread in April 1782 that he had, in fact, secured such an appointment, he took great delight in reporting it.[8] But father and son also knew that the age-old protocols of court appointments made it rather unlikely. Appointments were for life, compounded by the practice of appointing from within, particularly for senior positions. In the early 1780s, the Kapellmeister was Giuseppe Bonno (1711–88), who had held the position since 1774 having previously served for thirty-three years as composer (*Compositor*). When he died in March 1788 he was succeeded by Antonio Salieri (1750–1825) who, similarly, had worked as a composer at court, in his case for twenty-four years. Shortly before, in November 1787, a second composer, Gluck, had died, after thirteen years of service. It was only at this juncture – the promotion of one composer and the death of another – that Mozart's ambitions could finally be realized and he was duly appointed as composer. This satisfaction would have been tempered by the realization that, since Salieri was only six years older than him, Mozart would have to wait a very long time before succeeding to the highest position.

Approximately 3 per cent of the population of Vienna were identified as belonging to the nobility, over 7,000 individuals, divided into four groups: princes, counts, barons and knights.[9] Contrary to perceptions that are still commonplace, the number of households that employed a full-time retinue of musicians was very small indeed, but music as a recreation serviced by the casual employment of musicians as performers and teachers was socially widespread, and Mozart acted in both capacities. Between February and April 1784, for instance, Mozart performed several times at the palaces of Prince Dimitri Galitzin (long-serving Russian ambassador) and Count Johann Baptist Esterházy (a distant cousin of Haydn's employer), and those two plus no fewer than twelve princes and princesses and fifty-five counts and countesses subscribed to the three concerts that Mozart himself organized that season.[10] Piano pupils were invariably women but, as Mozart's letters hint, this income stream was a fitful one, discontinued when the aristocracy left for their country estates in the summer, and summarily cancelled at other times of the year too.

[7] MBA, vol. 3, p. 220; LMF, p. 814 (17 August 1782).
[8] MBA, vol. 3, p. 201; LMF, pp. 799–800 (10 April 1782).   [9] Luca, *Topographie*, pp. 13–21.
[10] MBA, vol. 3, pp. 303–04, 305–07; LMF, pp. 869–72 (3 March and 20 March 1784).

A natural consequence of this strong tradition of private patronage was that public concert life was not as well developed in Vienna as in some European cities, notably London and Paris. Most concerts were one-off occasions for the benefit of a named individual and mainly took place in the theatres, including the two court theatres (the Burgtheater and the Kärntnertortheater), on evenings when there were no theatrical performances. As Mozart's letters from the early 1780s reveal, he was particularly anxious to take part in the charity concerts of the Tonkünstler-Societät, an organization established in 1771 to raise money for the widows and orphans of musicians. The society had evolved an annual pattern of presenting a pair of concerts during Lent and a second pair of concerts in Advent, each pair usually featuring the same repertoire and held in one of the court theatres. By the 1780s the concerts had become highlights in the musical calendar, and Mozart's desire to become involved was central to his ambition. The programmes typically featured an oratorio (or extracts from an oratorio) together with concertos and symphonies. Mozart became a regular participant, appearing in nine concerts between 1781 and 1791, as a soloist in his piano concertos, a composer of symphonies and, a crucial indicator of acceptance, the composer of the cantata *Davide penitente*, performed at the pair of concerts in Lent 1785.[11]

One of the most far-reaching musical decisions that Joseph II made as emperor was to return the court theatres to the direct management of the court in 1776, following a period of eleven years when they had been run by contracted impresarios. The emperor was genuinely interested in the theatre – spoken drama as well as opera – and liked to exercise artistic and managerial authority on behalf of what he expected would be a responsive and appreciative public; in thought and deed it was the outlook of an enlightened despot. In 1776 he had set up the National Theatre to promote plays written in German rather than in the traditional French. Two years later, the language policy was extended to opera, and until 1783 only *Singspiele* were performed, effectively marginalizing the status of Italian opera in the eyes of the public. Traditionalists did not like this new emphasis, and in 1783 Joseph re-engaged an Italian company to perform comic Italian opera at the Burgtheater. But as Joseph hoped, and certainly lived long enough to witness, this apparent volte face did not lead to the demise of German opera in Vienna; some continued to be performed in the Burgtheater and the Kärntnertortheater, and many more in

---

[11] David Black, 'Mozart's Association with the Tonkünstler-Societät', in Simon P. Keefe (ed.), *Mozart Studies 2* (Cambridge: Cambridge University Press, 2015), pp. 55–75.

the two suburban theatres outside the control of the court, the Leopoldstadt theatre (north of the inner city) and the Theater auf der Wieden (south of the inner city).[12] It was against these interlocking patterns of changes in management and artistic preferences that Mozart's Viennese operas were composed: *Die Entführung von Serail* for the German opera troupe, *Le nozze di Figaro* and *Così fan tutte* for the re-established Italian opera (*Don Giovanni* was also performed, following its premiere in Prague) and *Die Zauberflöte* for the Theater auf der Wieden.

The most striking difference between Mozart's professional life in Salzburg and the one he led in Vienna was the part that Catholic liturgical music played: from being central to his creative life in Salzburg, it did not figure at all in Vienna for much of the 1780s. This was not a matter of deliberate choice by Mozart, but a direct consequence of a concentrated period of reform of the role of the Catholic Church in the Austrian territories. Between 1782 and 1784 in a series of measures, Joseph II suppressed one third of the monasteries, redirected the role of the remaining two-thirds to parish work and to education, curtailed the considerable duplication of church services in Vienna, abolished most church processions and many pilgrimages, disbanded the many brotherhoods that supported church activities (including music) and determined a new, much reduced role for music in the liturgy.[13] Mozart would have witnessed this upheaval and its impact on the many musicians employed in Vienna's churches, over four hundred in number, and, though he never commented on these changes, they were the reason why composing church music was not a priority early in the 1780s. Only towards the end of the 1780s did church music begin to feature once more in Mozart's thinking. His employment at the imperial court from 1787 and his strategic thinking about how that career might unfold over the years seem to have encouraged him to compose five movements (four settings of a Kyrie and one of the Gloria), portions of masses that could be completed if and when an opportunity presented itself. This hypothesis is given further credence by Mozart's plan, apparently never enacted, to petition Joseph II's successor, Leopold II, for a more senior position as a composer of church music at the court and for occasional public occasions too, a genre of music, he correctly

[12] Derek Beales, *Joseph II, Volume II: Against the World, 1780–1790* (Cambridge: Cambridge University Press, 2009), pp. 457–64. Hadamowsky, *Wien. Theatergeschichte*, pp. 266–77, 484–88, 504–06. Otto Michtner, *Das alte Burgtheater als Opernbühne. Von der Einführung des Deutschen Singspiels (1778) bis zum Tod Leopolds II. (1792)* (Vienna: Österreichischen Akademie der Wissenschaften, 1970), pp. 25–297, 455–503.
[13] Beales, *Against the World*, pp. 271–98, 314–25.

pointed out, in which he was vastly more experienced than Kapellmeister
Salieri. A year later, in May 1791, Mozart turned his thoughts to the
possibility of a post at the cathedral, St Stephen's. The Kapellmeister,
Leopold Hofmann (1738–93), had been ill and Mozart offered to act as
his assistant, which, in accordance with standard practice, would have
almost certainly guaranteed him the post on Hofmann's death. In the
event, Hofmann did not die until 1793, when he was succeeded by Johann
Georg Albrechtsberger (1736–1809).[14]

Mozart's adult career in Vienna was determined by the many changes in
the musical environment that occurred between 1781 and 1791. In range
and in degree these changes amounted to one of the most eventful musical
decades of the eighteenth century in the city. Mozart had to navigate his
way through this period, responding to the new, the changing and the
traditional, in patronage, concert life, operatic life, church music and
musical commerce. The shifting dynamic of these constituent elements
made for an environment that was unique in its challenges and produced
a diversity of musical output that was not achieved by any other Viennese
composer of the time.

---

[14] David Black, 'Mozart and the Practice of Sacred Music, 1781-91' (PhD thesis, Harvard University,
    2007), pp. 168–72, 183–92, 286–94.

Germany

Paul Corneilson

In the eighteenth century, Germany was not a separate state, but rather the collective lands where German was the principal (spoken) language. Mozart lived in or spent significant time in several important cities in Germany (including Salzburg, Vienna and Prague, which are covered elsewhere in this book) and visited many others (Augsburg, Munich, Mannheim, Dresden, Leipzig, Berlin, Frankfurt), and so he would have been well aware of the distinctive regions of Germany, their political systems, social customs and currencies. He also personally met the rulers of these lands and had the privilege of interacting with them more or less on an equal level.[1]

From the late Middle Ages, the so-called Holy Roman Empire served as the governing body, with the Habsburg dynasty providing the emperor for most of the modern period.[2] But each kingdom, province, duchy and ecclesiastical domain had its own rulers (kings, dukes, archbishops, etc.) and systems of government, and some territories retained their own languages (Italian, Hungarian, French, Polish), even if they were allied to the Empire. Formally, the emperor was elected by the electoral college (Kurfürstenrat), which had been established in 1356 by the Golden Bull of Charles IV. In the late eighteenth century, the *Kurfürsten* included the secular and spiritual elector-princes given in Table 11.1.

The secular prince-electors were hereditary, and in the eighteenth century several lines of families died out without a direct heir. For instance,

---

[1] Derek Beales, 'Mozart and the Habsburgs', in *Enlightenment and Reform in Eighteenth-Century Europe* (London: I. B. Tauris, 2005), p.92, points out that eighteenth-century musicians, especially composers of Mozart's talent and rank, were among the few subjects who were able to talk to their sovereigns in a familiar way.

[2] See the recent book by Peter H. Wilson, *Heart of Europe: A History of the Holy Roman Empire* (Cambridge: Harvard University Press, 2016). For an account of the Hapsburg dynasty from the eighteenth to twentieth centuries, see Pieter M. Judson, *The Habsburg Empire: A New History* (Cambridge: Harvard University Press, 2016). Voltaire famously quipped that it was neither holy, Roman nor an empire.

Table 11.1 *German Elector-Princes during Mozart's Lifetime*

Electoral Title	Principal Residence	Family Name (Other Titles)	Rulers in Late 18th Century
King of Bohemia	Vienna	Habsburg (Emperor, King of Hungary)	Joseph II (r. 1765–90); Leopold II (r. 1790–92)
Duke of Bavaria	Munich	Wittelsbach (Bavarian line)	Maximilian III Joseph (r. 1745–77); Carl Theodor (r. 1778–99)
Count Palatine	Mannheim	Wittelsbach (Neuburg and Sulzbach lines)	Carl Theodor (r. 1742–99)
Duke of Saxony	Dresden	Wettin (King of Poland)	Friedrich August II (r. 1733–63); Friedrich August III (r. 1763–1806)
Margrave of Brandenburg	Berlin	Hollenzollern (King of Prussia)	Friedrich II (r. 1740–86); Friedrich Wilhelm II (r. 1786–97)
Duke of Brunswick-Lüneberg	London	Hanover (King of Great Britain)	George III (r. 1760–1820)
Archbishop of Mainz	Mainz		Emmerich Joseph von Breidbach zu Bürresheim (r. 1763–74); Friedrich Karl Joseph von Erthal (r. 1774–1802)
Archbishop of Cologne	Bonn		Maximilian Friedrich of Königsegg-Rothenfels (r. 1761–84); Maximilian Francis (r. 1784–1801)
Archbishop of Trier	Koblenz		Clemens Wenceslaus (r. 1768–1803)

in January 1742, Elector Palatine Carl III Philipp of Neuburg arranged for his two granddaughters, Elisabeth Auguste and Maria Anna, to marry Duke Carl Theodor of Palatine-Sulzbach and the Duke Clement Francis of Bavaria.[3] (Soon after the wedding, Charles Albert of Bavaria was elected Holy Roman Emperor as Charles VII, the only non-Habsburg to become Emperor, though he only ruled for three years.) Carl III Philipp died

---

[3] The wedding celebration included a new opera, *Meride*, by Carlo Grua, which opened the Mannheim opera house; see Paul Corneilson, 'Reconstructing the Mannheim Court Theatre', *Early Music*, 25 (1997), pp. 63–81.

within the year and was succeeded by his nephew Carl Theodor.[4] While Mozart was visiting Mannheim in 1777, the Elector of Bavaria, Maximilian III Joseph, died on 30 December, and his cousin Elector Palatine Carl Theodor inherited the Electorate of Bavaria, which was thereafter known as the Electorate of Palatinate-Bavaria with Munich as the residence.[5]

The reason for going into so much detail on the political history is to show that these events did affect Mozart's career. In the autumn of 1777, Mozart left Salzburg to seek a position, preferably at a German court, and visited Munich and Mannheim in the hope of joining the Hofkapelle.[6] He was led to believe that there might be a position available at Mannheim, where the elector had recently established a National Theatre, and Mozart gave lessons to two of the elector's natural children in an effort to curry favour. He also told Carl Theodor that 'my greatest wish is to write an opera here'.[7] Mozart befriended some of the court musicians and singers, including the Cannabichs, the Wendlings and the tenor Anton Raaff, all of whom wielded influence with the elector. In order to cover all his bases, Mozart also dedicated a set of six accompanied sonatas (K. 301–306) to Electress Elisabeth Auguste and presented her with a copy of the engraving in January 1779.

The death of Maximilian III Joseph was a double blow against Mozart. First, it meant that Carl Theodor had to leave Mannheim immediately for Munich to secure his claim to the Bavarian Succession.[8] This in turn led the carnival opera (Anton Schweitzer's *Rosemunde*) to be cancelled and virtually all other musical activities ceased.[9] Second, Carl Theodor ultimately moved his court to Munich permanently, which resulted in no openings in the combined Mannheim-Munich music establishment.

---

[4] On Carl Theodor, see the sumptuous exhibition catalogue, Alfried Wieczorek et al. (eds.), *Lebenslust und Frömmigkeit: Kurfürst Carl Theodor (1724–1799) zwischen Barock und Aufklärung*, 2 vols. (Regensburg: Pustet, 1999). For a brief survey of music in its social context at Mannheim, see Eugene K. Wolf, 'The Mannheim Court', in Neal Zaslaw (ed.), *The Classical Era* (London: Macmillan, 1989), pp. 213–39.

[5] The only child of Carl Theodor and Elisabeth Auguste, a son Francis Louis Joseph, was born on 28 June 1762 but died the following day. Thus when Carl Theodor died in 1799, the title passed to another cousin, Maximilian IV Joseph, Duke of Zweibrücken (who later became Maximilian I Joseph, King of Bavaria from 1806 to 1825).

[6] On the organization of the Mannheim Hofkapelle, see Bärbel Pelker, 'The Palatine Court in Mannheim', in Samantha Owens et al. (eds.), *Music at German Courts, 1715–1760: Changing Artistic Priorities* (Woodbridge and Rochester, NY: Boydell Press, 2011), pp. 131–64.

[7] MBA, vol. 2, p. 110; LMF, p. 362 (8 November 1777). Translation slightly amended.

[8] See Derek Beales, *Joseph II, Volume I: In the Shadow of Maria Theresa, 1741–1780* (Cambridge: Cambridge University Press, 1987), chapter 13.

[9] Mozart visited the Princess Weilburg at Kirchheim-Bolanden in mid January with the eldest two Weber daughters, Josepha and Aloysia, and their father Fridolin, in order to make a little money.

Finally, it also meant that when Mozart received a commission for an opera from Carl Theodor less than two years later, *Idomeneo* was performed in Munich, rather than Mannheim, though most of the singers and orchestra had formerly been at Mannheim.[10]

Mozart timed his itinerary to arrive at Mannheim for the gala days in early November 1777 to celebrate the name day of the elector. In his first letter written from Mannheim on 31 October, Mozart mentions having attended a rehearsal of an oratorio by Handel (Part I of *Messiah*) and a psalm setting by Georg Joseph Vogler, which would have been performed on 1 November, All Saints Day. A few days later, he described the performance in great detail, and noted that the Mass by Kapellmeister Ignaz Holzbauer on Sunday, 2 November, was much better than the one by Vogler on 1 November (letter of 4 November). The court almanac for 1777 describes the events for 4 November:

> On the fourth, St. Charles Borromeo, there is a great gala at court in honour of the name day of his Electoral Highness, our most benevolent ruler. On this high festival all the nobles, ministers, and cavaliers, together with all secretaries of administration, will most graciously appear in his [the elector's] grand apartment for congratulations and hand-kissing, after which around eleven o'clock his Electoral Highness and the entire court establishment will process between both bodyguards [Swiss Guard and Palatine Guard], arranged to the left and right of the palace corridor, to the High Mass [in the court chapel], wherein the Most Holy Sacrament is exposed [in the form of a monstrance], and, after the Elevation, the Te Deum laudamus is sung. During the High Mass at the Gloria in excelsis, again at the singing of the Te Deum, and finally at the last holy blessing, the cannons are fired from the ramparts. Thereafter a public banquet is held, to which the food is carried by the electoral chamberlains.[11]

The following day, on 5 November, Holzbauer's opera *Günther von Schwarzburg* was performed (see Mozart's short review in his letter of 14 November), and on 6 November there was a concert at the Rittersaal in the palace. Almost in passing – first in a letter to his cousin Maria Anna Thekla on 5 November and then in a letter to his father on 8 November –

---

[10] The classic study is Daniel Heartz, 'The Genesis of *Idomeneo*', *Musical Quarterly*, 55 (1967), pp. 1–19. For background on Carnival opera in Munich, see Karl Böhmer, *W.A. Mozarts 'Idomeneo' und die Tradition der Karnevalsopern in München* (Tutzing: Hans Schneider, 1999).

[11] *Kurpfälzischer Hof- und Staats-Kalender auf das Jahr 1777*, facsimile, with an introduction by Stefan Mörz (Mannheim: Universitätsbibliothek Mannheim, 2000). To see how little this ceremony had changed in more than twenty years, compare this to the description in the almanac of 1755, quoted in Wolf, 'The Mannheim Court', p. 219. In 1755, an opera was performed on the elector's name day.

Mozart mentions that he played two selections at the Academie on 6 November at the command of the electress. There was also a play given on 7 November, which the Mozarts attended with the Cannabichs.[12] A couple of weeks later, on 19 November, the Feast of St. Elisabeth, the name day of the electress, there were similar celebrations at court.

The Mozarts often visited Munich during Carnival to see the operas, attend the balls and partake in the other festivities of the season. Wolfgang received a commission to write an opera buffa, *La finta giardiniera*, for Carnival 1775. A few years later he wrote *Idomeneo* for Carnival 1781. Naturally, Leopold and Nannerl attended the latter premiere, thus depriving us of correspondence that might have further explained the cuts made in the third act of the opera. Wolfgang certainly heard Schweitzer's *Alceste* in Carnival 1779, and probably also heard Franz de Paula Grua's *Telemaco* in Carnival 1780.[13] Leopold continued to visit Munich during Carnival in the following years, attending Salieri's *Semiramide* in 1782 and Holzbauer's *Tancrède* in 1783.[14] After Wolfgang's departure, Leopold began to tutor two of the Marchand children, Heinrich on violin and Margarethe on keyboard and voice, and in 1785 he visited their parents in Munich then went to Vienna to see his son. By 1786 Leopold had taken in his grandson Leopold (Nannerl's child) and had to wait to visit Munich until arrangements could be made to care for young Leopold. He was still able to hear Salieri's *La fiera di Venezia* (originally written for Vienna in 1772 and earlier performed in Mannheim) with Gretl, and made his last trip to Munich in Carnival 1787 to hear Georg Joseph Vogler's *Castore e Polluce*, again with Gretl singing.[15]

---

[12] Maria Anna Mozart specifies that Wolfgang played a concerto, then later improvised and played a sonata at the academy. The ambassador to the Saxon court, Andreas von Riaucour, also reported on this concert, but he only mentions that the Princess Marianne sang two arias. See Paul Corneilson, 'Opera at Mannheim, 1770-1778' (PhD thesis, University of North Carolina, Chapel Hill, 1992), p. 394.

[13] The Munich public did not like German serious opera, and so, after *Alceste*, Carl Theodor reverted to Italian opera seria in 1780. See Böhmer, *W.A. Mozarts 'Idomeneo'*, pp. 159–64.

[14] On Salieri's opera, see John A. Rice, 'Salieri's *Semiramide* and the End of the Metastasian Tradition in Munich', in Theodor Göllner and Stephan Hörner (eds.), *Mozarts 'Idomeneo' und die Musik in München zur Zeit Karl Theodors* (Munich: Bayerischen Akademie der Wissenschaften, 2001), pp. 151–63. On 8 May 1782 Mozart asked Leopold about Salieri's opera, but none of Leopold's letters to Wolfgang in Vienna have survived.

[15] These trips are documented and discussed by Ruth Halliwell in *The Mozart Family: Four Lives in a Social Context* (Oxford: Clarendon Press, 1998).

Leopold Mozart was born in Augsburg, and some of his family remained there. Wolfgang met his cousin again in 1777, and the two carried on a raucous correspondence for the next year or so. But Augsburg was a 'free city', like Frankfurt and Hamburg, with no court *Kapelle* that Mozart could join, and it seems clear that Mozart had set his sights on obtaining a court appointment at one of the major courts. When nothing was available in Munich or Mannheim or Paris, Mozart reluctantly returned to Salzburg as court organist. Only after the success of *Idomeneo* at Munich in 1781 did he have the courage to resign (or be dismissed) from Archbishop Colloredo's court to seek opportunities in Vienna.

Having received an appointment as court composer in 1787 (see Chapter 16, 'Patronage'), it is curious that Mozart decided to make a trip to Dresden, Leipzig and Berlin in 1789. Perhaps after the death of Frederick II in 1786, Mozart was finally able to travel freely through Saxony to Prussia. Was Mozart really hoping to get a position in Berlin, or was he simply looking to make some extra income, giving concerts or receiving commissions for new works? In any event, it now seems clear that Mozart borrowed money from Prince Lichnowsky to make the trip.[16] Although Maynard Solomon goes to great lengths to propose an illicit affair between Mozart and Josepha Duschek, the wife of Franz Xaver Duschek, the two of them planned their trips independently.[17] Mozart arrived in Prague on 10 April 1789 and two days later reached Dresden. On 13 April, Mozart was asked to perform for the elector and hastily arranged a concert at the Hotel de Pologne, which included the String Trio K. 563 and selections from *Figaro* and *Don Giovanni* sung by Mme Duschek; on the following day he played his Piano Concerto in D, K. 537, at court. For his efforts, Mozart received a very handsome snuffbox. (We learn these details from a letter to his wife, dated 16 April 1789.) Next Mozart went to Leipzig, where he

---

[16] Apparently the debt had not been paid when Mozart died. Peter Hoyt reported on his theory at the American Musicological Society meeting in 2010. Prince Lichnowsky sued Mozart over a debt and won a judgment of 1,435 florins and 32 kreutzer in Austrian currency just before the composer died. Hoyt calculated the money of the lawsuit probably resulted from a loan of 1,000 thalers in Prussian currency made on 2 May 1789, when the prince left Berlin and Mozart needed money to pay for his own transportation back to Vienna.

[17] Maynard Solomon, *Mozart: A Life* (New York: HarperCollins, 1995), pp. 437–54, invented an elaborate *tête-à-tête* between the two, but this has been soundly refuted by Bruce Alan Brown, 'In Defense of Josepha Duschek (and Mozart): Patronage, Friendship, and Evidence', in Kathryn Libin (ed.), *Mozart in Prague: Essays on Performance, Patronage, Sources, and Reception* (Prague: Mozart Society of America, 2016), pp. 155–74. On Mme Duschek as a singer, see Paul Corneilson, '"aber nach geendigter Oper mit Vergnügen": Mozart's Arias for Mme Duschek', in *Mozart in Prague*, pp. 175–200; on K. 528 and its relationship to Jommelli's 'Bella mia fiamma', see Geoffrey Chew, 'The Public and Private Affairs of Josepha Duschek: A Reinterpretation of Mozart's *Bella mia fiamma, addio* KV 528', *Early Music*, 40 (2013), pp. 639–57.

stayed several days before going to Potsdam. There he hoped to have an audience with Friedrich Wilhelm II, but there is no evidence that they ever actually met. Admittedly, the exact timetable of his trip is difficult to reconstruct (four of Mozart's letters to Constanze are missing between 22 April and 9 May), but he eventually returned to Leipzig, where he gave a benefit concert at the Gewandhaus; the programme survives, and it shows that he performed two symphonies (in D and C, according to annotations on the programme), two keyboard concertos, as well as two arias for Mme Duschek.[18] In Leipzig, Mozart also met Johann Friedrich Doles, the Cantor of the Thomaskirche, and heard the Thomaner perform J. S. Bach's *Singet dem Herrn ein neues Lied*, acquiring a copy of the motet for himself.[19] Mozart returned to Berlin and at least played for the queen, claiming that he was 'fortunate enough to be enjoying the King's favour'.[20] Mozart also heard his *Entführung aus dem Serail* in Berlin,[21] and he eventually completed three string quartets (K. 575, 589, 590) that were intended to be dedicated to the Prussian king.

Still more curious is Mozart's trip to Frankfurt for Leopold II's coronation in October 1790. According to Georg Nikolaus von Nissen, Mozart was only accompanied by his brother-in-law Franz de Paula Hofer and had to pawn some of his wife's valuables ('silberne Toilette und Pretiosen') to finance the trip.[22] Why wasn't Mozart part of the official group of court musicians, which included Salieri, Ignaz Umlauf and '15 Kammermusici'?[23] If Mozart was 'on the threshold of his fortune'[24] at this stage of his career, why did he choose to sell some possessions to go to Frankfurt? Perhaps Mozart was overly optimistic about what he could gain financially by giving concerts in Frankfurt and other cities in the Rhineland.[25] The one concert documented, on 15 October 1790 at the Frankfurt Schauspielhaus, was not a success.[26] But perhaps Mozart was using the coronation as an

[18] MDL, p. 300; MDB, p. 342. The programme is reproduced in Corneilson, 'Mozart's Arias for Mme Duschek', p. 193.

[19] Christoph Wolff discusses the trip and Mozart's interest in Bach's music in *Mozart at the Gateway to His Fortune: Serving the Emperor, 1788–1791* (New York: Norton, 2012), pp. 50–73.

[20] MBA, vol. 4, p. 90; LMF, p. 928 (23 May 1789).

[21] This anecdote, originally published in the *Allgemeine musikalische Zeitung* (1799) by Friedrich Rochlitz, is included in John A. Rice, *Mozart on the Stage* (Cambridge: Cambridge University Press, 2009), pp. 230–31, along with an engraving depicting the scene (fig. 10.1 on p. 232).

[22] Georg Niklaus Nissen, *Biographie W. A. Mozart's* (Leipzig, 1828), pp. 545, 683.

[23] Otto Jahn, *W. A. Mozart*, 2 vols. (2nd edition, Leipzig, 1867), vol. 2, p. 458.

[24] As mentioned by Mozart in MBA, vol. 4, p. 104; LMF, p. 936 (March/April 1790).

[25] See Austin Glatthorn, 'The Imperial Coronation of Leopold II and Mozart, Frankfurt am Main, 1790', *Eighteenth-Century Music*, 14 (2017), pp. 89–110.

[26] MDL, pp. 329–30; MDB, pp. 374–75.

excuse to travel back to Mannheim and revisit his friends there. His *Figaro* was performed in Mannheim in late October, and Mozart attended a rehearsal; in Mainz, he performed for the elector and was paid 165 florins.[27] Finally, on the way back to Vienna, Mozart visited Carl Theodor in Munich one last time. According to the early biographer Franz Niemetschek (and confirmed by Mozart's widow to the Novellos): '[Mozart] counted the time spent in Munich as among the most pleasant days of his life, and never forgot the cordial friendship which he there enjoyed with so many estimable people.'[28] Thus it seems likely that Mozart felt as much at home in some of the German cities as he did in the imperial city of Vienna.

[27] MDL, p. 331; MDB, p. 376.
[28] *Leben des k.k. Kapellmeisters Wolfgang Gottlieb Mozart, nach Originalquellen beschrieben* (Prague, 1798), p. 21.

CHAPTER 12

Italy

Sergio Durante

Italy was a reality of some sort in Mozart's imagination long before his first trip to the country began in December 1769. Not only was Italian culture a diffuse 'myth' in Europe but its influence was also strong in Salzburg, notably in relatively recent architecture and in music. The association between Italy and music was essentially twofold: it was connected to the high reputation gained during the seventeenth and early eighteenth centuries as a result of work by many emigrant musicians; and it related to the Italian language itself, the primacy of which as the ideal one for music was undisputed at the time. Both factors might be regarded at least in part as commonplace but were not without effect on Mozart's life: over the years he came to master and take full advantage of the language while occasionally suffering from preconceptions about the supposed superiority of Italian musicians, both in Salzburg with respect to the court music and later in Vienna in the realm of music theatre.

Mozart's first recorded vocal piece, the aria K. 19c (=21) composed in London on a text from Metastasio's *Ezio* in 1765, demonstrates an adequate understanding of the language, and his first experiences of writing Italian, in early letters from Italy itself, reveal a taste for the ironic use of the language in spite of lexical and syntactic uncertainties. Around 1770 Italy was divided into a number of different states as a result of various historical developments. Although all could be grouped together as *Ancien Régime* states, differences were significant, in particular regarding the relationship between church and state on the one hand (a theme on which the Mozarts themselves commented) and between central and peripheral powers on the other (political, administrative or judiciary, whether of a feudal, patrician or bureaucratic nature). Despite all these differences, to which one should add the multiplicity of dialects in use, Italy also offered a degree of homogeneity at least within the upper classes that became familiar to the Mozarts. Italian intellectuals, especially during the eighteenth century, increasingly recognized common cultural ground based on history, culture and descendance (imaginary though it might be) from the ancient Roman civilization, a primacy of sorts also recognized elsewhere in Europe. A major role in such cultural identification was played by the Accademia dell'Arcadia, the interstate cultural network of savants founded in Rome in 1689 and active through numerous *colonie* in the main cultural centres of the peninsula. At the other end of the spectrum, however, members of the ruling class were often associated with European potentate networks within which national identity was far less relevant than family connections or feudal-based dependency, a situation substantially affecting the Mozarts' musical activities in Italy.

The degree to which Leopold and the young Wolfgang perceived the different conditions of the Italian states during the three journeys of 1770–73 is open to question, but there is no doubt that their social and professional success was related to such differences and especially to the degree of influence that the Habsburg monarchy (or associated individuals) exerted locally. We should also acknowledge that the impressions of Italy gathered from the letters are essentially Leopold's rather than those of Wolfgang who, at this point of his life, probably leaned on the opinions of his father in most matters, still enjoying the privilege of a relatively carefree and exciting – but also professionally trying – existence. In his communications from Italy (mainly postscripts) Wolfgang seems more interested in maintaining contact with Salzburg than in adding to Leopold's observations on Italian customs. But his attention is caught, significantly, by the especially slow tempo to which Italians dance minuets.

The first Italian journey represents the overlapping of two different projects: the exposure of the miraculous talents of Wolfgang (as during the earlier Grand Tour, albeit now with the end of his child-prodigy status fast approaching) and the somewhat premature search for an important professional position. In addition, a sizeable amount of time was devoted to visiting Italian historical sites and natural beauties.

Wolfgang acknowledged being in Italy once in Verona and the territory of the Venetian Republic, that is, after having left the territories of the empire and the Italian Rovereto.[1] Leopold related back to Salzburg the warm welcome they usually received – with the exception of that from Michael II Thurn und Taxis in Mantua who snubbed them. The differences in audiences did not pass unnoticed, such as between those at Verona's Accademia filarmonica (run and attended exclusively

---

[1] MBA, vol. i, pp. 301–2 (7 January 1770); the text of the letters is given in the translation by Stewart Spencer in Cliff Eisen et al. (eds.), *In Mozart's Words*: https://www.hrionline.ac.uk/mozartwords/

by the aristocracy) and at Mantua (within the Austrian Lombardy) where the military and the high bourgeoisie were admitted at the recently opened Teatro della Reale Accademia 'as it is a foundation set up by her majesty the Empress'.[2] This difference derived from Maria Theresia's reforms, which extended social participation while containing aristocratic privileges.[3] Leopold noted that on more than one occasion Wolfgang had to perform gratis 'because everyone is admitted free of charge'[4] a fact evidently not as obvious to him as to the local patrons. (The case of church performances was different in that free performances were generally thought to represent acts of devotion.) Leopold's incidental comment on the real income possibilities in Italy proved to be correct: eventually 'Nothing much will come of Italy: our only pleasure consists in the fact that there is more enthusiasm and insight here and that the Italians appreciate what Wolfgang knows'.[5]

In comparison to the Austrian Lombardy, the Republic of Venice reacted conservatively to including new social strata within the central administration; equally, the public discourse on social renewal concerned the clergy's excessive number and the accumulation of property in monastic institutions. Another local characteristic was latent friction between the Venetian aristocracy (exerting the central control of the state) and the nobility of the mainland cities, jealous of their historical prerogatives and occasionally intolerant of the capital, significantly referred to in official documents as the 'Dominante'. In different ways, frictions between the central power and the local aristocracy also affected the State of Milan in the decades before 1770. Economic reforms and increased subjugation of the clergy to the state had been achieved under the aegis of the Genoese minister Gian Luca Pallavicini, who succeeded in establishing a balance between central and peripheral powers more favourable to Vienna and to the intended reforms of the state. Pallavicini, who would later patronize and host the Mozarts in Bologna, also negotiated with the envoys of the Duke of Modena in 1753 the wedding contract that led eventually to the marriage of Maria Beatrice Ricciarda d'Este, the last of her bloodline, and Ferdinand Habsburg, an event of great political importance in that it foreshadowed the inclusion of the Este territories within the empire. The lavishness of the celebrations that took place in October 1771 and Mozart's contribution to the festivities with the *serenata teatrale Ascanio in Alba* need to be situated in this context.

---

[2] MBA, vol. 1, pp. 305–9 (26 January 1770).   [3] MBA, vol. 1, pp. 305–9 (26 January 1770).
[4] MBA, vol. 1, pp. 305–9 (26 January 1770).   [5] MBA, vol. 1, pp. 314–6 (17 February 1770).

Milan represented the most fruitful stopover for the Mozarts, both on the first journey for social occasions and the commission of *Mitridate* and on the later ones for *Ascanio in Alba* and *Lucio Silla*. This was largely due to the strong support of Count Karl Joseph (Gotthard) von Firmian, plenipotentiary minister of Lombardy, a man of German upbringing imbued with considerable experience of international culture. Firmian promoted the careers not only of the young Mozart but also of J. J. Winckelmann and A. Kaufmann. In light of the minister's cultural outlook, the commission of *Ascanio in Alba* (which was suggested by Firmian to Maria Theresia) from the celebrated Milanese poet Giuseppe Parini for the text and Mozart for the music assumed a symbolic value beyond the festivities themselves. While the second Milanese visit acquired a negative aura on account of Maria Theresia's advice against the hiring of Wolfgang in 1771, the full meaning of her reference to the Mozarts as 'useless people' should be understood in the context of the already rich local musical life and not just as a crude derogatory comment. Nevertheless, some kind of personal aversion to the Mozarts on the part of members of Habsburg family cannot be excluded: it surfaces in Leopold's letters commenting on both the Grand Duke Pietro Leopoldo in Florence and his sister, Queen Maria Carolina, in Naples.[6] If such animosity did in fact exist, we may surmise that it was generated more by Leopold's attitude to social climbing than by considerations of aesthetic significance. The pleasure that the Mozarts (father and son) took in luxury clothing and in mixing with the élites (in Rome, Leopold boasted of pretending to be a steward to the imperial ambassador)[7] might also offer a clue to the aloof annoyance of the Habsburgs.[8] In any case, even in early 1773 Leopold still acted and hoped for a Florence position that, in the event, never materialized.[9]

Where relations with other musicians are concerned, they vary between respectful and ritual in the case of famous individuals (Jommelli in Naples and Piccinni in Milan), about which virtually no detail is recorded, and more-friendly interactions with fellow composers such as Mysliveček.[10]

---

[6] On encountering the Grand Duke in Florence and the Queen in Naples see, respectively, MBA, vol. 1, pp. 330–2 (3 April 1770) and MBA, vol. 1, pp. 365–7 (30 July 1774).

[7] MBA, vol. 1, pp. 363–5 (27 June 1770).

[8] J. A. Hasse from Vienna, March 23, 1771 to G. M. Ortes in Venice: 'The young Mozart is certainly extraordinary for his age [...] his father, as I hear, is equally disgruntled wherever he goes [...] he idolizes his son a little too much, and he does what he can to spoil him, but I have such a high opinion of the natural common sense of the boy, that I hope he will not be ruined despite all the adulation of his father and will grow up into a good man'. From L. Pancino (ed.), *J.A. Hasse e G. Ortes. Lettere (1760–1783)* (Turnhout: Brepols, 1990), p. 229 (my translation).

[9] MBA, vol. 1, pp. 413–5 (9 January 1773).   [10] MBA, vol. 1, pp. 398–400 (27 October 1770).

They also include disdain for the nuisances of theatrical *cabala*, provoked mainly by capricious singers and described as inevitable in the activity of any Kapellmeister.[11] It is noteworthy that such disturbances appeared to Leopold especially intense on the Italian stage, suggesting more than just local colour: the strong competition characteristic of a complex, overcrowded opera market prompted more than elsewhere in Europe unfair competition of which capriciousness is probably a symptom.

In Bologna the Mozarts came into contact with a special, unusually large community of musicians either connected with the Accademia Filarmonica specifically or woven into the social fabric of a city that constituted a major Italian centre for the recruitment of singers.[12] The central figures of Carlo Broschi Farinelli and Giambattista Martini represented professional and symbolic enrichment par excellence: Broschi was a living embodiment of music history; and Martini offered the Mozarts a unique opportunity to discuss the history of music.[13] Wolfgang's inclusion in the Accademia Filarmonica was a sign of deep appreciation for the exceptionally talented composer. But we should not overlook the fact that he was awarded his diploma 'alla forestiera', that is, not for the purpose of working in the churches of Bologna (the main reason for local musicians to associate with that institution) but as an honourable recognition, awarded under payment of a fee. The Bologna period was particularly enjoyable on account of the hospitality of the Genoese Count Gian Luca Pallavicini, who had been since 1733 in the service of Austria as a high officer in the army and who was in 1742–45 governor and general commander in the duchy of Mantua and later on governor of the Austrian Lombardy (see above). In this respect, the two periods spent in Bologna (where Pallavicini lived as a retiree), could be regarded as a continuation of the brilliant reception in Milan, reinforced in this case by the appreciation of local musicians. At a great private concert on 26 March 1770, the audience reportedly comprised 150 members of high society, while the representatives of the music community included the learned G. B. Martini and G. B. Predieri, maestro di cappella of the Pallavicini household. The second Bologna stay was characterized by the luxurious hospitality at Pallavicini's villa at Croce del Biacco and by the friendship with the count's only son, a boy of Wolfgang's age who was 'already an Imperial

[11] MBA, vol. 1, p. 400–1 (3 November 1770).
[12] See MBA, vol. 1, pp. 327–30 (27 March 1770) and MBA, vol. 1, pp. 337–40 (21 April 1770).
[13] MBA, vol. 1, pp. 394–5 (6 October 1770): 'We visit him [Martini] every day and discuss the history of music.'

chamberlain'.[14] The other significant friendly encounter took place in
Florence with violinist and composer Thomas Linley, Mozart's equal in
age and as a child prodigy.

The visit to Rome implied important musical occasions but, on the
whole, was a continuation of the Grand Tour at the centre of
Christianity, a place of symbolic significance for both father and son;
the mention of the 'miraculously' preserved bodies of saints (such as St
Caterina Vigri in Bologna and S. Rosa in Viterbo) hint at superstition in
otherwise enlightened minds. Later in Naples Leopold was scandalized
by the popular idolatry of San Gennaro that placed this local saint above
Christ.[15] The arrogance of the clergy, encouraged by the proximity with
the papal court, caught Leopold's attention in Rome; he also appears
informed and interested in the debate about the destiny of the Jesuits,
hundreds of whom had become recent residents of Bologna – affecting,
among other things, the housing market – after their expulsion from
Portugal, Spain and from the duchy of Parma and the kingdom of Naples
and Sicily in Italy. While Leopold was generally prudent in statements
made, on one occasion he opened his heart: 'it is bad enough that the
most appalling pamphlets are being published in catholic countries and
even in Italy, all of them inveighing against the papal authority and the
immunity of the clergy'.[16] If Wolfgang's opinions were in tune with his
father's, the harsh comment on Voltaire at the news of his death in 1778
can be understood as a consequence of the anticlericalism of the philosopher. About Febronianism, the intellectual movement aimed at limiting the influence of the papacy in state matters, Leopold observed quite
neutrally: 'the court in Rome won't be particularly pleased by many of
these points, especially the one that establishes that the Council is more
important than the Pope, which is as much as to say that the Pope isn't
infallible'.[17] All of the above subjects were secondary in the eyes of
Leopold and Wolfgang to the conferment of the Speron d'oro knight-
hood by Pope Clemente XIV, the high point of the second Roman visit
on 4 July 1770. (It might not be a coincidence that the honour was
bestowed on Wolfgang by Cardinal Lazzaro Opizio Pallavicini, cousin
of his patron in Bologna.) Among numerous private performances in
Roman *conversazioni*, the one at the Collegium germanicum stands out
for its national connection.[18]

---

[14] MBA, vol. 1, pp. 379–80 (11 August 1770).   [15] MBA, vol. 1, pp. 358–60 (9 June 1770).
[16] MBA, vol. 1, pp. 392–3 (29 September 1770).   [17] MBA, vol. 1, pp. 385–6 (1 September 1770).
[18] MBA, vol. 1, pp. 344–5 (2 May 1770).

Despite the fact that the Mozarts greatly enjoyed the high-class hospitality and transportation privileges of their aristocratic patrons, both father and son preferred the family atmosphere experienced in the house of a bourgeois, the German-born but Venice-naturalized merchant Johannes Wider. Here the young Mozart savoured the simple intimacy unlikely to be found in aristocratic milieus, spiced up with home dancing and games learned from the seven daughters of the house (ranging from five to twenty-eight years of age and including fourteen-year-old Marianna) who initiated him in the ways of the 'real Venetian'. Despite the frequent opportunities for performance and contacts with the high nobility, the Mozarts did not receive in Venice the attention they expected, a state of affairs predicted by G. M. Ortes who was repeatedly in contact with them.[19] Despite the aloofness of local aristocracy, Wolfgang performed a number of times, including at an accademia at the residence of Elisabetta Maffetti Dandolo, an interesting, emancipated figure whose private behaviour later attracted criticism from the local authorities.[20] In Venice Wolfgang also caught the eye of impresario Michele dall'Agata who offered a contract to compose the second and most prestigious opera for the carnival season of 1772 at the main theatre San Benedetto. The project never materialized (for unknown reasons); it would have been Wolfgang's first opera independent of political support. A similar but less formalized offer was received by Wolfgang in Naples from the renowned impresario of Teatro S. Carlo (and former singer) Giovanni Tedeschi Amadori: both projects suggest that a career in Italy in the commercial theatres might have been possible after all.

In Naples the political situation was not particularly favourable to the search for a court position. The most important musical event was organized by the wife of the imperial ambassador, Countess von Kaunitz, together with a group of four great ladies.[21] As to the court, Queen Maria Carolina seemed more cordial on the surface than genuinely interested in her fellow countrymen; in any case the real power, Leopold rightly observed, was in the hands of prime minister Bernardo Tanucci, opposed by the queen at this time in conjunction with the indifference of the unfit

---

[19] Letter of March 2, 1771 to J. A. Hasse: 'I do not think they [the Mozarts] will be very happy in this city, where they might have thought to be looked after, as it must have happened elsewhere . . . And here in reality, people do not care to demonstrate esteem for other people, however worthy of it they might be, and it is no small feat that they show esteem to those who look for it' (*J. A. Hasse e G. Ortes. Lettere*, p. 228; my translation).

[20] On Elisabetta Maffetti Dandolo, see Paolo Cattelan, *Dandula. L'ultimo sorriso di Mozart* (Venice: Marcianum, 2013).

[21] MBA, vol. I, pp. 352–3 (26 May 1770).

king Ferdinand IV, famously nicknamed 'il re lazzarone'. The real Neapolitan 'lazzaroni' (populace) shocked Leopold with their insolence, comparable only to behaviours he had experienced in London.

Yet another figure connected with the Habsburgs (although at a lower level than Pallavicini or Firmian), was Marquis Don Giuseppe Ximenes d'Aragona, who had spent his active life as Austrian ambassador in Stockholm, St Petersburg and Munich, and had finally retired to Padua around 1760 to become a patron of Tartini among others and to organize *accademie* and oratorio performances. His commission of *Betulia liberata* K. 118, reported in Leopold's letters, prompted the composition of one of the most important works of the period (and the only complete oratorio by Wolfgang) which, however, appears not to have been performed in Padua at the time.

The impact of the Italian experience in the context of Mozart's music is not easy to assess in detail but the three journeys certainly represented a time of substantial growth for him, confirming at the same time that he matched the local standards, had relatively little more to learn and nothing to fear. Appreciation by the Mozarts of individual, albeit mostly unidentified, pieces of Italian instrumental music is a recurring theme in the correspondence. However, their main interest was opera, especially opera seria. They attended buffa as well, but commented, if briefly, only on seria works. Jommelli's *Armida*, witnessed in Naples, earned a compliment but also attracted criticism for its excessively learned and old-fashioned style.[22] Unconditional praise was reserved for Paisiello's *Annibale in Torino*, attended at a lavish production in the eponymous city.

The second and third journeys to Italy (August–December 1771 and October 1772–February 1773) were much more focussed than the first on professional obligations; impressions of the country are relatively rare. In any case, Wolfgang's relationship with Italy did not end with his last visit. In 1778 he expressed a great desire to return there with Aloysia Weber and to work for the theatre, a plan that never materialized.[23] More importantly, Mozart crossed paths time and again with the world of Italian opera outside Italy, in capital cities such as Vienna and Prague where he developed his ideas on the centrality of music (rather than verbal language) in the dramaturgical process more than would have been possible in Italy; in the land of opera itself, a diffuse ideology about the expressive primacy of the word and the vocal melody (with consequent

[22] MBA, vol. 1, pp. 356–8 (5 June 1770): 'beautiful but too clever and old-fashioned for the theatre'.
[23] MBA, vol. 2, pp. 251–5 (4 February 1778).

restraint in the use of the orchestra) hindered full exploitation of musico-dramatic resources. Within a larger continental context, the works setting Da Ponte's librettos and the revised version of *La clemenza di Tito* represent a huge step towards renewing the musical language of Italian opera. It should be remembered, however, that soon after Mozart's death, and as a result of the rise of national sensibilities and the decline of traditional aristocracy during the early nineteenth century, most of his Italian operas underwent a process of Germanization that led to the dissemination of new versions in German, more often than not including significant, even crucial dramaturgical variants. It is important to realize that the critical foundations for Mozart's operas were laid in this historical period and that they have affected until recently our understanding of his oeuvre, notably in the evaluation of works such as *Don Giovanni* and *Figaro* versus *Così fan tutte* (a work at odds with Romantic sensibility) and in the relatively recent reappraisal of the historical significance and value of the last masterpiece *Tito*.

CHAPTER 13

France

Jean-Paul C. Montagnier

'From Paris the name and fame of a man of great talent resounds through-out the whole world',[1] Leopold wrote to his son on 12 February 1778, thus echoing Johann Baptist Wendling's opinion that Paris was 'the only place where one can make money and a great reputation'.[2] Paris was indeed one of the greatest – if not *the* greatest – cultural centres of Europe, a place to visit at all costs. There, Mozart could compose for the Académie Royale de Musique (Opéra), for the Concert Spirituel and for the 'Académie des Amateurs' ('which pay five louis-d'or for a symphony'); could teach at 'three louis-d'or for twelve lessons'; and could have his music published by subscription.[3] Leopold knew all of this, explaining Mozart's three sojourns to the city in November 1763–April 1764, May–July 1766 and March–September 1778.

Mozart did not have a chance to see the prestigious Opéra where Jean-Baptiste Lully's *tragédies en musique* had been sung for so long. On account of the fire of April 1763, the Palais-Royal theatre was provision-ally established in the Salle des Machines of the Tuileries palace, where performances were to be given for almost seven years, the time needed for Louis-Pierre Moreau to rebuild the theatre in its original location. Accordingly, no work was staged by the troupe of the Académie Royale de Musique until late January 1764, when the directors François Rebel and François Francœur resumed performances at an average rate of three per week. Throughout the eighteenth century, the financial health of the Opéra had always been uncertain, and Jean-Philippe Rameau's death in 1767 did not help in this respect. Rebel and Francœur, and several of their successors (notably Pierre Montan Berton and Jean-Claude Trial), were therefore cautious and not open to novelty. To fuel the repertoire, they mainly relied on old titles and on some of Rameau's and Jean-Joseph Cassanéa de Mondonville's hits, such as *Castor et Pollux* and *Titon et*

---

[1] LMF, p. 478. [2] LMF, p. 401 (3 December 1777). [3] LMF, p. 401 (3 December 1777).

l'Aurore, which Mozart could have heard in 1764. Quite often, repertory scores were not staged in their original versions but peppered with the music of more recent authors. The 1771 revival of *Alcyone* (1706) by Marin Marais was a good case in point, a 'curious potpourri' with additions from works by Berton, André Campra, André Cardinal Destouches, Jean-Marie Leclair, Rameau, Rebel, Francœur and others.[4] The repertoire began to change slightly around 1769 with the appointment of Antoine Dauvergne at the head of the Académie Royale. In contrast to his predecessors, Dauvergne was receptive to foreign stage works, thus introducing fresh air into the venerable institution. It was he who, at the suggestion of the diplomat François Leblanc Du Roullet, brought Christoph Willibald Gluck to Paris in late 1773. There, the famous artist astutely sought the support of his former pupil Marie-Antoinette, and saw his *Iphigénie en Aulide*, based on Racine's play, triumph on 19 April 1774. This score was followed by five others, including *Armide* adapted from the Quinault libretto set by Lully a century earlier. Anne-Pierre-Jacques de Vismes, who took over the Opéra directorship in 1777, carried on Dauvergne's mission by asking Johann Christian Bach to produce a three-act version of *Amadis de Gaule*. If the first set of performances was not scheduled before December 1779, Bach's visit to Paris in August 1778 may have included hearing the singers who were to take part; on this trip he met Mozart for the last time too. De Vismes also invited Niccolò Piccinni to come and compose for the Académie Royale: *Roland* was thus premiered in February 1778 and instantly became an unmissable attraction. The Opéra directors commissioning settings of revised versions of Philippe Quinault's libretti in the hope of ensuring the success of new scores through their association with valued texts was not a new idea. Mondonville had composed a *Thésée* in 1767 that proved to be a disaster; the updated version of Lully's *Persée* put on at the Versailles Opéra Royal in May 1770 to celebrate the weddings of Louis XVI and Marie-Antoinette did not please either. But in the hands of Gluck, Bach and Piccinni, these resettings deeply and durably rejuvenated the declining *tragédie en musique*, and even fostered an aesthetic quarrel akin to the 'Querelle des Bouffons'. In 1778, Mozart attended these productions and witnessed the ensuing heated debates, notwithstanding his father's recommendation to remain aloof from them.

According to the *Journal de musique*, the first specialist periodical on music in French, the Comédie française and the Comédie italienne were

---

[4] Jérôme de La Gorce and Sylvette Milliot, *Marin Marais* (Paris: Fayard, 1991), p. 213.

two other important musical venues.[5] The former 'was the school of great virtues and that of manners' where spoken plays were staged accompanied by dances and singing, such as Pierre Augustin Caron de Beaumarchais's *Le Barbier de Séville* first given in 1775. The Comédie italienne, united with the Opéra-Comique in 1762, 'was the spectacle of Comic and Buffoonery' devoted to 'pièces en ariettes', that is plays with arias in the Italian style or with French strophic songs, often penned by François André Danican Philidor, Pierre-Alexandre Monsigny, Egidio Duni and then by one of its illustrious directors, André Ernest Modeste Grétry. Mozart saw Monsigny's *Aline, Reine de Golconde* there in 1766, and probably became acquainted with some of those *ariettes* on which he would subsequently write his sets of piano variations, such as 'Lison dormait dans un bocage' (K. 264) from Nicolas Dezède's *Julie* (1772), and Antoine-Laurent Baudron's song 'Je suis Lindor' from Beaumarchais's *Le Barbier de Séville* (K. 354).

On religious holidays and during Advent and Lent in particular, theatres were closed. To obviate public idleness, Anne Danican Philidor founded the Concert Spirituel in 1725, thereby offering twenty to twenty-five events a year to a paying audience in the Salle des Cent Suisses at the Tuileries. Originally, the agreement signed between Philidor and the Académie Royale de Musique stated that neither opera extracts nor music sung in French should be performed, but, by the time Mozart first visited Paris, the latter restriction had been withdrawn. Nonetheless and perhaps on account of standard practices, Antoine Dauvergne, who managed the Concert Spirituel from 1762 to 1773, still relied heavily on instrumental and Latin music including sonatas, concertos and symphonies mostly by French authors, excerpts from Rameau's stage works, solo motets and above all *motets à grand chœur* by famous composers such as Michel-Richard de Lalande, Jean Gilles, François Giroust and Dauvergne himself, not to mention the craze for Giovanni Battista Pergolesi's *Stabat mater*. The directorship of Pierre Gaviniès, Simon Leduc and François-Joseph Gossec (1773–7) and then that of Joseph Legros (1777–90) were greatly acclaimed, not only because of the excellence of the programming but also for the accuracy of the performances. Besides religious works and Italian airs, many symphonies and concertos by European composers – mainly from Germany and Austria – were given by an orchestra comprising almost sixty instrumentalists. They premiered Mozart's 'Paris' symphony (K. 297) on 18 June 1778 along with Felice Bambini's oratorio *Suzanne*, a two-voice

---

[5] *Journal de musique* (March 1770), vol. 2, p. 27.

motet by Gossec, two concertos, a cello sonata and three airs respectively by J. C. Bach, Niccolò Jommelli and Gluck.

Other concerts in Paris were organized by private patrons on a subscription basis. The most important of these was undoubtedly the Concert des Amateurs (or 'Académie des Amateurs' as Mozart put it in his above-mentioned letter). This concert that had been taking place at the Hôtel de Soubise since c. 1769 consisted of eighty amateur and professional performers under the baton of Gossec, and from 1773 onward, that of Joseph Boulogne, Chevalier de Saint-Georges. The orchestra, for which Gossec specifically intended his great symphonies with wind instruments, was regarded as the best in the capital. The Concert des Amateurs stopped for unknown reasons in 1781 but was replaced by the Concert de la Loge Olympique, which commissioned from Haydn six 'Paris' symphonies in 1784–5. The fact that a large number of French musicians were freemasons may account for their taste for Germanic symphonies and concertos composed by 'brothers'. This taste was also accommodated by Paris-based publishers such as the Bohemian François-Joseph Heina, who befriended Wolfgang and his mother in 1778 and issued the first print of seven of Mozart's works including the Piano Sonata in A minor K. 310.

If aristocrats and bourgeois played a major part in patronizing these private concerts, they also participated actively in cultural life by organizing musical events in their mansions. Salons – albeit too numerous to be listed here – were valuable venues for professional musicians. In the 1760s, the Prince de Conti (Louis-François de Bourbon) arranged regular concerts at the Temple palace and at his summer residence at L'Isle Adam. As an open-minded person, he promoted all kind of artists (Beaumarchais, Diderot, Duport, Gossec, Rousseau) and even hired the harpsichordist Johann Schobert, as well as the two horn players Heina and Jean-Joseph Rodolphe. Mozart's 1766 recital in the Conti salon was immortalized in *Le thé à l'anglaise*, an oil canvas by Michel-Barthélemy Ollivier. Similarly, Louis de Noailles – who introduced the Mozarts at Versailles in 1763 – maintained a highly esteemed ensemble made up of several German musicians, notably Carl and Anton Stamitz (whose *symphonies concertantes* were successfully performed at the Concert Spirituel), and hosted J. C. Bach in 1778. Mozart's Flute and Harp Concerto K. 299, commissioned by the Duke of Guines (Adrien-Louis Bonnières de Souastre), was intended for performance at salons of this kind.

A large array of church music – polyphonic, concertante or monodic (plainchant), or even played by organ virtuosos such as Claude Balbastre, Armand-Louis Couperin, Louis-Claude Daquin and Nicolas Séjan – could be heard either at the Chapelle Royale of Versailles or in countless Parisian churches. Among them, the choir schools of the Notre-Dame cathedral, the Saints-Innocents, Saint-Germain-l'Auxerrois and of the Sainte Chapelle were sought after, as their directors were also good composers. The most famous was François Giroust. After winning a competition set up by the Concert Spirituel in 1767, he served at the Saints-Innocents and then succeeded Charles Gauzargues (whom Mozart met in 1763–4) at the head of the Chapelle Royale music ensemble. Giroust and Mondonville were likely the most important composers of *motets à grand chœur* (or *grands motets*) during the Mozart years, even though those of Lalande were still enjoyed. The *motet à grand chœur* – a multi-movement work for soloists, five-part choir and orchestra – was the principal genre of French sacred music, originally designed as the sonorous background to the king's daily mass. Those of Mondonville were by and large operatic *divertisse-ments* not devoid of profundity, which thrilled listeners, whereas those of Giroust, strongly influenced by the symphonies performed in Paris at that time, made use of a large orchestra and called for regular phrases and clear structures including sonata forms.

On their way back to Salzburg, the Mozarts stopped at Lyon in 1766, where Jean-Marie Leclair 'le cadet' directed energy towards attracting new artists. On 13 August, Wolfgang and his sister took part in one of the weekly events organized each Wednesday at 5pm by the Académie des Beaux-Arts in the music room opposite the Saint-Bonaventure church. The Académie, founded by Jean-Pierre Christin and Nicolas Bergiron de Fort-Michon in 1713, remained active for sixty years, albeit experiencing financial ups and downs. It originally assembled about forty amateurs to give vocal and instrumental concerts throughout the year, except at Easter time and from 1 September until 11 November. As the Académie developed, the number of professional musicians coming from the Lyon Opera gradually grew. More often than not, programmes consisted of two extracts of operas and/or ballets, sometimes adapted to the musical forces available, and one *motet à grand chœur*. If these programmes quite frequently echoed those of the Concert Spirituel, they were at times innovative, because some provincial composers sent their scores to the Académie in the hope of being played. In this way, authors such as François Estienne and a certain Toutain continued respectable careers away from Paris. (Rameau made his public debut there in c. 1713–15 with performances of three of his motets.) From the 1760s onwards, symphonies and concertos by German and Italian composers as well as a myriad of short instrumental and vocal pieces – quite often performed by visiting virtuosos – increasingly replaced the traditional repertoire. Gluck's 'divertissement italien', *Le siège de Cythère* (the one-act version of *Cythère assiégée*) was even sung at the Académie in March 1762, thirteen years before being produced in Paris.[6]

The Lyon Opera house, set up in 1687, enjoyed a period of prosperity between 1739 and 1744, notably in 1743 with the production of Rameau's *Hippolyte et Aricie* ten years after its premiere. Yet, once established in the new theatre built by Jacques-Germain Soufflot in 1754–6, it became less dynamic and mainly staged *opéras comiques* by Philidor, Monsigny and Duni, as well as *opere buffe* in translation. The presence of Jean-Georges Noverre in 1750–2 and 1758–9, as well as representations of works by Gluck and Piccinni (who conducted his *Didon* in 1787) were other highpoints.

Musical life at Lyon was noticeably centred around the Académie, the Opéra and some wealthy patrons who now and then gathered amateur ensembles, since the music intoned in the Lyon churches remained generally stern and unadorned on account of local liturgical regulations.

After his mother's death, Mozart travelled on his own for the first time from Paris to Salzburg, stopping at Strasbourg in October 1778. Located midway between the French kingdom and the German Empire, Strasbourg offered different kinds of cultural activity from both of them. The city population was bilingual (Alsatian/French) and divided between Protestants and Catholics. The Strasbourg 'Académie' (Opéra) was initiated by Sébastien de Brossard in c. 1689, but operated on a non-regular basis until 1726, before being officially established in 1730. Even though it was supported by the governor and the intendant of the province, it was dissolved in 1751. Thereafter, *opéras comiques* and *opere buffe* such as Rousseau's *Le devin du village*, Grétry's *La fausse magie* and Pergolesi's *La serva padrona*, in addition to accepted and contemporary spoken plays, were put on in the Roßmarkt room run by the Théâtre français. As for the Théâtre allemand set in the clothmakers' guild room, it did not operate permanently, but only hosted well-known German touring companies. These two theatres vied with each other for supremacy, notwithstanding the different constituencies of their audiences: the former was frequented by the garrison officers and the nobility, and the latter by military troops and the bourgeoisie. It is thought that the recital Mozart gave on 17 October 1778 took place at the Théâtre allemand, but the venue where he gave his two other concerts (26 and 31 October) has not been established.

---

[6] Léon Vallas, *La Musique à l'Académie de Lyon au dix-huitième siècle* (Lyon: Éditions de la Revue musicale de Lyon, 1908), p. 109.

The *Concerts Municipaux* in Strasbourg lasted much longer than the Académie. Their origins may be found in the weekly 'Publicum exercitium musicum' instituted in 1605 by Christoph Thomas Walliser. The orchestra was made up of twenty or so professional musicians paid by the city. Under Johann Christoph Frauenholtz's directorship (1727–54), the Municipal Concerts were handled by the Académie and numbered thirty a year. From 1786 to 1793, Ignaz Pleyel, Franz Xaver Richter's assistant and eventual successor at the cathedral (in 1789), also organized the very successful Concert des Amateurs series with Johann Philipp Schonfeld, both Kapellmeister of the Temple Neuf (from 1777) and director of the Municipal Concerts (from 1781). It is possible that the modus operandi of this new undertaking was based on that of the Parisian Concert des Amateurs, as both of them brought together masonic musicians (Gossec and Schönfeld included). In fact, the 'Candeur' Masonic Lodge united Strasbourg aristocrats and traders with musical interests, such as Prince Max von Zweibrücken (who regularly attended the Pleyel-Schönfeld concerts) and Franck father and son (to whom Leopold recommended Wolfgang).

A large number of religious and spiritual works were sung in the Catholic and Lutherian churches in Strasbourg, especially at the cathedral and the Temple Neuf where a cantata was given at every Sunday service. However, when Richter arrived from Mannheim as *maître de musique* at the cathedral in April 1769, he boosted the musical life of the city dramatically by getting involved in the Municipal Concerts and by writing more than one hundred colourful masses and motets for the excellent cathedral choir and orchestra. These musical forces included no fewer than eight choirboys, sixteen vocalists and more than thirty instrumentalists, numbers roughly equivalent to the Versailles Chapelle Royale! There is no doubt that the Richter mass Mozart heard at the cathedral was 'charmingly written'[7] and performed. Strasbourg furthermore possessed beautiful organs by the famous builders André and, above all, Jean-André Silbermann. The latter's three-keyboard organ of the Temple Neuf contained forty-five stops and that of Saint-Thomas twenty-nine. The two were regarded as the 'best organs built by Silbermann' and were played publicly by Mozart.[8]

The lively musical world of late eighteenth-century France appeared to have a long-lasting influence on Mozart, as *Idomeneo* and several of his instrumental works would later testify. Paris was a cosmopolitan capital

---

[7] LMF, p. 630 (26 October 1778).   [8] LMF, p. 629 (26 October 1778).

that attracted artists from all around Europe. It was a place where young creators could discover new trends, digest them and carve out their own style, but also a city where they could be easily forgotten. The French, indeed, incessantly sought novelty, and were prompt to quarrel about aesthetic and philosophic tenets of music. In 1778, it may have been precisely these quarrels that deflected the attentions of French amateurs away from Mozart.

CHAPTER 14

Prague

Kathryn L. Libin

Musicians and audiences in the city of Prague played a remarkable role in Mozart's late career, enthusiastically embracing his music, supplying him with important commissions and stimulating his creativity. As capital of the kingdom of Bohemia and centre of a rich and varied musical culture, Prague offered Mozart a nearly ideal field of endeavour during his lifetime and ensured an unbroken legacy of appreciation for his music after his death. In this second largest city of the Habsburg realm, Prague's roughly 80,000 inhabitants lived within a fairly small geographical area, bisected by the Vltavá river and dominated by a royal castle, although in Mozart's time it was not an imperial seat. The city was densely populated by merchants, artisans, members of church and court, and aristocrats whose many palaces lined the streets beneath the castle walls. Though Prague was not immune to the church reforms and closures of Joseph II, in the 1780s it still retained many churches and monasteries with extensive musical establishments. Its university, founded by Emperor Charles IV in 1348, was the oldest in Central Europe, and in the 1780s non-Catholics were admitted as students and received instruction in German. It was a city with a vigorous concert life, full of fine musicians and of people educated in music. A number of factors made Prague fertile territory for Mozart's music and contributed to the extraordinary success that he enjoyed there.

One of the fundamental ingredients was an unusually high degree of musical literacy and accomplishment cultivated in Bohemia and Moravia. Charles Burney had noted the many Czech musicians who migrated from village to city to find employment, and marvelled at the musical training available in small parish schools: 'I went into the school', he wrote of one, 'which was full of little children of both sexes, from six to ten or eleven years old, who were reading, writing, playing on violins, hautbois, bassoons, and other instruments'.[1] Church officials and estate lords alike considered musical training an important attribute for rural peasantry, enabling them to participate in church choirs, village bands and house orchestras.[2] Religious orders, including the Jesuits, Augustinians, Benedictines and Knights of the Cross with the Red Star provided advanced levels of music education, with the many schools and rigorous standards of the Jesuits playing the most crucial role in supplying Prague with musicians of high quality. The intensive patronage of Prague's nobility was also a notable factor in its musical culture; from the activities of Count Wenzel von Morzin, whose 'most virtuosic orchestra' secured him early copies of the *Four Seasons* and other concertos from Vivaldi around 1718, to Count Johann Joseph von Thun-Hohenstein, whose private house players delighted Mozart with a welcome concert in 1787, aristocratic amateurs helped to build an international, especially Italianate, repertoire in Prague and employed many fine composers, singers and instrumentalists.

Perhaps most significant for Mozart, Prague was a city that since 1724, when Count Franz Anton von Sporck opened a theatre in the New Town to public audiences, had cultivated a sophisticated appreciation of Italian opera. Beginning under Sporck's auspices and continuing into Mozart's time, Italian singers and impresarios joined with Czech and German musicians to present operas by Vivaldi, Pergolesi, Gluck and others. It was an impresario of the Sporck theatre, Antonio Denzio, who produced the first operatic treatment of the Don Juan legend, the 1730 pastiche *La pravità castigata*, and thus laid the foundation for Mozart's contribution to that Prague tradition nearly sixty years later. The Kotce Theatre, which opened in 1738 in the market area of Prague's Old Town, employed a number of Italian impresarios, including G. B. Locatelli, who in 1750 produced Gluck's *Ezio*. In 1764 Giuseppe Bustelli leased the theatre, and among the seasoned Italian singers in his troupe was the *buffo* Pasquale Bondini (d. 1789). Bondini was not only a highly regarded performer but an ambitious and entrepreneurial impresario who would direct a Dresden-based company both there and in Leipzig and, after Bustelli's death in 1781, the Prague troupe as well.[3] Bondini's close ties to German theatres

[1] Charles Burney, *The Present State of Music in Germany, The Netherlands, and United Provinces* (London, 1775), 2 vols., vol. 2, pp. 4–5.
[2] Robert G. Rawson, *Bohemian Baroque: Czech Musical Culture and Style, 1600–1750* (Woodbridge: The Boydell Press, 2013), pp. 89–97.
[3] The theatrical connections between Dresden, Leipzig and Prague are explored in Ian Woodfield, *Performing Operas for Mozart: Impresarios, Singers and Troupes* (Cambridge: Cambridge University Press, 2012).

stimulated productions of *Singspiele* along with Italian opera. By the time Count Franz Anton von Nostitz opened a new public theatre designed by Anton Haffenecker, situated adjacent to the university in the fruit market of the Old Town, Prague possessed a highly engaged and knowledgeable opera-going public.

The first of Mozart's operas presented by Bondini in Prague was *Die Entführung aus dem Serail*, which opened in spring 1783 during the inaugural season of Count Nostitz's new 'National Theatre', whose motto – *Patriae et Musis* (To the Fatherland and the Muses) – was inscribed on its façade. A revealing account of the opera's premiere was provided by Mozart's Czech biographer, Franz Xaver Niemetschek, who wrote about Prague's encounter with *Die Entführung* and its impact on the city's relationship with the composer:

> [. . .] I was witness to the enthusiasm that its performance in Prague created among connoisseurs and non-connoisseurs! It was as though what one had hitherto heard and known was not music at all! Everyone was enchanted – everyone amazed at the novel harmonies and the original, previously unheard of passages for wind instruments. Now the Bohemians began to seek out his works; and in that same year, one already heard Mozart's keyboard pieces and symphonies at all the best musical concerts. From then on the preference of the Bohemians for his works was decided! The foremost connoisseurs and artists of our capital were also Mozart's greatest admirers, the most fiery heralds of his fame.[4]

The powerful affinity for Mozart's music described by Niemetschek led to the proposals that finally brought Mozart to Prague for his first and most successful visit, during the season of 1786–7 that introduced *Le nozze di Figaro*. By this time Bondini, no longer in robust health, had taken on a fellow singer and long-time colleague, Domenico Guardasoni (d. 1806), as deputy manager. Though Mozart and his wife arrived only in January, the furore over *Figaro* had begun with its first performances by the Italian company that autumn and had not abated; the *Prager Oberpostamtszeitung* of 12 December 1786 reported, 'No piece ... has ever caused such a sensation as the Italian opera *Die Hochzeit des Figaro*, which has already been given several times here with unlimited applause by Bondini's resident company of opera virtuosi'.[5] Niemetschek wrote of the public's

---

[4] Franz Xaver Niemetschek, *Lebensbeschreibung des K. K. Kapellmeisters Wolfgang Amadeus Mozart, aus Originalquellen* (Prague: Herrlischen Buchhandlung, 1798); facsimile reprint of 2nd, 1808 edition (Leipzig: VEB Deutscher Verlag für Musik, 1978), pp. 34–5. (All quotations from this source are given in my translation unless otherwise indicated.)

[5] MDL, p. 246; MDB, p. 280.

unprecedented enthusiasm for the music, which quickly appeared in piano, wind, string and dance versions so that 'soon Figaro's tunes echoed in the streets and parks'.[6] Niemetschek also relayed the excitement that Mozart's music aroused in the musicians who played it, and both he and Mozart's father Leopold made it clear that it was due to direct invitations from the theatre's musicians and patrons that Mozart went to Prague: 'His opera *Le nozze di Figaro* was performed there [Prague] with such great success that the orchestra and a company of *important* connoisseurs and music lovers wrote him letters of invitation and have sent him a poem which was written about him.'[7] Mozart's own account of his stay in Prague, where he and Constanze resided as guests of the musical patron Count Thun-Hohenstein in his Malá Strana [Lesser Town] palace, projects a state of glee: 'all these people leapt about to the music of my Figaro, arranged for noisy contredanses and German dances, so deeply happy. For here nothing is so talked about as Figaro; nothing played, blown, sung, and whistled but Figaro; no opera so attended as Figaro and ever Figaro. Certainly a great honour for me.'[8]

Performances of Mozart's instrumental music at this time, particularly a memorable occasion in the packed theatre where he played a concerto and improvised at the piano, further established his reputation in Prague. As Niemetschek wrote:

> We did not know in fact what to admire most, whether the extraordinary compositions or the extraordinary playing; together they produced such an overwhelming impression on our hearts, just like a sweet enchantment! But when at the end of the concert Mozart improvised alone on the piano for over half an hour, and our rapture had stretched to its highest extent, this state dissolved in loudly overflowing applause . . . This concert was certainly the most unique of its kind for the people of Prague, and Mozart likewise counted this day as one of the loveliest of his life.[9]

This visit, then, forged the strong bonds between Mozart and Prague that would secure the commission for *Don Giovanni* and draw him back to the city for its premiere in 1787.

When Mozart returned to Prague that autumn, he believed that *Don Giovanni* would open on 14 October as one of the festivities surrounding

---

[6] Niemetschek, *Lebensbeschreibung*, p. 38.

[7] Niemetschek, *Lebensbeschreibung*, p. 39. See also the letter by Leopold Mozart in MBA, vol. 4, p. 7; LMF, p. 902 (12 January 1787; extract only). The poem mentioned, by A. D. Breicha, is quoted in MDL, pp. 248–9; MDB, pp. 282–3.

[8] MBA, vol. 4, p. 10; LMF, p. 903 (15 January 1787) (my translation).

[9] Niemetschek, *Lebensbeschreibung*, p. 40.

the marriage of the Archduchess Maria Theresia to Prince Anton of Saxony; but when it became clear that the troupe, now under Guardasoni's direction, would not be ready in time, Emperor Joseph II demanded that *Figaro* be presented that day instead. *Don Giovanni* finally received its premiere on 29 October 1787, after a lengthy period in which Mozart rehearsed the singers in both operas and became intimately acquainted with their talents as well as those of the musicians in the orchestra. Among the many stories that circulated about the first Prague performance of this opera was that the orchestra was forced to perform the overture at sight, since Mozart had finished it only the night before. A reviewer in the *Allgemeine musikalische Zeitung* commented that the orchestra of the Nostitz theatre was small, but of high quality:

> it does not count famous concerto soloists or virtuosi among its members, but all its members are skilled and thorough, many are first-rate artists, fired by a sense of honour, who through renunciation of personal priority and a long period of continuous playing together, produce a remarkably unified whole that seems to come forth from a single soul. It has often, without any rehearsal, performed the most difficult pieces of Mozart to his complete satisfaction. One need only look at the instrumental parts of *Don Juan*, which Mozart wrote for this orchestra, to agree with my opinion.[10]

Contemporary reports indicate that *Don Giovanni* was a resounding success at its first performances; the fact that the opera also opened the 1788 season in Prague the following September confirms its popularity there.

Though Guardasoni relocated his Italian company to Warsaw in 1789, he received a summons to return to Prague two years later for the coronation festivities of new emperor Leopold II as king of Bohemia. Guardasoni was charged by the Bohemian Estates with producing a 'grand opera seria' in the National Theatre, hiring the finest singers, providing new scenery and costumes, suitably decorating the theatre, and commissioning a 'famous composer' to write the music.[11] Mozart received the commission for *La clemenza di Tito* and began work on it in the summer of 1791, swiftly preparing the opera for a September performance. Evidence suggests that Mozart dealt with this remarkably tight deadline by delegating part of the work to his student and assistant, Franz Xaver Süssmayr; apparently most of the *secco* recitative was written by Süssmayr, while Mozart himself took

[10] Translation from Thomas Forrest Kelly, *First Nights at the Opera* (New Haven: Yale University Press, 2004), p. 90.

[11] A translation of Guardasoni's contract for this coronation event appears in John A. Rice, *Mozart on the Stage* (Cambridge: Cambridge University Press, 2008), pp. 41–2.

charge of the overture, arias, ensembles and choruses. Mozart, with his wife and Süssmayr, left Vienna by stagecoach on 25 August and journeyed to Prague, arriving there three days later.

In Prague, preparations for the coronation were by then well under way. Court composer Antonio Salieri had already arrived from Vienna with numerous musicians and singers from the court chapel, as well as music (including three Mozart masses) for the solemn services that would take place throughout the ceremonies. The emperor with his entourage arrived on 29 August. Among the many entertainments hosted throughout the city were processions, plays, a 'Persian Fair' and a circus, banquets and balls, musical soirées and evenings of fireworks. A diarist who attended the coronation events, Count Johann Karl von Zinzendorf, reported that music from Mozart's *Don Giovanni* was heard at a formal dinner on 1 September; and on the following day, a full production of *Don Giovanni* took place at the National Theatre with the emperor and empress in attendance. Meanwhile Mozart himself was working long hours preparing the coronation opera, *Tito*, supervising its copying into parts for all the singers and musicians and rehearsing it with them. Several reports, including the official Prague Coronation Journal, mention that Mozart was ill during the final stages of production. On 5 September Mozart entered the opera in the catalogue that he kept of his works (the *Verzeichnüß*), indicating its completion; a dress rehearsal likely took place that afternoon. On the morning of Tuesday 6 September, the coronation ceremony itself finally took place in a service at St Vitus Cathedral, on Prague's castle hill. That evening Mozart's new opera was unveiled before the emperor and an audience of distinguished guests. It has often been noted that the opera failed to please the empress, Maria Luisa, who wrote to her daughter-in-law: 'In the evening at the theatre, the grand opera is not so grand, and the music very bad, so that almost all of us went to sleep. The coronation went marvelously'.[12] However, performances of the opera continued throughout the month of September to warm receptions from appreciative audiences, so it is possible that first-night attendees were simply jaded by all the pomp and spectacle they had already endured.

Each of the trips for premieres of major new operas found Mozart deeply engaged in composition, rehearsals and other production tasks and thus lasted many days and even weeks; he also made two shorter stops in Prague in 1789 on his journeys to Berlin and back. From surviving letters and other testimony, we know a fair amount about where Mozart went during his

[12] NMD, p. 70 (translation slightly amended).

visits to Prague. It is possible to trace his steps around the city's Old Town, with Count Nostitz's theatre at the centre of his activities both as participant and auditor, and also including the inns where he and librettist Lorenzo da Ponte stayed while working on *Don Giovanni*, and the famous library of the Clementinum that greatly impressed him during his first visit. Mozart also spent much time in the Malá Strana on the opposite bank of the river from the Old Town, staying at the Thun palace and later, briefly, at the 'Unicorn' inn, having a mass performed in the celebrated St Nicholas church and playing on the great organ of the Strahov monastery. His close friendship with soprano Josepha Duschek and her husband made him a frequent guest at their villa, Bertramka, which at that time was enveloped by vineyard, park and orchard and would have offered him serene refuge from the city.

When word of Mozart's death on 5 December 1791 reached Prague, the city mourned him in a great public Requiem Mass on 14 December in the St Nicholas Church. According to contemporary reports, the music for the service was a requiem by Bohemian composer Antonio Rosetti, and 120 of the city's finest musicians – many of whom would personally have known and worked with Mozart – took part in a performance that filled the vast church with grieving listeners. In 1837, conscious of its role in securing Mozart's legacy, Prague would become the first city to erect a civic memorial to Mozart. Most important, however, was the robust commitment of Guardasoni and his troupe to keeping Mozart's operas in the repertory; in the years after Mozart's death, audiences in Prague and Leipzig regularly heard not only *Don Giovanni* but also *Così fan tutte, Le nozze di Figaro, Il flauto magico* and *La clemenza di Tito*, and by 1795 the music from *Idomeneo* began to circulate in a keyboard arrangement by Prague organist Johann Wenzel. Even as the taste for Italian opera declined during the first decade of the nineteenth century, Mozart's operas and other music continued to find a warm reception in Prague that has endured into the twenty-first century; *Don Giovanni*, in particular, has acquired near mythic significance in the city. It can still be heard daily in the marionette theatre of the Old Town, and Mozart operas remain popular every season at the old National Theatre, now known as the Stavovské divadlo, or Estates Theatre, where Mozart directed both *Don Giovanni* and *La clemenza di Tito*.

Prague was very much a crossroads at the heart of Central Europe, with close connections not only to Vienna but also to the musical worlds of Dresden, Leipzig and Warsaw to the east and north, and Venice and Naples to the south. The musicians with whom Mozart played in

Prague, the other composers whose work intersected with his and the impresarios and patrons who supported and nurtured this culture derived from all these places and others in the same orbit. In Mozart's late career, as opportunities in Vienna seemed to diminish, new ventures and enthusiastic supporters drew him to Prague, which embraced him as its own and has never relinquished that claim.

CHAPTER 15

London

Hannah M. Templeton

When the Mozart family arrived in England in April 1764, they were
further from Salzburg than any of their friends or acquaintances had ever
travelled. Crossing the English Channel whetted Leopold's appetite for the
new experiences that lay ahead. He wrote to his friend and landlord Johann
Lorenz Hagenauer:

> To see English people in Germany is nothing to write home about; but to
> see them in their own country and by choice is quite different. The sea and
> especially the ebb and flow of the tide in the harbour at Calais and Dover …
> then … to be driven by the finest English horses that run so fast that the
> servants on the coach seat could scarcely breathe from the force of the air –
> all this was something entirely strange and agreeable.[1]

Mozart was only eight years old when the family arrived in London on 23
April – too young to be writing letters home or documenting his own
thoughts – but Leopold kept detailed records of the fifteen months the
family spent in the capital. His twelve surviving letters to Hagenauer and his
London *Reisenotizen*,[2] alongside numerous objects and prints that the family
acquired, help to contextualize the Mozarts' music-making and understand
their wider engagement with the capital's cultural and intellectual life. As
well as documenting the family's musical activities, Leopold's letters contain
a wealth of non-musical content, covering the expense of living in London,
English customs, weather, food, politics and religion. They also document
the variety of places the family visited as tourists – including the menagerie at
the Tower of London, Greenwich, the Foundling Hospital for abandoned
children and the British Museum. The letters convey Leopold's frequent
amazement and wonder at the new world in which he was immersed.

---

[1] Cliff Eisen (ed.), *Wolfgang Amadeus Mozart: A Life in Letters*, trans. Stewart Spencer (London:
Penguin Books), p. 36 (28 May 1764).

[2] Leopold's *Reisenotizen* are a set of travel notes listing the contacts he made in locations on the tour.
For a transcription of the London *Reisenotizen*, see MBA, vol. i, pp. 192–6.

By the mid 1760s, London had close to 750,000 inhabitants and was rapidly expanding. Its position at the centre of a prosperous trading empire provided both commercial stability and social diversity, contributing to a varied musical life that was distinct from other European cities. On the continent, concert life was primarily court-controlled, meaning that the Mozarts' success in a new place was dependent upon making an early appearance before the monarch. In London, however, there was relatively little state administration of musical activities; musical patronage came from both members of the aristocracy and other wealthy individuals, including merchants and professionals of the ever-expanding middle class. Consequently, London's musical life was varied, competitive, and commercially driven, offering unrivalled opportunities for individual impresarios and entrepreneurs. The London concert scene demanded a high turnover of foreign musicians from the continent, who were all eager to establish themselves in the capital.

When the Mozarts arrived in England, Leopold was the only family member with any grasp of the English language. He does not refer to his own language skills in his letters, but his purchase of a French–English dictionary shortly after arriving in London suggests that he was not fluent.[3] The Mozarts were nevertheless able to forge initial contacts in London through letters of recommendations that they had obtained in Paris, one containing an introduction to the royal family and another allowing them to attend mass at the French Embassy Chapel. Despite the relative lack of court control over London's musical life, Leopold still prioritized meeting King George III and Queen Charlotte, appearing before them privately within a week of their arrival, on 27 April 1764. He used this acquaintance to his family's advantage: it helped to open up their passage into wider musical life, affording introductions to the many members of the nobility and aristocracy who acted as musical patrons, as well as other professional musicians active in Westminster. Leopold also referenced his children's royal performances in newspaper advertisements for their subsequent public concert appearances.

At the Mozarts' royal appearances, Wolfgang's musical abilities were tested. As Leopold's letter of 28 May explains:

> The king gave him not only works by Wagenseil to play, but also [J.C.] Bach, Abel and Handel, all of which he rattled off *prima vista*. He played the king's organ so well that everyone rates his organ playing far higher than his

---

[3] Alexandre de Rogissard, *Novelle Grammaire Angloise* (London, 1763). Leopold's copy, containing his signature and dated 8 May 1764, is held at the Mozarteum in Salzburg.

harpsichord playing. He then accompanied the queen in an aria that she sang and a flautist in a solo. Finally he took the violin part in some Handel arias that happened to be lying around and played the most beautiful melody over the simple bass, so that everyone was utterly astonished.[4]

It is likely that the King and Queen facilitated the Mozarts' contact with composers Johann Christian Bach and Karl Friedrich Abel, who were both chamber musicians in Queen Charlotte's service. Both are listed directly underneath the king and queen in Leopold's *Reisenotizen*. Significantly, these early acquaintances were all native German speakers, and the Mozarts appear to have enjoyed a friendly relationship with both the royal couple and German composers. Leopold also took great pleasure in recounting how, a week after their initial appearance, King George had opened his carriage window to greet the family while they were out for a walk in St James's Park. In addition to their first meeting on 27 April, the Mozarts appeared before the family on two further occasions: 19 May and 25 October 1764.

Many of the Mozarts' musical contacts were made early on in their stay and Leopold's *Reisenotizen* can, in part, be used to establish the existing networks with which he engaged. Twenty-nine professional continental singers and instrumentalists are listed within the first three pages. Below Bach and Abel, Leopold lists a group of Italian musicians who were all employed as singers by the Italian Opera Company at the King's Theatre during the 1763–4 season, and whom Leopold met while having lunch with Antonio Mazziotti, the leading male singer for the Opera that season. On the following page, Leopold lists several instrumentalists, all of whom either played for the Opera or were in the service of the royal household.

The Mozarts' public concerts frequently drew upon the musical talents of Leopold's new professional acquaintances. This can be seen in their first public performance, which took place on 5 June 1764 at the Great Room in Spring Gardens. Carefully timed for the day after the king's birthday, the concert was attended by over two hundred people. Two new arrivals, violinist François-Hippolyte Barthélémon and cellist Giovanni Battista Cirri, were named as soloists. Interestingly, too, Leopold notes that many of the participating instrumentalists and singers would not accept a fee, suggesting a sense of reciprocity amongst visiting musicians. By appointing Barthélémon and Cirri as soloists in the concert, Leopold was providing them with the opportunity to become more prominent on the London concert scene. Likewise, in largely refusing to accept fees, the more

---

[4] *Mozart: A Life in Letters*, p. 38.

established performers allowed Leopold to maximize his profit from the event. Leopold continued to draw upon networks of professional musicians throughout his family's time in London: at the end of the 1763–4 season, all of the opera house singers returned to the continent, and a second group of Italian singers in the *Reisenotizen* represents musicians engaged for the 1764–5 season.

The large number of aristocracy, nobility and members of England's political class in the London *Reisenotizen* also confirm Leopold's success at forging contacts within the capital's private concert sphere. Performances for the nobility and gentry were among the most profitable and prestigious for the Mozarts. In a letter dated 13 September, he writes: 'During the coming months I shall have to use every effort to win over the aristocracy and this will take a lot of galloping round and hard work. But if I achieve the object which I have set myself, I shall haul in a fine fish or rather a good catch of guineas.'[5] Because of their 'private' nature, details of specific events are rare, although an account of one such occasion survives in a letter from Lady Margaret Clive (wife of Robert Clive of India) describing the Mozarts' concert at her home in Berkeley Square:

> Tomorrow I shall have a great deal of Company indeed all the people of quality etc I am on an intimate footing with, or that like me and music, to hear Manzuoli sing here, accompanied by Mr Burton on the harpsichord, on which the little Mozarts, the boy aged 8 and the girl aged 12 will also play most completely well and this together with two good Fidlers [*sic*] and a bass will be all the concert I shall have, & which I hope will be a good return for all the routs I have been invited to.[6]

Importantly, the Mozarts' private appearances were not limited to the aristocracy. Leopold's *Reisenotizen* also list a number of wealthy merchants and traders for whom the family performed. Although some of these patrons lived in Westminster, their professional activity took place primarily in the City of London, the capital's financial and trading nexus. Leopold made the acquaintance of Aaron Franks, for example, a jeweller, ship-owner, and governor of London's Foundling Hospital for abandoned children. Franks was well known for hosting musical events at his country home, and music writer and historian Charles Burney documents seeing

[5] LMF, p. 52.
[6] Margaret Clive letter of 12 March 1765, discovered by Ian Woodfield and reproduced in Woodfield, 'New Light on the Mozarts' London Visit: A Private Concert with Manzuoli', *Music & Letters*, 76/2 (1995), p. 195.

Wolfgang Mozart perform there.[7] While it is tempting to view merchants and traders as somehow less prestigious than the aristocratic patrons of Westminster, they were highly respected by members of Britain's political and upper classes. Indeed, concerts provided frequent opportunity for interaction between these different social groups.[8]

Leopold visited the City of London in person; his letter of 27 November 1764 describes London's Royal Exchange in detail, noting the 'hundreds [and] thousands of people coming and going' during trading hours.[9] It was perhaps this encounter that led the Mozarts to give a series of daily concerts during these hours in the Great Room at the Swan and Hoop Tavern, situated on Cornhill in the immediate vicinity of the Royal Exchange, towards the end of their stay.[10] Several contemporaneous guidebooks and surveys of London emphasize the area's respectability, claiming it to be one of the richest in the world and noting 'the great Number of eminent Bankers and Goldsmiths' who conducted their business in the vicinity.[11] In all likelihood, then, the Swan and Hoop attracted a wealthy clientele, and performing there was an astute business move on Leopold's part. How Leopold became aware of the Swan and Hoop as a performance venue is not clear; it is possible that he was introduced to it through another travelling musical family, that of the glass harmonica player Marianne Davies. Leopold recounts a warm reunion between the two families in 1771, although the date of their first meeting is unknown. The Davieses regularly performed at the Swan and Hoop during their many visits to London, including while the Mozarts were in London, suggesting that it was a successful venture for them.

The Mozarts' contact with so many London-based musicians and different performance situations meant that Wolfgang was exposed to a huge variety of music over the fifteen months of their residency. Leopold's earliest musical acquaintances in the capital provided models for his son's musical development: Leopold's letter of 28 May 1764 describes Mozart

---

[7] Charles Burney letter of 13 December 1790, reproduced in NMD, p. 5.

[8] See Linda Colley, *Britons: Forging the Nation 1707–1837* (New Haven, CT: Yale University Press, 2009), pp. 60–4.

[9] MBA, vol. 1, pp. 170–1. (Not in LMF.)

[10] The Swan and Hoop performances in the City of London did not mark the end of the Mozarts' appearances in Westminster; they continued to appear before private patrons throughout their time in London.

[11] For example, see William Maitland, *The History and Survey of London: From its Foundation by the Romans to the Present Time* (London, 1756), vol. 2, pp. 808, 996; Joseph Pote, *The Foreigner's Guide; or, a Necessary and Instructive Companion, Both for Foreigner and Native, in Their Tour through the Cities of London and Westminster* (4th edition. London, 1763), p. 88.

playing through J. C. Bach's trios at the clavier; Mozart also transcribed Abel's Symphony No.6 in E♭ Major, Op. 7, once mistakenly catalogued as one of his own compositions (K. 18). The Mozarts also kept abreast of the capital's latest musical developments, including the premieres of J. C. Bach's *Adriano in Syria*, Mattia Vento's *Demofoonte* and two multi-author *pasticcio* operas, *Ezio* and *Berenice*.

Another strand of London's diverse musical life was a 'club culture' largely devoted to the performance of sixteenth- and seventeenth-century polyphony. These clubs were amateur societies, their members primarily learned gentlemen, that held evening meetings for amateur study and singing in London taverns.[12] There were increasing opportunities for the wider public to hear this music, too, for example at London's pleasure gardens at Ranelagh and Vauxhall. The Mozarts visited both locations, with Leopold enthusiastically writing:

> *Vauxhall* amazed me and is impossible to describe. I imagined the Elysian Fields. Just picture yourself an uncommonly large garden with all manner of tree-lined avenues, all of which are lit as in broad daylight by many 1000s of lamps, all enclosed within the most beautiful glass. In the middle is a kind of tall, open summerhouse, in which can be heard an organ and a full orchestra, with trumpets and timpani and all the other instruments.[13]

Here, English catches, glees and the 'ancient' music valued by London's club culture could be heard alongside the latest J. C. Bach trios, popular opera arias, Handel oratorios or music by contemporaneous English composers such as William Boyce and Thomas Arne.

During his time in the capital, Wolfgang began to hone his abilities as a composer under Leopold's careful guidance. He composed his first symphonies, of which K. 16 and K. 19 survive; a set of keyboard sonatas that were published and dedicated to the queen, K. 10–15; a concert aria, K. 21; and a short chorus, 'God is Our Refuge' K. 20. The family's two public concerts in February and May 1765 included performances of Wolfgang's first symphonies, and it is also possible that his first concert aria, 'Va, dal furor portata' K. 21, received its public debut around this time. On the whole, Wolfgang's London compositions can be firmly situated within the modern, continental style that the young composer was fully immersed in. 'God is Our Refuge', however, is distinct in both character and style from any of his other London works. Composed as a gift for the British

---

[12] For a detailed study of London's musical club life, see Brian Robins, *Catch and Glee Culture in Eighteenth-Century England* (Woodbridge and Rochester, NY: Boydell & Brewer, 2006).

[13] *Mozart: A Life in Letters*, p. 43 (28 June 1764).

Museum, it most immediately appears to be a short pastiche of seven-teenth-century English polyphony, demonstrating Wolfgang's awareness of England's enthusiasm for antique musical styles and his own ability to compose in a more esoteric idiom.[14]

***

The Mozarts' London visit holds a prominent position in received narra-tives of Wolfgang's upbringing. Leopold has often been viewed as an exploitative, mercenary individual, intent on profiting financially from his children's prodigious talents by touting them around concert halls and courts, often to the detriment of their wellbeing. The family's success on the London scene is widely thought to have declined over the course of their visit, with later appearances at venues like the Swan and Hoop Tavern being viewed as a desperate attempt to recoup losses before returning to Salzburg. Such interpretations, however, fail to take into account the diversity of London's musical life and the extent to which the Mozarts capitalized on a variety of opportunities as they arose. Wolfgang's exposure to, and understanding of, such a breadth of musical styles was unrivalled for a musician of his age, and his compositional output during the period situates him as a modern, cosmopolitan musician in training, aware of the full extent of his patrons' musical tastes.

The variety of people with different skills, interests and professions listed by Leopold recasts the London visit as part of a broader intellectual journey. The level of detail provided in Leopold's letters, the places the family visited, and the range of prints, scientific instruments and books that the family purchased in London all suggest that Leopold placed great value on the all-round – not just musical – education of his children. This is made clear in a later letter he wrote to his daughter, Nannerl, offering advice on bringing up her own children: 'My whole attention was invari-ably devoted at my children's education and training. First and foremost are good manners and knowledge, enlightened and sound common sense and skill … these … cannot be taken away.'[15] And it is clear that the childhood travels left a lasting impression on Mozart. Writing as a young adult from Paris in 1778, he observed: 'I can assure you that people who do not travel – at least people in the arts and sciences – are pitiful creatures!'[16]

---

[14] For more on Mozart's London works, see Simon P. Keefe, 'Wolfgang Amadeus Mozart the Child Performer-Composer: New Musical-Biographical Perspectives on the Early Years to 1766', in Gary E. McPherson (ed.), *Musical Prodigies: Interpretations from Psychology, Education, Musicology, and Ethnomusicology* (New York: Oxford University Press, 2016), pp. 550–75.

[15] *Mozart: A Life in Letters*, p. 495 (after 21 November 1784).

[16] *Mozart: A Life in Letters*, p. 360 (11 September 1778).

PART III

Career Contexts and Environments

CHAPTER 16

Patronage

Paul Corneilson

Today, a patron is someone who gives financial or other support to a person, charity or organization, but in the eighteenth century the word retained part of the original Roman meaning of the word: a *patronus* was the former owner and protector of a freed slave. Not literally of course, but the relative position of a patron to his or her protégé was clear. This was certainly true for Mozart, whose patrons were all older, wealthier and of a higher social status than him. Nevertheless, it is important to distinguish between those who supported him directly through employment or friendship and those who supervised him (like Count Orsini-Rosenberg) or loaned him money (like Johann Michael Puchberg). Rather than attempt an exhaustive study of all the people who patronized Mozart throughout his career, I will focus on three individuals who were his patrons at various points during his career: Carl Heinrich Joseph, Count Sickingen (1737–91); Gottfried, Baron van Swieten (1733–1803); and Joseph II (1741–90). These case studies will help us to see how Mozart exploited his patrons not only for economic gain but also for social and artistic support.

Count Sickingen served as privy councillor to Elector Palatine Carl Theodor and minister plenipotentiary in Paris from 1768 until his death. Sickingen was a noted chemist, whose work on aluminium and other metals has been recognized.[1] He also assembled a remarkable collection of operas, arias and instrumental music, and was able to use his contacts in Mannheim, Italy and Paris to acquire the latest works in score and in parts. Mozart was introduced to him the day after arriving in Paris, through the tenor Anton Raaff and flautist Johann Baptist Wendling, and described him in a letter of 24 March 1778 as 'a great connoisseur and passionate amateur of music'.[2] A couple of months later, Mozart spent a day with him

---

[1] See Eva Flegel, *Minister, Mäzen, Metallforscher: Carl Heinrich von Sickingen (1737–1791) und seine Versuch über die Platina (1782). Leben und Werk eines Laienforschers im Zeitalter der Aufklärung* (Frankfurt: Peter Lang, 1997).

[2] MBA, vol. 2, p. 326; LMF, p. 516 (translation slightly amended).

on 28 May, in which for eight hours the two of them sat at the keyboard playing 'all kinds of music' that was also 'praised, admired, reviewed, discussed, and criticized'.[3] According to Mozart, Count Sickingen owned thirty scores of operas, and the exact works (in some cases the exact copies of his manuscripts) have now been identified.[4] The thematic catalogue lists several of his own compositions, including a symphony, a ballet and two arias. One of the *scena ed aria* by Count Sickingen (no. 165 in the catalogue) is to the same text that Mozart later set in Munich for Josepha Countess Paumgarten, 'Misera, dove son! – Ah, non son io che parlo' (K. 369, dated 8 March 1781).

Through June 1778 and into the summer months, Mozart spent increasingly more time with Sickingen, previewing his 'Paris' Symphony for Raaff and Sickingen before its premiere on Corpus Christi at the Concert Spirituel. When Baron von Grimm (a somewhat reluctant patron of Mozart) ordered the composer to leave Paris, Count Sickingen intervened and offered Mozart a place to stay so that he could check the engraver's proofs of his six accompanied sonatas for keyboard and violin (K. 301–306). In spite of Grimm's threat to disassociate himself from Mozart completely had he resided elsewhere in the capital prior to eventual departure, Mozart left Grimm's house on 11 September and stayed in Paris with Count von Sickingen until 26 September 1778. (There Mozart might have even dined in the company of Benjamin Franklin, at the time representing the Thirteen American Colonies at the court of Louis XVI. A dinner invitation from Sickingen to Franklin is extant, but unfortunately no reply survives.)[5]

Mozart does not mention receiving any money from Count Sickingen while in Paris, but he gained two even more valuable things: friendship from someone with connections throughout Europe and access to operas he otherwise would not have known. Sickingen must have been sympathetic to Mozart's desire to get a full-time position away from Salzburg,

---

[3] MBA, vol. 2, p. 368 (29 May 1778; translation slightly amended).

[4] His collection was first discussed in Paul Corneilson and Eugene K. Wolf, 'Newly Identified Manuscripts of Operas and Related Works from Mannheim', *Journal of the American Musicological Society*, 47 (1994), pp. 244–74. In 2009 I identified the second half of his thematic catalogue and summarized its contents in 'Count Sickingen's Music Collection', *Society for Eighteenth-Century Music Newsletter*, 19 (2012), pp. 1, 9–12.

[5] 'Ce vendredi [11 September 1778] a Paris Barriere du Roule. Mr: Leroy Et d'autres personnes de La Connaissance de Monsieur franklin, se rassembleronts Lundi 14 7bre [Monday, 14 September] chez Le Comte de Sickingen, et on s'y occuppera de quelques recherches sur la Platine; si Cette Societé et Le motif qui La rassemble pouvaient Engager Monsieur franklin a faire L'honneur au Comte de Sickingen de Diner ce jour Chez Luy, il En serait infiniment flatté; il a L'honneur de le saluer. R.S.V.P.' *The Papers of Benjamin Franklin*, http://franklinpapers.org/franklin/ (accessed on 8 June 2017).

and he offered to help Mozart find one in Mannheim or Mainz, where his brother Wilhelm (1739–1818) was the minister of state to his cousin, Baron Friedrich Karl Joseph Erthal, the Elector of Mainz (1774–92).[6] Although nothing came of this in 1778, Mozart put his knowledge of the opera collection, which included works by Gluck, Salieri, Piccinni, Traetta, Jommelli and Johann Christian Bach, to good use in 1781, when he was commissioned to write *Idomeneo* for Carl Theodor's court in Munich, with Raaff in the title role. In December 1783 in Vienna Mozart asked his father to send the score of *Idomeneo* so that he could play it for Sickingen, who was visiting him there.[7]

Gottfried, Baron van Swieten was the eldest son of Dr Gerhard van Swieten (1700–72), who in 1745 became the personal physician to Empress Maria Theresa and eventually also served as director of the court library. The young Gottfried 'excelled in his studies, spoke and wrote many languages, and thus became a good prospect for diplomatic service'.[8] He served as a diplomat in Brussels, Paris and Warsaw before becoming ambassador to the court of Frederick the Great in Berlin from 1770 to 1777. In the Prussian capital he studied with Johann Philipp Kirnberger, a former pupil of J. S. Bach, and was in the musical circle of Princess Anna Amalia, where Bach and Handel were played and admired. Years later, in the first issue of the *Allgemeine musikalische Zeitung* (1798–9), van Swieten wrote:

> I belong, as far as music is concerned, to a generation that considered it necessary to study an art form thoroughly and systematically before attempting to practice it. I find in such a conviction food for the spirit and for the heart, and I return to it for strength every time I am oppressed by new evidence of decadence in the arts. My principal comforters at such times are Handel and the Bachs and those few great men of our own day

[6] Peter Clive, *Mozart and His Circle* (New Haven: Yale University Press, 1993), pp. 140–1, mentions that C. F. D. Schubart wrote a novella, *Zur Geschichte des menschlichen Herzens* (1775), which contains 'guarded allusions' to the two brothers keeping their father, who was a fanatical alchemist and squandering the family fortune, imprisoned on the family estate at Sauerthal. This story partly inspired Friedrich Schiller's *Die Räuber*, which had its premiere at Mannheim in 1782.

[7] On 6 December Mozart said he wanted to perform *Idomeneo* at the subscription concerts during Lent 1784; MBA, vol. 3, p. 295. Then on 24 December he mentioned Sickingen; MBA, vol. 3, p. 299.

[8] Daniel Heartz, *Mozart, Haydn and Early Beethoven, 1781–1802* (New York: Norton, 2009), p. 62. For a study of van Swieten's influence in Vienna, see Edward Olleson, 'Gottfried van Swieten: Patron of Haydn and Mozart', *Proceedings of the Royal Musical Association*, 89 (1962–1963), pp. 63–74; Otto Biba, 'Gottfried van Swieten', in Ulrich Prinz (ed.), *Europas Musikgeschichte: Grenzen und Öffnungen* (Stuttgart: Internationale Bachakademie, 1997), pp. 120–37; and Teresa M. Neff, 'Baron van Swieten and Late Eighteenth-Century Viennese Music Culture' (PhD thesis, Boston University, 1998), esp. chapter 3.

who, taking these as their masters, follow resolutely in the same quest for greatness and truth.[9]

C. P. E. Bach's six string symphonies Wq 182 were commissioned by van Swieten (completed by 1773), and Bach also dedicated the third collection of 'Kenner und Liebhaber' pieces to van Swieten (1781).[10] Van Swieten wrote some music himself, including three comic operas: *Les talents à la mode; Colas, toujours Colas*; and the lost *La chercheuse d'esprit*. He also wrote ten symphonies, of which at least seven survive.[11]

In 1777 van Swieten was appointed prefect of the Imperial Library and served in that capacity until his death in 1803. Under Joseph II, he was appointed a Councillor of State and Director of the State Education Commission in 1781, then also as director of a new Censorship Commission in 1782. Thus, he was de facto minister of culture and directly responsible for many of Joseph's reforms in education. In 1784 van Swieten proposed a copyright law for the Austrian empire, which, had it not been rejected by Joseph II, would have benefitted Mozart as a freelance composer.[12] Van Swieten was ultimately blamed by Joseph II for the failure of some of the reforms, and was dismissed from the commission by Leopold II on 5 December 1791 (the day Mozart died).

Mozart first met van Swieten in Vienna in 1768, when he was involved in planning the young Mozart's early opera, *La finta semplice*. (Leopold claims in his petition to Joseph II dated 21 September 1768 that Wolfgang had played the entire opera in van Swieten's apartment.) Later in 1781 they met at the salon of Countess Thun (another patron of Mozart), where Mozart played excerpts from his opera *Idomeneo*. Baron van Swieten and Countess Thun also witnessed the premiere of the Sonata in D for two pianos, K. 448, played by Mozart and Josepha Auernhammer on 23 November 1781. More important, there were informal concerts at van Swieten's rooms every Sunday afternoon, as Mozart reports in a letter to his father on 10 April 1782, 'where no music is played other than that of Handel and Bach'. This study of the fugues by the Bachs (J. S., W. F. and C. P. E.)

[9] Quoted in Tia DeNora, *Beethoven and the Construction of Genius: Musical Politics in Vienna, 1792–1803* (Berkeley and Los Angeles: University of California Press, 1998), p. 26.

[10] See the introduction by Sarah Adams to the edition in *Carl Philipp Emanuel Bach: The Complete Works*, III/2. A facsimile of the five surviving autograph scores of the symphonies are published by The Packard Humanities Institute (2015).

[11] Four arias by van Swieten are listed in Count Sickingen's thematic catalogue. See Note 4. Several of van Swieten's symphonies have been edited by Teresa Neff and were published by Artaria Editions in 2011.

[12] Nicholas Till, *Mozart and the Enlightenment: Truth, Virtue and Beauty in Mozart's Operas* (New York: Norton, 1993), p. 130.

resulted in the Prelude and Fugue in C, K. 394; and Mozart also made arrangements for string quartet of Bach fugues, K. 405, later writing his own Fugue in C minor K. 426.[13] Although the importance of Mozart's encounter with the music of Bach and Handel has been questioned, there can be little doubt that Mozart became a fan of their music, and his Gigue in G, K. 574 (written in Leipzig in 1789), is another example of homage to Bach.

In 1786 van Swieten established the Gesellschaft der Assoicierten Cavaliere (Society of Associated Cavaliers), and Mozart became the music director in 1788, conducting his own arrangements of Handel's *Acis and Galathea* (1788), *Messiah* (1789), the *Ode for St. Cecilia's Day* and *Alexander's Feast* (both 1790), and C. P. E. Bach's *Auferstehung und Himmelfahrt Jesu* (1789).[14] (Later, the Society performed Haydn's *Die Sieben letzten Worte*, and van Swieten supplied the texts for *The Creation* and *The Seasons*.) In a letter to Michael Puchberg, probably from spring of 1790, Mozart refers to an enclosed note from Baron van Swieten that potentially could put Mozart 'on the threshold of my fortune'.[15] Even after Mozart's death, van Swieten continued to support his family, first by organizing a performance of the Requiem on 2 January 1793, and later by arranging to assist his son Karl Thomas with his education in Prague.

Joseph II was the eldest son of Maria Theresa and her consort Francis I. Upon the death of his father, Joseph served as Holy Roman Emperor from 1765 to 1790 and, following the death of his mother, as ruler of the Habsburg lands from 1780 to 1790. Joseph in turn was succeeded as emperor by his brother Leopold II (1747–92). While we tend not to think of Joseph II as one of Mozart's patrons, he was in fact a big supporter of Mozart. Joseph was poorly portrayed in Peter Shaffer's play and screenplay, *Amadeus*, as musically incompetent, indecisive and overly reliant on his advisors. As Joseph's biographer, Derek Beales, has shown, he actually had a hands-on approach to his theatre and music in general, was

---

[13] See Ulrich Leisinger, 'Bachian Fugues in Mozart's Vienna', *Bach Notes: The Newsletter of the American Bach Society*, 6 (2006), pp. 1–7.

[14] Maynard Solomon, *Mozart: A Life* (New York: Harper Collins, 1995), p. 523, suggests that Mozart *possibly* received payment of 225fl. in 1788–90 for conducting these works, but Count Zinzendorf reported Mozart obtaining 150fl. for the benefit concert in November 1788. This is comparable to what Haydn received for *The Creation* about ten years later. See Neff, 'Baron van Swieten', p. 57.

[15] See LMF, p. 936 (March/April 1790). Since van Swieten's note is lost, we do not know what could have made Mozart's prospects 'better than ever'. It might have been wishful thinking on Mozart's part, though Christoph Wolff quoted the phrase as part of the title of his recent book, *Mozart at the Gateway to His Fortune: Serving the Emperor, 1788–1791* (New York: Norton, 2012).

a competent performer on cello and keyboard, and cultivated one of the best opera troupes in Europe.[16]

Joseph's German National Theatre, founded in 1776, paved the way for Mozart's *Die Entführung aus dem Serail* (1782), and, when interest began to lag in German Singspiel, there was a blossoming of opera buffa under his patronage.[17] True, Joseph did not enjoy opera seria; Mozart thus wrote no new seria works between *Idomeneo* (1781) and *La clemenza di Tito* (1791, for the coronation of Leopold II in Prague).[18] Instead, we have the three Da Ponte operas, two of which were commissioned for and first performed in Vienna (*Le nozze di Figaro* in 1786 and *Così fan tutte* in 1790) and a third (*Don Giovanni*) that was commissioned and first performed in Prague in 1787 but revised for Vienna less than a year later. The one-act Singspiel, *Der Schauspieldirektor* (1786), actually grew out of a competition Joseph set up between German and Italian opera.

At a time when Mozart might have been shut out of the court, Joseph appointed him court composer on 7 December 1787, with a salary of 800 gulden.[19] This required relatively little effort aside from writing dance music for the balls, for which Mozart wrote some three-dozen minuets (K. 568, 585, 599, 601, 604) and a similar number of *deutscher* and *ländler* (K. 536, 567, 571, 600, 602, 605, 606). For those who claim Joseph never did enough for Mozart, counter-evidence comprises an official explanation in court documents when Mozart died and his post became vacant: 'Mozart in fact received the title of Kammer Kompositor with a salary of 800 fl. per year from H.M. the late Emperor solely out of consideration that so rare a genius in the world of music should not be obliged to seek abroad for recognition and his daily bread'.[20] Beethoven later benefitted

---

[16] Derek Beales, *Joseph II, Volume II: Against the World, 1780–1790* (Cambridge: Cambridge University Press, 2009), particularly chapter 13, 'Joseph in Vienna: his Routine and his Impact, Especially on Music'. See also Beales, 'Court, Government, and Society in Mozart's Vienna', in Stanley Sadie (ed.), *Wolfgang Amadè Mozart: Essays on His Life and Music* (Oxford: Clarendon Press, 1996), pp. 3–20.

[17] See Dorothea Link's chapter 23 in this volume on Mozart's Viennese singers.

[18] That Mozart wanted to produce *Idomeneo* in Vienna is clear from his letters in 1781 and 1782. Eventually, the opera was revived in a private performance at Prince Auersperg's palace in March 1786, for which Mozart wrote two replacement numbers, K. 489 and 490. For more detail on the revival, see Simon P. Keefe, *Mozart in Vienna: the Final Decade* (Cambridge: Cambridge University Press, 2017), pp. 310–17.

[19] Dorothea Link, 'Mozart's Appointment to the Viennese Court', in Dorothea Link and Judith Nagley (eds.), *Words about Mozart: Essays in Honour of Stanley Sadie* (Woodbridge: Boydell Press, 2005), pp. 153–78.

[20] MDL, pp. 269–70, 378; MDB, pp. 306–7, 430; the latter passage is also quoted in Derek Beales, 'Mozart and the Habsburgs', in *Enlightenment and Reform in Eighteenth-Century Europe* (London and New York: I.B. Tauris, 2005), p. 97.

from patronage of a group who did not want him to suffer the same fate as Mozart.[21]

During the war with the Ottoman Empire, Mozart wrote several vocal works that mention Joseph by name, including two Masonic pieces, *Die Maurerfreude* K. 471 and the song K. 483, and two further songs, 'Ich möchte wohl der Kaiser sein' K. 539 (written for the bass Friedrich Baumann in March 1788) and 'Beim Auszug in das Feld' K. 552 (dated 11 August 1788).[22] Whether Mozart subscribed to the patriotism espoused in the verses is not known, although it is clear that most of Vienna got caught up in the celebrations when Belgrade fell in October 1789.[23] But Joseph II did not live long enough to enjoy the victory, and, unfortunately for Mozart, Leopold II was not as keen a supporter. Mozart was not part of the official entourage of court musicians to Frankfurt for Leopold's coronation in October 1790, and the commission to write *La clemenza di Tito* for his coronation in Prague in September 1791 came only after Salieri had turned it down.[24]

---

[21] See Eliot Forbes (ed.), *Thayer's Life of Beethoven* (Princeton: Princeton University Press, 1967), pp. 453–9.

[22] These works and their texts are discussed in Beales, 'Mozart and the Habsburgs', pp. 101–6, and a translation of K. 552 is given in the appendix, pp. 107–10.

[23] See Beales, 'Mozart and the Habsburgs', p. 104.

[24] For further discussion see chapter 24, 'Mozart's Italian and German Singers'.

CHAPTER 17

Mozart as Impresario

Martin Harlow

In 1786 Mozart produced the music for a singspiel, *Der Schauspieldirektor*, performed in February in the presence of Emperor Joseph II and his entourage at the Schönbrunn palace, outside of Vienna. This was a tongue-in-cheek tale of an impresario, Frank, engaging two singers who vie for top billing as prima donna, and for the highest fee. Mozart's remuneration for his composition, preparations and performance was fifty ducats. In real life, as well as on stage, the solo performers in *Der Schauspieldirektor* fared well. Aloysia Weber and Caterina Cavalieri (the feuding ladies) and Johann Valentin Adamberger were leading singers, each securing the same fee as Mozart, as additional payments to already substantial court salaries.[1] This 'Impresario' typifies the contemporary hegemony of performance over works performed. As a freelance musician Mozart knew that successful impresarial activity – the organization, promotion and direction of performances – was a prerequisite for financial stability. He had, after all, been schooled by his father in the art and science of self-promotion, particularly through the tours from their Salzburg home that extended back to his infancy.

From their first substantial tour, to Vienna (October 1762–January 1763), Leopold's main objective was to show off his children to imperial and noble audiences, in order to procure money and gifts and to enhance the prospects of future patronage. Leopold's letters to his landlord Johann Lorenz Hagenauer record the financial outcomes of their endeavours. With no developed public musical life, Leopold organized concerts, assuming associated financial risks. Waiting for noble invitations to perform was risky, as fees were discretionary and unpredictable. Heading for Vienna, in Passau, after a five-day wait, Wolfgang played for the Prince-Bishop. The miserly four gulden received left Leopold eighty gulden out of pocket. In Vienna, performing to the Prince Saxe-Hilburghausen secured a healthier

---

[1] MDL, p. 230; MDB, p. 263.

six ducats (twenty-six gulden). The Mozarts made an impact sufficient for the court paymaster to offer a hundred-ducat inducement to stay in the city, a sum exceeding Leopold's Salzburg salary.

'The Grand Tour', made between 1763 and 1766, was designed to include a number of German courts and exploit Paris as one of Europe's richest cities. Private performances, for the elector in Munich, the French royal family in Paris, and the king and queen in London, brought in good sums. But Leopold knew that concert promotion in a large city would be most profitable. An excess of a thousand gulden was taken at a Paris concert in the theatre of M. Felix, and again at Wolfgang's London debut in St James' in June 1764. Leopold's hope to make 'some thousands of gulden' during the London season was probably realistic.[2] But not all such endeavours proved successful: on the return to Salzburg, a concert in Lausanne in September 1766 had an audience of only seventy. Rewards for private performances frequently came in trinkets: in Donaueschingen, where Wolfgang wrote cello pieces for the prince, around 200 gulden was received, along with diamond rings for the children. The Salzburg diarist Beda Hübner estimated the Mozarts' tour income as 12,000 gulden, in gifts alone. Expenses to the family were estimated at 20,000 gulden.[3]

The 'Grand Tour' illustrates the frailty of musical entrepreneurship that Mozart would eventually encounter alone: balancing investments against projected incomes, assessing the whims of patron, and evaluating local markets for concertizing. Later journeys were also dotted with financial successes and disappointments. A trip to Vienna between 1767 and 1769 held promise, but the commission fee for the opera buffa *La finta semplice* never materialized. Leopold estimated outgoings of 160 ducats. Trips to Italy between 1769 and 1773 were also more artistically than financially fruitful. In 1772, aged sixteen, Mozart took employment with the Salzburg archiepiscopal court on a 150-gulden salary. He was not to find fortune in Salzburg, so Leopold took Wolfgang to Vienna in summer 1773, again in search of a post, but nothing came of the trip. Long discontented with his hometown, Wolfgang commenced his ill-fated trip towards Paris in September 1777, chaperoned by his mother, who was to die in the city on 3 July 1778. The courts of Munich and Mannheim, with their large musical retinues, offered promise, and wealthy Paris supported many musicians. This tour was the first occasion on which Mozart assumed the incumbent duties – hitherto undertaken by his father – of organizing travel

[2] MBA, vol. 1, p. 169; LMF, p. 51 (13 September 1764).
[3] Stanley Sadie, *Mozart: The Early Years 1756–1781* (Oxford: Oxford University Press, 2006), pp. 110–11.

and accommodation and making contacts. The prize remained a court appointment, but along the way Mozart needed to put on successful concerts simply to cover costs.

Leopold advised on effective concert promotion:

> Ask your host who is the Kapellmeister or musical director of the town; or, if there isn't one, who is the best musician. Ask to be taken to him, or, according to his standing, ask him to come to you, and speak to him; that way you will quickly know whether the cost of putting on a concert is too great, whether you can obtain a decent keyboard instrument – whether an orchestra can be got together, whether there are music-lovers – you might even find whether there is anyone who out of a love of music would play some part in the undertaking etc.[4]

Concerts were given in Munich, but no evidence suggests Mozart earned money during his three-week stay. A plan for ten connoisseurs to pay one ducat every month for Mozart to live, compose and perform in Munich, was sceptically received by Leopold, who urged him to continue his journey. In Mannheim from late October 1777, a concert arranged by the keyboard maker Johann Andreas Stein brought in ninety gulden. Wolfgang gauged that the tour was already twenty-seven gulden down. Collecting a gold watch from the elector (he now had five), he wrote that 'On a journey one needs money'.[5] Other concerts returned small profits, including forty-two gulden with Aloysia Weber in Kirchheimbolanden (early 1778). No appointment was forthcoming in Mannheim, and Mozart embarked for Paris in March 1778. There he took pupils and relayed to his father an offer to be organist at Versailles on a 900-gulden salary, a post Mozart declined. Leopold's bafflement and exasperation over his son's attitude to money was shared by others, including Mozart's host in Paris, Baron Friedrich Melchior Grimm: 'he is too good-natured, too little active, too easily caught out, too little concerned with the ways of advancing his career'.[6]

By August 1778 Leopold had secured for Wolfgang a new salary with reasonable terms back in Salzburg, and Mozart left Paris the next month. In Strasbourg (October 1778), anxious not to risk engaging an orchestra, he gave a solo concert, making only thirty-three gulden with a modest audience in attendance. A subsequent concert with orchestra confirmed his concerns: 'I took in a little more certainly, but the cost of the orchestra (who are very

---

[4] MBA, vol. 2, p. 150; LMF, p. 394 (27 November 1777; translation adapted).
[5] MBA, vol. 2, p. 119; LMF, p. 369 (13 November 1777; translation adapted).
[6] Leopold reports, in French, the views of Baron Grimm. See MBA, vol. 2, p. 446; also LMF, p. 600 (13 August 1778).

bad but demand to be paid handsomely), the lighting, the guard, the printing, the crowds of attendants at the entrances and so forth made up a considerable sum'.[7] Leopold's patience was up, and he listed his investment, 863 gulden, over fourteen months, and censured his son's unfulfilled projects, 'empty words amounting to nothing whatever'.[8] Finances could be rectified only by Wolfgang's prompt return to Salzburg. The family were reunited in January 1779, and knowledge of the Mozarts' next twenty-two months is limited in the absence of correspondence. They may have made music with the amateur orchestra founded by Count Czernin, but opportunities for self-promotion were rare. A commission for *Idomeneo*, for a modest 125 gulden, was therefore sufficient to lure Wolfgang to Munich in late 1780. The next spring Mozart followed the Archbishop to Vienna, for festivities related to the promotion of Joseph II to sole ruler following his mother Maria Theresia's death.

Mozart's first staple income in Vienna was from piano pupils: he taught two daily in 1781, Frau von Trattner and the Countess Rumbeke. A piano contest with Muzio Clementi brought in 225 gulden, which corresponded to months of teaching income and half his former Salzburg salary. By early 1782 Josepha Auernhammer was also a pupil: 'I really need only one more, because four pupils are quite enough. With four I should have twenty-four ducats [per month] ... With this sum a man can live quietly and in the retired way which we desire.' Mozart reassured his father of financial opportunities: regular pupils, an opera commission and a concert per year, and the publication of engraved music or manuscript works available on subscription. Ad hoc concerts would bring 'additional' income (*Accidentien*).[9] Most lucrative would be the big yearly concert. Under edict, theatre productions were forbidden during the periods of Lent and Advent, on Holy Days, Fridays and birth and death days of the imperial family. Restrictions permitted performers to promote 'benefits' in the court theatres – *Akademien* (academies) – bearing all expenses and yielding profits. Lent became the most productive time for concert-giving. Mozart's first academy was on 3 March 1782, including extracts from *Idomeneo* and a piano concerto (K. 175, with a new Rondo, K. 382). And it was the first of six consecutive years in which Mozart gave a Lenten benefit.[10]

---

[7] MBA, vol. 2, p. 501; LMF, p. 627 (26 October 1778).
[8] MBA, vol. 2, pp. 508–11; extracts only in LMF, pp. 633–4 (19 November 1778).
[9] MBA, vol. 3, p. 195; LMF, pp. 794–5 (23 January 1782; translation amended).
[10] A recently discovered notice in the *Bayreuther Zeitung*, 12 March 1787, suggests a Mozart benefit concert on 28 February 1787. See Dexter Edge and David Black, *Mozart: New Documents*, at https:// sites.google.com/site/mozartdocuments/documents/1787-02-28.

Leopold retained a perception of Wolfgang's indolence and poor money management in the early years of his son's Viennese decade. He wrote to Countess Waldstätten: 'If he [Wolfgang] lacks for nothing, then he is at once satisfied and becomes easy-going and lazy. If he is forced into activity, he then bestirs himself and wants to make his fortune at once'.[11] The countess was generous to the Mozarts, reassuring Leopold about Constanze's suitability, accommodating her before the wedding, and even settling a debt for Wolfgang. In gratitude, Mozart invited the countess to take a box at his 23 March 1783 academy. This was also attended by the emperor, who contributed twenty-five ducats. Mozart relayed a triumphant success: 'Suffice it to say that the theatre could not have been more crowded and that every box was full'.[12] Receipts were reported as 1,600 gulden.[13] The following Lent was extraordinarily busy, including three subscription concerts in the Trattnerhof rooms in March, for 174 subscribers yielding 1,044 gulden, and participation in seventeen other concerts. Profits from the academy on 1 April 1784 are unknown, but its reported success was no doubt both artistic and financial.

The Lent 1785 season is particularly well documented,[14] and coincided with a visit by Leopold to Vienna. Concerts in the Burgtheater took place on an almost daily basis between 9 February and 20 March, given by visiting and resident performers, singers, and members of the theatre orchestras. Ignaz Willmann, the Bonn instrumentalist, used the first to showcase his children, Magdalena (singer), Walburga (piano) and Maximilian (cello), respectively thirteen, fifteen and seventeen years of age. *Morgengesang am Schöpfungstage*, a choral work to a text of Klopstock, was the central item on the programme. Ignaz also promoted another concert, comprising a performance of Haydn's opera *L'isola disabitata*. Violinist visitors were Johann Bora, director of the Orchestra of the King of Sardinia, and the Pole Feliks Janiewicz, and visiting wind players included the flautist, Cecilia Cataldi, a 'Romanerin'; the bassoonist Francesco Caravoglia; and Wenzel Schlauf, oboist to the Count Batthjány. Another oboist was the well-known virtuoso Ludwig Le Brun performing with his wife, the singer Franziska Le Brun, both of whom were in the service of the

[11] MBA, vol. 3, pp. 222–3; LMF, p. 816 (23 August 1782; translation amended).
[12] MBA, vol. 3, p. 261; also LMF, p. 843 (29 March 1783). For more on this academy, see Simon P. Keefe, *Mozart in Vienna: The Final Decade* (Cambridge: Cambridge University Press, 2017), pp. 164–7.
[13] Cramer, *Magazin der Musik*, vol. 1, p. 578 (9 May 1783). Also MDL, p. 191; MDB, p. 215.
[14] On account of extant copies of the daily newspaper, *Das Wienerblättchen*. See also Joseph Krauss *Vollständiges Verzeichniss der National-Schauspiele und Besetzung ... Nebst einen Anhang von musikalischen Akademien* (Vienna, 1786).

Elector of Bavaria. They gave three academies, Leopold reporting takings of 1100, 900 and 500 gulden. The fifteen-year-old Munich violinist Heinrich Marchand, a pupil of Leopold, was one of the youthful performers. Marchand's concert on 3 March made a 78-gulden profit after expenses of 115 gulden. A second academy took place on 14 March, and he played a concerto the following day at a Tonkünstler-Societät benefit. Mozart's *Davide Penitente* K. 469, a reworking of the Mass in C minor K. 427, was performed on the same occasion.

Court theatre orchestra members, court singers and their families were clearly afforded priority where putting on academies was concerned. Cellists Joseph Weigl, principal of the Burgtheater orchestra, and Philipp Schindlöcker of the Kärntnerthortheater both gave concerts. A viola player in that orchestra, Basilius Bohdanowicz, also presented a singspiel *Die Eroberung der Festung* with novelty items between its two acts. First came a 'symphony in 24 vocal parts, without texts and instruments' followed by a violin sonata, 'which will be played by 3 people with 3 violin bows on one violin'.[15] Wind players also had opportunities: the annual benefit of the Kaiserlich-königlich Harmonie, the emperor's wind ensemble, was on 12 March; and Anton Stadler, a clarinettist member of the Harmonie for whom Mozart wrote several works, had his own academy a week later including on the programme the oratorio *Der Tod Jesu*. Josepha Hortensia, an actress in the German spoken theatre company and daughter of the playwright and actor Johann Müller, performed a piano concerto at her 17 February concert. Leopold reported dining with the Müllers three days later, no doubt with Wolfgang and Constanze also present. Joseph Scheidl, a violinist in the Burgtheater orchestra and subsequent concertmaster of the Tonkünstler-Societät,[16] promoted his eight-year-old piano prodigy son Cäsar at an academy on 21 February.

Concerts were also given in spring 1785 by those singers in the Italian opera buffa company who would go on to premiere roles in *Le nozze di Figaro* in May 1786: Francesco Benucci (Figaro), Nancy Storace (Susanna), Luisa Laschi (the Countess), and Stefano and Maria Mandini (Count Almaviva and Marcellina). Singer Elizabeth Distler, daughter of the Logenmeister of the court theatre Johann Anton Distler, gave a benefit at which Mozart performed his Piano Concerto in D minor K. 466, four days after its premiere at one of his Mehlgrube subscription concerts. Elizabeth

---

[15] Mary Sue Morrow, *Concert Life in Haydn's Vienna: Aspects of a Developing Musical and Social Institution* (Stuyvesant, NY: Pendragon, 1989), p. 260.

[16] Carl Ferdinand Pohl, *Denkschrift aus Anlass des hundertjährigen Bestehens der Tonkünstler Societät* (Vienna: Im Selbstverlage des Vereines, 1871), p. 96.

then featured as a second soprano soloist, alongside Caterina Cavalieri, in *Davide penitente* performed in the two Tonkünstler-Societät concerts. These events, whose profits went to society funds to support widows and families of deceased musicians, saw musicians give their services for free. Artists who had promoted their own benefits contributed: Stefano Mandini and Franziska Le Brun sang, and Ludwig Le Brun and Marchand performed concertos.

Viennese instrumental performers giving concerts in spring 1785 included Mozart's piano pupil Auernhammer and the violinist Josepha Ringbauer. Organizing their second Lenten concerts were the composer-pianist Anton Eberl and the flute, harp and piano player Josepha Dermer. Mozart's own academy was on 10 March 1785 when he premiered the Piano Concerto in C, K. 467, and played a fantasy on fortepiano with pedal keyboard. Leopold described to daughter Nannerl Wolfgang's unexpected 559-gulden profit. Lent 1785 was a lucrative time for Mozart as impresario: his six subscription concerts in the Mehlgrube – offered on Fridays so as not to clash with Burgtheater academies – were attended by 'over 150 people', with gross takings exceeding 2,025 gulden. Concert returns outstripped monies from other sources: Artaria paid Mozart 450 gulden for the six 'Haydn' quartets published later in 1785.[17] Although Leopold was sniffy about Mozart's fine quarters in Schulerstrasse, at an annual rent of 460 gulden, his son could clearly afford them at that time.

Joseph II relaxed Lenten restrictions in 1786, permitting theatrical performances at the Kärntnertortheater. With only three days a week now available, concert opportunities diminished. Mozart gave a benefit on 7 April, one of a handful recorded that season, when he premiered his Piano Concerto in C minor K. 491. Little changed in 1787, with German plays stifling concert activity. After the success of *Figaro* in Prague in December 1786, Mozart gave concerts in the city in early 1787, as if forced away from Vienna to achieve the successes that he had hitherto enjoyed at home. Trips to Dresden and Leipzig in 1789 and Frankfurt in 1790 were, perhaps, similar in intent. His 15 October 1790 concert in Frankfurt, however, was 'a splendid success from the point of view of honour and glory, but a failure as far as money was concerned'.[18]

---

[17] On Mozart as publisher of chamber music during this period, see Keefe, *Mozart in Vienna*, pp. 220–80.
[18] MBA, vol. 4, p. 118; LMF, p. 946 (15 October 1790).

Theories abound over Mozart's want for money in his last years,[19] and circumstances surrounding petitions to fellow mason Michael Puchberg were complex.[20] Puchberg lent money at least sixteen times to Mozart from 1788, but half of these loans were for less than one hundred gulden. In the context of Mozart's former earning power, Puchberg should have felt confident of being paid back. But Mozart wrote to Puchberg, in summer 1789, that 'I cannot earn anything even if I want to', describing a concert series planned in his apartment, which had secured only one subscriber.[21] Plans for a small-scale subscription series, in a domestic setting during the heat of the summer, speak of some desperation on Mozart's part. There is no evidence that Mozart's popularity waned,[22] but opportunities for profitable, self-promoted concerts had diminished by this time. The Viennese craving for novelties, retrenchment and high inflation as Joseph embarked on conflicts with the Turks in 1788, the reduction of noble music establishments and the concomitant rise in freelance competitors made the Viennese musical environment more challenging. Income on the Mozarts' family tours had been predicated on sustained good health. Illness dogged Mozart's family in his final years.

Leopold's assessment of his son as financially naive, profligate and slothful seems unfair. Mozart had the gifts and sufficient financial acumen to profit from the Viennese musical environment, the 'land of the clavier'. A guaranteed court income of 800 gulden from late 1787 gave some stability, but straitened times meant he was unable to sustain his earlier success. Although a lack of documentary evidence will always blur the picture, after 1787 circumstances conspired against Mozart, limiting his concertizing and having an impact on his endeavours as a self-promoting impresario.

[19] See Andrew Steptoe, 'Mozart and Poverty: A Re-examination of the Evidence', *Musical Times*, 125 (1984), pp. 196–201; Julia Moore, 'Mozart in the Market-Place', *Journal of the Royal Musical Association*, 114/1 (1989), pp. 18–42; William J. Baumol and Hilda Baumol, 'On the Economics of Musical Composition in Mozart's Vienna', in James M. Morris (ed.), *On Mozart* (Cambridge: Cambridge University Press, 1994), pp. 72–101.

[20] Michael Lorenz, 'Mozart's Apartment on the Alsergrund', *Newsletter of the Mozart Society of America*, 14/2 (27 August 2010), pp. 4–9. Mozart's move from the centre of Vienna appears not to have reduced his expenditure.

[21] MBA, vol. 4, p. 92; LMF, p. 930 (12 July 1789; translation amended).

[22] Dexter Edge, 'Mozart's Reception in Vienna, 1787–1791', in Stanley Sadie (ed.), *Wolfgang Amadè Mozart: Essays on his Life and his Music* (Oxford: Clarendon Press, 1996), pp. 66–117, especially 93–4 and Keefe, *Mozart in Vienna*, pp. 501–42.

CHAPTER 18

Publishing

Rupert Ridgewell

On 20 February 1784 Mozart wrote from Vienna to his father Leopold ostensibly to ask his advice about 'something of which I know nothing whatever':

> If I have some work printed or engraved at my own expense, how can I protect myself from being cheated by the engraver? For surely he can print off as many copies as he likes and therefore swindle me. The only way to prevent this would be to keep a sharp eye on him. Yet that was impossible in your own case, when you had your book printed, for you were at Salzburg and the printer was at Augsburg. Why, I almost feel inclined not to sell any more of my compositions to any engraver [i.e. publisher], but to have them printed or engraved by subscription at my own expense, as most people do and in this way make good profits.[1]

The nature of Leopold's advice, presumably conveyed in a lost letter of 24 February, is unknown and Mozart does not appear to have pursued the option of having his works engraved and printed at his own expense. The letter is nonetheless of great interest because it offers a rare insight into Mozart's attitude towards music publishing. Even allowing for an element of flattery towards his father, implied by the reference to Leopold's self-published violin tutor,[2] the letter tells us three important things: by dispensing with the publisher as 'middleman', Mozart saw an opportunity to increase his potential income by issuing his music directly to the public; he was concerned above all to protect himself from unauthorized printing, which would harm potential sales; and he identified a trend emerging at the time for composers to publish their own music, which notably led composers such as Franz Anton Hoffmeister and Leopold Kozeluch to establish their own publishing businesses in the mid 1780s.

[1] MBA, vol. 3, p. 302; LMF, p. 868.
[2] Leopold Mozart, *Versuch einer gründlichen Violinschule, entworfen und mit 4. Kupfertafeln sammt einer Tabelle versehen* (Augsburg, 1756). For a translation see *A Treatise on the Fundamental Principles of Violin Playing*, trans. Editha Knocker (London: Oxford University Press, 1948).

It is not difficult to imagine why Mozart baulked at the prospect of joining that trend. The costs associated with self-publication would have been significant, leaving the composer open to bills for acquiring paper and engraving plates, as well as payments to engravers, printers and for advertising. Even if such an outlay had been within Mozart's grasp in 1784, the practicalities and effort required were surely beyond him at a time when he was in great demand as a pianist and was composing at a furious pace.

Mozart's music was nevertheless published widely in the 1780s. It was fortuitous that his arrival in Vienna in 1781 coincided with the beginnings of a rapid rise in the printing of music, itself part of a wider trend in publishing triggered by Joseph II's liberalization of commercial regulations and censorship. At least fifty-three first editions of Mozart's music were published in Vienna during the ten years in which he was resident in the city, covering a large proportion of his output during that period, together with many other reprints and later editions. Many works were also published in other cities across Europe, contributing significantly to his early reputation and the wide dissemination of his music.[3]

Knowledge of contemporary publishing practice is crucial for understanding Mozart's engagement with the trade. Unlike today, composers were not contracted to specific publishers in the eighteenth century, allowing Mozart to engage with multiple publishers and to explore other avenues of distribution, such as the sale of manuscript copies either to the general public or to specific buyers.[4] Contemporary norms also largely determined the type of music that appeared in print at that time, with a focus on solo and chamber music, as well as songs and operatic excerpts. Sacred music was more likely to be disseminated in manuscript rather than in print, while orchestral music was issued in parts for performance rather than in score, if it was published at all.

The principal publisher of Mozart's music in Vienna was Artaria, a family firm established in 1768 that sold prints, maps, portraits and books, as well as music.[5] As a prominent firm located in the centre of

---

[3] For a bibliography of Mozart first editions, see Gertraut Haberkamp, *Die Erstdrucke der Werke von Wolfgang Amadeus Mozart*, 2 vols. (Tutzing: Hans Schneider, 1986).

[4] Mozart attempted to sell manuscript copies of his piano concertos K. 413–415 in 1783, before they were published by Artaria. Mozart's advertisement first appeared in the *Wiener Zeitung* on 15 January 1783. See MDL, pp. 187–8; MDB, p. 212. In 1786, he also attempted to sell copies of various works to Sebastian Winter, an employee of Joseph Maria Benedikt, Prince von Fürstenberg, in Donaueschingen. See his letter to Winter in MBA, vol. 3, pp. 565–7; LMF, pp. 897–900 (8 August 1786).

[5] For information about Artaria's full range of commercial activities, see Rupert Ridgewell, 'Inside a Viennese *Kunsthandlung*: Artaria in 1784', in Emily Green and Catherine Mayes (eds.), *Consuming*

Vienna, with burgeoning trade contacts and distribution networks around Europe, Artaria might be regarded as representing a more traditional publishing model of the type that Mozart railed against in his letter to his father in 1784. Artaria is nevertheless known to have issued forty-five editions of Mozart's music during his lifetime, including the first appearances in print of sixty works. Despite this comparatively large output, the significance and scope of the relationship is rather unclear. References to Artaria in Mozart's correspondence testify to sporadic dealings between 1781 and 1784, but the detail they impart is sketchy.[6] The letters are silent on the business of preparing an edition for publication, giving no indication that Mozart collaborated with the publisher in any significant way, while the inventory of Mozart's estate lists only six editions published by Artaria of his own music.[7] Studies of Artaria's Mozart editions also paint a somewhat inconsistent picture, with some examples that apparently point to the composer's direct involvement in the publication process (most notably in the case of the six 'Haydn' quartets), and others that suggest a somewhat haphazard approach to textual accuracy.[8]

As a result of this obvious lacuna in the correspondence, and in accordance with the romantic notion that Mozart was somehow immune to the nitty-gritty of commercial negotiation, biographers have tended to downplay the role that publishing potentially played in Mozart's daily life.[9] But it may be argued that the gap in documentation is unsurprising, given that Mozart hardly needed to correspond with Artaria when it was possible to visit the firm in the centre of Vienna to negotiate directly. The nature of that discussion could have addressed such topics as the publisher's

---

Music: Individuals, Institutions, Communities, 1730–1830 (Woodbridge and Rochester, NY: University of Rochester Press, 2017), pp. 29–61.

[6] See Mozart's letters dated 25 July 1781, 10 February 1784, 3 March 1784 and 9 June 1784 in MBA, vol. 3, pp. 140, 300, 303, 318–19; LMF, pp. 754, 866, 869, 880.

[7] A transcription and facsimile of Mozart's estate inventory is given in Ulrich Konrad and Martin Staehelin (eds.), *'allzeit ein buch'. Die Bibliothek Wolfgang Amadeus Mozarts* (Weinheim: VCH, 1991). His library of music and printed books included Artaria editions of the following works: the Symphonies K. 319 and K. 385; the Piano Variations K. 353 and K. Anh. 209; the Piano Concerto K. 413; and the Fantasy and Sonata K. 475/457.

[8] For discussion of Artaria's edition of the 'Haydn' string quartets, see Wolf-Dieter Seiffert, 'Mozart's "Haydn" Quartets: An Evaluation of the Autographs and First Edition, with Particular Attention to mm. 125–42 of the Finale of K. 378', in Cliff Eisen (ed.), *Mozart Studies 2* (Oxford: Clarendon Press, 1997), pp. 175–200; Simon P. Keefe, 'Composing, Performing and Publishing: Mozart's "Haydn" Quartets', in Keefe (ed.), *Mozart Studies 2* (Cambridge: Cambridge University Press, 2015), pp. 140–67, and Keefe, *Mozart in Vienna: The Final Decade* (Cambridge: Cambridge University Press, 2017), pp. 220–51.

[9] For an exception among biographers, see Keefe, *Mozart in Vienna*, especially chapters 5 and 10, pp. 220–80, 449–500.

requirements or expectations in relation to future output; the remuneration that Mozart demanded or expected for his compositions; the way in which the work would be transmitted to the publisher, via a manuscript score or parts prepared by Mozart himself or by a copyist; and arrangements surrounding the checking and correction of proofs. Given Artaria's documented relationships with other composers, such as Haydn, Dittersdorf and Sterkel, it would have been highly uncharacteristic of the firm to publish so much of Mozart's music without his involvement at some level, even if the firm did not necessarily deal with each composer in the same way.

The degree to which Mozart earned money from publishing his music is one area that has attracted scholarly attention and goes to the heart of our understanding of the composer–publisher dynamic. According to an anecdote that appeared in the *Allgemeine musikalische Zeitung* in 1798, 'no one abused [Mozart's] carelessness concerning money more than music dealers and theatre directors', and Mozart's piano compositions 'didn't even bring in a penny'. Written by the journal's editor, Friedrich Rochlitz (1769–1842), this anecdote was one of many fabrications intended to fuel popular interest in Mozart's life and the circumstances surrounding his death and should therefore be read with a healthy dose of scepticism.[10]

Some scholars nevertheless agree that Mozart's publishing income was limited. Otto Jahn, for example, assumed that publishing did not offer a significant return during Mozart's lifetime because 'the music trade at that time had not yet achieved the extent and significance that it later did'.[11] Similarly, Julia Moore states that Mozart cannot have expected more generous payments than Beethoven later received, 'since the market for published music was substantially smaller at the end of the eighteenth century than during the first decades of the nineteenth'.[12] Others have by contrast estimated high potential earnings based on 'typical' fees paid to Mozart's composer colleagues during the 1780s. Maynard Solomon, for example, dismisses Rochlitz's anecdote and proposes that Mozart earned

[10] See Maynard Solomon, 'The Rochlitz Anecdotes: Issues of Authenticity in Early Mozart Biography', in Cliff Eisen (ed.), *Mozart Studies* (Oxford, 1991), pp. 1–59; reprinted in Simon P. Keefe (ed.), *Mozart* (Farnham and Burlington, VT: Ashgate Publishing, 2015), pp. 91–149.

[11] Otto Jahn, *W.A. Mozart*, 4 vols. (Leipzig, 1858), vol. 3, p. 25. Jahn credited the early nineteenth-century expansion in publishing – and therefore Mozart's posthumous reputation – primarily to the activities of his own publisher, Breitkopf & Härtel.

[12] Julia Moore, 'Mozart in the Marketplace', *Journal of the Royal Musical Association*, 114 (1989), p. 25. See also William J. Baumol and Hilda Baumol, 'On the Economics of Musical Composition in Mozart's Vienna', in James M. Morris (ed.), *On Mozart* (Cambridge: Cambridge University Press, 1994), p. 94.

2,864 gulden in publishing fees from Artaria, Franz Anton Hoffmeister and Christoph Torricella between 1781 and 1791, with standard payments ranging from one ducat per lied or dance to seventy-five gulden per quartet or concerto.[13]

Both positions are problematic, for different reasons. The notion that publishers did not have the resources to be able to offer substantial payments to composers is itself based on speculation rather than hard data and attempts to correlate a vague assessment of the size of the market with the financial calculations that potentially come into play when a publisher negotiates a fee payment with a composer. This negotiation may be based on various different criteria, such as an assessment of the potential sales of works in different genres (keyboard sonatas, for example, might be expected to sell more copies than a symphony issued in parts), the perceived popularity or status of the composer himself and the extent to which the retail price was set according to established norms or whether the market could accept an adjustment. Similarly, the idea that fee payments were set according to pre-existing tariffs for works in different genres is based on relatively little evidence relating mostly to a single composer – Joseph Haydn – rather than a representative sample of different composers. Is it realistic to assume that publishers made standard payments across the board, that all composers were treated equally regardless of stature or any other criteria?

The extent to which fee payments acted as an incentive to publish or to which publishers commissioned works from composers merits consideration. Did Mozart ever compose specifically for publication, or was the impetus to write more likely to come from another activity or opportunity, such as a public or private performance, for which publication was merely a source of supplementary income and/or exposure? Definitive answers are hard to come by given the lack of information about the circumstances surrounding the composition of many of the works that appeared in print during Mozart's lifetime. The issue is, however, brought to the fore by consideration of his relationship with the composer-publisher Franz Anton Hoffmeister, who published at least fifteen editions of his music up to the end of 1791. These editions covered a variety of chamber music, including a string quartet, a violin sonata, a piano trio, various works for solo piano and piano duet and a couple of arrangements for flute quintet (another

[13] Maynard Solomon, *Mozart: A Life* (New York: HarperCollins, 1995), pp. 525–6. Other biographers who have estimated Mozart's publishing income include H. C. Robbins Landon, *1791: Mozart's Last Year* (London: Thames & Hudson, 1988), pp. 45–7 and Volkmar Braunbehrens, *Mozart in Vienna 1781–1791*, trans. Timothy Bell (New York: Grove Weidenfeld, 1990), p. 140.

eight editions have been posited by scholars at various times, even though no copies of them appear to be extant).[14] Many of these works appeared in Hoffmeister's ambitious subscription scheme, launched in 1785, which featured monthly instalments of music in three categories: piano music, flute music, and chamber music for strings.[15] Each instalment featured music by various composers for different instrumental combinations, thereby offering subscribers a diverse selection of music to play and enjoy.

This was an innovative publishing project for music in Vienna at that time. Crucially, Hoffmeister relied upon the provision of music on a regular basis from participating composers, and there is tantalizing evidence to suggest that payments were made based on the revenue accrued.[16] It is therefore possible that composers could anticipate regular income in return for continuing collaboration. Mozart's contributions fit comfortably within the parameters of the scheme, but their dates of publication and allocations to particular instalments are not always obvious. As a regular contributor, it seems possible to suppose that Mozart was aware of Hoffmeister's ongoing requirement for music in certain genres and instrumental configurations and composed music to fit. At the very least, this prospect deserves closer scrutiny, even if it conflicts with traditional views of his creativity. The singleton status of the so-called 'Hoffmeister' string quartet, K. 499, for example, may be explained by its appearance in Hoffmeister's series. Rather than being composed as part of a set of three or six string quartets, as was customary at the time, the quartet appeared in a monthly instalment of chamber music alongside works by Hoffmeister and Ignaz Pleyel.[17]

By supporting Hoffmeister's scheme, Mozart may well have been seeking a way to address some of the concerns outlined in his letter to Leopold. Rather than dealing with a traditional publisher like Artaria, Mozart may have welcomed the opportunity to work with a composer colleague who

[14] On the arrangements for flute quintet of Mozart's operatic ensembles 'Dite almeno in che mancai' K. 479, and 'Mandina amabile' K. 480, see Rupert Ridgewell, 'A Newly Identified Viennese Mozart Edition', in Keefe (ed.), *Mozart Studies 2*, pp. 106–39.

[15] Hoffmeister's publications are listed in Alexander Weinmann, *Die Wiener Verlagswerke von Franz Anton Hoffmeister* (Vienna: Universal Edition, 1964).

[16] For further details of the scheme, see Rupert Ridgewell, 'Biographical Myth and the Publication of Mozart's Piano Quartets', *Journal of the Royal Musical Association*, 135/1 (2010), pp. 41–114.

[17] The exact position of the quartet in the series chronology is not securely documented, but it is likely to have been issued in the instalment for May 1786 ('Cahier 7'), which finally appeared towards the end of 1786. Based on their proximity in Hoffmeister's plate number sequence to Mozart's quartet (which was issued with the plate number 76), the other works in the instalment were almost certainly a string quintet by Pleyel (plate number 74), a duet for violin and viola by Hoffmeister (75) and Hoffmeister's Trio Concertante No. 3 (73).

offered not only something rather different to the normal publishing model but also an innate understanding of the craft of composition. The degree to which the venture succeeded on its own terms, however, is questionable. Hoffmeister faced financial problems from an early stage and his intended monthly publishing schedule slipped drastically over time. Mozart's contributions also declined after an initial burst of enthusiasm in 1785 and 1786, and his sole surviving letter to Hoffmeister, dated 20 November 1785, appears to be a request for payment that had been promised but not delivered.[18]

Viewed in a wider context, Mozart's engagement with the publishing scene reflected an important development in the second half of the eighteenth century, namely urban musical life moving away from the feudal model of patronage towards a more commercial, consumer-driven market. In this climate, it was for the publisher to seek novelties and to engage composers, according to perceptions of public demand and musical taste. At a time when the concept of intellectual property had yet to be established, any longer-term benefits arising from making music available in print were not fully acknowledged and in any case of secondary importance. Thus Mozart makes no mention in his 1784 letter or elsewhere of any desire to use the technology of print to fix the text of his works for posterity. The very fact that he was able to explore various ways to publish his music nevertheless reflects the developing role of the composer in society, as opportunities arose that allowed individuals to make a living outside the traditional confines of aristocratic or ecclesiastical employment.

[18] MBA, vol. 3, p. 454, including a facsimile on p. 496; LMF, p. 894 (20 November 1785). See also Ridgewell, 'Biographical Myth and the Publication of Mozart's Piano Quartets', pp. 55–7.

CHAPTER 19

Theatrical Life in Mozart's Vienna

Lisa de Alwis

Mozart's move from Salzburg to Vienna surely contributed to his great productivity in the final decade of his life. In addition to its multifaceted cultural influences, the imperial capital boasted a vibrant theatrical scene. But the particular decade of Mozart's residency, 1781 to 1791, was also significant: had he lived in Vienna earlier or later, he would not have enjoyed quite the same experience. These years coincide with the reign of Emperor Joseph II, who was just coming into his own as sole ruler when Mozart arrived, following the death in 1780 of his co-regent and mother, Maria Theresia, who exerted a powerful influence on him. In his new position, Joseph was able to put his own policies in place, which generally included greater freedoms, more tolerance and less emphasis on Catholicism than hitherto. He also had an important impact on the theatre and theatrical culture in Vienna.

The Court Theatres

In the mid eighteenth century, under Maria Theresia, French was given pride of place as the main language spoken at court, whereas Italian was considered more suitable for the theatre (at least opera). German, especially as spoken in Viennese dialects, was the language of the lower classes. Since the tastes of this segment of the population tended, in the eyes of the authorities, towards the objectionable, German works were often subjected to heavy censorship. In the Enlightenment-era project of educating the public to become morally upright, French and Italian works were rather mildly censored, since only the elite understood these languages.

In 1778, as part of an attempt to raise the profile of German as an operatic language, Joseph added a German troupe that was supposed to have its own repertoire to compete with the Italian and French fare so enjoyed by audiences. At the same time, in order to save money, Joseph dismissed the court theatre's expensive Italian opera buffa singers and ballet troupe. But the German Singspiel that was offered instead was not parti-cularly successful – unlike Italian opera, it did not have a long and venerable tradition upon which to draw. While its greatest success came with Mozart's *Die Entführung aus dem Serail* (1782), many other offerings were simply translations of French and Italian works. These changes were consistent with Joseph's wishes to unite German-speaking lands and to instil a deeper sense of German nationalism in the population as a whole. As with many of his ideas, though, the implementation of theatrical reforms was too sudden and impractical, with many employees losing their jobs in the process, and Joseph earned the displeasure of the aristocracy.[1] In 1783, Joseph, finally conceding to the wishes of the nobility, removed the German troupe and rehired an Italian one, thus enabling Mozart, Salieri and others to write Italian operas for the Habsburg capital. The librettist Lorenzo Da Ponte was employed as court poet to write librettos for Salieri, the official court composer, as well as for composers under contract, such as Martín y Soler and Mozart. The collaboration between Da Ponte and Mozart is one of the most famous in all of opera, yielding *Le nozze di Figaro, Don Giovanni* and *Così fan tutte*.

By the end of Mozart's lifetime, the court supported three troupes that gave performances in two court theatres, the Burgtheater and Kärntnertortheater: a ballet ensemble, a troupe of actors for German plays and an Italian opera troupe. In general, operas were offered in rotation with ballets and plays, with fifteen or so staged each season including a new work at least once every two months. The more popular an opera was, the more it was repeated. Older repertory was rarely heard during the eighteenth cen-tury: each season might include an acclaimed opera from the previous season or two but not an old one in the sense we would understand the word today.

By tradition, operas were usually not performed during Lent. One notable exception was the performance of Da Ponte's *L'ape musicale* (The Musical Bee), which included vocal music by various composers, including Mozart and Salieri. Although the idea for this pasticcio was a good one, with the inclusion of many popular pieces, it worsened Da Ponte's already strained relationship with Salieri because the poet chose for most of the arias his favourite Italian soprano (and mistress) the famous 'La Ferrarese' or Adriana Del Bene and neglected Salieri's preferred singer and student (and later mistress) Caterina Cavalieri.[2]

---

[1] John Rice, 'Vienna under Joseph II and Leopold II' in Neal Zaslaw (ed.), *The Classical Era* (London: Macmillan, 1989), p. 135.

[2] John Rice, *Antonio Salieri and Viennese Opera* (Chicago: University of Chicago Press, 1998), p. 458.

Four years earlier, Salieri had quite dramatically sworn that he would rather chop off his fingers than work with Da Ponte again after a failed first collaboration on *Il ricco d'un giorno* (Rich for a Day).[3] Da Ponte, for his part, blamed Salieri's music for the failure of the opera, noting that upon the composer's return from Paris, his ears were full of a 'shrill screaming music', and that his once beautiful style had been 'drowned in the Seine'.[4]

A good example of Joseph's liberal policies towards press freedom that continued until his successor Leopold II shut them down in 1791 is a slanderous pamphlet published that year entitled *Anti-Da Ponte*.[5] An anonymous author takes the poet to task for the various crimes against the arts that he has committed and even subjects him to a mock trial with Mozart, Salieri and other notables as character witnesses. Da Ponte's dismissal as theatre poet by Leopold that same year (together with La Ferrarese) was probably due in part to the accusations in the pamphlet. In his memoirs, Da Ponte recounts (and in all probability largely invents) a dialogue with the emperor in which Leopold becomes Da Ponte's mouthpiece, stating 'Salieri is an insufferable egotist . . . I don't want either him or his German woman [Cavalieri] in my theater anymore'.[6] Although much of Da Ponte's memoirs must be taken with a pinch of salt, John Rice has argued that Leopold's actions, particularly with regard to Cavalieri, are consistent with what the librettist reports: Leopold fired her and several other female singers who were associated with Salieri.[7]

Since Mozart's operatic work in Vienna was largely contractual, meaning that he had no permanent position and was paid per piece, he was pragmatic about work undertaken. Although he enjoyed writing dramatic music, he would do so only if he had a clear sense that a piece would be approved by the authorities and consequently staged. As he considered setting *Die Entführung aus dem Serail*, for example, he made it clear he would not begin work on the music until Count Rosenberg, director of the court theatres, deemed the libretto worthy of producing. Otherwise, he wrote to his father in 1781, 'I would have the honour of writing for free'.[8] Even composers with permanent positions such as Salieri had to write what was asked of them: total creative freedom was afforded Beethoven some years later, but that was an exceptional case.

[3] Otto Michtner, *Das alte Burgtheater als Opernbühne* (Vienna: Hermann Böhlaus Nachf., 1970), pp. 193–4.
[4] Lorenzo Da Ponte, *Memoirs* (New York: New York Review of Books, 2000), p. 117.
[5] Lisa de Alwis (trans. and ed.) *Anti-Da Ponte* (Malden, MA: Mozart Society of America, 2015).
[6] Da Ponte, *Memoirs*, p. 185.   [7] Rice, *Salieri and Viennese Opera*, p. 504.
[8] MBA, vol. 3, p. 132; LMF, p. 746 (16 June 1781; translation amended).

The Suburban Theatres

On account of Joseph's liberal policies towards theatres, some local troupes, which had previously had temporary, seasonal housing, were able to find permanent homes. These included the two examined below: the Theater in der Leopoldstadt and the Freihaustheater auf der Wieden, where Mozart's *Die Zauberflöte* was first performed. Other important theatres include the Theater in der Josefstadt, and the Theater an der Wien, both of which still stand today. These venues attracted a wide range of audience members from different classes and were quite competitive with the court theatres, mainly because a lot of money was put into decorations and theatrical effects. Reviewers of the time mention that certain effects, such as magical transformations, always worked seamlessly in the suburban theatres but were often delayed in the court theatres thus ruining their impact.[9]

Viennese traditions, including those of stock characters similar to the characters of the Italian commedia dell'arte, were able to flourish in the suburban theatres. Most popular among such characters was Hanswurst, a silly, cowardly peasant focussed on his own bodily needs, who often manages to outwit authority figures. The character's roots in improvised theatre also remained evident in scripted pieces, in that he often comments on politics or current scandals in spite of efforts by Maria Theresia to outlaw improvisation all together as well as the ongoing battles of her successors' censors to control what was said on stage.

Works in the suburban theatres almost always included a Hanswurst-like figure, and although many of the works performed were spoken ones, there was usually a musical element comprising simple, repetitive songs, in which the content of the text was more important than the music itself. In commenting on musical life in Vienna's theatres, Mozart complained to his father in 1781 that 'the music of Hanswurst has not yet been eradicated'.[10] The complaint comes in the context of a discussion about serious versus comic music in the theatres. Mozart's thoughts on the matter were quite strict; he maintained that an opera seria should not include any comic numbers and that an opera buffa, correspondingly, should consist only of lighter fare. Interestingly, Mozart himself ended up creating genres of opera that mixed the comic and the serious in the same sense that a Shakespearean tragedy often integrated comic moments or even whole

---

[9] *Kritisches Theater Journal von Wien* (6 November 1788), p. 261.
[10] MBA, vol. 3, p. 132; LMF, p. 746 (16 June 1781; translation amended).

sections into the drama. Leopold Mozart shared his son's opinion of Viennese theatre: 'That the Viennese, generally speaking do not care to see serious and sensible things [performances], have little or no understanding of them, and only want to see foolish stuff, dances, devils, ghosts, magic, Hanswurst, Lipperl, Bernardorn, witches and apparitions is well known, and their theatres prove it every day.'[11] The Mozarts' opinion about Viennese popular theatre notwithstanding, Papageno from *Die Zauberflöte* owes most of his character traits to Hanswurst and his theatrical successors.

The Theater in der Leopoldstadt shares its name with Vienna's second district and was founded in 1781 by Karl Marinelli, an actor in a travelling troupe, who applied for a so-called privilege from the emperor to erect a permanent house. The personnel consisted mainly of married couples, in accordance with how most travelling troupes were constituted. The repertory they performed was largely comic and included Johann Laroche, who created the wildly popular Viennese stock character of Kasperl, essentially the successor to Hanswurst.[12] Since the troupe's repertory was limited, Marinelli brought in musicians and singers to augment the new theatre's offerings with opera. In 1786, Marinelli hired the composer Wenzel Müller as Kapellmeister, and, other than a short period in Prague, Müller remained in the post until his death in 1835. His light, melodic music was heard in the full breadth of the theatre's repertory as operas, pantomimes and incidental music for plays were added to the regular rotation of works. Müller's handwritten diary, which covers every day of the theatre's existence until 1830, provides valuable information about political incidents in Vienna, the attendance of various famous figures at the theatre (including members of the imperial family) as well as about fires and floods and illnesses and deaths that all affected daily life. With the help of librettist Karl Friedrich Hensler, comic, musical plays based on the experiences of a Kasperl character involved in a relatively simple plot full of local allusions became the bread and butter of the Theater in der Leopoldstadt. Hensler also created several traditions that later became inextricably linked to the city's culture. Most famous was the character das Donauweibchen (the nymph of the Danube), from the play of the same name. Hensler's affinity for German ghost stories as well as his interest in Schiller, Lessing and Goethe are also evident, but in a foreword to a collection of his works he emphasized that they were written purely for

---

[11] MBA, vol. 1, p. 254; LMF, p. 80 (30 January 1768).
[12] Otto Rommel, *Die Alt-Wiener Volkskomödie* (Vienna: Anton Schroll & Co., 1952), p. 417.

entertaining the audience and not for artistic edification.[13] Marinelli also hired a second Kapellmeister, Ferdinand Kauer, who, in addition to his compositional duties (which included writing the music for *Das Donauweibchen*), created and directed a theatrical school for children. The performers mainly comprised offspring of the theatre personnel, who also appeared in many of the plays as well as in children's operas written by Kauer. Children's operas and ballets, particularly those dealing with magical subjects, eventually became very popular, but children's participation in theatrical performances was unregulated until the second decade of the nineteenth century, when substantial evidence of sexual abuse, mainly by members of the aristocracy, came to the attention of the emperor.

The first director of the Theater auf der Wieden, Christian Rossbach, was unable to keep it financially solvent, so in 1788, Johann Friedel, the leader of a travelling acting troupe, took over with his partner and lover, Eleonore Schikaneder. Friedel, fairly well known as a writer, preferred higher-class works, such as those of Lessing and Schiller, and disliked the Viennese taste for – and preponderance of – *Lokalstücke* that emphasized local traditions and experiences. On Emperor Joseph's ultimate failure to endow German-language theatre with the same prestige as French and Italian works, Friedel had a clear opinion: 'One cannot say that German rulers don't support German theatre; one must rather say that German theatre does not deserve to be supported by them.'[14]

In 1789, Friedel added operas to the theatre's roster and hired members of a German-language troupe to perform translated versions of Italian comic operas. Since it was generally always members of the troupe performing each evening, theatre posters of the time advertised shows simply with the names of the characters in the plot; in the role of Pamina at the Theater auf der Wieden in 1791, for example, the audience could expect to hear Anna Gottlieb, a soprano who generally sang dramatic leading roles. In addition to the date and time of the performance, it was important for advertising purposes that posters emphasized either a new attraction or an extremely popular work being performed for the umpteenth time.

Friedel's writings corroborate much of what is known about theatrical performances of this time, for example that famous or particularly effective pieces may have been well attended but that not everyone was there to

---

[13] Rommel, *Die Alt-Wiener Volkskomödie*, p. 443.
[14] Johann Friedel, *Briefe aus Wien: verschiedenen Inhalts an einen Freund in Berlin* (Leipzig: 1784), pp. 394–5.

experience the performance. 'The theatre', Friedel explains, 'is the place for the rendez-vous', and there are many 'miniature duodramas' (presumably romantic liaisons between audience members with the music as background entertainment). Friedel claims that these activities intensified when the emperor was not in attendance and that some of the loges in the theatre could be considered 'little beerhouses'.[15]

According to theatre reviewers in several newspapers, the early performances at the Theater auf der Wieden were mediocre as Friedel gave performers insufficient rehearsal time and (for example) put on six different works on six consecutive days; the public, unhappy with Friedel for his poor business decisions, felt that the job should be given to a more experienced man.[16] And they got their wish when Friedel, who had been ill for some time, died in 1789 at the age of thirty-eight. Eleonore Schikaneder, in the unusual position of being a woman in charge of a theatre, reconciled with Emanuel, her estranged husband, and brought him back to run it with her. Schikaneder is best known as the librettist of *Die Zauberflöte*, but he also played the first Papageno and was, like Da Ponte, one of the more colourful figures in Vienna during Mozart's Viennese decade. He befriended the Mozarts in 1780 when his troupe performed in Salzburg for an extended period. The Mozarts were especially happy to attend Schikaneder's shows because he gave them complimentary tickets for the entire season. And Schikaneder sometimes went shooting with them on Sundays, playing a game called Bölzelschiessen, in which air guns were used to hit targets painted with various, sometimes obscene scenes.

On 12 July 1789, Schikaneder presented his first work at the Theater auf der Wieden, a comic opera entitled *Der dumme Anton im Gebürge* (Stupid Anton in the Mountains). The title character was played by Schikaneder, and the Anton series became so popular that Schikaneder produced several sequels. Mozart wrote to his wife in the summer of 1790 that he too enjoyed the Anton operas;[17] he even composed a set of variations for the piano, K. 613, based on one of its arias, 'Ein Weib ist das herrlichste Ding auf der Welt' (A woman is the most wonderful thing in the world). The music for most of the shows at the theatre was written by Johann Baptist Henneberg, the Kapellmeister of the theatre, who often collaborated with Johann Benedikt Schack and Franz Xaver Gerl, members of Schikaneder's troupe

---

[15] Johann Friedel, *Briefe aus Wien*, p. 408.
[16] Otto Erich Deutsch, *Das Freihaustheater auf der Wieden: 1787–1801* (Vienna: Deutscher Verlag für Jugend und Volk, 1937), pp. 10–11.
[17] MBA, vol. 4, p. 110; LMF, p. 940 (2 June 1790).

and later creators of the roles of Tamino and Sarastro in *Die Zauberflöte*. This collaborative approach to writing music for the Theater auf der Wieden was a necessity on account of time pressures related to rehearsing and performing new works. Mozart, who worked under contract and did not have permanent employment at the Theater auf der Wieden, also contributed to the collaborative compositional environment and at least one piece, a duet from Schikaneder's *Der Stein der Weisen* (The Philosopher's Stone), has been attributed to him. Schikaneder began presenting magical operas of this sort as soon as he took over the theatre, beginning with Paul Wranitzky's *Oberon, König der Elfen* (Oberon, King of the Elves), and its success prompted the Theater in der Leopoldstadt to produce its own similarly successful magical opera, *Das Glück ist kugelrund, oder Kaspars Ehrentag* (Luck is Rotund, or Kaspar's Day of Glory). Both theatres continued with the trend of magical operas, and their directors also revisited older magical works to fill out the repertory. In general, such operas were either completely light-hearted, such as all works involving Kaspar, or they mixed the serious and the comic, such as *Oberon*, and *Die Zauberflöte*. The main competitor with Mozart and Schikaneder's *Die Zauberflöte* in 1791 was Wenzel Müller and Joachim Perinet's *Kaspar der Fagottist*, an extremely popular magical opera about which Mozart, upon attending a performance, noted that 'there's absolutely nothing to it'.[18]

****

One cannot underestimate the importance of Viennese theatre, particularly opera, in the late eighteenth and early nineteenth centuries. People living in German-speaking cities went to the theatre to hear works not only by Mozart, Salieri and Martín y Soler but also by Müller and Kauer, which were equally popular. Kauer's *Das Donauweibchen* became one of the most performed works of the nineteenth century; countless versions of its libretto still exist, as well as several sequels. Although they were intended and condoned as a distraction from various political problems that people in Austria were experiencing, the carefree, even silly works that came after Mozart's time, contributed to the fun-loving character of Vienna as a city, a reputation that was eventually cemented in the Viennese waltzes of Johann Strauss Jr. Much more could be added to this overview of the intertwining forces that created the unique environment of Mozart's final decade. There is more to be learned about the interactions between members of theatre troupes and their audiences, about the circumvention

---

[18] MBA, vol. 4, p. 137; LMF, p. 954 (12 June 1791; translation amended).

of the censors, about the factions supporting various sorts of theatre and about the many cultural norms of the time that can be surprising to the modern reader. By broadening our view to encompass issues beyond the music and biography of Mozart and by placing them in a larger context, we can better understand both the concerns of individuals and the larger movements of the period. In so doing, we also add texture to our relationship with Mozart's sublime achievements.

CHAPTER 20

Mozart and Finances

Jessica Waldoff

The notion that Mozart could not manage his finances has long served the myth that he was a child in all matters but music. Friedrich Schlichtegroll, Mozart's first biographer, took this view from reminiscences supposedly provided by Nannerl (but very likely supplemented by Albert von Mölk): 'Apart from his music he was almost always a child, and thus he remained ... he could not manage his financial affairs.'[1] Franz Xaver Niemetschek, among others, embellished the story: 'with an insecure and irregular income, added to the frequent accouchements and lengthy illnesses of his wife in an expensive town like Vienna, Mozart in fact very nearly starved'.[2] This idea has influenced both scholarly and popular biographies for more than two centuries and helped to develop the caricature we find in Peter Shaffer's *Amadeus*. It is still with us, even though scholars have shown that Mozart did not starve, that he flourished in Vienna through his own industry and that his periods of difficulty and debt are best understood in context. The truth, as often happens, is less compelling and more complicated than the fiction invented to take its place. As a freelance artist, Mozart earned a substantial income, but it was variable and subject to factors in the marketplace beyond his control such as the political climate, the Turkish War and the economic recession, as well as changes in concert culture, patronage and popular taste.[3]

---

[1] MDL, p. 405; MDL, p. 462.

[2] Niemetschek, *Mozart: The First Biography* (1798), trans. Helen Mautner (New York and Oxford: Berghahn Books, 2007), p. 29.

[3] Assessments of Mozart's income and circumstances differ; see, among others, Andrew Steptoe, 'Mozart and Poverty: A Re-Examination of the Evidence', *The Musical Times*, 125 (1984), pp. 196–201; Julia Moore, 'Mozart in the Market-Place', *Journal of the Royal Musical Association*, 114/1 (1989), pp. 18–42; Ruth Halliwell, *The Mozart Family* (London: Oxford University Press, 1998); and Christoph Wolff, *Mozart at the Gateway to his Fortune: Serving the Emperor, 1788–1791* (New York: Norton, 2012). See also a new biography by Simon P. Keefe, *Mozart in Vienna: The Final Decade* (Cambridge: Cambridge University Press, 2017).

Mozart's financial independence began with his break from the Archbishop's service in 1781. His decision to stay in Vienna without a court appointment meant he had no fixed income. This was not a choice without risk; on the other hand, in Salzburg where he held court positions – as concertmaster (1772) and as organist (1779) – his salary (450 gulden) had been considered family income and not his own. (He wrote to his father in 1781: 'you are drawing two salaries'.)[4] Mozart's lifelong quest for a court appointment in a prestigious musical city was finally achieved with the post of *Kammermusikus* (chamber composer) in December 1787. It provided an annual salary of 800 gulden and made minimal demands on his time, requiring only that he write dances for court balls.

From the moment of his arrival in Vienna, Mozart's letters were full of plans to seek his fortune there – to play for the Emperor, to give a public concert, to write opera, to compose an oratorio to be put on during Lent, to perform with the Tonkünstler-Societät. On 23 January 1782, having lived in the city for less than a year, he outlined the formula by which he intended to make a living.

> I have three pupils now. – that brings me eighteen ducats a month . . . with four I should have twenty-four ducats, or 102 gulden, 24 kreuzer: – with this sum a man and his wife can manage in Vienna if they live quietly and in the retired way which we desire . . . I can certainly write at least one opera a year. I can give a concert each year. I can have some things engraved and published by subscription. There are also other concerts where one can make money, particularly if one has been living in a place for a long time and has a good reputation. But I should prefer not to count on such takings but rather to regard them as windfalls.[5]

It was overly ambitious, of course, to expect to compose one opera per year, but Mozart knew a great deal about how to make his way in the world – how to manage pupils, please an audience, compose for both public and private venues, network (in the modern sense) and develop a 'good reputation'. His financial security for the next decade would depend on a combination of teaching, performing, composing and publishing.

Teaching provided an essential means of support. Only two weeks after his arrival in Vienna, Mozart reported that he had a pupil, Countess Rumbeke.[6] From 1781 to 1784 he taught on a regular basis: 'As for pupils,

---

[4] MBA, vol. 3, p. 102; LMF, p. 721 (4 April 1781).
[5] MBA, vol. 3, p. 195; LMF, p. 795 (23 January 1782; translation slightly amended).
[6] MBA, vol. 3, p. 101; LMF, p. 720 (28 March 1781).

I can have as many as I want, but I do not want many. I intend to be better paid than others, and I would prefer to have fewer.'[7] He had as many as four clavier pupils at a time, among them, Josepha Auernhammer, Maria Theresia Trattner, and Barbara Ployer.[8] He charged six ducats (twenty-seven gulden) for twelve lessons, which he later adjusted to six ducats per month with the proviso that he would be paid even when lessons were missed.[9]

So, how many lessons did Mozart give each year and what income came to him as a result? If we multiply Mozart's figure of 102 gulden 24 kreuzer by twelve months, the total is 1,228 gulden 48 kreuzer, but that number is almost certainly too high. Wealthy ladies were probably not in town during the summer months. We also do not know how well his scheme of being paid for missed lessons held up: a letter of 22 December 1781 reported that Frau Trattner would not pay for missed lessons.[10] If we assume he could give lessons for about nine months of the year and may not always have had four students, the annual income from teaching was more likely in the neighbourhood of 600–800 gulden.[11] It is more difficult to estimate how teaching contributed to Mozart's income from 1785 to 1789, though he continued to have students, including for composition. In 1790–1, he mentioned teaching again in his letters and appeared to have two clavier pupils.[12]

Mozart's most important source of income through 1786 was performing. His early letters from Vienna are teeming with reports of concerts, invitations to perform, and compositions written for these occasions: 'my special line is far too popular for me not to be able to support myself. Vienna is certainly the land of the clavier!'[13] In short order, Mozart had organized a highly lucrative career for himself, arranging public and private concerts and appearing regularly in concerts put on by others.

From 1782 through 1786, Mozart gave a public concert or 'academy' for his own benefit each year during Lent in the Burgtheater. Financial information survives for only two. His concert of 23 March 1783, newspaper reports tell us, brought in receipts of 1,600 gulden. This is an enormous sum, but we do not know what portion was required to cover

[7] MBA, vol. 3, p. 120; LMF, p. 736 (26 May 1781; translation slightly amended).

[8] MBA, vol. 3, p. 197; LMF, p. 797 (13 February 1782).

[9] MBA, vol. 3, pp. 131, 195; LMF, pp. 744, 795 (16 June 1781 and 23 January 1782).

[10] MBA, vol. 3, p. 187; LMF, p. 789 (22 December 1781).

[11] In a letter of 12 October 1782, Mozart indicates that he can earn more than the salary offered to the instructor of the Princess Elizabeth of Wurtemberg (400 fl.) from two pupils: MBA, vol. 3, p. 238; LMF, pp. 827–8.

[12] MBA, vol. 4, p. 108; LMF, p. 939 (on or before 17 May 1790).

[13] MBA, vol. 3, pp. 124–25; LMF, p. 739 (2 June 1781; translation slightly amended).

his costs (some scholars guess as much as half).[14] Leopold reports that the concert of 12 March 1785 earned a *profit* of 559 gulden. This is a more useful figure and may help us to estimate profits from other benefit concerts.[15]

Mozart arranged subscription concerts, chiefly during Lent and Advent. These were public concerts in smaller venues for which he sold tickets in advance; subscribers paid for a series of three or six whether or not they could attend all the concerts. For the Lenten concerts at the Trattnerhof in 1784, he proudly sent his father a list of 174 subscribers.[16] At a cost of six gulden per ticket, a gross of 1,044 gulden is implied, but without knowing his costs we cannot calculate profit with any certainty. In 1785 Leopold tells us that Mozart charged a souvrain d'or (13 gulden 30 kreuzer) to over 150 subscribers for the Lenten series at the Mehlgrube, suggesting a gross of 2,025 gulden. Maynard Solomon assumes an average profit of 187 gulden per concert, which would have meant a profit (1,122 gulden) in this case of a little more than half the gross.[17]

Salon concerts given in a patron's residence offered another highly lucrative source of income. Mozart reported missing a private performance at Countess Thun's attended by the Emperor for which Adamberger and Madame Weigl received fifty ducats each (225 gulden).[18] Mozart himself received 225 gulden from the Emperor after his competition with Clementi in December 1781. But patrons paid at their discretion and the performer could not dictate terms. Mozart was given 450 gulden by the Elector of Saxony for a private performance in 1789, but only a 'meagre' 135 gulden by the Elector of Mainz for a similar performance in 1790.[19] Prince Colloredo gave the performers, including Mozart, five ducats (22 gulden 30 kreuzer) each for a private concert in March 1781.[20] Some patrons paid with trinkets: the Mozart family returned from their travels with a princely treasure of gold watches, snuff boxes and assorted other finery. Mozart found this frustrating and had written in a letter of 1777 that he was considering wearing two watches (one on each leg of his trousers) to avoid being presented with another.[21]

[14] For one report, see MDL, pp. 190–1; MDB, p. 215.
[15] MBA, vol. 3, p. 378; LMF, p. 888 (12 March 1785).
[16] MBA, vol. 3, pp. 305–7; LMF, pp. 870–2 (20 March 1784).
[17] Maynard Solomon, *Mozart: A Life* (New York: HarperCollins, 1995), p. 524.
[18] MBA, vol. 3, p. 105; LMF, p. 723 (11 April 1781).
[19] See NMD, p. 56; and Mozart's letter of 23 October 1790 (Mozart gives the sum as 15 carolins): MBA, vol. 4, p. 119; LMF, p. 947.
[20] MBA, vol. 3, p. 101; LMF, p. 720 (28 March 1781).
[21] MBA, vol. 2, p. 119; LMF, p. 369 (13 November 1777).

Once the income from benefit, subscription and private concerts is added up, plus anything earned from other appearances, what was the total? Leopold, who was present for all of the Lenten concerts of 1785, reported to his daughter: 'I think that my son can now deposit 2000 gulden in the bank if he has no debts to pay'.[22] Lent was the busiest time of year for concerts – Mozart gave twenty-two Lenten concerts in 1784 – and performing during Advent and at other times of year would have yielded significant income as well. Mozart was perhaps able to earn as much as 3,000 gulden from performing during his most active years.

Composing contributed significantly to Mozart's income through commissions and publications. Opera commissions were the most profitable, and we find Mozart in his letters longing to write opera and hunting down librettos. The standard fee for an opera was 450 gulden. It was also common for the proceeds of one 'benefit' performance to be given to the composer (though we know for certain this happened only in the cases of *Don Giovanni* in Prague and *Die Zauberflöte*). During his Vienna years, Mozart received 450 gulden each for *Die Entführung aus dem Serail* (1782), *Le nozze di Figaro* (1786) and *Don Giovanni* (Prague, 1787). He received 225 gulden for *Der Schauspieldirektor* (1786) and *Don Giovanni* (Vienna, 1788). For his last three operas, we cannot be sure of the fee. Mozart claimed he was paid 900 gulden (double the usual fee) for *Così fan tutte* (1790), but the records show only one payment of 450 gulden.[23] For *La clemenza di Tito* (1791), we have no records, but Mozart was offered 900 gulden plus expenses by Guardasoni in 1789, and Salieri reports that *he* was offered 900 gulden to compose the coronation opera. It seems reasonable, therefore, to conclude that Mozart received double the usual fee on this occasion.[24] For *Die Zauberflöte* (1791), it is unclear whether any fee was paid upfront. Given the vagaries of life in the suburban theatre and the expense associated with the production, it may be that he was promised a profit-sharing arrangement instead or in addition. A recently recovered newspaper account shows that he received the box office receipts for 5 October 1791.[25] Some other commissions were lucrative as well, such as the Requiem for which Mozart was reportedly offered fifty or sixty ducats

---

[22] MBA, vol. 3, p. 380; LMF, p. 889 note 1 (19 March 1785; translation slightly amended).
[23] Dexter Edge, 'Mozart's Fee for *Così fan tutte*', *Journal of the Royal Musical Association*, 116/2 (1991), pp. 211–35.
[24] See MBA, vol. 4, p. 80; LMF, p. 920 (10 April 1789), and NMD, p. 68.
[25] Dexter Edge, 'Mozart Rewarded with the Receipts from the Third Performance of *Die Zauberflöte*', in Dexter Edge and David Black (eds.), *Mozart: New Documents*, first published 16 March 2015, https://sites.google.com/site/mozartdocuments/.

(225–270 gulden). Mozart arranged four works by Handel (1788–90) for Baron van Swieten's Society of Associated Cavaliers. In the case of *Acis and Galatea*, he was also able to give a public performance for his own benefit.[26]

It is difficult to determine Mozart's income from publishing, though it was surely substantial at times. The sale of his six 'Haydn' quartets in 1785 for 450 gulden is a familiar example, but should be regarded as the exception, not the rule. In 1790 he complained that he was forced to give away another set of quartets (K. 575, 589 and 590) for next to nothing.[27] Mozart expressed concern about maximizing his profit and cutting out the middleman on several occasions. In 1783 he advertised the sale of his concertos K. 413–415 by subscription to avoid sharing the profit with a publisher, but it seems unlikely that his scheme succeeded because he eventually sold the concertos to Artaria in 1785. He also worried about his work being copied and sold by others, a not uncommon practice at the time.[28] Solomon has used figures paid to other composers, including Haydn, to estimate Mozart's income from publication, which may have been as much as 900 gulden in 1785, but was probably closer to 200–550 gulden in later years.[29] In the last years of his life, Mozart put more effort into composing music for the home market, suggesting a shrewd assessment of where he might make the most profit.[30]

If we pause here to estimate Mozart's income, it appears that he was able to earn a reasonable sum from teaching (600–800 gulden or more in some years), a very substantial sum from performing (perhaps as much as 3,000 gulden in his best years), significant sums from commissions (675 gulden in 1786), and something from publishing (200–500 gulden, depending on the year). Adding these figures together and leaving some margin for error, we arrive at an annual income of about 4,000 gulden for the years through 1786 when Mozart was most active as a performer. He may even have come close to this figure in 1787, given his concerts in Prague (1,000 gulden), the benefit performance of *Don Giovanni* (600 gulden), and his inheritance of 1,000 gulden from his father's estate. In 1788–90, however, his income would have dropped, even with the addition of his new salary (800 gulden). Performing opportunities in Vienna were greatly reduced due to changes in concert culture (a new policy in 1786 allowing theatrical performances during Lent, for example, limited opportunities for benefit concerts in the court theatres), the political and economic difficulties caused by the

[26] Solomon, *Mozart*, p. 423. [27] MBA, vol. 4, p. 110; LMF, p. 940 (12 June 1790).
[28] MBA, vol. 3, p. 302; LMF, p. 868 (20 February 1784). [29] See Solomon, *Mozart*, pp. 525–6.
[30] On solo and chamber work for publication between 1786 and 1791, see Keefe, *Mozart in Vienna*, pp. 449–454.

Turkish war (which put a strain on the nobles and removed many from the city) and the death of the Emperor (resulting in no concerts during Lent in 1790). Mozart made a trip to Berlin, Dresden and Leipzig in 1789 to play concerts and seek new opportunities, but this expensive venture did not prove profitable. He borrowed during this period due to a combination of difficult circumstances and costs associated with health care. In 1791, his situation improved with commissions for two operas and the Requiem, substantial publishing fees, income from two pupils and the promise of support from abroad (patrons from Amsterdam and Hungary offered him an annual income).[31]

When viewed in contemporaneous terms, both Mozart's court salary and income were competitive. Ignaz Umlauf earned 850 gulden. Salieri's salary was 853 gulden 20 kreuzer; when he was appointed Kapellmeister in October 1787, it was increased to 1,200 gulden. Some musicians were paid more, singers in particular. During the years of the Nationalsingspiel, Aloysia Lange received 1,700 gulden and Valentin Adamberger over 2,000 gulden. Italian singers could earn even more: Nancy Storace was paid 4500 gulden for her final season with the Italian troupe; Francesco Benucci was offered just slightly less (4185 gulden) when he returned to Vienna in 1791. Instrumentalists, however, got significantly less: Leopold Mozart earned 350 gulden as assistant Kapellmeister in Salzburg, and string players in the Vienna Hofkapelle 300–400 gulden.

Mozart's standard of living was comfortably middle class. His most expensive apartment (1784–7) cost 450 gulden per year; his least expensive (second half of 1787) cost less than half that but was spacious and included a garden. Mozart dressed well and kept servants; he owned a horse, a carriage, a billiard table and he liked fine things such as coffee and tobacco. He entertained nobles and friends in his home and indulged in some expensive amusements such as the ball he and Constanze hosted in January of 1783 and the pantomime he and friends put on during carnival of the same year.[32] He sent his wife to Baden for expensive but necessary recuperative treatments and his son Karl to boarding school. But he had no job security, no health insurance and no savings.

When the tide turned in Vienna, just as Joseph II entered the Turkish war, Mozart struggled to match his musical activities to the changing marketplace. But, of course, one had to spend money to make money.

---

[31] See Constanze's petition for a pension in MDL, pp. 371–72; MDB, pp. 421–22. See also Mozart's mention of 2,000 gulden in MBA, vol. 4, p. 140; LMF, p. 957 (25 June 1791).

[32] MBA, vol. 3, pp. 252, 259; LMF, pp. 837, 842 (22 January and 12 March 1783).

This struggle appeared in his first letter to his friend and fellow Mason, Michael Puchberg, in June 1788: 'I dare ask you to help me out with a hundred gulden until next week, when my concerts start at the Casino. By that time I will definitely have received my subscription money.'[33] Mozart was accustomed to living close to the edge, but had been able to manage in better economic times. The current situation, however, was very different and was subsequently exacerbated by Constanze's illness in 1789 (an ulcerated leg). Günther G. Bauer has estimated the cost of care associated with births, deaths and cures at Baden during the last three years of Mozart's life to be almost 2,000 gulden.[34] Between 1788 and 1791, he borrowed 1,415 gulden from Puchberg, all in small sums. He arranged to borrow from others as well: 100 gulden from Franz Hofdemel (another Masonic brother) through a bill of exchange signed on 2 April 1789, which was then cashed (that is, repaid) later that year; 1,000 gulden from Heinrich Lackenbacher on 1 October 1790, which was probably guaranteed by Hoffmeister in exchange for a claim on Mozart's future publications; and a significant amount from Count Lichnowsky that resulted in a court judgment against Mozart of 1,435 gulden 32 kreuzer (though Lichnowsky apparently dropped this suit after Mozart's death).[35] All of Mozart's known requests to Puchberg as well as his other debts from the period are summarized in Table 20.1. The pattern is clear: Mozart wanted to borrow a large sum, enough to work and plan, but Puchberg made him frequent small loans – just enough to get by or pay pressing bills. After Mozart finally borrowed a larger sum in the autumn of 1790 (from Lackenbacher), his requests to Puchberg were infrequent and small.

During this period, Mozart repeatedly expressed a desire to raise enough money to compose without day-to-day worries. It is clear that he felt more anxiety about securing loans than about carrying debt. Personal debt was not unusual in Mozart's day, and the need for it certainly as frequent as in ours.[36] He also pawned some items, economized in small ways and turned his considerable energies to initiatives likely to pay off in the new economy: opera, publishing for the home market, finding a position with a larger fixed income and teaching. When Mozart had money, he was generous about loaning it. On his death, two friends owed him money: Franz Anton Gilowsky (300 gulden) and Anton Stadler (500 gulden). We also know he

---

[33] MBA, vol. 4, p. 65; LMF, p. 915 (June 1788; translation adapted).

[34] Günther G. Bauer, *Mozart: Geld, Ruhm und Ehre* (Bad Honnef: K.H. Bock, 2009), p. 259.

[35] MDB, pp. 338, 348, 371–2.

[36] Volkmar Braunbehrens, *Mozart in Vienna: 1781–1791*, trans. Timothy Bell (New York: Grove Weidenfeld, 1986), p. 140.

Table 20.1 *Mozart's Requests to Puchberg and Other Known Debts*

Request	Request	Money Received	Comments
1788			
June	100 gulden	100 gulden	Mozart mentions existing debt of 8 ducats (36 gulden)
Before 17 June	1000–2000 gulden	200 gulden	needs capital to work and plan; 200 gulden owed to landlord
27 June	a fairly substantial sum	none	only a larger sum will provide a long-term solution
early July	raise money on pawnbroker's tickets		asks for immediate assistance
1789			
March, to Hofdemel	*100 gulden*	*100 gulden*	*bill of exchange signed 2 April and cashed 2 July 1789*
12 July	500 gulden	none	Constanze's illness, Mozart's illness, difficulty working
17 July	a large sum (same request)	150 gulden	misfortunes and upcoming expenses
December	400 gulden	300 gulden	can't wait for *Così* payment to pay chemists and doctors
1790			
20 January	100 gulden	100 gulden	additional 100 gulden would be helpful
20 February	a few ducats	25 gulden	Mozart must settle a matter that can't be postponed
21 March/April	what you can	150 gulden	opportunity ('Gateway to my fortune') will be lost without aid
8 April	what you can easily spare	25 gulden	a temporary embarrassment
23 April	what you sent last time	25 gulden	no reason given
May	at least 600 gulden	100 gulden	living expenses plus an urgent debt of 100 gulden may be forced to resort to moneylenders
17 May	what you can spare	150 gulden	needs help to meet present expenses, sold quarters for next to nothing
12 June	what you can spare	25 gulden	
14 August	the smallest sum	10 gulden	will be better off in a week or two

Date			
1 October	*1000 gulden*	1000 gulden	*Mozart receives a two-year loan from Lackenbacher at a rate of 20% interest*
1791			
13 April	*30 gulden*	20 gulden	anxiously awaiting his quarterly pay, due the following week
27 April	*no money*	borrow instruments	apologizes for delay on repaying debt in previous letter
25 June	*25 gulden*	a small sum	Constanze needs money in Baden; 2000 gulden arriving in Mozart's name
before November	*1435 gulden 32 kr.*	*a large sum*	*Judgement in Lower Austria Court against Mozart for debt to Prince Karl Lichnowsky, plus court costs of 24 gulden (suit dropped after Mozart's death)*

Note: Requests made to others (not Puchberg) are given in italics.

loaned Lichnowsky 100 gulden while on their journey. From the financial numbers alone, Mozart's habits of borrowing do not seem surprising, especially when we consider that he lived in a world with no social safety nets. Over a period of three years, he borrowed the equivalent of his annual income to meet expenses, finance business ventures and pay for health care. On 25 June 1791, he wrote to Puchberg that a sum of 2,000 gulden would be arriving shortly in his (Mozart's) name from which Puchberg might repay himself. Whether Puchberg did so or not is unclear, but the instruction suggests that Mozart's period of borrowing was at an end.[37] By 1791, in fact, Mozart had largely recovered from his financial difficulties. With earnings that year of around 4,000 gulden, he was comfortable again and had begun to pay off his debts.

To understand Mozart's finances, one must accept a number of uncertainties, including significant gaps in the historical record. What emerges clearly from the surviving evidence, however, is his approach to earning. Hard-working, ambitious, confident (perhaps overly so) and certainly not risk-adverse, he met the vicissitudes of eighteenth-century life with entrepreneurial ingenuity and extraordinary resilience.

[37] MBA, vol. 4, p. 140; LMF, p. 957.

PART IV

Performers and Performance

CHAPTER 21

Instrumentalists in Salzburg and Abroad

Ulrich Leisinger

In one important respect Mozart was a typical composer of his era: with few exceptions he wrote music with the intention of having it performed as soon as it was finished and so usually had precise knowledge about the musicians who were to participate in the premieres.[1] This is true not only for singers, where Mozart was proud to conceive arias that fitted them as accurately as a well-made suit,[2] and other soloists, but also for accompanists. For almost a decade, from November 1769 until August 1777, Wolfgang served as one of the concertmasters of the orchestra of the Salzburg archiepiscopal court which not only participated regularly in church ceremonies but also in concerts at the Residenz. Furthermore, the court musicians formed the core of private music-making activities in Salzburg for which larger forces or particularly skilled ensemble players were required. The Mozarts were not only acquainted with the other court musicians, they were also on friendly terms with some of them and met them at private occasions. According to the Salzburg *Hofkalender* in the 1760s and 1770s, up to fifteen violin and viola players, two cellists and four double-bass players formed the string section while two oboists, three bassoonists and three horn players served as wind players; these forces were supplemented by two organists, two timpanists and ten trumpet players.[3] In church music three trombones were also used regularly. Setting aside the trumpeters who mainly participated in festive ceremonies and at the cathedral, the Kapellmeister, supported by the vice Kapellmeister and several concertmasters, had an ensemble of around thirty-five musicians at his disposal. This constituted at the time one of

---

[1] For the Salzburg court musicians see Ernst Hintermaier, 'Die Salzburger Hofkapelle von 1700 bis 1806. Organisation und Personal' (PhD thesis, University of Salzburg, 1972). For biographical data about many Salzburg musicians and their relationships to the Mozart family see Gerhard Ammerer and Rudolph Angermüller (eds.), *Salzburger Mozart Lexikon* (Bad Honnef: K.H. Bock, 2005).

[2] MBA, p. 304; LMF, p. 497 (28 February 1778). All translations from MBA are by the author.

[3] Hintermaier, 'Die Salzburger Hofkapelle', pp. 538–45.

the largest orchestras in the German-speaking lands. The British diplomat Louis (Lewis) de Visme visited Salzburg in autumn 1772 and reported to his friend Charles Burney on 30 November 1772:

> I passed lately some days at Salzburg and had a great deal of Musick at the Archbishop's, as he is a Dilettante & plays well on the Fiddle. He takes pains to reform his Band, which, like others, is too harsh. He has put Fischietti at the head of it, Composer of Il mercato di Malmantile & il Dottore &c. There is among them an excellent Composer for the Bassoon & other wind Musick. Secchi & Raineri (for so Reiner is to be called for the future by my direction) are to go there on purpose to play before him, that he may learn their stile & write for them.[4]

Possibly Johann Michael Haydn was the composer for woodwinds who was to be trained since Mozart is explicitly named afterwards both as a player of piano four-hands with his sister as well as a composer of symphonies.

The absence of flautists in the *Hofkalender* and official salary lists is striking; it goes without saying, though, that the oboists also played the flute. This explains why Mozart and his Salzburg contemporaries switched between flutes and oboes for some movements of their orchestral works. One therefore has to wonder about the specific circumstances that motivated Mozart to compose a symphony like K. 184 in E♭ major during his Salzburg years which requires both at the same time. Through-composed (like the Symphony in G, K. 318 several years later) it is – in modern terminology – an overture rather than a symphony and may have served as incidental music, possibly for *Thamos* K. 345 for which Mozart is known to have written, at different times, choruses and entr'actes.[5]

Clarinets were not used as orchestral instruments, particularly in church music, until the end of the eighteenth century.[6] This makes it clear that a piece like the 'Concerto ò sia Divertimento' in E♭, K. 113 is unlikely to have originated in Salzburg (in fact it was composed in Milan in 1771 according to an inscription on the autograph score) and explains why a woodwind particella exists on Salzburg paper where the Milanese woodwind parts for two clarinets and two horns were expanded to a total of eight (two oboes, two English horns, two horns, two bassoons), and the clarinet parts at the same time eliminated.[7] This does not mean that clarinets were never heard

---

[4] NMD, p. 23.
[5] On Mozart's *Thamos* see Neal A. Zaslaw, 'Mozarts Incidental Music to "Lanassa" and his "Thamos" Motets', in James P. Cassaro (ed.), *Music, Libraries, and the Academy: Essays in Honor of Lenore Coral* (Middleton, WI: A-R Editions, 2007), pp. 55–63.
[6] Hintermaier, 'Die Salzburger Hofkapelle', p. 539.
[7] All autograph material for K. 113 is preserved at the Staatsbibliothek zu Berlin.

in Salzburg; they could be found among the bands of military musicians of the Salzburg court.

In spite of de Visme's remarks and the Mozarts' predilection for mocking fellow musicians in private communications such as letters (which we tend to consider objective even though they are not free of gossip), the overall quality of the Salzburg court orchestra must be regarded as high. In his orchestral music, Mozart like Michael Haydn wrote demanding but not exceedingly difficult instrumental parts; he did not exhaust the technical limits of orchestral players, such as by using very high registers or extremely long-held notes.[8] The versatile education and training of eighteenth-century musicians resulted in many of them being accomplished players of more than one instrument. One of the first appearances of the newly appointed double-bass player Joseph Thomas Cassel, active in Salzburg from 21 June 1777 until his death on 28 December 1788, was at a private concert in the Tanzmeisterhaus to celebrate Maria Anna Mozart's name day on 25 July 1777; Cassel presented himself on this occasion as the soloist in a Mozart flute concerto, apparently K. 313 in G.[9] The *Hof- und Feldtrompeter* Johann Andreas Schachtner (1731–95) is known to have played the violin in chamber music at the Mozart's on more than one occasion.[10] Also the quality of amateur musicians in Salzburg must not be underrated: Mozart succeeded in assembling no fewer than eight competent horn players for the extravagant Notturno in D for four ensembles K. 286, each of which required a pair of horns. Johann Rudolph Franz de Paula, Count Czernin (1757–1845), himself a good violinist, founded an amateur orchestra in 1778 which played regularly in the Lodron Palais and gave public performances of serenades.

For concertos or ambitious chamber music, Mozart clearly had the capabilities of his players in mind. The Salzburg keyboard concertos were not written exclusively for himself, but were often intended for the use of the family's keyboard student, such as the so-called 'Lützow concerto' for Countess Maria Antonia von Lützow (1750–1801) and the 'Lodron concerto' for Countess Antonia Lodron (1738–80) and her daughters Maria Aloysia and Maria Josepha, the younger of the two being only eleven years old and in receipt of a very manageable keyboard part. During his Salzburg years Mozart does not seem to have composed for the professional keyboard players at the Salzburg court, Cajetan Adlgasser and Michael Haydn;

---

[8] For the standard compass of eighteenth-century orchestral instruments see Johann Georg Albrechtsberger, *Gründliche Anweisung zur Composition* (Leipzig: Breitkopf, 1790), pp. 416–40.

[9] MDL, p. 144; MDB, p. 161.   [10] MBA, vol. 4, p. 181.

it even appears that the Mozarts prevented their more extravagant and technically compelling solo keyboard works from circulating in their home city.

When discussing Mozart's violin concertos, it becomes clear how difficult it is to distinguish educated guesses from fast and loose speculation. Five concertos and two individual movements survive in Mozart's hand; the autograph of the Rondo in C, K. 373 was lost during the nineteenth century, fortunately only after André had issued a reliable edition. Two further concertos K. 268 in E♭ and K. 271a for which no authorized source is known to survive are to be counted among Mozart's works of doubtful authenticity. It seems natural that Mozart, a more than competent violin player, would have written most of the concertos for his own use at court in his capacity as concertmaster. From the family letters it becomes apparent, however, that at least one concerto was written for Joachim Kolb (1752–1817), who was a very skilled amateur violinist; Joachim Ferdinand Schidenhofen admired in his diary Kolb's good tone and the force and velocity of his playing, although he apparently sometimes played poorly. Kolb is known to have performed 'his' concerto on 15 August 1777 in the Tanzmeistersaal, on 26 September 1777 in the Eizenbergerhof and on 9 July 1778 in front of the house of Joachim Rupert Mayr von Mayrn.[11] Given these dates it is plausible that the concerto in question was the Concerto in D, K. 271a dated 16 July 1777 according to a note on a non-autograph source. K. 271a, however, is technically the most demanding of all Mozart concertos, making more use of high registers than any of the concertos whose authenticity is beyond doubt. Without knowing more about Kolb's capabilities as a violinist, it is difficult to determine whether the extravagant violin part of this concerto was specifically designed for Kolb or whether its apparent incompatibility with the authentic concertos excludes Mozart's authorship.

There remains little doubt that Mozart, who is known to have performed several of his concertos to great applause in Salzburg and abroad, was not the most technically versatile violin player in Salzburg. Joseph Hafeneder (1746–84), son of a violinist and student of Leopold Mozart, became a court musician in 1769; his salary was doubled in 1775, and he was additionally appointed violin tutor at the Kapellhaus. The surviving compositions by Hafeneder show that he must have surpassed Mozart as a violin virtuoso; in 1778 Leopold Mozart informed his son about a notturno

---

[11] See, respectively MDL, pp. 144–45; MDB, p. 161 (from Schidenhofen's diary), and MBA, vol. 2, pp. 18, 436; LMF, pp. 281, 592 (28 September 1777, 3 August 1778).

presented to Countess Antonia Lodron composed mainly by Hafeneder in which Count Czernin and Joachim Kolb took on the obbligato violin parts which contained 'amazing solos'.[12]

The three individual movements with solo violin K. 261 in F, K. 269 in B♭ and K. 373 in C were written for Antonio Brunetti (1744–86), who was employed at the Salzburg court in 1776 and serving as concertmaster when Wolfgang resigned in 1777 to travel to Mannheim and Paris. K. 261 and K. 269 were apparently meant as replacement pieces for the slow movement of K. 219 and the finale of K. 207 respectively, whereas K. 373, labelled 'ein Rondeau zu einen Concert für Brunetti' in Mozart's letter of 8 April 1781,[13] served a similar purpose for a hitherto unidentified concerto from Brunetti's performance repertoire. No documents survive to explain for whom Mozart may have written the Sinfonia Concertante in E♭ for violin, viola and orchestra K. 364 around 1779 or who he may have had in mind as soloists for the violin, viola and violoncello parts in his unfinished Sinfonia Concertante in A, K. 320e written around the same time. While the archive of Salzburg Cathedral has been transmitted almost intact, all traces of the secular portion of the prince-archbishop's library were lost in the early decades of the nineteenth century, making it impossible to determine whether there were viola, violoncello or double-bass players who might have excelled as soloists during Mozart's Salzburg years.

More information – but still inconclusive – survives for Mozart's Salzburg woodwind concertos. The recipient of Mozart's Bassoon Concerto in B♭, K. 191, dated 4 or 5 July 1774 on the now-lost autograph, is yet to be determined. Even if Gioseffo Secchi (dates unknown) or Felix Rainer (1732–83), mentioned in de Visme's letter to Burney, ever played in Salzburg, they were not appointed to the court. Legend has it that Mozart composed the work for Baron Thaddäus von Dürniz (1756–1807), a dilettante in Munich, who later moved to a family manor near Straubing in Bavaria, but there is no evidence that Mozart and Dürniz met before the end of 1774 during preparations for the Munich premiere of *La finta giardiniera*. The one surviving catalogue of Dürniz's vast musical library is restricted to keyboard music; according to a posthumous report, Dürniz owned Mozart's bassoon concerto but only a copy of the 1802 print.[14]

Mozart is known to have a written an oboe concerto for Giuseppe Ferlendis (1755–1833) who served as a court oboist in Salzburg for little

---

[12] MBA, vol. 2, p. 374; LMF, p. 549 (12 June 1778).
[13] MBA, vol. 3, p. 103; LMF, p. 722 (8 April 1781).
[14] See *Fremden-Blatt*, no. 224 (Vienna, 17 August 1867).

more than a year from 1 April 1777 onwards. Since Mozart left Salzburg on 23 September 1777, the concerto can be dated securely to a period of five months. It is most likely, but not proven beyond doubt, that this concerto was K. 314 in C major (better known as a flute concerto in D). The charming piece does not allude to special features of Ferlendis's playing and thus could be used on later occasions by other oboe players: Leopold Mozart recommended selling a copy to the court of Oettingen-Wallerstein where Markus Perwein (dates unknown), a former Salzburg court musician, was employed. Wolfgang also left a copy with Friedrich Ramm (1745–1813), the principal oboist of the electoral court in Mannheim, later in Munich. Years afterwards, on 15 February 1783, he asked his father to send the score from Salzburg to Vienna as he sensed an opportunity to sell the concerto to Anton Mayer, who served as oboist to Prince Esterházy between 1781 and 1790.[15] This shows that Mozart did not always write with just one player in his mind but was able to compose in a style appealing to several leading players.

The extended journeys Mozart undertook brought him into contact with many capable instrumentalists. On the first trips the prodigious children Wolfgang and Nannerl were received with universal acclaim. Many musicians, particularly from the German communities in Paris and London, visited the Mozarts in their lodgings or invited them to their homes to present their newest compositions; particularly touching is the anecdote about Johann Christian Bach playing and improvising at the keyboard with young Mozart on his lap.[16] During the Grand Tour, Mozart did not yet compose instrumental pieces for specific performers. The sonatas for piano with violin accompaniment (and sometimes also a violoncello) printed as Opus 1–4 adapt well to the then fashionable style. Opus 1 and Opus 2 contain a number of movements that had originated as solo piano pieces to which the violin part was added only later; in Opus 3, the six trios K. 10–15, young Mozart followed the model of Carl Friedrich Abel's trios Op. 5 (London 1765) in assigning the higher accompanimental part to a violin or flute, but the part contains double stops and goes below the compass of the eighteenth-century flute, meaning that players would have had to adapt them on the spot. The extant symphonies require the standard orchestra of two oboes, two horns, two violins, viola and bass and could be played at sight by any well-trained amateur orchestra.

---

[15] The concerto and the various oboists are mentioned in MBA, vol. 2, pp. 59, 100–101, 282, and vol. 3, pp. 256–57; LMF, pp. 320, 355, 482, 840 (15 October 1777, 4 November 1777, 14 February 1778, 15 February 1783).

[16] Georg Nikolaus Nissen, *Biographie W. A. Mozart's* (Leipzig: Breitkopf & Härtel, 1828), p. 67.

Although Mozart wrote some instrumental music on his three trips to Italy between 1769 and 1773, these journeys mainly benefitted his composition of operas. Mozart adjusted quickly to the capabilities of local orchestras and made use of, for example, pairs of flutes and oboes and up to four horns in his Milan operas *Mitridate, re di Ponto* K. 87, *Ascanio in Alba* K. 111 and *Lucio Silla* K. 135. Nothing is known about the identity of the horn player for whom Mozart composed the demanding first horn part in 'Lungi da te, mio bene' from *Mitridate*; that it went beyond the standards of the time can be determined from the fact that this aria survives in one contemporary source from Milan in an alternate version without solo horn.[17] From Mozart's Italian travels, the violinist Thomas Linley (1756–78), an exact contemporary, can be singled out as an instrumentalist whose abilities were immediately recognized and admired.[18]

During the trip to Mannheim and Paris, Mozart sought the company and support of fellow musicians. In Mannheim he befriended numerous instrumentalists including Christian Cannabich (1731–98), Kapellmeister to the Palatine court, the flautist Johann Baptist Wendling (1723–97) and the aforementioned oboist Friedrich Ramm. He travelled with Cannabich and Wendling to Paris where he wrote the lost sinfonia concertante K. 297B for them and their fellow musicians from the court orchestra Johann Wenzel Stich, called Punto (horn), and Georg Wenzel Ritter (bassoon).[19] In Mannheim and Paris, Mozart also became acquainted with some amateur musicians for whom he composed rather reluctantly. They included the flute player Ferdinand Dejean (1731–99), the apparent recipient of an arrangement of the oboe concerto as well as quartets with solo flute, and Adrien-Louis Bonnières de Sonastre, Duc de Guines (1735–1806), for whom Mozart composed the Concerto for Flute and Harp in C, K. 299 to be played with de Guines' daughter, Marie-Louise-Charlotte. Mozart remained on good terms with the professional musicians from Mannheim after their move to Munich with the electoral court. Mozart built on that relationship once in Munich in winter 1780–1 for the premiere of his opera *Idomeneo*. The Oboe Quartet in F, K. 370 for Friedrich Ramm and the obbligato woodwind parts for flute, oboe, bassoon and horn in the aria 'Se il padre perdei' from *Idomeneo* demonstrate the remarkable virtuosity of these players.

---

[17] Paris, Bibliothèque national de France, shelfmark: D 8541.
[18] See MBA, vol. 1, pp. 332–3, 388–9; LMF, pp. 160–1 (10 September 1770; the letter from Linley to Mozart on 6 April 1770 is not given in LMF).
[19] MBA, vol. 2, p. 332; LMF, p. 522 (5 April 1778).

CHAPTER 22

Instruments and Instrumentalists in Vienna

Martin Harlow

Given the number of musicians who lived and worked in Vienna during the ten years of Mozart's residency from March 1781 and those who must have performed for and with him, our awareness of his extended musical network is surprisingly patchy. Existing family letters, the main evidence for his personal contacts, reduce significantly after the death of Mozart's father in May 1787. And even before 1787, Mozart and family tended to report only on mutually familiar musicians. From letters we do gain glimpses of Mozart's wider circle. Concerning the replacement of the Salzburg violinist Joseph Hafeneder, Mozart reported to his father on the qualities of Zeno Franz Menzel, 'a handsome and clever young fellow' and 'a very good sight reader', whom Mozart engaged as an orchestra member for his 1 April 1784 Lenten benefit concert.[1] Menzel is not mentioned in letters after 1784, although he remained an active violinist, becoming a member of the court's Kärntnertortheater orchestra in 1785. Serendipitous records of this kind can be misleading: many musicians such as Menzel, performers in the musical establishments of the nobility, freelancing musicians, visiting artists and gifted and well-trained amateurs, will have had associations with Mozart that simply went unrecorded.

An important source of income, Mozart's piano pupils feature prominently in surviving correspondence: Josepha Auernhammer, Maria Theresia von Trattner, Marie Karoline de Rumbeke, Barbara Ployer, Franziska and Gottfried von Jacquin, Franz Jakob Freystädtler and Magdalene Pokorny. Mozart was keen to report on pupils to his father, and careful not to criticize them unduly. Of his pianist peers, however, Mozart was routinely disparaging. Muzio Clementi, with whom Mozart

---

[1] MBA, vol. 3, pp. 309–10; LMF, pp. 873–4 (10 April 1784). Menzel was one of the players 'stolen' by Prince Lichtenstein for a performance of a Righini opera, occasioning the cancellation of his 21 March 1784 benefit. See Dexter Edge, 'Mozart's Viennese Orchestras', *Early Music*, 20/1 (1992), pp. 78–9.

had a piano contest in late 1781, was 'a mere *mechanicus*';[2] from the low salary of the court keyboard teacher Georg Summer, one could 'infer the strengths of this master';[3] the playing of Georg Friedrich Richter, in whose concerts Mozart performed in 1784, was 'too coarse, too laboured, and without any taste and feeling'.[4] Mozart was wary of competitors, and sought for himself the best equipment. He had responded ecstatically to the fortepianos of the Augsburg maker Johann Andreas Stein in 1777 and borrowed a Stein instrument from Countess Thun soon after arriving in Vienna. Before 1784 he acquired a fortepiano by the Viennese maker Gabriel Anton Walter, adding a pedal instrument (in effect a second instrument operated by the feet), on which he gave public concerts in 1785.

Mozart probably performed on Thun's Stein piano at the Tonkünstler-Societät benefit on 3 April 1781, 'at which all musicians play for nothing'.[5] Mozart played solo, and a symphony of his was also given. It is tantalizing to imagine Mozart meeting, so soon after his arrival, many of the best Viennese orchestral performers in the unusually large-scale concert for this society.[6] Mozart's desire to give a concert for his own benefit was not realized until 3 March 1782, when extracts from *Idomeneo* and his Piano Concerto in D, K. 175 (with a new Rondo, K. 382) were performed. While the orchestral personnel for this concert is unknown, Mozart's work with the Burgtheater orchestra commenced on 3 June 1782 at the first rehearsal for his singspiel *Die Entführung aus dem Serail*. Of the thirty-six members of that ensemble, only three are mentioned in Mozart's correspondence.[7] One was the violinist Franz de Paula Hofer, who was to become the husband of Mozart's sister-in-law Josepha Weber and who accompanied Mozart on his 1790 visit to Frankfurt. The two others were the clarinettist Anton Stadler (1753–1812) and the horn player Joseph Leutgeb (1732–1811).

Anton Stadler and his younger brother Johann, also a clarinettist, had performed in Vienna by 1773.[8] Contemplating departure from Vienna in late 1781, they applied for work at Wallerstein;[9] at the intervention of the

---

[2] MBA, vol. 3, p. 191; LMF, p. 792 (12 January 1782; translation amended).
[3] MBA, vol. 3, p. 236; LMF, p. 826 (5 October 1782; translation amended).
[4] MBA, vol. 3, p. 312; LMF, p. 875 (28 April 1784; translation amended).
[5] MBA, vol. 3, p. 99; LMF, p. 718 (24 March 1781; translation adapted). Mozart numbered the orchestra at 180, although this would have included the choir.
[6] Edge, 'Mozart's Viennese Orchestras', p. 79. MBA, vol. 3, p. 106; LMF, p. 724 (11 April 1781).
[7] For transcriptions of personnel lists in court records see Dorothea Link, *The National Court Theatre in Mozart's Vienna* (Oxford: Oxford University Press, 1998), pp. 399–448.
[8] They performed a two-clarinet concerto in a Tonkünstler-Societät concert on 21 March 1773.
[9] The letter of application is reproduced in facsimile in Pamela Poulin, 'The Basset Clarinet of Anton Stadler and Its Music' (PhD thesis, University of Rochester, NY, 1976), pp. 16–18.

Emperor Joseph II himself, they were hired as permanent members of the Burgtheater orchestra from February 1782. Shortly thereafter the orchestra's oboes (Georg Triebensee and Johann Went), clarinets (the Stadlers), horns (Martin Rupp and Jakob Eisen) and bassoons (Wenzel Kauzner and Ignaz Drobney) received additional remuneration as members of a new wind octet, the *Kaiserlich-königlich* Harmonie. The contemporary interest in original and arranged Harmoniemusik occasioned Mozart's interest in this genre and the writing of the 'Gran Partita' K. 361 and (in 1781–2) wind serenades K. 375 in E♭ and K. 388 in C minor. This eight-man ensemble, serving double duty in the theatre orchestra, remained unchanged throughout Mozart's Vienna years. So these musicians were the first performers of the wind parts of Mozart's stage works premiered at the court theatre.

Virtually all of Mozart's works were conceived for specific performances and performers. For particular singers, he wished an aria 'to fit a singer as perfectly as a well-made suit',[10] and he was equally attuned to attributes of specific instrumentalists and their instruments. Mozart had exploited the fine wind players in the Munich orchestra in *Idomeneo*: Ilia's second-act aria 'Se il padre perdei', includes obbligato writing for flute (Johann Baptist Wendling), oboe (Friedrich Ramm), horn (Georg Eck or one of the Lang brothers, Franz Joseph or Martin Alexander) and bassoon (Georg Wenzel Ritter). Using solo players of a court orchestra in this way was commonplace. In three arias for Caterina Cavalieri, from works premiered in Vienna in 1778, there are solo obbligatos for Burgtheater players. Aspelmayr's *Die Kinder der Natur* includes a violin (Thomas Woborzil) in Therese's aria 'So gut, wie er mir schiene'; Umlauf's *Die Bergknappen* features an oboe (Vittorino Colombazzo) in Sophie's aria 'Wenn mir der Himmel lacht'; and Ulbrich's *Frühling und Liebe* includes a quintet of wind soloists in Gianina's aria 'Singt, ihr süßen Philomenen'.[11] A response to the proclivities of Cavalieri, and the skills of the Burgtheater wind players, is manifest in Constanze's second-act aria 'Marten aller Arten' from *Die Entführung*. Leopold Mozart wrote to his daughter describing a later Salzburg performance of the singspiel, naming the solo instrumentalists as Reiner (flute), Feiner (oboe), Matthias Stadler (violin) and Fiala (cello).[12] No correspondence cites the soloists for the premiere, though court records reveal them to be Prowos (flute), Triebensee (oboe),

---

[10] MBA, vol. 2, p. 304; LMF, p. 497 (28 February 1778).
[11] The final performance of Ulbrich's work was twelve days after the 16 July 1782 premiere of *Die Entführung*.
[12] MBA, vol. 3, p. 344; LMF, p. 884 (19 November 1784; letter from Leopold to Nannerl).

Woborzil (violin) and Joseph Weigl (cello). Constanze's aria 'Traurigkeit ward mir zum Lose', with its prominent flutes, oboes, basset-horns (instruments played by the Stadlers) and bassoons, and the solo winds in Belmonte's third-act 'Ich baue ganz auf deine Stärke', for the tenor Johann Valentin Adamberger, also seem to represent creative exploitations of the *Kaiserlich-königlich* Harmonie personnel. This is also the case in other Viennese theatrical works by Mozart. *Der Schauspieldirektor* (1786) has a prominent wind octet in the trio 'Ich bin der erste Sängerin' and some of the most memorable moments of *Le nozze di Figaro* (1786) foreground the Harmonie players. In the Countess's arias 'Porgi amor' and 'Dove sono', and in the penultimate scene of the opera 'Pace, pace, mio dolce tesoro', the woodwinds make telling individual contributions. Mozart fashioned these parts for specific players known to him from his earliest days in Vienna. The serenading wind sextet at the commencement of the second-act duet and chorus 'Secondate, aurette amiche' from *Così fan tutte* (1790) was doubtless written with the Stadlers, Kauzner and Drobney, Rupp and Eisen in mind.[13]

In addition to music for himself and his students, Mozart wrote for a number of distinguished instrumentalists during his Viennese decade. For his fellow employee of the Archbishop of Salzburg, Antonio Brunetti, he composed the Rondo for violin and orchestra in C, K. 373 shortly after arriving in Vienna and for Mantuan violinist Regina Strinasacchi, visiting Vienna in spring 1784, the Violin Sonata in B♭, K. 454. He performed with other notable musicians, famously as viola player in a string quartet of composers, Joseph Haydn, Carl Ditters von Dittersdorf and Johann Baptist Vanhal.[14] Distinguished instrumentalists also performed obbligatos in Mozart arias. His friend, and chamber music companion, the violinist August von Hatzfeld, was the soloist in 'Non temer, amato bene' K. 490, a new aria for a revival of *Idomeneo* in 1786. An entirely different setting of the same text featured in the farewell concert of Nancy Storace in 1787, K. 505, where Mozart created a keyboard obbligato for himself as well. The 1791 aria 'Per questa bella mano' K. 612, was for the bass Franz Xaver Gerl, the first Sarastro in *Die Zauberflöte* (1791) and features a demanding double bass obbligato for Friedrich Pischelberger, the clearly exceptional principal player at Emanuel Schikaneder's Freihaus

[13] For more on wind writing in *Figaro* and *Così fan tutte* for the Burgtheater orchestra, see Simon P. Keefe, *Mozart in Vienna: The Final Decade* (Cambridge: Cambridge University Press, 2017), especially Chapter 9, pp. 410–46.

[14] Michael Kelly, *Reminiscences* (London: H. Colburn, 1826), vol. 1, pp. 240–1.

theatre. The obbligato in Sesto's first-act aria 'Parto, parto' from *La clemenza di Tito* (1791) was for Anton Stadler.[15]

Musical evidence – the clarinet and basset-horn writing in *Die Entführung* and Mozart's Harmoniemusik – suggests that Mozart and Stadler made acquaintance in 1781, but no documented association materializes until March 1784, when Stadler's Lenten *Akademie* included movements of the 'Gran Partita'. Many of Mozart's other works with clarinets and basset-horns also would have been written with the Stadlers in mind.[16] It was surely Anton who was the intended clarinettist for the Quintet for piano and winds in Eb, K. 452 (1784) and the 'Kegelstatt' Trio for clarinet, viola and piano in Eb, K. 498 (1786) though no hard evidence confirms it. The clarinets used by the Stadlers in the Burgtheater included those by Theodor Lotz, a Pressburg maker who moved to Vienna in 1785.[17] A 'Bass-Klarinet' (now known as the basset clarinet) was made by Lotz for Anton and was first reported in use at his Lenten benefit on 20 February 1788, when he played a concerto on it. For Stadler's Lotz instrument, with an extended lower compass, Mozart conceived the Clarinet Quintet in A, K. 581 and the Clarinet Concerto in A, K. 622.[18] Evidence of Stadler's collaboration with composers suggests that Mozart would have been keen to learn from Stadler's playing and the advances to his instrument.[19] Stadler's surviving clarinet music reveals traits found in Mozart's works: a penchant for swift registral transfer, exploitation of the *chalumeau* register and the expressive use of *cantabile* in the clarinet register.[20]

Lotz was not alone in contriving advancements to wind instruments. An indicative range available for purchase in Vienna can be gleaned from a 1789 advertisement from the maker Friedrich Lempp.[21] Instruments included oboes, cors anglais, bassoons, clarinets, bass serpents (newly invented and a specialty of his apprentice son Martin), basset-horns

---

[15] On instrumental writing for the aforementioned performers in each of these works, see Keefe, *Mozart in Vienna*, pp. 311–15 (K. 490), 369–70 (K. 505), 569–70 (K. 612), 594–6 ('Parto, parto' from *Tito*).

[16] For a more extensive discussion of works for Stadler see Colin Lawson, *Mozart: Clarinet Concerto* (Cambridge: Cambridge University Press, 1996), pp. 22–4.

[17] Roger Hellyer, 'Some Documents relating to Viennese Wind-Instrument Purchases, 1779-1837', *Galpin Society Journal*, 28 (April 1975), p. 51. Payments to Lotz are recorded between 1784 and 1786.

[18] Fragmentary clarinet quintets K. 516c and K. 581a are also for basset clarinet.

[19] See Martin Harlow, 'The Clarinet in Works of Franz Xaver Süssmayr: Anton Stadler and the Mozartian Example', *Acta Mozartiana*, 57/2 (December 2010), pp. 147–65.

[20] Stadler's works are listed in Lawson, *Clarinet Concerto*, pp. 91–2.

[21] *Wiener Zeitung* (25 February 1789), p. 464. For a survey of wind and brass makers in Mozart's Vienna see Richard Maunder, 'Viennese Wind-Instrument Makers', *Galpin Society Journal*, 51 (1998), pp. 170–91.

(including those newly invented in E♭ and G), flutes, piccolos and fifes, vox humanae and cornets. These could be made of different materials, including boxwood, blackwood, ivory and silver, at different costs. And foreign purchasers could acquire instruments at their local pitch by sending a tuning fork. Innovation and novelty were paramount: Friedrich Hammig advertised in 1791 'all kinds of wind instruments' but especially 'a newly invented type of basset-horn, whose special feature is the depth and power of its tone'.[22]

The maker of Joseph Leutgeb's horns is not known, but Viennese brass-instrument manufacture in the 1780s was dominated by a small number of families, notably the Kerners and Starzers.[23] Leutgeb was a native Viennese, who worked for the Esterházy court in 1760s and as a Salzburg court musician in 1764 and who subsequently travelled as a solo player, giving concerts in 1770 at the Concert Spirituel in Paris. He settled back in Vienna in 1777, living there for the remainder of his life. Leutgeb was a member of the court theatre orchestra until the end of the 1782–3 season; thereafter court records note fees to Leutgeb for ad hoc duties. By this point Leutgeb had turned fifty and his companion hornist Scrivanek's positions were taken by younger men, Rupp and Eisen. Leutgeb was a family friend of the Mozarts, receiving financial support from Leopold, and was the recipient of Mozart's horn concertos K. 417 in E♭ (1783), K. 495 in E♭ (1786) and K. 412 in D (1791). The Horn Quintet in E♭, K. 407 was also composed for him. Although several of Mozart's autograph scores include mocking comments at Leutgeb's expense, his confidence in this ageing player must have been considerable.

As with the brass manufacturers, we know of only a small group of local string instrument makers, including the Bartl family, Stadlmann and Thir.[24] An eclectic mix of wind, brass and string instruments, in quality and provenance, would have been a familiar feature of Mozart's musical environment. Mozart sought out the best and probably most innovative local musicians and visiting instrumentalists, spawning compositions as enduring records of these associations. For all these instrumental musicians in 1780s Vienna, there were challenges, as noble musical establishments diminished and the expenses of the Turkish wars began to have an impact. The abundant production of printed music and manuscript copies suggests

[22] *Wiener Zeitung* (12 November 1791), p. 2912.

[23] Anton Kerner's reputation was sufficient to warrant bogus foreign instruments appearing with his stamp, a situation he railed against publicly. See *Wiener Zeitung* (19 December 1789), pp. 3232–3.

[24] Richard Maunder, 'Viennese String-Instrument Makers, 1700–1800', *Galpin Society Journal*, 52 (1999), pp. 27–51.

a sustained thirst for instrumental music performance, however, in both private and public spheres, and Mozart tapped into these opportunities, working with Artaria and other Viennese publishers and disseminating his music in manuscript through the likes of Lausch, Traeg, Torricella and Sukowaty.

The violinist Ignaz Schweigl (d. 1803) serves as an example of a Viennese musician practically unknown today whose activities were contemporaneous – and perhaps intersected – with those of Mozart. In a treatise, *Verbesserte Grundlehre der Violin*, self-published in 1786, Schweigl styled himself 'Instrumental Musikus'. Though clearly a teacher, Schweigl was also a performer (a violinist at the Kärntnertortheater by 1791), arranger, publisher and composer.[25] His treatise also advertised music. After his own piano version of Dittersdorf's recent opera *Der Apotheker und Doktor*, chamber music is offered in the customary sets of six: string quartets by Silverio Müller, Michael Haydn and Michael Ritter von Esser (a violinist familiar to the Mozarts). Sets of string trios by Maddelena Laura Syrmen and Felice Giardini are also listed, as well as duets for two violins by Cajetan Wutky and Giovanni Battista Gervasio. 'Deutsche and Welsche' from beloved opera arias are offered in keyboard arrangements and lieder by J. J. Grünwald and Franz Anton Hoffmeister are listed. A fuller range of Schweigl's professional interests can be gleaned from an advertisement in March 1785.[26] From the 'Golden Eagle, Wieden, no. 85' were offered for sale, at an all-in price of seven gulden, an unstrung harpsichord with six sonatas by Joseph Anton Steffan, six sonatas for mandolin and two trios by Vanhal. A horn, 'capable of playing all tones', with 327 duets for 'noble Tafelmusik', was packaged at twelve ducats. Two 'ordinary' violins could be had together for seven gulden, but a 'good' violin cost twenty-two ducats (ninety-nine gulden). The disparity in prices is striking. Music was then offered in copies, with a premium price to be paid 'for the newest or best music'. And this offer was a substantial one: violin concertos by Steinmetz [Carl Stamitz?], Carl Ditters von Dittersdorf, Giuseppe Tartini, Jean-Baptiste Davaux, Leopold Hofmann, Josef Mysliveček, Antonio Rosetti, Dokski [?], Lorenz Wagenhofer and Neimann [?]; mixed partitas by Haydn, Hoffmeister, Dittersdorf, Syrmen, Davaux, Crammer [Franz Krommer?], Steinmetz, Vanhal, Joseph Kriner, Johannes Sperger, Johann [Mederitsh-] Gallus, Scheigel [Ignaz Schweigl?], Rosetti and Weiner [?];

---

[25] For discussion of Schweigl's compositions, see John A. Rice, *Empress Marie Therese and Music at the Viennese Court, 1792–1807* (Cambridge: Cambridge University Press, 2003), pp. 140–42.

[26] *Das Wienerblättchen* (3 March 1785), 'Anzeigen', p. 3.

symphonies by Joseph Haydn, Rosetti, František Adam Míča, Leopold Koželuch and Ignaz Holzbauer; concertos for two horns by Dittersdorf, Václav Pichl, Rosetti, Haydn and Johann Franz Xaver Sterkel, and seven (unspecified) concertos for 'second horn'.

There is no evidence linking Schweigl to Mozart, although it seems impossible that the former's musical activities were unknown to the latter. There will have been many Menzels and Schweigls in Mozart's Vienna, instrumentalists forging a career through a range of musical endeavours. Documents connected to Mozart reveal what will have been only a small part of his circle of musicians and instrumentalists. Many thus-far hidden musicians no doubt played an important part in the life and work of the composer in his final decade.

CHAPTER 23

The Opera Singers in Vienna

Dorothea Link

The opera singers with whom Mozart worked in Vienna in the 1780s belonged to one or more of three opera companies. The first was the court Italian opera, established in 1783, which was of an international calibre and which recruited its singers largely from Italy. The second was the court singspiel, which operated from Easter 1778 to Lent 1783 and again from October 1785 to Lent 1788 and whose singers came from German-speaking centres. The company occasionally shared its lower-rank singing actors with the court Schauspiel (acting company) to which it belonged administratively and artistically.[1] The two times the singspiel was dissolved, its first-rank singers were absorbed into the Italian company, where they assumed the status of second-rank singers. The third opera company played in the suburban Theater auf der Wieden; its singers could also be actors, composers, playwrights and impresarios. The difference in status and quality of the companies and their singers can be determined from the salary figures. The prima donna of the court Italian company, at different times Nancy Storace, Celeste Coltellini, Luisa Laschi Mombelli and Adriana Ferrarese, was paid 4,500 florins, the prima donna of the court singspiel, Aloysia Weber Lange, was paid 1,706f 40x, and the prima donna of the Theater auf der Wieden, Josefa Weber Hofer, was paid 832f.[2] In what follows, I will situate Mozart's Viennese singers within their respective companies and Vienna's operatic life as Mozart interacted with them.

Die Entführung aus dem Serail was first performed on 16 July 1782 in the final year of the singspiel's first run, when it had attained a certain degree of

---

[1] The actor Johann Heinrich Friedrich Müller established and directed the singspiel in its first two years, after which it was assigned to the five-member directorate of the Schauspiel and thence to Gottlieb Stephanie d. Jüngere, who also directed the singspiel at its revival in 1785. See *H. F. Müllers Abschied von der k. k. Hof- und National- Schaubühne* (Vienna, 1802), p. 264.

[2] Hofer's contract for 1791–2 is reproduced in Emil Karl Blümml, *Aus Mozarts Freunds- und Familienkreis* (Vienna: Strache, 1923), pp. 128–30. Salaries for the singers in the court theatre can be found in Dorothea Link, *The National Court Theatre in Mozart's Vienna* (Oxford: Clarendon Press, 1998), pp. 404–48. A gulden (abbreviated f. or fl. for florin) contains 60 kreuzer (abbreviated x).

stability. The prima donna at that time was Aloysia Weber Lange (1,706f 36x). Also in the company since 1 May 1781 was the *seria* singer Antonia Bernasconi (salary 2,133f 20x) but in what capacity is unclear. Hers was a puzzling appointment, as the emperor did not want her and as she was of little use to the company.[3] However, her prowess as a singer of tragic roles, such as Alceste, which she had created for Gluck in Vienna in 1767, and Aspasia, created for Mozart in *Mitridate* in Milan in 1770, unexpectedly became useful in the autumn of 1781 when the court found it expedient to mount three serious Gluck operas for the imperial visit of Grand Duke Paul and Grand Duchess Maria Feodorovina of Russia.[4] In the comic operas, according to Mozart, she sang so badly no one wanted to write for her.[5] Mozart was spared that fate with his *Entführung*, but he also was denied Lange as his prima donna. Instead, Catarina Cavalieri (1,200f), Antonio Salieri's student and protégé, was cast in the main role of Konstanze. Cavalieri may not have possessed Lange's subtle musicianship, but she could sing brilliant and loud coloratura, a strength of which Mozart took full advantage, most memorably in 'Martern aller Arten'. From among the company's four lower-rank female singers, Therese Teyber (600f) was chosen to sing Blondchen. The singspiel's male singers included one of Germany's finest basses, Ludwig Fischer (2,400f), whose exceptionally resonant bass notes and superb acting skills Mozart exploited to great comic effect in the role of Osmin. Valentin Adamberger (2,133f 20x) came from a background of singing *seria* roles in Italy and brought with him a beautiful tenor voice and excellent vocal technique, which allowed Mozart to indulge in writing virtuosic music for him as Belmonte. His acting was said to be wooden, but in this opera Johann Ernst Dauer (1,200f) more than compensated as the lively Pedrillo. Engaged as a comic tenor for the singspiel, he soon also performed in the Schauspiel. The actor Dominik Jautz (800f) was borrowed from the Schauspiel for the speaking role of the Pasha Selim.

For *Le nozze di Figaro*, first performed on 1 May 1786, Mozart was allotted the cream of the Italian opera company. The prima donna Nancy Storace (4,500f), who portrayed Susanna, may not have had an outstandingly beautiful voice, but she possessed excellent acting skills and a high

---

[3] Joseph to Count Rosenberg, 1 October 1781, in Rudolf Payer von Thurn (ed.), *Joseph II. als Theaterdirektor: Ungedruckte Briefe und Aktenstücke aus den Kinderjahren des Burgtheaters* (Vienna: Heidrich, 1920), p. 26.

[4] *Iphigenie auf Taurus, Alceste* (sung in Italian) and *Orfeo ed Euridice*. Bernasconi sang in a total of twenty-five performances of these operas.

[5] MBA, vol. 3, p. 153; LMF, pp. 761–2 (29 August 1781).

level of musicianship, both of which left their mark on the opera.[6] By the rules of the theatre she was entitled to a large vocal display-piece before the last finale, but Mozart dropped it in favour of the virtuosically slighter but musically more demanding aria 'Deh vieni, non tardar'. In Francesco Benucci (4,185f) Mozart had the best Figaro he could wish for, as Benucci was a cut above the typical *primo buffo caricato,* both in possessing a solid vocal technique and in exercising good taste in his comic acting.[7] Stefano Mandini (4,185f), who today would be considered a baritone, was then classified as either a *mezzo carattere* or a *basso buffo,* depending on whether he sang tenor-clef or bass-clef roles.[8] In the 1783 Vienna production of Paisiello's *Il barbiere di Sevilla,* Mandini had played the tenor lover Count Almaviva. In the story's sequel in *Le nozze di Figaro,* he again played Almaviva, but now the character has changed from a lover to a powerful nobleman, so Mozart wrote the role for Mandini's baritonal voice. Luisa Laschi (3,375f), who a few years later matured into the company's prima donna, was as yet inferior in rank and salary to Storace, but Mozart made the role of the Countess equal in depth and interest to that of Susanna, in effect creating two prima donna roles. Noticeably, he did not give Laschi much coloratura to sing although coloratura was conventionally reserved for a countess or other exalted person. When Cavalieri took over the role in the opera's revival three years later, Mozart rewrote her second-act aria so as to add the appropriate coloratura. For Laschi, though, Mozart wrote long cantabile lines, which came to typify her singing.

The second-rank singers included Francesco Bussani (2,520f), who played Bartolo and Antonio. He had been engaged for the company in 1783 as a tenor but soon switched to lower roles. The comic tenor Michael Kelly (1,800f) played Basilio and Don Curzio. Dorothea Sardi Bussani (1,350f), who had joined the company only a few weeks before the opera's premiere, created Cherubino. Mandini's wife, Maria, sang Marcellina, and the twelve-year old Anna Gottlieb, the daughter of husband-and-wife actors employed in the Schauspiel, played Barberina.

Despite the large number of characters in the opera, there was no role suitable for a *seria* tenor. Otherwise Mozart might have written for

---

[6] For a vocal portrait of the singer see Dorothea Link (ed.), *Arias for Nancy Storace, Mozart's First Susanna* (Middleton, WI: A-R Editions, 2002), pp. vii–xvii.

[7] A *buffo caricato* is a highly regarded type of buffo singer, who specializes in humour based on the stylized antics characteristic of the commedia dell'arte tradition. See Dorothea Link (ed.), *Arias for Francesco Benucci, Mozart's First Figaro and Guglielmo* (Middleton, WI: A-R Editions, 2004), p. x.

[8] Regarding Mandini's voice type, see Dorothea Link (ed.), *Arias for Stefano Mandini, Mozart's First Count Almaviva* (Middleton, WI: A-R Editions, 2015), pp. xii–xviii.

Domenico Mombelli, one of the most celebrated tenors in the late eighteenth century. He was recruited from the Teatro San Carlo in spring 1786 at a salary of 4,500 gulden, the highest to that point, but his presence in Vienna over the three years of his engagement, and again for two years in 1794, left hardly a trace. Very few of the roles that he sang are known, and, of those, only one was composed for him, the tenor role in Joseph Weigl's *Il pazza per forza*. Surprisingly, he was not cast in Salieri's *Axur, re d'Ormus*, the imperial wedding opera of 1788 that marked the greatest dynastic event in Joseph's reign. Instead, the *mezzo carattere* tenor Vincenzo Calvesi (3,600f) created the demanding tenor role.[9]

When Mozart received his commission for *Le nozze di Figaro* in the summer of 1785, the singspiel was being revived, and he could conceivably have been asked to compose another German opera as he frequently professed wanting to do. The following February he got his chance to compose not a full singspiel but a scenario consisting of several musical numbers to fit into the spoken play *Der Schauspieldirektor*. As part of the entertainment for his imperial visitors, Joseph had instructed the German company, comprising the Schauspiel and the singspiel, and the Italian opera company to face off in an artistic competition, in which they each presented a one-act stage work with themselves as the subject matter. Representing the singspiel were Lange as Mme Herz, Cavalieri as Mlle Silberklang and Adamberger as Vogelsang. All three were former singspiel singers who had been kept on for the Italian company, but in October Lange had returned to the singspiel, where Adamberger was to join her after Easter. Cavalieri, except for this one event, remained with the Italians.

Composed for Prague in the autumn of 1787, *Don Giovanni* was presented in Vienna on 7 May 1788. For this production Mozart was unlucky with his singers. For starters, he wound up with a cast of largely second-rank performers. The only first-rank singers were Benucci, who sang Leporello, and Laschi, now Laschi Mombelli (and now 4,500f), who sang Zerlina. The coloratura of Donna Anna's role did not suit her, while Zerlina offered the greatest room for acting and coquettish singing, especially with Benucci opposite her.[10] Mozart reinforced the pairing of the two stars by composing a new comical duet for them in Act 2, 'Per queste tue manine'. Among the second-rank singers, Francesco Albertarelli (2,250f), new to the company, sang Giovanni. Had Mandini not taken a year's leave

---

[9] Dorothea Link (ed.), *Arias for Vincenzo Calvesi, Mozart's First Ferrando* (Middleton, WI: A-R Editions 2011), pp. ix–xx.

[10] While she usually portrayed serious roles, she also created to great acclaim the impish Amore in Vicente Martín y Soler's *L'arbore di Diana* (1787).

of absence just then, he would almost certainly have sung the role; indeed, Salieri biographer and conductor Ignaz von Mosel in later years distinctly remembers as a sixteen-year-old hearing Mandini sing Giovanni![11] The newly recruited tenor Francesco Morella (1,800f) sang Don Ottavio. He seems to have been the only tenor available. Mombelli would have made for a dream Ottavio, but he had opened the season two weeks earlier singing opposite the returning prima donna Coltellini. Calvesi, too, was unavailable for, like Mandini, he had taken a leave of absence. Adamberger was nominally back in the Italian company, but his duties were now split between the opera and the Hofkapelle, and in truth he never was very active in the Italian company. So Morella it was. Interestingly, he may not have been as vocally weak as is usually thought, although the evidence can go both ways. The original orchestral parts show that early in the production Morella was to have sung both 'Dalla sua pace', the new aria that Mozart wrote for him, and 'Il mio tesoro', the more difficult Prague aria, even if in the end the latter was cut.[12] Bussani sang Masetto and possibly the Commendatore, but as he used to sing tenor he would not have had the sepulchral voice now associated with the latter role. Cavalieri (now 2,133f 20x) was assigned the role of Elvira; her vocal capabilities inspired Mozart to enlarge the role by adding a new aria, 'Mi tradì quell'alma ingrata'. Lange (still 1,706f 40x) sang Donna Anna. Despite her success in the singspiel, she was often said to have had a weak voice and now was said to have lost her voice.[13] Whether true or not, she sang no further roles and was let go at the end of the season.

Compounding the casting problems were the pregnancies of Laschi Mombelli and Lange. Management had prepared for Laschi Mombelli's confinement by having Teyber, now Teyber Arnold (and now 1,400f), replace her as Zerlina for the month of July when she was off,[14] but there was no replacement for Lange, so the opera could not be performed in

---

[11] In *Jahrbücher des deutschen Nationalvereines für Musik und ihre Wissenschaft* (1841), quoted in Christopher Raeburn, 'Mosel und Zinzendorf über Mozart', in Walter Gerstenberg, Jan LaRue and Wolfgang Rehm (eds.), *Festschrift Otto Erich Deutsch zum achtzigsten Geburtstag* (Kassel: Bärenreiter, 1963), p. 156.

[12] Wolfgang Rehm, Critical Report for *Don Giovanni*, NMA, II/5/17 (2003), p. 57.

[13] Joseph Lange, *Biographie des Joseph Lange, k. k. Hofschauspielers* (Vienna, 1808), p. 151, relates that the Kaiser was told she had lost her voice, which was why her contract was not renewed. The reason given for not keeping her on, as entered into the court records, is that her voice was too weak. Rosenberg to Kaiser Franz, 11 September 1794, quoted in Elizabeth Grossegger, *Das Burgtheater und sein Publikum*, part 2, vol. 1, *Pächter und Publikum, 1794–1817* (Vienna: Verlag der Österreichischen Akademie der Wissenschaften, 1989), p. 116.

[14] Laschi Mombelli sang until the day before the delivery on 1 July and returned to the stage on 4 August.

almost all of August, all of September and most of October.[15] Surprisingly, the opera still managed to rack up fifteen performances that season, second only to Salieri's *Axur* with twenty-four performances.

Così fan tutte, produced on 26 January 1790, once again featured a stellar cast with four first-rank singers. The prima donna Adriana Ferrarese (4,500f) sang Fiordiligi.[16] At her debut her voice was described as the best heard in living memory within Vienna's walls, even if her acting did not measure up to her singing. As soon became apparent, she was also limited in the kind of music that suited her, but as long as she was provided with music featuring large leaps between chest and head registers and endless passages of coloratura, she shone. Mozart made a virtue of her limitation: as Fiordiligi she had only to play herself. Calvesi was back and, as this year's only first-rank tenor in the company, created Ferrando. Mozart wrote a dazzling role for him. While the other singers were each given two arias, Calvesi alone was given three, including the fiendishly difficult 'Ah lo veggio quell'anima bella' with its thirteen high B♭s, its breathless, close phrasing and a melody that repeatedly crosses the break between the head and chest registers. Benucci created Guglielmo, a role dramatically more constrained than usual for him, in consideration of which Mozart may have wanted to give him a chance to display his singing talent. The grand aria 'Rivolgete a lui lo sguardo' K. 584 that he wrote for Benucci could have allowed him to join the singing match between the Fiordiligi and the Ferrando, but in the end Mozart removed it from the opera. Luisa Villeneuve, who had sung Cherubino in the 1789 revival of *Le nozze di Figaro*, radiated charm and finesse in the role of Dorabella.[17] The secondary roles, Alfonso and Despina, were filled by the Mozart veterans, Francesco and Dorothea Bussani.

Mozart composed the singspiel *Die Zauberflöte*, premiered 30 September 1791, for Emanuel Schikaneder's company in the Theater auf der Wieden. Much like a travelling troupe, the company relied heavily on the versatility and varied experiences of its singers. Schikaneder was an actor, singer,

---

[15] Lange's advanced pregnancy prevented her from singing in late August, perhaps earlier, as we know from Joachim Daniel Preisler's report of 20 August when he visited her and her husband. She gave birth on 2 September and was apparently back on stage for the performance of *Don Giovanni* on 24 October.

[16] Direct proof for the salary figure is lacking, as the relevant account books are missing. However, 4,500f had been and continued to be the top salary paid to singers; also in failed negotiations with singers, the line was drawn at 4,500f (or 1,000 ducats), for example for Storace when she wanted to return from London in 1788 and for Mandini when he wanted to return from Paris in 1791.

[17] She had made her Vienna debut in the other trouser role, that of Amore in *L'arbore di Diana*. Mozart also composed three substitute arias for her, K. 578, K. 582 and K. 583.

playwright and impresario; he wrote the libretto for *Die Zauberflöte* and created the role of Papageno. He had been employed at the court theatre in 1785–6 (for 1,400f), first for the Schauspiel, then the singspiel when it recommenced. Benedikt Schack, the tenor who created Tamino, was also a prolific composer of singspiels, many in collaboration with the bass, actor and composer Franz Xaver Gerl, the first Sarastro. Johann Joseph Nouseul, an actor, singer and impresario, sang Monostatos. He and his wife had been engaged for the court theatre's Schauspiel in 1779, but after one and a half seasons he was let go while she carried on. Hofer, the Queen of the Night, had unsuccessfully auditioned for the Italian opera in 1784, after fifteen months of lessons in voice and Italian at the court's expense.[18] Gottlieb, the first Barberina, sang Pamina. Family members performed the smaller roles: Barbara Gerl created Papagena, Elisabeth Schack sang one of the Three Ladies, Urban Schikaneder appeared as one of the priests, Anna Schikaneder played the First Boy. Some idea of how the cast sounded might be obtained from a comment made by Baron von Reitzenstein, who spent a good part of 1789 and 1790 in Vienna. In his survey of the city's seven theatres, he observes that the German singers in the suburban theatres remain far behind the Italians, who possess a technique unique to them, that of *cantabile* or *portamento* singing.[19]

The hierarchical position of the singers within and across companies is not in any way reflected in the music Mozart composed for them: the brilliance of the Queen of the Night's arias, for example, does not betray any of Hofer's weaknesses. Quite the contrary: Mozart writes to her strengths, her thrilling staccato notes in the high celestial register, and that sound image gets abstracted from the conditions that gave rise to it to become the very expression of godly rage. In some way, the singers' vocal peculiarities, while making an imprint on the music composed for them, recede into the background, as they yield to the sublimity of the music that lifts the operas far above the particulars of their inception.

---

[18] The singing and Italian lessons are recorded in the theatre account books, A-Whh, Hofarchiv, General Intendanz der Hoftheater, Rechnungen der k.k. Theatral- Hof- Directions Cassae, S.R. 20 (1783–84), expenditure no.118, and S.R. 21 (1784–85), expenditures nos. 134 and 142. Joseph to Rosenberg, 13 March 1784, 'I like your idea of trying out M[elle] Weber in a role to see how she fares in front of an audience', in Payer von Thurn (ed.), *Joseph II. als Theaterdirektor*, p. 49. Zinzendorf, 14 July 1784, identifies the opera in which she appeared as *I viaggiatori felici* and also gives his verdict, 'Marchesi [was] dull, la Weber forced her voice, la Storace pretty, kept her rondo short with just the cavatina', quoted in Link, *National Court Theatre*, p. 230. The few existing contemporary descriptions of Hofer agree that she was a very poor actress. Of her singing, one writer in 1789 observes that she had a strong and expressive voice, which, however, was a little rough in places. (My translations.) See also Paul Corneilson, 'Josepha Hofer, First Queen of the Night', *Mozart-Studien*, 25 (2018), pp. 477–500.

[19] Baron Carl von Reitzenstein, *Reise nach Wien* (Hof, 1795), p. 347.

CHAPTER 24

Mozart's Italian and German Singers

Paul Corneilson

Mozart adored his singers, and he loved to write for the voice, above all Italian opera. In one of the earliest reports of his musical abilities – in a report submitted to the Royal Society by Daines Barrington – the writer mentions that 'little Mozart was much taken notice of by Manzoli' (that is, the castrato who had come to London in 1764), and Barrington asked Mozart to improvise a 'love song, such as his friend Manzoli might sing at the opera'. Following this extempore song, complete with a simple recitative, Barrington asked for a 'song of rage, such as might be proper for the opera stage'. Mozart obliged, and Barrington noted that 'in the middle of it he had worked himself up to such a pitch, that he beat his harpsichord like a person possessed'.[1] Before Mozart returned to Salzburg he had written down his first arias, K. 21 and 23. His first three-act opera, however, was a buffa opera *La finta semplice* (1768), which Joseph II supposedly encouraged the twelve-year-old to write but which was not performed in Vienna, in part due to intrigues against it by the Italians at court.[2]

In December 1769 Leopold took a leave of absence to take Wolfgang over the Alps to Italy. This trip was undertaken not only to continue his studies in Italian prosody and counterpoint but also to seek opportunities to write operas. Leopold must have begun a systematic method of introducing Wolfgang to writing arias for opera seria, focussing on settings of texts from Metastasio's *Artaserse* (K. 88) and several from *Demofoonte* (K. 77, 82, 83 and 74b, all dating from 1770). In addition to spending time in Bologna, where he became a pupil of Padre Martini and eventually earned admission to the Accademia filarmonia, and in Rome, where he

---

[1] Barrington's complete report is published in MDL, pp. 86–91; MDB, pp. 95–100. John Rice discusses Mozart's studies with Manzoli and Johann Christian Bach in London in 'Mozart as Soprano', *Mozart-Jahrbuch 2006*, pp. 345–53. See also Ian Woodfield, 'New Light on the Mozarts' London Visit: A Private Concert with Manzuoli', *Music & Letters*, 76 (1995), pp. 187–208.

[2] Leopold wrote a long letter in protest addressed to Joseph himself; see MDL, pp. 74–7; MDB, pp. 80–3.

performed for the Pope and was given the prestigious medal of the Knight of the Golden Spur, the Mozarts made the acquaintance of Count Agostino Litta in Milan. Probably through the influence of the count (who had also been a patron of J. C. Bach), Mozart was given a commission to write the Carnival opera, *Mitridate, re di Ponto*, for the Regio Ducale Teatro.[3] The cast included the prima donna Antonia Bernasconi (who had created the role of Alceste in Gluck's opera in 1767) and the tenor Guglielmo d'Ettore in the title role. By all accounts, this was a baptism of fire for the young composer. While he was able to please Bernasconi (see his letter of 17 November 1770), he was forced to rewrite one of d'Ettore's arias four times, and the tenor ultimately preferred to use another aria by Quirino Gasparini.[4] Nevertheless, Mozart was invited back to write the serenata *Ascanio in Alba* for the wedding celebrations of Archduke Ferdinand and Princess Maria Beatrice Ricciarda of Modena in autumn 1771. The title role was taken by Mozart's old friend, Giovanni Manzoli, with the soprano Antonia Maria Girelli Aguilar as Silvia.[5] Hasse also contributed an opera seria *Ruggiero* (his last work, a setting of Metastasio's last libretto), as a special favour to the mother of the groom, Empress Maria Theresa. While Mozart's serenata might not have 'killed' Hasse's opera (as Leopold claimed in a letter of 19 October 1771), its success did lead to a second commission for an opera seria, *Lucio Silla*, for Carnival 1772. For this last work for Milan, Mozart had an excellent prima donna as Giunia, Anna de Amicis Buonsollazzi, whom the Mozarts had first met in Mainz in 1763.[6] His primo uomo, Venanzio Rauzzini, was equally renowned, and, in addition to the role of Cecilio, Mozart wrote for him the solo motet 'Exultate, jubilate' K. 165.

In the mid 1770s the Mozarts probably spent time in Munich each year during Carnival, but because the entire family went there, there are no letters documenting these visits. Mozart would have heard several famous

---

[3] See Anthony Pryer, 'Mozart's Operatic Audition. The Milan Concert, 12 March 1770: A Reappraisal and Revision', *Eighteenth-Century Music*, 1 (2004), pp. 265–88.

[4] See Harrison Wignall, 'Guglielmo d'Ettore: Mozart's First Mitridate', *Opera Quarterly*, 10 (1994), pp. 93–112.

[5] Mozart had heard Aguilar (called la Bastardella) sing in Parma and noted that she had '(1) a beautiful voice, (2) a marvelous throat, (3) an incredible range'. He transcribed some passages in a letter of 24 March 1770; see MBA, vol. 1, pp. 323–24.

[6] She was returning to Italy following her initial triumph in London, where she sang in two operas by J. C. Bach, *Orione* and *Zanaida*. See Ulrich Leisinger, 'Anna Lucia De Amicis Buonsollazzi – Mozarts erste Giunia', in Leisinger (ed.), *Mozart – Lucio Silla: Ein frühes Meisterwerk* (Salzburg: Anton Pustet, 2013), pp. 147–70.

castrati, including Gaetano Guadagni, who sang Orfeo in a revised version of Gluck's opera for Carnival 1773.[7] Presumably, Wolfgang would have gone to the comic operas at the Salvator Theatre as well as the opera seria at the Cuvilliès Theatre. He received a commission to write an opera buffa for Carnival 1775, but since no printed libretto survives from this production, we cannot know for sure the singers who first performed *La finta giardiniera*, with the exception of the soprano Rosa Manservisi (whom Wolfgang met in Dresden in April 1789). If Rosa sang Marchesa Violante, then her sister Teresa probably sang Arminda or Serpetta. Don Anchise, the Podestà, might have been portrayed by Gasparo Obermayer, who appeared in many other buffa roles in the 1770s, and the Cavaliere Ramiro could have been sung by the castrato Tommaso Consoli. In any event, Mozart did write *Il re pastore* for the castrato Consoli in Salzburg (1775). Giovanni Valesi, who gave singing lessons to Valentin Adamberger (who created the role of Belmonte in *Die Entführung*) and who later appeared as the High Priest in *Idomeneo*, might have taken the role of Count Belfiore.[8] Domenico Panzacchi (later Arbace in *Idomeneo*), who started singing at the Munich court in the 1760s after performing in Italy and Lisbon (including in a few works with Anton Raaff), rarely took roles in comic operas. But he did sing leading roles in the Munich Carnival operas, including several Metastasian settings by Andrea Bernasconi.

In the 1760s and 1770s the Mannheim court opera became known for its 'reform' operas. The composers Tomasso Traetta, Gian Francesco de Majo and Johann Christian Bach specifically wrote Italian *opere serie* for the singers there.[9] Unlike many other cities and courts, where the opera companies tended to hire 'star' singers each season, the Mannheim ensemble was fairly stable for more than twenty years, with Dorothea Wendling taking the prima donna roles, her sister-in-law Elisabeth Wendling the

---

[7] See Patricia Howard, *The Modern Castrato: Gaetano Guadagni and the Coming of a New Operatic Age* (Oxford: Oxford University Press, 2014), especially pp. 158–9.

[8] For other alternative casts, see Stanley Sadie, *Mozart, the Early Years, 1756–1781* (New York: Norton, 2005), pp. 357–8, and Robert Münster, '... *ich würde München gewis Ehre machen': Mozart und der Münchner Hof* (Weißenhorn: Konrad, 2002), p. 48. My list relies on information about other comic operas performed in Munich around 1775, in Claudio Sartori, *I libretti italiani a stampa dalle origini al 1800*, 7 vols. (Cuneo: Bertola & Locatelli, 1990–94), and *Indice de' teatrali spettacoli*, facsimile in 2 vols., ed. Roberto Verti (Pesaro: Fondazione Rossini, 1996).

[9] See Marita P. McClymonds, 'Mannheim, *Idomeneo* and the Franco-Italian Synthesis in Opera Seria', in Ludwig Finscher, Bärbel Pelker, und Jochen Reutter (eds.), *Mozart and Mannheim* (Frankfurt: Peter Lang, 1994), pp. 187–96; Paul Corneilson, 'Opera at Mannheim, 1770–1778' (PhD thesis, University of North Carolina, Chapel Hill, 1992); and Nicole Edwina Ivy Baker, 'Italian Opera at the Court of Mannheim, 1758–1770' (PhD thesis, University of California, Los Angeles, 1994). See also my critical edition of Majo's *Ifigenia in Tauride* (1764) in Recent Researches in the Music of the Classical Era, 46 (Madison: A-R Editions, 1996).

seconda donna roles and (from 1770) Anton Raaff the leading tenor ones. During this time, the primo uomo roles were taken by Lorenzo Tonarelli (1753–66), Silvio Giorgetti (1766–71) and Francesco Roncaglia (1771–76). The bass Giovanni Battista Zonca and a second tenor Pietro Paulo Carnoli completed the casts in both comic and serious operas for this period.

The autobiography of the bass Ludwig Fischer (Mozart's first Osmin) provides information about his early training and first appointment at the Mannheim court. After being accepted as an apprentice in Mainz for the Elector Emmerich Joseph (r. 1763–74), Raaff returned to Mainz from Italy, Portugal and Spain, where he had become rich and famous. Fischer auditioned for him, and Raaff took him on as a student. 'He gave me very intensive lessons, and had me read Italian.' Eventually, Fischer 'was engaged to sing for the Kapelle and concerts'.

> I rehearsed Italian *opere buffe* with my master. Then an Italian singer got sick. I appeared on stage after two rehearsals. My master [Raaff] was not there. He was annoyed when I wrote to him, and he was afraid that I was going to ruin my entire career, but was all the more pleased when he heard how well it turned out. The Italians, no less annoyed, spread a rumor that I had been rehearsing the role for a long time. I went the next day, a Monday, to the Intendant, an Italian count, informed him of the matter and asked for satisfaction: 'Your Excellency knows that the opera Amore artigiano has already been assigned for over four weeks. I have still not seen a note of it. I will commit myself for the following Sunday, since the singer is still sick, to appear in his place.' The Intendant brought it to the Elector and His Highness gave an order: whoever was not ready on the following Sunday could expect his dismissal. The Italians were entirely negligent with their comic operas. I came to an agreement secretly with the Intendant; we wanted secrecy so that His Highness would know nothing of it. It was in Schwetzingen [the summer palace]; *Das Milchmädchen* was performed by Mlle Strasser (six years later my wife), a tenor Hartig, and I. The Elector came. It was a complete surprise to him; we even received presents. We also gave *Der Fassbinder* and *Das redende Gemälde*. Italian comic operas ceased.[10]

Indeed, Carl Theodor built a new National Theatre in Mannheim and commissioned Ignaz Holzbauer to write a serious German opera, *Günther von Schwarzburg*, for its opening in January 1777. Both Raaff and Fischer appeared in this work, along with the sopranos Franziska Danzi and Barbara

---

[10] Quoted in Paul Corneilson, *The Autobiography of Ludwig Fischer: Mozart's First Osmin* (2nd edition, Malden, MA: Mozart Society of America, 2016), p. 35. This volume includes an introduction, a facsimile of Fischer's autobiography (to c. 1790), the German text and English translation, plus commentary and music for seven arias that Fischer sang.

Strasser and the tenor Franz Hartig. Mozart heard the opera in November 1777 and wrote favourably about the music though he was initially not very impressed by Raaff (as explained in a letter of 14 November 1777).

During his sojourn at Mannheim (November 1777 to mid-March 1778), Mozart befriended several singers, including the young soprano Aloysia Weber, Dorothea Wendling and her daughter Elisabeth August (Gustl), and Raaff.[11] It was Raaff who took Mozart under his wing in Paris in the spring, and introduced him to colleagues and potential patrons (like Count Sickingen; see Chapter 16 'Patronage'). Mozart grew fond of Raaff and could even appreciate his old-fashioned style of singing (see letter of 12 June 1778). And Raaff, along with the Wendlings and music director Christian Cannabich, lobbied to have Mozart write an opera seria for Munich in Carnival 1781. Thus Mozart returned to his friends now in Munich in November 1780 to complete his work on *Idomeneo*. Mozart's letters home to Leopold document how thoroughly the opera was written to the strengths and preferences of his singers.

When Vincent and Mary Novello visited Mozart's widow in Salzburg in 1829, one of the questions they asked her was 'Which were the greatest favourites with him of his own compositions?' According to Vincent: '[Constanze] said he was fond of "Don Giovanni", "Figaro" and perhaps most of all "Idomeneo", as he had some delightful associations with the time and circumstances under which it was composed.'[12] The characterization of the two women's roles, Ilia and Elettra (sung by Dorothea Wendling and Elisabeth Wendling), reflect the course of their careers in singing opera seria at Mannheim.[13] Raaff, too, was treated with utmost respect, and Mozart took some trouble to find a fitting final aria text for him in the title role.[14] Not surprisingly, when Franz Xaver Niemetschek

---

[11] Mozart wrote the aria K. 294 for Aloysia, and gave her arias from *Lucio Silla* and K. 272 (see his letter of 30 July 1778). For Dorothea he wrote K. 295a; see Corneilson, 'An Intimate Vocal Portrait of Dorothea Wendling: Mozart's Concert Aria K. 295a', *Mozart-Jahrbuch 2000*, pp. 29–45. Gustl received K. 307–308; see Corneilson, 'A Context for Mozart's French Ariettes: The Wendling Family and Friedrich Schiller's *Kabale und Liebe*', *Current Musicology*, 81 (2006), pp. 53–72. For Raaff he wrote K. 295; see Manfred Hermann Schmid, 'Mozart, Hasse und Raaff: Die Mannheimer Arie KV 295 "Se al labbro mio non credi"', *Mozart-Studien*, 14 (Tutzing: Hans Schneider, 2005), pp. 101–37.

[12] Rosemary Hughes (ed.) *A Mozart Pilgrimage Being the Travel Diaries of Vincent & Mary Novello in the Year 1829*, transcribed and compiled by Nerina Medici di Marignano (London: Novello, 1955), p. 76. Mary confirmed this account (p. 77).

[13] See Corneilson, 'Mozart's Ilia and Elettra: New Perspectives on *Idomeneo*', in Theodor Göllner and Stephan Hörner (eds.), *Mozarts Idomeneo und die Musik in München zur Zeit Karl Theodors* (Munich: Bayerischen Akademie der Wissenschaften, 2001), pp. 97–113.

[14] See further details in Daniel Heartz, 'Raaff's Last Aria: A Mozartian Idyll in the Spirit of Hasse', *Musical Quarterly*, 60 (1974), pp. 517–43.

summed up Mozart's early masterpiece, he emphasized the quality of the singers and orchestra: '*Idomeneo* is one of his greatest works and richest in thought; the style is continuously pathetic and breathes heroic grandeur. Since he wrote this opera for great singers and for one of the best orchestras in Europe, his spirit was unrestrained and unfolded most luxuriously.'[15]

Mozart also became a great favourite in Prague, and at least part of his success was due to the support of another singer, Josepha Duschek. Originally from Salzburg, Duschek first met Mozart shortly after she had married the composer Franz Xaver Duschek. Mozart wrote the concert aria K. 272 for her in 1777 and promised her another aria while he was finishing *Idomeneo*.[16] Mme Duschek was one of Mozart's most faithful supporters, and she sang other arias by him in concerts and probably collected some of his music as well.[17] Mozart stayed with the Duscheks at Villa Bertramka during the preparation for *Don Giovanni* (October–November 1787) and *La clemenza di Tito* (August–September 1790).

Mozart, writing to Gottfried von Jacquin from Prague on 15 January 1787, proclaimed *Le nozze di Figaro* a great success in Prague: 'Nothing is played, sung or whistled but *Figaro*'.[18] In order to capitalize on the composer's popularity, Pasquale Bondini, the local impresario who was also active in Leipzig and Warsaw, commissioned a new comic opera from Mozart.[19] The tenor Antonio Baglioni, who had recently sung in Gazzaniga's *Il convitato di pietra* in Venice (Carnival 1787), probably brought a copy of the libretto and suggested the subject of *Don Giovanni*.[20] Baglioni created the role of Don Ottavio, and Luigi Bassi the role of Don Giovanni.[21] Leporello was performed by Felice Ponziani,

---

[15] *Leben des K.K. Kapellmeisters Wolfgang Gottlieb Mozart, nach Originalquellen beschrieben* (Prague, 1798), p. 110; translated by Helen Mautner in Niemetschek, *Life of Mozart* (London: Hyman, 1956), pp. 80–1 (modified).

[16] See Tomislav Volek, 'Josepha Duschek und Salzburg: Zur Arie "Ah, lo previdi" KV 272 und ihrem Kontext', *Mozart-Studien*, 14 (Tutzing: Hans Scheider, 2005), pp. 85–100. As I have argued, her request for a second aria was not fulfilled until several years later, when Mozart presented her with K. 528 in 1787. See Corneilson, '"aber nach geendigter Oper mit Vergnügen": Mozart's Arias for Mme Duschek', in Kathryn L. Libin (ed.), *Mozart in Prague: Essays on Performance, Patronage, Sources, and Reception* (Prague: Czech Academy of Sciences, 2016), pp. 175–200.

[17] Corneilson, 'Mozart's Arias for Duschek', pp. 190ff. See also Chapter 11, 'Germany' in this volume.

[18] MBA, vol. 4, p. 10; LMF, p. 903.

[19] On Bondini's troupe, see Ian Woodfield, *Performing Operas for Mozart: Impresarios, Singers and Troupes* (Cambridge: Cambridge University Press, 2011).

[20] See Rice, 'Antonio Baglioni, Mozart First Don Ottavio and Tito, in Italy and Prague', in Milada Jonášová and Tomislav Volek (eds.), *Böhmische Aspekte des Lebens und des Werkes von W.A. Mozart* (Prague: Akademie der Wissenschaften der Tschechischen Republik, 2011), pp. 295–322, esp. 304–6.

[21] Magnus Tessing Schneider, 'Laughing with Casanova: Luigi Bassi and the Original Production of *Don Giovanni*', in *Mozart in Prague*, pp. 403–20.

who, like Francesco Benucci in Vienna, performed the title role in *Figaro*. Other cast members included Giuseppe Lolli (Commendatore and Masetto), Teresa Saporiti (Donna Anna), Katherina Micelli (Donna Elvira) and Caterina Bondini (Zerlina). *Don Giovanni* became one of the most travelled of Mozart's operas in the years after its premiere and from an early stage was known in a hybrid version.[22]

Mozart claimed that Domenico Guardasoni offered him 200 ducats plus 50 ducats for travel expenses to write a new opera for the Prague troupe in autumn 1789 (letter of 10 April 1789). Instead Mozart and Da Ponte revised *Figaro* for Vienna in 1789 and wrote *Così fan tutte* (completed January 1790) also for Vienna. In the summer of 1791, however, Mozart did receive a contract to write the opera for Leopold II's coronation as King of Bohemia in September 1791. Baglioni was the only member of the *Don Giovanni* cast to perform in *La clemenza di Tito* (in the title role).[23] Guardasoni's contract specified that he should hire a famous Italian castrato and prima donna,[24] and to that end he brought Domenico Bedini to sing Sesto and Maria Marchetti Fantozzi to sing Vitellia in Prague.[25] Though it has been suggested that Mozart wrote 'Non più di fiori' for Mme Duschek in April 1791 (based on a concert poster advertising that she sang 'Ein Rondo von Herrn Mozart mit obligaten Bassete-Horn'), the evidence that the aria was written for Fantozzi after July 1791 is overwhelming.[26] In any event, Mozart did not have much time to spend with the cast of *Tito* and probably assigned the simple recitatives to Franz Xaver Süssmayr, who accompanied him to Prague.

In his biography of Shakespeare, Peter Ackroyd observes: 'Shakespeare sees his characters as an actor would, not as a poet . . . And the central point is that Shakespeare sees before him not just the character but the actor playing the character'.[27] This applies equally to Mozart, who did not write

---

[22] Ian Woodfield shows that many early copies of the opera conflated the two versions; see *The Vienna Don Giovanni* (Woodbridge and Rochester, NY: Boydell Press, 2010).

[23] See Rice, 'Antonio Baglioni', especially pp. 303–4.

[24] The contract is translated in NMD, pp. 67–8.

[25] John A. Rice, 'Mozart and His Singers: The Case of Maria Marchetti Fantozzi, the First Vitellia', *Opera Quarterly*, 11 (1995), pp. 31–52.

[26] See Tomislav Volek, 'Über den Ursprung von Mozarts Oper *La clemenza di Tito*', *Mozart-Jahrbuch 1959*, pp. 274–86, and Volek, 'Nochmals: über den Ursprung von Mozarts Oper *La clemenza di Tito*', in *Böhmische Aspekte des Lebens und des Werkes von W.A. Mozart*, pp. 265–77. The strongest counter-arguments are made by Sergio Durante, 'The Chronology of Mozart's *La clemenza di Tito* Reconsidered', *Music & Letters*, 80 (1999), pp. 560–94, and John Arthur, 'Some Chronological Problems in Mozart: The Contribution of Ink Studies', in Stanley Sadie (ed.), *Wolfgang Amadè Mozart: Essays on His Life and Music* (Oxford: Clarendon Press, 1996), pp. 35–52.

[27] Ackroyd, *Shakespeare: The Biography* (New York: Anchor, 2006), p. 263.

generic arias for a soprano, tenor or bass, but rather for specific singers. And
doing so gave him pleasure, as he wrote to his father regarding the aria
K. 295 for Raaff: 'I assured him in return that I will arrange the aria for him
in such a way that he would certainly enjoy singing it; for I love it when an
aria is so accurately measured for a singer's voice that it fits like a well-
tailored dress'.[28]

---

[28] Letter of 28 February 1778, as translated by Robert Spaethling in *Mozart's Letters, Mozart's Life*
(New York: Norton, 2000), pp. 134–5.

CHAPTER 25

Mozart the Performer-Composer

Simon P. Keefe

For Mozart as for many other musicians in the eighteenth century, performing and composing represented two sides of the same coin. Numerous treatises implicitly or explicitly referenced the ideal scenario of a composer performing their own music. And Mozart described good sight-reading as playing a piece in such a way 'that you might suppose that the performer had composed it himself'.[1] Players and singers were expected to continue the creative work of a composer, irrespective of whether they themselves had written the music, for example by introducing tasteful elaboration and embellishment to the notated text; each piece thus existed at a place on a composition-performance continuum determined inter alia by genre and intended purpose, and relationship between author and executant.

Improvisation at the keyboard, a stock in trade for Mozart throughout his career, represented his most complete merging of performing and composing into a single creative act. In improvising for an audience, Mozart had these activities reinforce each other, as critics recognized when referencing both his playing and features of the music produced (such as 'ideas', themes, harmony). For one writer, witnessing the young child prodigy in action: 'Now we will be overcome with complete astonishment when we see sitting at the clavier a boy aged 6 and hear him not dally with sonatas, trios and concertos but play valiantly, improvising for hours off the top of his head, now cantabile, now in chords, producing the best ideas according to today's taste'.[2] The distinguished Paris-based intellectual Friedrich Melchior Grimm commented a few months later in December 1763:

> what is unbelievable is to watch him improvise for an hour and thereby let loose the inspiration of his genius and a mass of beautiful ideas, which he

---

[1] MBA, vol. 2, p. 228 (my translation); also LMF, p. 449 (17 January 1778). All translations from MBA and MDL are my own, unless otherwise indicated.

[2] MDL, p. 22; also MDB, p. 21.

again knows how to make follow one another with taste and without confusion. The most consummate Kapellmeister could not be more profound than him in the science of harmony and modulations, which he knows to lead down the least familiar but always exact routes.[3]

And Placidus Scharl, writing of the young Mozart in memoirs from 1808, neatly summed up the prevailing critical view of Mozart as improviser: 'inexhaustible ideas' made him 'author and performer simultaneously'.[4]

Compliments for Mozart's improvisations continued to flow during the final decade of his life when based in Vienna (1781–91). Franz Xaver Niemetschek, one of Mozart's earliest biographers, described his playing on a visit to Prague in January 1787: 'Mozart at the end of the academy improvised alone at the pianoforte for more than half an hour and enhanced delight to the highest degree. And actually this improvising exceeded everything that we could imagine from piano playing, the highest degree of compositional art united with the most perfect skill in playing.'[5] The critic Johann Schink, attending Mozart's academy on 1 April 1784 in Vienna, was astonished by the improvisation: 'what richness of ideas! What variety! What changes in passionate tones! We swim away with him unresistingly on the stream of his emotions!'[6] And Johann Daniel Preisler, a Danish actor temporarily resident in Vienna, commented similarly about hearing Mozart improvise at home on 24 August 1788: 'This small man and great master twice *extemporized* on a *pedal piano*, so wonderfully! so wonderfully! that I didn't know where I was. The most difficult passages and the loveliest *themes* interwoven.'[7]

In other areas of activity, particularly piano concertos, performing and composing shared equal billing for Mozart. He acknowledged as much in an announcement in the third person enticing potential audience members to an academy at the Burgtheater in Vienna on 10 March 1785: 'he will play not only a *new*, just *finished Fortepiano Concerto* [K. 467], but will also use a particularly *large pedalled Fortepiano* [with a keyboard at his feet to emphasize low notes]'.[8] Improvisations and embellishments were an important feature of Mozart's performances of concertos: he had no need or desire in his own renditions to stick rigidly to the notated keyboard text now preserved in autograph scores. And in one case, the Piano Concerto

[3] MDL, pp. 27–8; also MDB, p. 26.   [4] MDL, p. 440; also MDB, p. 512.
[5] Niemetschek, *Leben des K. K. Kapellmeisters Wolfgang Gottlieb Mozart* (1798), ed. E. Rychnovsky (Munich: Bibliothek zeitgenössicher Literatur, 1987), p. 27 (my translation).
[6] MDL, p. 206; also MDB, p. 233.
[7] MDL, p. 285; MDB, p. 325 (translation from the original Danish as given in MDB).
[8] MDL, p. 212; also MDB, p. 239.

No. 26 in D, K. 537 ('Coronation'), large chunks of solo music are missing from the autograph – including the entire left-hand part of the slow movement – meaning that Mozart must have improvised material here in concert (or at least memorized unnotated music). But he had to ensure in piano concertos that he was admired for compositional work as well as his own playing. Leopold Mozart marvelled at both to daughter Nannerl (albeit only implicitly referencing performance on this occasion) after an academy on 13 February 1785 in Vienna: 'I . . . had the pleasure of hearing so splendidly all the interplay of the instruments that tears filled my eyes from sheer delight. When your brother left, the Emperor passed down a compliment hat-in-hand and shouted out "Bravo, Mozart!" When he came back to play, he was applauded.'[9] Small changes to piano and orchestral parts in autographs, with timbral and textural as well as soloistic implications, reflect an aspiration to be appreciated both as a composer of refined and powerful instrumental music and as a solo performer of technically and expressively virtuosic material.[10] It is no coincidence in 1780s Vienna that piano concertos and solo improvisations, which promoted performer and composer together, were at the heart of Mozart's academies at the Burgtheater and his subscription concerts at the Trattnerhof residential building on the Graben and Mehlgrube restaurant on the Neuer Markt.

Elsewhere in Mozart's keyboard repertory, performing experiences are captured in the notated texts of autographs. In two works, the accompanied sonatas K. 379 in G (1781) and K. 454 in B♭ (1784), Mozart gave premieres in advance of notating his own keyboard parts in full. K. 379, for example, was 'composed yesterday [7 April 1781] between eleven and twelve – but in order to finish it, I wrote out only the accompaniment part for Brunetti [the Salzburg violinist with whom Mozart played on 8 April at a concert at Archbishop Colloredo's Viennese residence] and remembered my own part.'[11] Similarly, Italian virtuoso violinist Regina Strinasacchi, co-performer of K. 454 with Mozart on 29 April 1784 in Vienna, received her part only in the immediate run-up to the academy; Emperor Joseph, in attendance, is said to have caught sight of the score after the event and expressed amazement at the empty spaces where keyboard material should have been written. In both sonatas, the autograph scores bear witness to the initial notation of the violin music and later

---

[9] MBA, vol. 3, p. 373; also LMF, p. 886 (16 February 1785).
[10] For discussion of changes of this kind see Simon P. Keefe, *Mozart in Vienna: The Final Decade* (Cambridge: Cambridge University Press, 2017), especially Chapter 4, pp. 168–219.
[11] MBA, vol. 3, p. 102; also LMF, p. 722 (8 April 1781).

inclusion of keyboard music: the latter is often squashed into an amount of space dictated by that originally assigned to the former, indicating later accrual of piano writing to the score. The keyboard texts themselves were probably influenced by Mozart's memories of the premieres: passages where attention is unambiguously directed towards the actions of performers, such as the improvisatory parts of the first and last movements of K. 379 and the rich, sinewy interaction between fortepiano and violin in the slow introduction of K. 454, seem born of practical experiences of great musicians freely and imaginatively interacting with each other. In any case, the subsequent publisher of K. 454, Vienna-based Torricella, evoked memories of a premiere several months earlier in encouraging players to purchase the edition, remembering it as having been 'recently played at the theatre by the famous Mlle Strinasachy [*sic*] and Herr Mozart to universal applause, and therefore [needing] no further recommendation'.[12]

Mozart's intimate relationship with renditions of his own music also affected what he wrote primarily or exclusively for others to perform. In line with standard eighteenth-century practice, he tailored opera and concert arias to the needs of individual singers. Not only did he respond actively to vocal desires, predilections, strengths and weaknesses, he also combined knowledge of individual voices with attention to how best to blend them with instruments: Aloysia Lange, Mozart's sister in law and recipient of a number of arias, is regularly heard with a solo oboe, and Johann Valentin Adamberger, the first Belmonte in *Die Entführung aus dem Serail* (1782) and interpreter of later Mozart arias too, with a full complement of wind instruments. Mozart's music for leading instrumental practitioners such as horn-player Joseph Leutgeb and clarinettist Anton Stadler also explored timbral as well as exclusively soloistic opportunities.[13]

Another area testifying to Mozart's performing interests and concerns is music for publication. While works such as the six quartets dedicated to Haydn (1782–5) and the string quintets in C and G minor K. 515 and K. 516 (1787) are routinely venerated as beautifully chiselled compositions, as if set in stone by their creator, they were influenced in the transition from autograph to printed text by performing experiences that reflect continuing textual and interpretative evolution in Mozart's mind. Artaria, the leading Viennese music publisher of the late eighteenth century, assigned up to six months between receiving a work and bringing it into the public

---

[12] MDL, p. 200; also MDB, pp. 226, 227–8.
[13] Mozart's writing for individual singers and instrumentalists in combination with distinctive wind timbres is discussed in detail in Keefe, *Mozart in Vienna*.

domain, sometimes enabling composers to play through – and make alterations to – handwritten performing copies of the work before the onset of the engraving process. Such copies survive for the C major string quintet; they contain dynamic annotations by Mozart not found in the autograph but included in the first Artaria edition.[14] A similar process can be surmised for the 'Haydn' quartets in spite of performing copies no longer being extant: pre-publication copies and renditions are documented in Mozart's correspondence, and substantial differences between articulation and especially dynamic markings in the autograph and first edition can surely be attributed to Mozart rather than to editorial intervention.[15] Having an opportunity to play, hear and contemplate a chamber work between submission to Artaria and appearance in print encouraged Mozart to clarify and reinterpret his own music, in particular through added and altered performance markings. In another work published by Artaria in 1790, the Piano Trio in G, K. 564, an unusual kind of primary source shines a light on Mozart's contemplation of performance. The keyboard part was copied into the score in another hand from an unknown source and a stave left empty above and below it for Mozart to write the violin and cello parts. As well as including violin and cello material, Mozart added dynamics and articulation for the piano: the sonata came alive for him, then, when envisaged as a complete, performable entity.

Like the works he wrote, Mozart's career was shaped by involvement as a performer-composer. During the Grand Tour of northern Europe in 1763–6, he was promoted as a prodigious performer-composer not just as one or other in isolation. For Leopold, his young son's reputation could only be enhanced in this way, and the scale of his achievement rendered all the more remarkable. When trying to entice paying customers to a benefit concert in Spring Garden near St James's Park, for example, Leopold wrote in the *Public Advertiser* (31 May 1764): 'Every Body will be astonished to hear a Child of such tender Age playing the Harpsichord in such a Perfection—It surmounts all Fantastic and Imagination, and it is hard to express which is more astonishing, his Execution upon the Harpsichord playing at Sight, or his own Composition.'[16] In effect, Mozart learned his compositional craft as a performer on this trip: compositional weaknesses, including harmonic and gestural unevenness in the accompanied sonatas K. 8/iii and K. 14/i respectively, are probably attributable to a desire to

[14] See Ernst Herttrich, 'Eine neue, wichtige Quelle zu Mozarts Streichquintetten KV 515 und 516', in Paul Mai (ed.), *Im Dienst der Quellen zur Musik: Festschrift Gertraut Haberkamp zum 65. Geburtstag* (Tutzing: Hans Schneider, 2002), pp. 435–45, and Keefe, *Mozart in Vienna*, pp. 455–8.
[15] Keefe, *Mozart in Vienna*, chapter 5.   [16] MDB, p. 34 (in English).

exploit concomitant performing opportunities. Exuberant ornamentation and embellishments in the early accompanied sonatas also give a flavour in notated form of the enthusiastic performances that audiences of Mozart's renditions would have enjoyed across Europe in 1763–6.[17] Eleven years after returning from the Grand Tour, Mozart embarked on an extended trip to southern Germany and France (1777–9) without his father on this occasion and with the intention of exploiting skills as a performer-composer to procure a post away from Salzburg. While ultimately unsuccessful in Munich, Mannheim and Paris, at least in his principal career aspiration, Mozart focussed his mind on the future and where he wanted to direct his energies. As stated to Leopold in early 1778, he would rather '*so to speak* neglect the clavier than composition, because the clavier is only my secondary thing, though thank God, a very strong secondary thing'. (Leopold responded in angrily pragmatic fashion that Mozart should first make his name as a pianist in Paris and then – as a composer – exploit the reputation he had earned.[18]) Mozart also made crystal clear from Paris on 11 September 1778 that if a return to a court post in Salzburg were to be countenanced it would have to be in an enhanced role of quasi Kapellmeister rather than as the straightforward violinist of earlier years.[19]

Once Mozart had decided to stay in Vienna in spring 1781 and had extricated himself from his Salzburg position, he needed to make a living as an independent composer, performer and performer-composer who could no longer rely on the security of a court salary, nor the financial support of his father (as had been the case on the 1777–9 trip). Given his previous achievements as a keyboard player, it is no surprise that he repeatedly exploited the cachet of combined keyboard performance and composition (including improvisations) in order to help navigate a path through the early Viennese years in particular: in 1781–2 he wrote and played a highly successful new rondo finale, K. 382, for an old work (K. 175 in D from 1773); he gave acclaimed performances of the concerto K. 415 in C in 1783; and he composed and played twelve new piano concertos at subscription concerts and academies between 1784 and 1786. Contrary to popular opinion, he did not fall from favour as a performer-composer and concertizer between 1786 and his death in 1791 but was less successful

---

[17] For discussion of Mozart's music from the Grand Tour, see Simon P. Keefe, 'Wolfgang Amadeus Mozart the Child Performer-Composer: New Musical-Biographical Perspectives on the Early Years to 1766', in Gary McPherson (ed.), *Musical Prodigies: Interpretations from Psychology, Education, Musicology, and Ethnomusicology* (New York: Oxford University Press, 2016), pp. 550–75.

[18] MBA, vol. 2, pp. 264, 295–6; also LMF, pp. 468, 492 (7 and 23 February 1778).

[19] MBA, vol. 2, p. 473; LMF, pp. 612–13.

financially than in the first half of the decade – in part because of the economic downturn the onset of the Turkish War brought about in 1787 – and had less time available in his busy schedule for concert activities. He was warmly praised as a performer-composer visiting Dresden and Leipzig in 1789 and Frankfurt in 1790.[20] Also, after probably his final appearance at a public concert on 4 March 1791 playing the recently completed Piano Concerto no. 27 in B♭, K. 595, one critic wrote that 'everybody admired [Mozart's] art, in composition as well as execution'.[21]

In the aftermath of Mozart death, he was remembered as having had no equal 'in keyboard playing and composition' and being 'the greatest master of the keyboard'.[22] Ernst Ludwig Gerber, in an entry for Mozart in a dictionary of musicians written before Mozart died, remained a bit perplexed by some of his works but in absolutely no doubt about his status as one of the leading fortepianists of his generation.[23] As first-hand memories of Mozart faded, his compositions and compositional activities inevitably assumed centre stage in biographical and critical work, not least in Gerber's revision and expansion to his original dictionary twenty-or-so years later, which carried a significantly longer Mozart article.[24] But the vivid, 'live' quality of works Mozart wrote for himself and the energetic, engaged mind of the distinguished performer writing music for others, can only be properly appreciated once due consideration is given to his role, status and experiences as an extraordinarily gifted performer-composer.

---

[20] NMD, pp. 56, 59; MDL, pp. 304, 330; MDB, pp. 347, 375.

[21] MDL, p. 339; also MDB, p. 387.

[22] MDL, pp. 369–70 (also MDB, pp. 419–20); and *Bayreuther Zeitung* (13 December 1791), p. 1089.

[23] Gerber, *Historisch-biographisches Lexikon der Tonkünstler* (Leipzig, 1790 and 1792), 2 vols., vol. 1, cols. 977–9.

[24] Gerber, *Neues historisch-biographisches Lexikon der Tonkünstler* (Leipzig, 1812–14), 4 vols., vol. 3, cols. 475–98.

CHAPTER 26

Instrumental Performance Practice

John Irving

Mozart wrote literally hundreds of instrumental works. They include canons; church sonatas; concertos for piano, violin and wind instruments; dance music (contredanses, German dances) for various occasions; divertimentos (sometimes called cassations, notturni or serenades) for strings, wind or full orchestra; keyboard fantasias, sonatas and variations; marches; miscellaneous works including those with parts for unusual instruments like the glass harmonica and mechanical clocks; piano trios, quartets and a quintet for piano and winds; string quartets, quintets and a trio; symphonies; violin sonatas and variations; and a whole host of arrangements or completions of works by others (notably fugues by members of the Bach family, concertos made from the sonatas of J. C. Bach and others, and duos for violin and viola which were probably written to assist former Salzburg colleague Michael Haydn, who was unable through illness to complete a projected set of six).

A short chapter cannot do justice to performance practices of each and every type of instrumental work listed above and necessarily must be selective. We can celebrate the fact that, in the early twenty-first century, we are privileged to have choice – both as performers and listeners – where the performance of Mozart's instrumental works is concerned. As listeners, we can choose among different interpreters, among 'period' and 'modern' approaches to performance, between a public or private listening experience (in a concert hall, or at home on radio, TV, CD or personal listening device). As players, we can choose between different resources, principally of two kinds: instruments and playing styles, and texts (and how to interpret them). Introducing the range of choices and exploring some consequences of making such choices provides the focus for my chapter.

Arguably, the single most significant development in Mozart performance during the last half-century – especially regarding his instrumental music – has been the turn towards 'period performance'. While Mozart's instrumental works are, happily, still performed on modern instruments too, the use of faithful modern copies of historical originals, supported by awareness of relevant historical attitudes towards interpretation of his music, has become mainstream. All responsible music conservatoires around the world routinely include historical performance programmes; major publishers have produced, and continue to produce, in-depth studies of historical performance practice engaging scholars from across a wide range of specialisms; music journals debate the finer points of that scholarship, influencing performance choices; national funding bodies award major grants for the further pursuit of this scholarship and its application, occasionally in the form of new recordings and other forms of public dissemination. The time is long past when an artist such as Malcolm Bilson needed to argue the case (in the pages of *Early Music*) that there was no longer a skills gap between players of Mozart's keyboard music on period pianos as opposed to modern instruments. Indeed, there are several complete recordings of Mozart's sonatas on fortepiano, including from Alexei Lubimov (Warner Classics), Ronald Brautigam (BIS), Bart van Oort (Brilliant Classics) and Kristian Bezuidenhout (Harmonia Mundi), all of whom can be heard regularly in concert halls performing this repertoire.

Amid such a sea change, it is something of a relief that one can still hear Mozart performed well on modern instruments. A notable recent example is the recording (Linn, 2008) of his last four symphonies by the late Sir Charles Mackerras and the Scottish Chamber Orchestra – winner of several awards and the fruit of Mackerras' protracted study of period performance concerns (including many Mozart projects with the Orchestra of the Age of Enlightenment during the last two decades of his career). By contrast with his earlier recording of these works with the Prague Chamber Orchestra (Telarc, 1991), the 2008 versions are notably quicker, crisper in articulation, more transparent in texture, phrased on a level more suited to an aesthetic of local gesture – an approach altogether more conversational in tone. Using valveless horns and trumpets, Mackerras's later accounts of symphonies 38, 39, 40 and 41 set a new benchmark not just for recordings, but for performances in the concert hall, laying down a challenge to symphony orchestras to equal the clarity and rhetorical vigour with which groups such as the Academy of Ancient Music (Christopher Hogwood), The English Concert (Trevor Pinnock) and The London Classical Players (Sir Roger Norrington) had been approaching Mozart's orchestral works for over two decades.

Within this challenge lay a requirement to abandon luxurious tempos, seamless legato phrasing and perhaps even vibrato: performance factors that had much to do with the civic settings for symphonic musical performance that developed in (for example) Berlin, Leipzig, Amsterdam, Paris, Vienna and London during the nineteenth century and have continued since. Large concert halls primarily celebrated the power of musical culture to glorify civic pride; their size as well as external and internal decoration went far beyond the functional. In Mozart's day, by contrast, his symphonies, piano concertos, instrumental solo and chamber music were performed in spaces of varying sizes (salons, ball-rooms, theatres, upstairs rooms in taverns, aristocratic palaces, university auditoria). For the performer on modern instruments, such a sophisticated ecology of performance possibilities has been largely lost. Because perfor-mance memory does not survive beyond a generation or two, it becomes increasingly difficult, over time, to think beyond situations inherited in the recent past: through one's teachers and their experience, through one's own concert attendance, through the experience of performance collea-gues, and so on. The scale of the musical gestures in these different genres (for which there are numerous clues in Mozart's carefully-notated auto-graphs – two important examples being frequent short slurs, and staccato dots and strokes) was aimed at listeners with a grasp of rhetoric, of the affective potential of musical figures, keys, tempos and temperaments. To claim that these were all uniformly tailored in Mozart's imagination to just one particular type of civic space such as a concert hall is unhisto-rical, to say the least. Yet there are those who make exactly such a claim to a tradition of performance stretching backwards as if in an unbroken chain to the composer himself. Important ingredients within that 'tradition' include:

- fairly steady tempos, especially at the Andante, Adagio, Larghetto end of the spectrum (giving a marked contrast to the quicker outer move-ments of a three-movement work, for instance);
- a uniformly legato approach to phrasing (in long, seamless lines – each phrase having a trajectory that reaches its climax about three-quarters of the way through);
- smoothly graduated dynamic changes (crescendos and diminuendos);
- a 'tasteful' rallentando just before the end of a movement (typically combined with expansive physical gestures signalling, in a large acoustic space, where this might not otherwise be noticed, that the end is nigh);
- near-continuous nourishing of the tone by vibrato, allied with a succession of relatively long bow strokes and use of higher finger-positions (and avoiding open strings at all costs);

- uniformity of tone across the range (a factor made possible on wind instruments by the development of complex key-systems during the nineteenth century, in contrast to, for example, the quite shocking tonal variations emitted by boxwood five-keyed clarinets or natural horns with their array of tuning crooks).

Such fingerprints of 'concert hall performance' of Mozart's symphonies could easily be multiplied (including the number of desks of violins that might be appropriate in a symphony performance; whether a continuo keyboard instrument might be necessary; and, more controversially, whether a conductor is actually needed).

Players of historical instruments soon become sensitive and responsive to their inbuilt lack of uniformity in respect of tone and tone production. For string players, this revolves around such factors as the lack of a chin rest (for violinists), the lack of a spike (for cellists) and the consequent impact on the amount of position shifting, players often staying in the lower positions and using open strings (gut, not metal) more frequently. The setup of the instruments (height of bridge, length and angle of neck, tension of strings) also plays a large part in the delivery of a more transparent sound. Of equal significance are the types of bow and the nature of bowing. The modern 'Tourte' bow was not in common use in the Vienna of Mozart's day, and classical bows of his time did not share their design, differing from earlier models in length and shape (especially Tourte's hammer-head point of the stick, giving far greater power in that region of the bow). While earlier bow designs (in which the stick often curved away from the hair) allowed for some application of arm weight at the tip, the natural response of the bow favoured generally shorter strokes predominantly nearer to the heel and middle; Tourte's later design (the bow stick curving inwards towards the hair) allows for far greater power across the length, and with it an extended repertory of bow strokes going well beyond those outlined in a much-circulated treatise on the violin published by Mozart's father in 1756 (which no doubt influenced Mozart's conception of string playing). During the nineteenth century, string instruments were routinely altered to produce a much louder sound, capable of filling a large auditorium, and on these instruments the Tourte bow really came into its own. But in the process, the physicality of string playing took on a muscularity that led it further away from the string sound imaginable to Mozart.

This trend is also noticeable where woodwind instruments are concerned. For instance, the clarinets of Mozart's time were made of boxwood and produced a much more mellow tone than the later, harder blackwood models. They had only a few keys (typically five) and many of the chromatic notes were produced by special fingerings (known as 'forked fingerings') in which adjacent tone holes were left alternately open or closed. This technique affects both tuning and tone colour (a feature deliberately 'ironed-out' by nineteenth-century developments to keywork). But for Mozart, the tonal variation was an inherent quality of the clarinet, and one he exploited to the full in chromatic writing in the 'Kegelstatt' Trio K. 498, the Quintet for Piano and Winds K.452 (both for the B♭ instrument) and in the Clarinet Quintet K. 581 and Clarinet Concerto K. 622 (for the A instrument). In the last two works, the tonal qualities were further affected by Mozart writing for a basset clarinet (with its extended range at the bottom, adding to the variation of colour across the range). Knowledge of these factors, and experience in their artistic application, affords players of period clarinets access to dimensions of expressive contrast in Mozart's works that ceased to exist during the nineteenth century and through most of the twentieth.

A similar case can be made for the piano. Perhaps the most noticeable difference from a modern piano's tone is the immediacy with which the fortepiano sound occurs on striking a key. In contrast to the thickly-felted hammers of the modern instrument, a Viennese fortepiano's hammers were covered in finely graded strips of leather, transmitting energy directly from the hammer to the string. The material and dimensions of the strings are important factors too: compared with the modern piano, the tone of each note diminishes rapidly. From the player's perspective, this kind of tone-production is a bonus in terms of clarity, whether of successive semiquavers in extended passagework or in textures involving the 'Alberti bass' (in which the left-hand arpeggiated figures never overpower the melody above). However well-trained the player, and however finely regulated the modern piano, Mozart's piano writing never achieves the nimbleness and conversational immediacy that can be achieved on the type of instrument that originally fired his imagination in the 1770s and 1780s.

Mozart's experience of the South German and Viennese pianos of Johann Andreas Stein and Gabriel Anton Walter is well documented. In October 1777, writing from Augsburg to his father in Salzburg, he detailed his approval of Stein's instruments, noting the cleanness of their sound, the evenness of touch across the range and the reliability of their action (with escapement mechanism). From about 1782 he owned a five-octave piano by Walter, which he regularly used for concerts in the capital (notably in performances of his piano concertos). The design of this instrument (in particular the grading of the hammer size, their coverings of thin strips of leather rather than felt, the shape and thickness of the soundboard whose grain runs in parallel with the strings – themselves quite thin and typically of brass or iron) gives far greater colour variation across the registers than a modern grand, whose sound is, once again, designed for uniformity across its range, focussed at one point near the centre of the soundboard for maximum projection into a large concert-hall space. So when, for example, Mozart transfers a cadential motive across different registers of the instrument (as he does in the closing bars of the Adagio of the B♭ Sonata K. 570), the change of colour when played on a Viennese fortepiano is quite striking, a feature of the texture that comes newly to life on such an instrument, affording the player a range of interesting interpretive opportunities (from which, of course, the player of the modern piano can learn).

It is important to note that the action in Mozart's Walter during his lifetime was significantly different from most modern reproductions of this type of Walter instrument. Mozart's widow had the instrument modernized by Walter about a decade after her husband's death, at which stage the action was changed from a so-called 'Stossmechanik' – in which the hammers hung from a rail and were activated by an intervening rod positioned on the key lever – to a 'Prellmechanik', in which the hammers were placed on the key levers in a pivot point called a Kapsel, with upward rotation of the hammer regulated from the far end of the key. The Prellmechanik gives the player a much more immediate control of the hammer flight and consequently a more direct sense of connection to the sound. At the same time, Walter transformed the operation of the sustain mechanism, by means of a knee-lever beneath the keyboard, whereas in Mozart's day it had been activated by hand-operated stops at either end of the keyboard. This latter point is of no small significance to players: how much 'pedal' should be applied in Mozart's later piano works, given that, on the instrument on which so many of them were conceived (from 1782 onwards), the damper rail could only be lifted by hand (and most of the time the player's hands are quite fully occupied playing the notes)?

Individual tonal qualities of the kinds of historical instruments for which Mozart was writing merge in an ensemble context. Comparing performances on modern instruments with those on period instruments, the most commonly reported difference has to do with the ease with which players of string or wind instruments can be heard against the piano. This too is connected to the rapid tonal decay of the Viennese piano sound, creating textural space for the ensemble as a whole. A particularly telling test-case is the Quintet for piano and winds K. 452. At many points in this work the piano's textures are quite full: for example, bars 18–32 of the Larghetto, revisited and expanded at bars 91–117; and in the rondo finale, bars 103–22 (including the wonderful chromatic horn descent beginning at bar 116, whose alternating 'open' and 'stopped' notes when played on natural horn reveal this passage quite literally in its true colours). The mighty, overtone-rich sound of the modern concert grand piano easily overwhelms the rest of the ensemble at such points, diminishing the impact of Mozart's delicate polyphonic texture in favour of punchy, harmonic successions. Period instruments encourage us to focus instead on the lateral intervallic movements among the winds, giving a conversational quality to these passages, newly revealed in – indeed, clarified by – their diverse colours.

Finally, what of textual resources – how might these affect our choices as performers (and listeners)? Pedagogical traditions stretching back well over a century have encouraged performers to assume total respect for the letter of the notated score. (One consequence has been the rise to prominence of the Urtext edition, one supposedly presenting the composer's intentions in pure form, as a purportedly dependable foundation for performers.) This is not the place for a philosophical debate on the relation of performance authenticity to a notated score of which it is a particular instantiation. But we may nevertheless note here the comparatively recent emergence of the phenomenon whereby a score (a representation of a work) is thought of *as if* the work itself (ergo, a faithful performance of the score is a performance of the work). For Mozart, the situation may well have been different. He was known as a fabulous improviser in concerts (for example, of cadenzas and *Eingänge* to his piano concertos – some representative examples of which survive, useful as models for linking together sections separated by fermatas). By his own admission, he frequently departed from his notated texts, decorating them sometimes quite profusely. (A charming example of how he decorated a simple phrase in the Andante of the Piano Concerto in D, K. 451 still survives in the performance materials used by his sister Nannerl in Salzburg in summer 1784.) Most telling of all, perhaps, is the surviving autograph of the C minor Piano Concerto K. 491. The variation finale contains contrasting versions of the right-hand passagework of bars 45–8, 60–2 and 69–71, for which no definitive version is indicated. (In the first of these passages, there are no fewer than four versions, all of which fit the harmony exactly.) These may be seen not, successively, as replacements, but as alternative ways of melodically elaborating the same tonal space. Such an approach to Mozart's own playing of this work is revealing, perhaps, to today's performers: treat Mozart's notated scores with the greatest respect towards their purpose. They are not a confining prescription for behaviour but are suggestions enabling (indeed empowering) creativity of thought: not 'must be', but 'might be'.

CHAPTER 27

Vocal Performance Practice

Sarah Potter

Mozart's gift for vocal writing has made his music as rewarding for the singer as for the listener: with his operatic and liturgical work loved by generations, every professional soloist carries work by Mozart in their repertoire. Perhaps surprisingly, then, singing Mozart in the twenty-first century is not without controversy. Performers and listeners often have a very clear idea of how they expect Mozart's music to be sung (perhaps with particular ornamentation or accompanied by period instruments), but their expectations may not always sit comfortably within the context of Classical music-making.

When considering historical approaches to any kind of musical performance it is essential to keep in mind the dichotomy between performance ideals described in treatises or other writing and the reality of performances actually taking place.[1] There is no shortage of information describing Classical approaches to singing, and such material provides an excellent foundation for further consideration of evidence relating specifically to Mozart and his singers. This chapter will redefine expectations of Mozartian singing within a reliable Classical context, keeping in mind the practicalities and physical constraints of performance reality.

The Classical Singer

In general discussion of music, the term 'classical' is often used to describe a performer who has received some degree of formal training: it would not be unreasonable to expect a 'classical singer' to perform vocal works by Mozart with some proficiency. Many extend this definition further and relate that formal vocal training directly to a specific vocal technique that requires the lowering of the larynx. The (twenty-first-century) classically trained singer is trained to use a lowered larynx technique, predominantly

---

[1] George Kennaway, 'Do as Some Said, or as Most Did? – A Foucauldian Experiment with Nineteenth-Century HIP', *Current Musicology*, 92 (2011), pp. 79–101.

to facilitate the continued projection of the voice (without amplification) without damage to the vocal apparatus.

By habitually lowering the larynx whilst singing, an individual can increase the length of the vocal tract (the tube from the mouth to the opening of the throat), adjusting its acoustic properties and capitalizing upon the effects of the 'singer's formant', a peak in sound energy that occurs around the frequency at which the sound of an orchestra decays (in the region of 3kHz).[2] This technique allows the trained singer to project their voice over an accompaniment without straining or forcing, regularly and reliably. Teachers and performers might describe the physical config-uration required by referencing raised cheekbones, an 'open throat', or a high soft palate – but the outcome remains a lowered larynx. Training in advanced breath control is also closely linked to a lowered larynx techni-que, as the optimization of breath capacity, and the resultant gravitational force upon the larynx, can assist the singer in finding and maintaining a low larynx position. It is important to emphasize that this technique should not result in any tension or discomfort, within the vocal apparatus or in any other area of the body. A trained singer habituates a low larynx position over many years in order to enjoy greater vocal power at low physical cost: habitual larynx-lowering is the key to maintaining vocal health over a lengthy (twenty-first-century) singing career. If you observe a skilled singer on one of today's professional stages you will immediately notice the power of their voice, which will demonstrate a round but incisive tone immediately distinguishable from that of an untrained singer. A lowered-larynx technique encourages a more focussed (less breathy) tone and gives the impression of an even, rich timbre throughout the range.

The association of the classically trained singer with a lowered-larynx technique is, in turn, often extended to the Classical singer and to singers and singing predating the Classical period. There is, in fact, no evidence that the Classical (or earlier) singer would have used a low-larynx approach to voice production.[3]

Voice Production

Research confirms that approaches to voice production have changed dramatically over time, as have expectations of expressive singing. Singers

---

[2] Johan Sundberg, *The Science of the Singing Voice* (De Kalb, IL: Northern Illinois University Press, 1987), p. 97.

[3] The term 'bel canto' has similarly become associated with low-larynx singing in recent decades: there is no evidence of low-larynx voice production during the period of bel canto composition.

have always possessed the same equipment, but we must be careful not to imagine Classical singers within the context of twenty-first-century singing styles and techniques.

In the centuries predating reliable internal investigation (using a laryngoscope, for example), theorists relied upon more general observation to corroborate any theory of voice production. As a result of these somewhat unreliable means, technical advice to the Classical singer was usually very general in nature and lacked the scientific discussion of more recent writing. A number of eighteenth-century theorists suggested methods of voice production now objectively confirmed as false, supporting the view that Classical teachers and performers did not yet properly understand the physiology of voice production, let alone manipulation of larynx height.

Whilst writers in this period had difficulty analysing the inner workings of the larynx, they could easily observe the general movement of the voice box from *outside* the body. Both Johann Quantz (1697–1773) and Domenico Corri (1746–1825), for example, described the larynx visibly ascending in the throat as the singer's voice rose in pitch, and descending in the throat as the singer's voice lowered in pitch.[4] Acknowledgement of a relationship between pitch and larynx height was repeated unchallenged by others and later confirmed by the emerging voice-science movement in the mid nineteenth century. This unconscious movement of the larynx can easily be confirmed by feeling the throat whilst speaking, or by observing a person without formal low-larynx training when singing. The widespread acceptance of this seemingly incidental information is key evidence that Classical (and earlier) singers did not attempt to manipulate the height of the larynx but instead employed a neutral approach to larynx height where the larynx moved in accordance with pitch, without conscious intervention by the singer. Classical singing was an exclusively neutral-larynx pursuit.

Further evidence for neutral-larynx usage by Classical singers includes a preference for the chest voice in vocal writing. When presented using neutral-larynx movement, the head voice does not display the weight and depth of its low-larynx equivalent but expresses the characteristics of voices we would now recognize as being without formal training (weakness at high pitch, relatively limited range, some breathiness of tone and lower perceived volume, for example). A neutral-larynx approach emphasizes

---

[4] Johann Joachim Quantz, *Versuch einer Anweisung die Flöte traversiere zu spielen* (Berlin: Johann Friedrich Voß, 1752); Domenico Corri, *The Singer's Preceptor* (London: Longman, Hurst, Rees and Orme, 1810).

what many would recognize as register 'breaks', because the larynx can only ascend so far in the throat before the singer must make adjustments to accommodate any further rise in pitch.

Having accepted the Classical voice as closer to that of the untrained voice, it is easier to comprehend the successful teenage debuts of many female singers. When a female singer uses a neutral approach to larynx height throughout her career, the voice is reasonably constant from an early age. This also makes the existence of castrati a little more understandable: if successful, his modification ensured the continuation of the youthful neutral-larynx voice that his female counterparts enjoyed without intervention. (Other male singers, of course, had to contend with adolescent vocal changes.) Signs of a young voice 'maturing' whilst receiving twenty-first-century training might be explained by the habituation of a lowered larynx position and the vocal qualities it affords.

Discussion of the manipulation of larynx height began only in the mid nineteenth century, around the time that Manual Garcia II (1805–1906) first published his observations on the effects of larynx lowering and its possible application in vocal expression, in 1841.[5] Remarkably, writers described the lowered larynx only as an expressive device and never as means for greater power; continual larynx lowering was not suggested in vocal literature until the turn of the twentieth century. The relatively low volume of the Classical voice would fit appropriately within the context of chamber performances and period instruments. Possible early proponents of a selectively lowered larynx include nineteenth-century singers Giuditta Pasta (1797–1865) and Maria Malibran (1808–36), who were praised for their ability to sing notes in one of two voices upon demand (either with a neutral or low larynx position), and Gilbert-Louis Duprez (1806–96), who was reported to have first produced the high tenor C in what appeared to be an extended chest voice, but most likely used a lowered larynx to produce qualities of depth usually associated with the chest register.

Stylistic Devices

Unconcerned by larynx height, Classical singers used a variety of other devices to deliver dramatic and affecting performances. Both the *messa di voce* and portamento were considered fundamental to the art of expressive singing.

---

[5] Manuel Garcia, *Traité complet de l'art du chant* (Paris, 1841). See Gregory W. Bloch, 'The Pathological Voice of Gilbert-Louis Duprez', *Cambridge Opera Journal*, 19/1 (2007), pp. 11–31.

The *messa di voce* was often described as a teaching tool used to develop muscle memory and encourage flexibility. Most writers described it simply as a gradual increase in volume followed by an equal decrease in volume, although singers may well have combined the device with a vibrato effect where the expressive context allowed. An interpretation focussing on dynamic contour alone is not implausible, as variety in both phrasing and articulation was considered essential to stylish Classical singing. As an ornament, the *messa di voce* was considered most suited to long, static notes and, like all devices in this period, was best used in moderation.

Early nineteenth-century writers described two forms of portamento: the first 'carrying' the initial syllable up to the destination pitch, and the second drawing the second syllable from the original pitch up to the destination pitch. The first form was the default option (presumably as it preserved the clarity of the text) and the second either derided or reserved only for exceptional use. There was a great deal of ambiguity in the description of the many facets of the portamento in this period, particularly in relation to the desired audibility of the intervening pitches within the portamento and the speed of its delivery. The device can be found in a variety of situations in source material, ascending and descending, and spanning up to an octave. Each element of the portamento (speed, emphasis, rhythm) could be adjusted to portray the whole spectrum of emotion, from melancholy to joy, but, as ever, Classical writers warned that interpretation should be governed by moderation and emotional context.

Performance by a Classical singing-actor required the whole gamut of expressive adaptation. This also included trills, turns, scalar and arpeggiated figures, rhythmic and tempo adjustment, grace notes and appoggiaturas and other stylistic devices now witnessed but rarely in vocal performance. Twenty-first-century singers will be familiar with the practice of starting trills from above the written note, with adding decorative ornamentation and with using an appoggiatura on the penultimate syllable of a phrase to emphasize a tapered ending, but this level of simplification fails to reflect the real diversity of Classical practice. Writers would often advise a student to listen to more accomplished singers in order to learn the nuances of expressive singing, but such detail can be observed in the annotations of Corri and others and has been discussed in the scholarship of Toft, Brown and Neumann.[6]

[6] Dominico Corri, *A Select Collection of the Most Admired Songs, Duetts, &c* (Edinburgh: John Corri, [n.d.]); Robert Toft, *Bel Canto: A Performer's Guide* (Oxford: Oxford University Press, 2013); Clive Brown, *Classical and Romantic Performing Practice 1750–1900* (Oxford: Oxford University Press, 1999); Frederick Neumann, *Ornamentation and Improvisation in Mozart* (Princeton, NJ:

Annotated repertoire from this period depicts much more frequent breathing than currently expected, in part due to the neutral use of larynx height (where a more breathy timbre is produced by air escaping though the vocal folds).[7] The Classical singer had no technical need to modify their instinctive breathing patterns because they did not use a lowered larynx position; use of the diaphragm to maximize breath capacity and maintain a low larynx position necessitates the outward movement of the abdomen, and so the prevalence of corset wear actually prevented female singers from meeting twenty-first-century phrasing and voice production ideals. There is no evidence that expectations of either factor differed for male singers in this period. Classical writers did not tend to criticize singers' breathing, as they were expected to break phrases in order to observe punctuation. Singing in this period was directly related to oration and so looked to the effects of emotion upon the speaking voice for inspiration. Classical singers could sigh, sob, choke or cough if the situation demanded it, and the need to take breath provided regular opportunity to portray realistic emotion that might reasonably interrupt or distort vocal sound.

Classical treatises often prescribed dedication to vocalize (songs without words) before repertoire with written text, prioritizing the training of both muscle memory and aural skills. It was common for treatises to include exercises in a great variety of keys, time signatures and tempos, and sometimes to consist of these exercises alone. The inclusion of example cadenzas in a treatise can be observed well into the nineteenth century, and it is plausible that the reuse of common frameworks gave rise to the canonical ornamentation and cadenza forms we still hear in popular works (the top C in the 'Alleluja' from Mozart's *Exsultate Jubilate* K. 165, for example). Mozart's writing exhibits two common cadential figures in particular: the cadenza proper, which extends the thematic material in virtuosic style (often indicated by a fermata), and the *Eingang*, an ornamental figure used to link two sections of an aria (often introducing the return of the main theme).[8] The Classical singer was expected to execute a cadenza in just one breath, and to maintain the general character by referencing themes from the main body of the aria. Evidence suggests that singers might take breath immediately before a cadenza, but its length would have been dictated by the capabilities of neutral-larynx singing.[9] Mozart's

---

Princeton University Press, 1986). Toft also discusses gesture in eighteenth- and nineteenth-century vocal performance.

[7] Corri, *A Select Collection.*
[8] See Neumann, *Ornamentation and Improvisation*, pp. 216–29, 264–74.
[9] See annotations in Corri, *A Select Collection.*

manuscripts and letters confirm that he sometimes provided cadential embellishment he had composed in accordance with the talents or limitations of a particular singer.

Perhaps the most contentious issue in the twenty-first-century performance of Classical vocal music is the use of vibrato effects. The view that some level of vibrato is inherent in the voice is now commonplace, and this is indisputable to a degree: the voice is produced by vibration of the vocal folds, and so some level of sound variation is to be expected. To interpret this as evidence for unavoidable or continuous vibrato usage, however, is inappropriate. The neutral-larynx voice displays some inherent breath variation, and it is this very gentle wavering of intensity that is described as evoking the sound of bells, musical glasses or the glass harmonica in Classical writing. Mozart derided the noticeably frequent use of intensity vibrato in correspondence with his father, and, like many in the eighteenth and nineteenth centuries, described sustained use of vibrato effects as a vocal defect.[10] Terminology remained somewhat inconsistent in this period, but both pitch and intensity variation were described as ornaments to be used in moderation; vibrato effects can be added, emphasized, reduced and controlled for expressive effect by a skilful singer using a neutral approach to larynx height.[11]

The Mozartian Singer

The Mozartian singer was first and foremost a Classical singer, and therefore used a neutral approach to larynx height, emulating the spoken voice and applying principles of moderation and variety in order to present a truly expressive performance. The neutral-larynx voice fits most convincingly with the Classical style of expression as it more easily mimics the effects of emotion upon the speaking voice. In correspondence with Aloysia Weber, Mozart emphasized the importance of true vocal verismo, advising her:

> [. . .] to watch the expression marks – to think carefully of the meaning and the force of the words – to put yourself in all seriousness into Andromeda's situation and position! – and to imagine that you really are that very person. With your beautiful voice and your fine method of producing it you will

---

[10] MBA, vol. 2, p. 378; LMF, p. 552 (12 June 1778).

[11] The involuntary intensity variation that the low-larynx singer experiences when performing high frequencies at high volume is irrelevant to the practice of the Classical singer.

undoubtedly soon become an excellent singer, if you continue to work in this way.[12]

This brief chapter seeks not to endorse the emulation of specific performances or performers nor to prescribe a 'correct' approach to the performance of Mozart's vocal repertoire but to encourage the reader to consider historically plausible approaches to Mozart's vocal works, and Classical singing more broadly. Principles for singing Mozart in context might include:

- variation of the musical text in accordance with expressive context;
- emulation of the speaking voice (as when affected by emotion);
- moderation in the application of all devices (including vibrato effects);
- acknowledgement of a neutral-larynx approach to voice production;
- recognition of stylistic devices not currently in common usage;
- interpretation of source material within a Classical context.

This chapter does not focus solely upon historical accounts of Mozartian singers and singing, but lays important groundwork for reliably interpreting such accounts within a Classical context. Truly Mozartian singing is much more than a well-placed ornament, a delicate trill or appoggiatura here and there, or the use of a period accompaniment; it requires the whole spectrum of human feeling to be communicated using the Classical singer's language of expression. Taking inspiration from Mozart's talent for expressive variation, the twenty-first-century singer should not be afraid to experiment with the styles and devices highlighted in this chapter.

---

[12] MBA, vol. 2, p. 420; LMF, p. 581 (30 July 1778).

PART V

Reception and Legacy

CHAPTER 28

Reactions to Mozart in His Lifetime

Ian Woodfield

'Music has suffered an irreparable loss. Last night, Herr Mozart, artist and darling of our age, surrendered his beautiful, harmonious spirit, and from now on will mingle his heavenly tones with the choirs of the immortals.' This shocking news appeared in the *Bayreuther Zeitung* on 13 December 1791. The paper's correspondent added a short obituary, noting how untimely the death was, as the composer still had much to offer the musical world. A masonic cantata, his last work, had been a 'masterpiece of noble simplicity'.[1] Dated 6 December, it is the earliest known announcement of Mozart's passing. As further details of the tragic circumstances began to emerge, there was a growing consensus that his music was generally loved and admired, and in light of its acknowledged commercial value, there was an immediate hunt for unpublished works.[2]

The mood of general goodwill received a jolt when a report of the Prague commemoration was published on 17 December.[3] The city had staged a moving service of remembrance, an impressive event by any standards: huge crowds, tolling bells, solemn trumpets and drums, and elaborate flowers. The requiem was by Francesco Rosetti, and there was a contribution from Josefa Duschek, a long-time friend of the deceased. Readers would have been left in no doubt that Mozart was regarded with warm affection in the city, but the account ends on a discordant note, raising a contentious issue: the fact that during his final years the composer's operas had by no means been universally appreciated. This was hardly the

---

[1] *Bayreuther Zeitung* (13 December 1791), no. 148, p. 1089. Dexter Edge, 'The Earliest Dated Report of Mozart's Death', *Mozart: New Documents*, compiled by Dexter Edge and David Black, first published 20 July 2014, updated 16 December 2017, http://sites.google.com/site/mozartdocuments

[2] The *Kurfürstlich gnädigst privilegirte Münchner Zeitung* (29 December 1791), no. 205, p. 1082, Wien, vom 24 Dez., described this search and raised the possibility of fakes: 'Die ungestochenen unbekannten Werke dieses großen Meisters werden izt überall aufgesucht, und um hohes Geld verkauft. Mitunterlaufen dann natürlicher Weise auch Werke anderer Meister, die man für Mozartische ausgiebt.'

[3] *Prager Oberpostamtszeitung* (17 December 1791); given in NMD, p. 123.

occasion to name names, but the writer did not pull his punches: 'they could accuse him of only a single fault . . . that he was too rich in ideas'.

The account of the commemoration in Prague was reprinted in several cities, local editors taking significantly different approaches to the text that they had been offered.[4] In Pressburg, the substance of the account was deemed acceptable but not its tendentious ending, which was omitted.[5] In Laibach, by contrast, the implicit national claim was brought out into the open: in Bohemia musical merit is treasured.[6] A key test was how Vienna would react. On 24 December, the piece appeared in the *Wiener Zeitung*, but only after major surgery. The warm personal tone of the original was muted through the use of a noticeably cooler vocabulary; 'lebhaftsten' (most animated), for example, replaced 'zärtlichsten' (most tender). Mozart was no longer 'our Mozart' but 'the artist'.[7] The claim that Prague had been able to call on musicians of high renown for the church service, seen as exaggerated, was played down. Since it was obvious that the concluding attack on unnamed critics of Mozart was aimed at members of the Vienna Italian opera establishment, this passage was cut altogether.

It was left to a journal published in Berlin to name and shame Vienna. A private letter from Prague dated 12 December, two days before the commemoration, was published in the *Musikalisches Wochenblatt*. The purpose of the communication was to provide an account of the coronation opera by Mozart, but, on the point of signing off, the correspondent had received the sad news of the composer's death, prompting him to speculate about the cause. At the end, he came out with the charge that he had been undervalued in his home city: 'now that he [Mozart] is dead the Viennese will at last realise what they have lost in him . . . Neither his *Figaro* nor his *Don Juan* was successful in Vienna.'[8]

The idea that Mozart's style could be too difficult for some listeners – the underlying allegation in the commemoration report – can be traced back to his early maturity. In his late teenage years, praise for his compositional prowess was usually unqualified: *Thamos* was 'beautifully written' and *La finta giardiniera* 'generally applauded', while an unidentified symphony 'excited applause . . . on account of its beautiful composition'.[9] But during

---

[4] The *Leipziger Zeitung* (20 December 1791), p. 1482, confined itself to the bare facts.

[5] *Preßburger Zeitung* (24 December 1791), no. 103, p. 1093.

[6] *Laibacher Zeitung* (30 December 1791), no. 104: Prag den. 16 Christm:, 'Diese Feyerlichkeit war auszeichnend, war ein redender Beweis, wie sehr in dem edeln Königreich Böhmen musikalische Verdienste geschätzt werden.'

[7] *Wiener Zeitung* (24 December 1791), no. 103, p. 3271. Given in MDL, pp. 375–6; MDB, p. 427.

[8] MDL, p. 380; MDB, p. 432.   [9] MDB, pp. 148, 150, 155.

his 1777 journey to Augsburg and Mannheim, a change of tone started to manifest itself: isolated harbingers of the critique to come. A reviewer described his harmony as 'full', 'strong', 'unexpected' and 'elevating'. The quality represented by the third adjective – not here intended as criticism – would soon start to cause trouble.[10] His musical language, maturing rapidly, almost always attracted praise, but the praise was often now accompanied by reservations. In 1778, a Parisian reviewer noted the 'richness of ideas and motifs' in the first two movements of an unnamed symphony, but the counterpoint on show in the third was 'the kind of music that may interest the mind without ever touching the heart'.[11]

Mozart was certainly well aware of this issue. In a letter dated 28 December 1782, he described three new piano concertos as: 'a happy medium between what's too difficult and too easy'. He continued: 'there are passages here and there that only connoisseurs can fully appreciate, yet the common listener will find them satisfying as well'.[12] Audience reactions suggested that the compromise was effective in instrumental genres, especially those involving his own instrument, the piano. A young amateur pianist in Berlin was successful in executing the 'emotional passages' and the 'peculiar traits' of a composer who occasionally delights in the 'strangest paradoxes'. Pointedly, however, the critic observed that what might work in a few passages of a concerto might not succeed in *Don Giovanni*.[13]

An exception to the generally favourable reception of Mozart's instrumental music was a critique of the string quartets that emerged in 1786. There are indications that Ditters von Dittersdorf was in part responsible for ensuring the circulation of a rather negative appraisal. In his celebrated conversation with Joseph II, as he recalled it many years later, he commended the 'wealth of ideas' in his rival's music but complained that this left the listener 'out of breath'. When the emperor asked him to compare the quartets of Haydn with those of Mozart, he replied that the beauties of the former are immediately apparent, while those of the latter require repeated hearings. Joseph concurred, observing that Haydn's have 'simplicity and beautiful polish', Mozart's 'many tasteful ornaments'.[14] A few months later, an anonymous letter, very much in Dittersdorf's style, was published by Cramer. It made use of a culinary analogy to assert that

[10] MDB, p. 168. [11] MDB, p. 185.

[12] As given in Robert Spaethling, *Mozart's Letters, Mozart's Life* (London: Faber, 2000), p. 336.

[13] MDB, p. 410. The reviewer indicated that he would return to this issue, but he did not do so, as far as is known.

[14] This version of this celebrated conversation appeared in the *Allgemeine musikalische Zeitung* (March 1799), col. 382. Some comments were edited out before the autobiography was published.

Mozart had aimed too high in seeking originality and that his quartets were too highly seasoned: 'whose palate can endure this for long?'[15] In a similar vein, when Dittersdorf wrote to Artaria to offer his own set of quartets for publication, he observed that Mozart's were not to everyone's taste, 'owing to their overwhelming and unrelenting artfulness'.[16] The perception that his chamber music for strings was difficult appears to have had some effect, as the take-up for his quintet subscription was slow. An anonymous contributor to the *Magazin der Musik* in July 1789 summed up what (by now) had become a familiar dichotomy, observing that the quartets dedicated to Haydn display 'a decided leaning towards the difficult and unusual', albeit exemplifying the 'great and elevated ideas ... [of] a bold spirit'.[17]

Respect for the composer, but ambivalence over the level of complexity in his music, eventually became the dominant theme in the reception of his operas, shaping attitudes towards Mozart in his final years. At its premiere, *Die Entführung aus dem Serail* was received with great enthusiasm, the composer absolved of responsibility for the shortcomings of Christoph Friedrich Bretzner's libretto. A review in Johann Friedrich Schink's *Dramaturgische Fragmente* (Graz, 1782) noted that it had attracted much applause. Professing ignorance of technical matters, the writer was looking for music that 'affects the human heart' rather than mere 'ear-tickling', on which count he was not disappointed.[18] Mozart proudly informed his father on 6 December 1783 that his opera was being performed in Prague and Leipzig 'with the greatest applause'.[19] There is no reason to doubt its popular success, but even at this early stage hints that its difficulty might be an obstacle for some listeners were starting to emerge. An evaluator of Pasquale Bondini's production confessed that the music was too 'artificial' for his taste, while according to the *Magazin der Sächsischen Geschichte* (Dresden, 1785), the opera succeeded despite being 'somewhat heavily set'.[20]

A fully formed critique of Mozart as an opera composer emerged only in the autumn of 1788, following a renewal of interest in *Figaro* and *Don Giovanni*. The premiere of the former in 1786 had been a highly politicized affair, owing to the rivalry between the opera buffa and the Singspiel

---

[15] Karl Friedrich Cramer, *Magazin der Musik* (1787), p. 1273.

[16] Hubert Unverricht, *Carl von Dittersdorf: Briefe, ausgewählte Urkunden und Akten* (Tutzing: Hans Schneider, 2008), p. 85.

[17] MDB, p. 349. It is hard to know what to make of the report in the *Journal des Luxus und der Moden* (June, 1788; MDB, pp. 317–19), which describes how, despite execrable amateur performances, a piano quartet simply *had* to please owing to its composer's name.

[18] MDB, p. 210.   [19] MBA, vol. 3, p. 295; LMF, p. 862.   [20] MDB, pp. 218, 234.

troupes, and its impact was limited. *Don Giovanni's* success in Prague was not immediately replicated elsewhere, and its Vienna performance run was adversely affected by the Austro-Turkish war.[21] At the end of 1788, however, there was a distinct up-turn in the fortunes of both works, which started to appear regularly in the schedules of opera houses, at least in German-speaking cities. Over the next three years, a series of reviews in theatre journals, more discursive than those seen hitherto, resulted in something approaching a unified view of Mozart's achievements as a composer for the stage, easily the most detailed appraisal of his work to appear during his lifetime. The tone of this critique, while admiring, was also carping. The discourse revolved around a substantial menu of overdone virtues: fertile invention (too many themes); rich orchestration (too many wind instruments); inventive modulation (too many rapid or distant key changes); and elaborate melodies (too many notes). With few exceptions, critics characterized the problem as a surfeit of excellence, claiming that audiences were not being served an inedible meal so much as a bewildering excess of gourmet delights.

The premise was that Mozart deserved respect as a composer of outstanding talent – the word genius appears so frequently as to debase its currency. Rhetorical hyperbole abounds. From the day that Adam chomped into his apple to the Congress of Reichenbach in 1790 at the end of the Austro-Turkish War, nothing finer than *Don Giovanni* had appeared.[22] But the accompanying bone of contention never varied: the composer's failure to control his tendency to write in a fashion challenging to the average music lover. That the composer's music had depth was generally acknowledged, and hidden beauties in the score, liable to surface only after repeated hearings, were a positive corollary. That was Goethe's experience. On 22 December 1785, he explained his initially cool response to *Die Entführung aus dem Serail* as an expression of his contempt for the text, but because everyone was heaping praise on the music, he persisted, and quickly modified his opinion.[23]

Some critics defined difficulty as textural complexity. From the perspective of a dramatist, Baron Adolf Knigge was worried by the density of the finales in *Figaro*, which in his view hindered singers from projecting distinctly and acting effectively. In an accompanying review of the

---

[21] For an account of the politics affecting the early reception of these two operas, see Ian Woodfield, *Cabals and Satires: Mozart's Comic Operas in Vienna* (Oxford: Oxford University Press, 2018).
[22] MDB, p. 380.   [23] MDB, p. 258.

music, highly laudatory in tone, Bernhard Anselm Weber confessed that he found the Act-3 sextet 'a little obscure and elusive'.[24]

Given the limited time available to rehearse, a poor first performance sometimes posed an obstacle to the initial reception of a challenging work. At the first night of *Così fan tutte*, a member of the audience felt that some of the singers had not mastered their roles.[25] Her reaction to Mozart's music was exactly in line with the prevailing consensus: too learned to be agreeable.[26] National stereotypes also tended to intrude, reinforced by the growing dominance of Singspiel versions of Mozart's Italian operas. Knigge took the view that few Italian singers had the dramatic gifts to do justice to *Figaro*.[27] Wind players came in for especially harsh criticism. A graphic description of their difficulties in *Die Entführung*, unable (save for two horns) to cope with their parts, referred to 'lamentable howling', enough to make one grind one's teeth.[28] A distinctive aspect of Mozart's operatic style, too demanding for many contemporaries, was its harmonic language. Knigge (or his musical advisor Weber) commented on the frequency of modulations and their enharmonic nature. He felt that the use of the augmented sixth chord was overdone, to the extent that the 'great sensation' of this harmony, sparingly used, was losing its effect on listeners.[29]

A criticism of a more practical nature, already current in 1786, was that Mozart scored his arias too heavily for singers' voices. Knigge, having discussed the matter with Weber, opined of *Die Entführung aus dem Serail*: 'The composer has been too loquacious with the wind instruments. Instead of only reinforcing the melody where that is required, and supporting the harmony as a whole, they often darken the former and confuse the latter, prevent simple beautiful singing and disturb the singer's delivery'.[30] Schink, reviewing *Don Giovanni*, felt that the voice should 'float gently along on the stream of accompaniment' and certainly not 'scream away' above the instruments.[31]

The overall effect of this accumulation of riches was a musical experience during which listeners were liable to start to feel overwhelmed. A reviewer wondered whether the music of *Die Entführung aus dem Serail* 'loses some

---

[24] MDB, p. 344.

[25] David Black, 'Report of the First Performance of *Così fan tutte*', contributed by Ivo Cerman, *Mozart: New Documents*, compiled by Dexter Edge and David Black, first published 12 June 2014, corrected 26 September 2017, http://sites.google.com/site/mozartdocuments.

[26] 'On a donné aujourd'hui un nouvel Opera dont la Musique de Mozart, est si savante qu'elle n'est pas du tout agréable.'

[27] MDB, p. 343.   [28] MDB, p. 333.   [29] MDB, p. 328.   [30] MDB, p. 328.   [31] MDB, p. 356.

of its effect from this almost extravagant over-abundance of ideas'.[32]
A dissenting and perceptive voice commended Mozart's control of pacing,
through the careful use of musical punctuation and pauses.[33] The most
telling objection to complexity of whatever kind, though, was that it
precluded the expression of true feeling; while perhaps acceptable to
a connoisseur, it would put off the man in the street. Of *Figaro*, a Berlin
critic wrote: 'How interesting for those that understand; how grand, how
overwhelming, how enchanting the harmony! For the general public too?
That is another question.'[34]

Mozart was very free with his opinions of musicians in his letters, but
he rarely recorded his reactions to what others said or wrote about him.
As far as is known, the only critique of his operas in his possession was the
one in Knigge's *Dramaturgische Blätter* (1789). Its review of *Le nozze di
Figaro* on 18 May is a rare example of unqualified enthusiasm for one of
his stage works, perhaps the reason why he acquired (and kept) a copy.[35]
Its list of music to admire was a long one: Figaro's arias, Cherubino's two
'delicious' songs, those of the Countess, the letter duettino, the charming
choruses, the conclusion of Act 3, Barbarina's cavatina, the trios in Act 1
and 2, and the Act 2 finale. A surprising inclusion, an individual melody
rather than a complete piece, was the moment in the Act 1 trio when
Basilio introduces the misogynistic words 'Ja so machen alle Schönen'
('Così fan tutte le belle'), hailed as 'a veritable stroke of genius'. It would
be quite understandable if sheer relief at finally receiving an appraisal free
from demoralizing caveats had prompted Mozart to adopt this title for
his next opera. The slightly obsessive use of his acknowledged 'Geniezug'
as the much-repeated main theme of the overture of *Così fan tutte* might
then have come with a touch of irony.

---

[32] NMD, p. 58.   [33] MDB, p. 355.   [34] MDB, p. 372.   [35] MDB, p. 345.

CHAPTER 29

Biographical and Critical Traditions

Simon P. Keefe

Extended biographical and critical writing on Mozart's life and work began soon after his death in 1791 and has flourished ever since. A large body of correspondence, reception-related documents, autographs and early editions, set against the backdrop of Mozart's totemic status in Western culture, has provided ample material and incentive for scholarly investigation, evaluation and analysis.

Three of the earliest writings on Mozart published in the 1790s, by Friedrich Schlichtegroll, Franz Niemetschek and Friedrich Rochlitz, as well as Georg von Nissen's *Biographie W. A. Mozart's* thirty years later, had a pronounced impact on the biographical tradition.[1] Schlichtegroll's 6,000-word obituary (1793) relied on testimony from those who knew Mozart personally, as he himself did not. Obtaining information, stories and anecdotes primarily from Salzburg sources, including Albert von Mölk who consulted Mozart's sister Nannerl, Schlichtegroll emphasized Mozart's childlike qualities (as well as activities in his childhood years), an orientation resonating in many biographies up to the present. Niemetschek (1798), reliant on Schlichtegroll for material on Mozart's early career, devoted more attention than his predecessor to Mozart's decade in Vienna, 1781–91, among other things documenting impressions of Mozart in action:

> The theatre [in Prague in January 1787] had never been so full of people as on this occasion; never a stronger, more unanimous delight as that awoken by his heavenly playing. We did not know what we should admire most, whether the extraordinary compositions, or the extraordinary playing; both

---

[1] See Schlichtegroll, 'Johannes Chrysostomos Wolfgang Gottlieb Mozart', in *Nekrolog aus das Jahr 1791* (Gotha, 1793), pp. 82–112; Niemetschek, *Life of Mozart* (1798), trans. Helen Mautner (London: Hyman, 1956); Rochlitz, as given in Maynard Solomon, 'The Rochlitz Anecdotes: Issues of Authenticity in Early Mozart Biography', in Cliff Eisen (ed.), *Mozart Studies* (Oxford: Clarendon Press, 1991), pp. 1–59; and Nissen, *Biographie W. A Mozart's* (1828) (Hildesheim: Georg Olms, 1991).

together made a complete impression on our souls similar to a sweet bewitchment.[2]

A proud, patriotic Czech, Niemetschek developed the still-persistent narrative of Mozart's full and proper appreciation in Prague not in Vienna. In 1798–1801, Rochlitz published a series of anecdotes about Mozart in the nascent *Allgemeine musikalische Zeitung*. Supposedly based on personal memories and on observations of others close to Mozart, Rochlitz freely mixed fact with imaginative fiction, often embroidering (without acknowledgement) information from Niemetschek. In spite of demonstrable falsities, the anecdotes need not be considered an entirely malign influence on subsequent writers: the famous accounts of the Requiem, for example, intensifying Mozart's compositional process and emotional fragility relative to Niemetschek's version and accentuating the commissioner's otherworldly qualities, ultimately enhanced nineteenth-century interest in the composer by providing a compelling, fatalistic story to coincide with the end of his life.[3] Mozart's widow, Constanze, provided information for Niemetschek and perhaps Rochlitz too, but exerted most influence in the biography set in train by her second husband Nissen (1828). Although it was cobbled together by Constanze and her friend Johann Heinrich Feuerstein after Nissen's death and cuts an ungainly figure, it gave an important first airing to large amounts of family correspondence, which has remained central to biographical endeavours ever since.

Much nineteenth-century writing took the inseparability of Mozart's life and music as a starting point. Alexander Ulïbïshev, who published a three-volume biography of Mozart (in French) in 1843, laid his cards on the table in the preface: 'To my very great surprise, I discovered between Mozart's works and the biographical circumstances attached to them, the same kind of correlation as that that strikes all minds and fills us with such astonishment in the history of the Requiem.'[4] Differences between Mozart's 'Haydn' string quartets and operatic music exposed links between life and works according to Ulïbïshev:

> As ever, the best explanation of the musician lies in the man himself. Was not Mozart, that merry companion, of a thoughtful disposition; was he not given to a dreamy imagination and predisposed to melancholy? Was not the

[2] Niemetschek, *Life of Mozart*, p. 36 (translation adapted).

[3] See Simon P. Keefe, *Mozart's Requiem: Reception, Work, Completion* (Cambridge: Cambridge University Press, 2012), pp. 16–19.

[4] Alexandre Oulibicheff (Alexander Ulïbïshev), *Nouvelle Biographie de Mozart* (Moscow: Auguste Semen, 1843), 3 vols., vol. 1, pp. x–xi (my translation).

poet-musician who exuded epic and tragic grandeur in the choruses of
Idomeneo, and who poured out such glowing passion in the arias of
Belmonte [in *Entführung*], able to carry out in his head the most complicated musical calculations? Did not all the contrasts of human nature
converge within this one man!⁵

For Otto Jahn too, author of a landmark biography in 1856, man and
musician were fused. Concerning the Requiem:

> human emotion, religious belief, and artistic conception go hand in hand in
> fullest harmony. On this unity rests the significance of the Requiem, for on
> this ground alone could Mozart's individuality arrive at full expression,
> and – working freely and boldly, yet never without consciousness of the
> limits within which it moved – produce the masterpiece which reveals at
> every point the innermost spirit of its author. In this sense we may endorse
> his own expression, that he wrote the Requiem for himself; it is the truest
> and most genuine expression of his nature as an artist; and is his imperish-
> able monument.⁶

Authors of fiction also promoted the merging of life and work.
Eduard Mörike's *Mozart auf der Reise nach Prag* (Mozart's Journey to
Prague, 1856), which caught Mozart on route to the premiere of *Don
Giovanni* and charming a distinguished family, connected his relaxed
and earnest moods with both his creative process and the nature of
music composed.⁷ Dramatic accounts of the commissioning and composition of the Requiem – including explicitly fictional tales from c. 1830
to 1860 – directly link Mozart's putative state of mind with the music
written.⁸ And the coming together of life and art in E.T.A. Hoffmann's
'Don Juan: Eine fabelhafte Begebenheit, die sich mit einem reisendem
Enthusiasten zugetragen' (Don Juan: a Fabulous Incident which Befell
a Travelling Enthusiast, 1813), which tells of a man attending a performance of *Don Giovanni* and unexpectedly encountering the singer of
Donna Anna in his box, parallels the biographical amalgamation of
Mozart as man and musician. Overwhelmed both by the music of the
opera and his encounter with Donna Anna during Act 1 and the interval,
the narrator explains:

⁵ Oulibicheff, *Mozart*, vol. 3, pp. 23–4; translation from Ian Bent (ed.), *Music Analysis in the Nineteenth
 Century: Volume 1, Fugue, Form and Style* (Cambridge: Cambridge University Press, 1994), p. 299.
⁶ Jahn, *Life of Mozart* (1856), trans. Pauline Townsend (London: Cooper Square Publishers, 1970), 3
 vols., vol. 3, pp. 391–2.
⁷ See Gernot Gruber, *Mozart and Posterity*, trans. R. S. Furness (London: Quartet Books, 1991), pp.
 147–8.
⁸ See Keefe, *Mozart's Requiem*, pp. 14–34.

> In Donna Anna's scene [in Act 2] I felt myself enveloped by a soft warm breath [which is how her earlier presence in the box was described]; its intoxicating spirit passed over me and I trembled with bliss. My eyes closed involuntarily and a burning kiss seemed to be imprinted on my lips. But the kiss was a long-held note of eternal passionate longing.

The Donna Anna character, deeply affected by her role that night, died a few hours later at 2 a.m., the precise moment that the narrator – back in his box to contemplate the masterwork in a now-empty theatre – experienced a 'warm electrifying breath' and the 'floating tones of an ethereal orchestra' as Anna sang the aria 'Non mi dir'.[9]

Mozart's 'classic' or 'romantic' status also became a critical theme in the nineteenth century. The common perception of Mozart initially as a romantic then as a classical figure simplifies nineteenth-century reception activity, even if the notion of Mozart as romantic did fade as the century progressed. Stendhal (1817) and E.T.A. Hoffmann (1810) provided quintessential romantic offerings. For Stendhal, Mozart's music is characterized by a yearning quality:

> One longs to hear one of his songs, from afar, deep in the red deciduous forest, played upon the horn. Mozart's gentle thoughts, and his shy happiness, precisely share the atmosphere of the autumnal day, where a gentle vapour clothes the charms of the countryside in sadness, and where the sun itself appears to shine in the woe of parting.[10]

And Hoffmann struck a similar note, albeit detecting stronger emotions at first: 'Mozart leads us deep into the realm of spirits. Dread lies all about us, but withholds its torments and becomes more an intimation of infinity. We hear the gentle voices of love and melancholy, the nocturnal spirit-world dissolves into a purple shimmer, and with inexpressible yearning we follow the flying figures beckoning to us from the clouds'.[11] Soon after Mozart's death, Niemetschek (1798) captured 'the real touchstone of [Mozart's] classical worth' in the need to listen to his music many times in order fully to appreciate it, and Ignaz Arnold (1803) remarked on the 'immense richness' and 'beauties' that are 'only evident through repeated study', again implying classic status.[12] By mid-century, Mozart was

---

[9] Quotations from R. Murray Shafer, *E.T.A. Hoffmann and Music* (Toronto: University of Toronto Press, 1975), pp. 67, 72–3.

[10] As given in Gruber, *Mozart and Posterity*, p. 114.

[11] Quoted from David Charlton (ed.), *E.T.A Hoffmann's Musical Writings:* Kreisleriana, The Poet and the Composer, *Music Criticism*, trans. Martyn Clarke (Cambridge: Cambridge University Press, 1989), pp. 237–8.

[12] Niemetschek, *Life of Mozart*, p. 55; Arnold, *Mozarts Geist* (Erfurt: Henningschen Buchhandlung, 1803), pp. 196–97.

regularly characterized as a classic in critical and scholarly discourse: in the 'cheerfulness, repose and grace' identified by Robert Schumann (1834); in Raphael Georg Kiesewetter's identification of the 'epoch of Mozart and Haydn' as a 'golden age' (1846); and in Jahn's biography (1856) and Ludwig Köchel's catalogue of Mozart's complete works (1862).[13] For Franz Brendel, in an influential historical volume (1852), Mozart was the classical figure par excellence, representing the beautiful in music, where the ideal and real and the mental and sensual simultaneously manifest themselves. As a 'culmination point', Mozart represented 'the most beautiful moment of development in all history'.[14] The philosopher Søren Kierkegaard (1843), while reluctant to assign classic status to entire repertories, was more than happy to accord it to *Don Giovanni*, the artistic work he revered above all others.[15]

Critical analysis of Mozart's music also flourished in the nineteenth century outside mainstream biographical work. Arnold (1803) offered, inter alia, protracted discussion of Mozart's instrumentation and orchestration, grounded in a notion of 'instrumental economy', and Simon Sechter (1843) published a sober and rational account of the finale of the 'Jupiter' Symphony that focussed on contrapuntal and thematic procedures.[16] In order to convey the 'true expression' of the first movement of the D minor string quartet K. 421, Jérôme-Joseph de Momigny (1806) set to Mozart's music the words of a distraught Dido about to lose Aeneas, with interjections from Aeneas as well.[17] And highbrow nineteenth-century musical journals such as the *Allgemeine musikalische Zeitung* devoted space to technical and aesthetic discussion of Mozart's works.

Analytical and critical discourse on Mozart's music developed rapidly from the early twentieth century onwards. (For recent theoretical and analytical trends, see Chapter 30.) Georges de Saint Foix (with Théodore de Wyzewa for the first two volumes of the five-volume set), Hermann

[13] See John Daverio, 'Mozart in the Nineteenth Century', in Simon P. Keefe (ed.), *The Cambridge Companion to Mozart* (Cambridge: Cambridge University Press, 2003), p. 178; Gruber, *Mozart and Posterity*, pp. 139, 151.

[14] Brendel, *Geschichte der Musik in Italien, Deutschland und Frankreich* (Leipzig: Hinze, 1852), pp. 502, 287, 322–3 (my translations).

[15] Kierkegaard, *Either/Or: A Fragment of Life*, ed. Victor Eremita, trans. Alastair Hannay (London: Penguin, 1992), pp. 61–135, at 63–4.

[16] See Arnold, *Mozarts Geist*. For Sechter's analysis, see Bent (ed.), *Music Analysis in the Nineteenth Century*, vol. 1, pp. 82–96.

[17] Momigny, *Cours complet d'harmonie et de composition* (Paris, 1806), 2 vols., vol. 2, pp. 388–403 and figure 30.

Abert and Alfred Einstein led the way in the biographical arena.[18] The combined biographical-stylistic study of Saint-Foix and Wyzewa (1912–46) is a systematic survey of Mozart's oeuvre that insistently pursues his status as a summative figure in music history who absorbed numerous influences along the way. Abert's magisterial biography, probably the greatest since Jahn's, includes both penetrating musical observations obtained from close readings of scores and rich historical, contextual and stylistic discussion (for example, on opera seria, opera buffa, *tragédie lyrique* and Singspiel). Setting his stall on revising and expanding Jahn in light of new historical orientations and the greater number of musical sources available than in the mid nineteenth century, Abert retained Jahn's belief in the inseparability of Mozart's life and music: 'it is the same forces that affect his outer life and his work as a composer . . . The true wellspring of his life was always his work as an artist'.[19] Not the least of Abert's achievements is to evaluate perennially controversial biographical elements – including the break from Salzburg Archbishop Colloredo in spring 1781 and Constanze's relationship with her husband – in fair and balanced ways. Einstein is much less generous than Abert towards Constanze, whom he characterizes as uneducated, unreliable and superficial – in short a wholly inappropriate spouse for a genius like Mozart – and tends towards well-worn biographical tropes about Mozart's naivety, disconnection from ordinary life and sense of impending death in 1791. As he explains:

> Mozart died in his thirty-sixth year; yet he went through all the stages of human life, simply passing through them faster than ordinary mortals. At thirty he was both childlike and wise; he combined the highest creative power with the highest understanding of his art; he observed the affairs of life and he saw behind them; and he experienced before his end that feeling of immanent completion that consists in the loss of all love for life.

On the whole, though, Einstein's musical insights are the equal of Abert's. And his final sentence, written in 1944, is a poignant reminder of the era in which he lived and worked (by now as an exiled German Jew in the US): 'It is as though the world-spirit wished to show that here [in Mozart's music] is pure sound, conforming to a weightless cosmos, triumphant over all chaotic earthliness, spirit of the world-spirit.'[20] Indeed, firmly held personal,

[18] Saint-Foix and Wyzewa, *W.-A. Mozart: sa vie musicale and son oeuvre* (Paris: Desclée de Brouwer, 1912–1946), 5 vols.; Hermann Abert, *W. A. Mozart* (1919–1921), trans. Stewart Spencer, ed. Cliff Eisen (New Haven and London: Yale University Press, 2007); Einstein, *Mozart: His Character, His Work* (1945), trans. Arthur Mendel and Nathan Broder (London: Panther Arts, 1971).
[19] Abert, *W. A. Mozart*, p. 729.
[20] Einstein, *Mozart: His Character, His Work*, pp. 76–88 (on Constanze), 80, 487 (quotations).

political and disciplinary views – including Brigid Brophy, Wolfgang Hildesheimer, Georg Knepler and Maynard Solomon's respectively Freudian, psychological, Marxist and psychoanalytical convictions[21] – have often resulted in vibrant contributions to the biographical literature.

From the mid twentieth century onwards, important critical activities have included the compilation of a new complete edition of Mozart's oeuvre; the investigation more systematically than hitherto of compositional processes and chronological issues; and the situating of Mozart's achievements in musical, dramatic, social, cultural and historical contexts that are simultaneously richer and more refined than in earlier scholarship. The lengthy gestation period and huge scope of the *Neue Mozart-Ausgabe* (New Mozart Edition), from 1955 to 2007 with more than 120 volumes (plus critical reports) published by upwards of seventy editors, inevitably created difficulties: some inconsistency in primary sources prioritized for editions produced problems not dissimilar to those encountered in the nineteenth-century *Alte Mozart-Ausgabe*;[22] and the belief nowadays that eighteenth-century composers neither desired nor strove for a *Fassung letzter Hand* – a final, unalterable version of a work – compromises any aspirations towards 'definitive' texts. But the NMA still represents a remarkable, collective accomplishment, advancing compositional, philological and performance-related knowledge about Mozart and his music and providing a solid foundation for hermeneutic work. Research into Mozart's handwriting, the types of paper used in autograph scores, and his sketches, drafts and fragments has increased and refined our appreciation of his working methods: we now know from studying autograph material that a number of major works (such as the piano concertos K. 449 in E♭, K. 488 in A, K. 503 in C, K. 537 in D and K. 595 in B♭) were begun a year or two ahead of their eventual completion dates, having been set aside in the intervening period, and that Mozart sketched, drafted and revised music considerably more than generally assumed up to the mid twentieth century. Thus, compositional processes and chronologies are often shown to be less fluent and more complex than previously thought.[23] And thorough, incisive contextualization of

[21] See Brigid Brophy, *Mozart the Dramatist* (New York: Harcourt, Brace and World, 1964); Hildesheimer, *Mozart* (1977), trans. Marion Faber (New York: Vintage, 1983); Georg Knepler, *Wolfgang Amadé Mozart* (1991), trans. J. Bradford Robinson (Cambridge: Cambridge University Press, 1994); Solomon, *Mozart: A Life* (New York: HarperCollins, 1995).

[22] See Cliff Eisen, 'The Old and New Mozart Editions', *Early Music*, 19 (1991), pp. 513–32.

[23] For important secondary literature in these areas, see for example Alan Tyson, *Mozart: Studies of the Autograph Scores* (Cambridge, MA: Harvard University Press, 1987); Wolfgang Plath, 'Beiträge zur Mozart-Autographie II: Schriftchronologie 1770-1780', *Mozart-Jahrbuch 1976/77*, pp. 131–73;

Mozart's instrumental and vocal outputs, partially motivated by attempts to demythologize him, have enhanced understandings of the man and musician: his achievements are those not of an ethereal genius disconnected from everyday life but of an exceptionally talented individual keenly attuned to the demands and practicalities of late eighteenth-century performing and compositional worlds and of the people and institutions inhabiting them.[24]

In the early twenty-first century Mozart competes for scholarly attention with a wider range of classical, popular and world music than ever before. But with a historical breadth, depth and methodological sophistication to rival work on any other individual musician, Mozart scholarship can build on its venerable past by continuing to shape biographical and critical agendas of the musicological future.

Ulrich Konrad, *Mozarts Schaffensweise: Studien zu den Werkautographen, Skizzen und Entwürfen* (Göttingen: Vandenhoeck and Ruprecht, 1992).

[24] For a representative sample of work from the last twenty-five years or so, see Simon P. Keefe (ed.), *Mozart* (Farnham: Ashgate Publishing, 2015).

CHAPTER 30

Mozart in Theory and Analysis

Stephen Rumph

Modern theories of common-practice music owe a considerable debt to Mozart. Over the last hundred years, his works have provided prize examples and, in some cases, primary stimuli for new analytical models. This chapter surveys four areas in which Mozart's music has figured significantly: theories of deep structure, form, musical topics and galant schemata. My brief sketch cannot hope to review the many distinguished analyses of individual works (the writings of Georges de Saint-Foix and Théodore de Wyzewa, Donald Tovey, Edward Dent and Charles Rosen are among the notable absences). The discussion will focus instead on scholars who have used Mozart's music to construct general theoretical systems.

Deep Structures

Much twentieth-century theory has been dedicated to excavating structures that lie below the thematic surface, and Mozart's Symphony in G minor K. 550 has been a favourite digging site. Heinrich Schenker proposed the most influential depth model, which he demonstrated in a classic analysis of K. 550 in *Das Meisterwerk in der Musik*, vol. 2 (Munich: Drei Masken Verlag, 1926). According to Schenker, the pitch structure of tonal music consisted of hierarchical realizations of a fundamental structure (*Ursatz*), a î-ŝ-î bass arpeggiation over which the fundamental line (*Urlinie*) descends from the third, fifth or octave. This deep structure is prolonged across the entire movement but unfolds at different time spans at the middle- and foreground levels. Reductive counterpoint reveals this underlying counterpoint, distinguishing structural chord tones from passing and neighbour tones. The lowest melodic notes in bars 1–9 of the Symphony in G minor thus unfold a ŝ-â-ŝ foreground line; at the middle-ground level, this same line functions as a ŝ-â-î descent in the secondary key, B♭; while at the background level, the opening theme initiates a $\hat{5}$-$\hat{4}$-$\hat{3}$-$\hat{2}$-$\hat{1}$ line that is not completed until bar 276.

Schenker was an unabashed elitist who felt burdened to save Mozart from the shallow accolades of a mass audience. His analysis of K. 550 probes below the accessible surface for long-range voice-leading progressions, 'paths whose confluences and crosscurrents are the only relationships in the world of tones that create musical action and tension'.[1] Schenker was guided by the metaphor of the musical work as an organism, as when he notes how the melodic leap of a sixth in bar 3 grows from the viola accompaniment where the same interval is 'planted in the inner voices, as if in a clump of soil' (p. 66). Despite his indifference to the expressive qualities of Mozart's thematic material, his penetrating analysis portrays an inner drama in which every isolated note and line embodies the teeming will of the tonal structure.

Rudolf Réti enlisted the Symphony in G minor in another deep-structural theory in *The Thematic Process in Music* (New York: Macmillan, 1951). Réti found the hidden source of musical unity in an underlying web of thematic interconnections. His analysis of K. 550 aimed to show the synergy between two 'form-building forces', the outer grouping of musical ideas and their inner motivic relationships. Mozart's symphony, which pairs exquisite formal construction with dense motivic work, served Réti well. He traced the wide-ranging transformation of two motivic ideas from the opening of the symphony, the semitone appoggiatura (bars 1–2) and the rising six (bar 3), both within and across movements. Like Schenker, Réti showed little interest in the character of the thematic material. His analysis overlooks, for instance, the origins of the semitone appoggiatura in the operatic 'sigh', a figure of pathos that pervades many works in a similar minor-mode vein. In his pursuit of inner substance, Réti ignored the overt expressivity of Mozart's symphony, and few readers will readily agree that 'the whole outer symmetry is but a charming attire, almost a camouflage' (p. 121).

The quest for deep structure took a linguistic turn in Leonard Bernstein's 1973 Norton Lectures, published as *The Unanswered Question: Six Talks at Harvard* (Cambridge, MA: Harvard University Press, 1976). Bernstein sought a musical equivalent to Noam Chomsky's generative grammar, in which linguistic utterances represent surface transformations of underlying structures. Chomsky sought to describe the

[1] Heinrich Schenker, *The Masterwork in Music* (1926), ed. and trans. William Drabkin (Mineola, NY: Dover Publications, 2014), vol. 2, p. 59.

innate mental apparatus that allowed children to master grammatical rules and generate an infinite number of new utterances. Bernstein proposed an analogous universal competence for musical 'language', adducing the Symphony in G minor as his primary case study. Bernstein's most convincing demonstration is an analysis of the metrical structure of Mozart's opening theme, which can be heard in pairs of either strong-weak or weak-strong bars. The ambiguity, as Bernstein showed, arises from the brevity of the 'vamping' introduction: had Mozart provided either a two- or three-bar introduction, the hypermeter would have been clearly established. Without a full introduction, the metrical structure remains undetermined, just as Chomsky's famous phrase 'the shooting of the hunters' remains ambiguous without reference to a deep structure (either 'the hunters shoot' or 'they shoot the hunters').

Fred Lerdahl and Ray Jackendoff undertook a more rigorous adaptation of Chomskyian linguistics in *A Generative Theory of Tonal Music* (Cambridge, MA: The MIT Press, 1983), which trades heavily on both K. 550 and the Sonata in A major K. 331. The authors defined the goal of their theory as the 'formal description of the musical intuitions of a listener who is experienced in a musical idiom' (p. 1). They proposed a system of rules for analysing four parameters – grouping and metrical structure, and time-span and prolongational reduction. 'Well-formedness rules' (WFR), as in linguistics, determine grammatically correct structures. The authors also posit distinctively aesthetic 'preference rules' (PR), which discriminate among multiple correct interpretations of a musical structure. For example, WFRs dictate that the opening of K. 550 must be segmented into a hierarchy of non-overlapping groups, in which the lower-level groups fill out the higher-level ones. One PR inclines the listener to assign group boundaries that correspond to longer timespans between attack-points, as in bar 3 or, on a lower level, between the third and fourth notes of the melody. While critics have questioned both the methodology and musical intuitions of Lerdahl and Jackendoff, *A Generative Theory* remains a compelling attempt to describe the mental structures responsible for musical competence and analysis.

Formenlehre

The turn of the twenty-first century saw a dramatic rebirth of *Formenlehre*, the theory of form, with two ambitious studies of the Viennese classical repertory. William Caplin's *Classical Form: A Theory of Formal Functions for the Instrumental Music of Haydn, Mozart, and Beethoven* (New York:

Oxford University Press, 1998) was followed soon after by James Hepokoski and Warren Darcy's exhaustive *Elements of Sonata Theory: Norms, Types, and Deformations in the Late-Eighteenth-Century Sonata* (New York: Oxford University 2006). Systematic theories of musical form, notably undertaken by A. B. Marx, Hugo Riemann and Hugo Leichtentritt, had dwindled by the end of the twentieth century, and analysis of Viennese classical forms had tended towards ad hoc description, as in Charles Rosen's *Sonata Forms* (New York: Norton, 1980) or James Webster's article 'Sonata Form' for the *New Grove Dictionary of Music and Musicians* (1980). The new studies renewed the search for fundamental principles, elaborating distinct frameworks for understanding the formal structures of Mozart and his contemporaries.

William Caplin proposed a theory of formal functions, drawing on the work of Arnold Schoenberg and his student Erwin Ratz. Caplin's analysis of lower-level thematic forms has proved most influential. He distinguished two principal types: the period (ABAB'), a balanced form in which both halves (antecedent and consequent) consist of two contrasting ideas (see the opening theme of K. 331); and the more dynamic sentence (AA'B), which begins with the sequential presentation of a single motive, followed by a more fragmentary continuation leading to a cadence (the opening theme of the Piano Sonata in G major K. 283). Caplin also identified hybrid forms that mix these functional elements, such as an antecedent (period) followed by a continuation or cadential passage (sentence). Indeed, his theory rests upon this independence of formal functions from their position within a formal schema. In a later essay, Caplin classified the various thematic elements as 'beginning', 'middle' and 'ending' functions, regardless of their position in a movement; his theory thus comprehends form as a complex, multi-layered temporal experience.[2] Also central to *Classical Form* is the distinction between 'loose- and tight-knit organization', judged by such criteria as harmonic and grouping structure, tonality and motivic uniformity.

Hepokoski and Darcy drew upon the reader-response theory of Wolfgang Iser and Hans-Robert Jauss for their 'dialogic' model of sonata form. They described sonata form as a series of cadential goals that individual movements achieve with varying levels of predictability. Most originally, they called attention to the 'medial caesura', the dramatic pause that punctuates the end of the transition and heralds the secondary theme.

---

[2] Caplin, 'What Are Formal Functions?' in Pieter Bergé (ed.), *Musical Form, Forms and Formenlehre: Three Methodological Reflections* (Leuven: Leuven University Press, 2009), pp. 21–40.

The second crucial goal is the 'essential expositional closure', the first convincing perfect authentic cadence in the new key followed by new material (renamed the 'essential structural closure' when it returns transposed in the recapitulation to confirm the tonic). Each formal event has a hierarchy of variants, beginning with a 'first-default setting' (for example, a half cadence in V for the medial caesura) and descending through less common options (a half cadence in I, a full cadence in V and so forth). Hepokoski and Darcy emphasized that each new realization of sonata form is heard in dialogue with other movements to which it conforms more or less closely. 'Deformations', examples that depart from any recognizable variant, prompt the listener to seek a hermeneutic explanation. Hepokoski thus suggested that Mozart's truncated overture to *Idomeneo*, which fails to reprise the secondary and closing themes, might be heard as a metaphor for analogous calamities within the drama (the sack of Troy, Ilia's shipwreck).[3]

Mozart enjoys an outsized place in *Elements of Sonata Theory*. Over a quarter of the book is devoted to Mozart's concertos and, as William Drabkin noted, almost three quarters of the printed examples come from Mozart's scores.[4] Arguably, Mozart's formal designs illustrate Hepokoski and Darcy's model more clearly than Haydn's quirkier, less uniform procedures. Yet this dependence on Mozart might raise the suspicion that one composer's music has served to some extent as an ideal type for an entire repertory; certainly, the chapters devoted to concerto form abandon any claim to universality. Nevertheless, 'sonata theory' has become an indispensable tool, and perhaps even the dominant paradigm, for the analysis of late eighteenth-century form.

Topic Theory

Leonard Ratner introduced an influential new approach to Mozart and his contemporaries in *Classic Music: Expression, Form, and Style* (New York: Schirmer Books, 1980). Ratner called attention to the wealth of musical allusions in late eighteenth-century music, which he dubbed 'topics' in a dubious reference to the topoi of classical rhetoric. In deriving their thematic material, as Ratner showed, composers imitated the features of characteristic genres (minuet, aria, fantasia) and styles (learned church counterpoint, brilliant concerto writing, Turkish military music). These

---

[3] Hepokoski, 'Sonata Theory and Dialogic Form', in *Musical Form, Forms and Formenlehre*, pp. 75–7.
[4] William Drabkin, 'Mostly Mozart' (review essay of *Elements of Sonata Form*), *The Musical Times*, 148/4 (2007), pp. 89–100.

topics imported cultural meanings into the musical work, deriving from their associations with social functions and theatrical representation. Topical analysis thus offered a potent rebuttal to the formalism that had characterized modernist reception of Mozart and musical 'classicism'.

Wye Jamison Allanbrook, a student of Ratner, explored the cultural meanings of topics in *Rhythmic Gesture in Mozart: 'Le nozze di Figaro' and 'Don Giovanni'* (Chicago: University of Chicago Press, 1983).[5] Beginning with a rich survey of eighteenth-century dances and meters, Allanbrook identified the pervasive influence of social dance in Mozart's comic operas, drawing out new interpretations of the familiar texts. For example, she showed how Mozart used the flowing 6/8 meter of the *pastorale* to evoke the feminine realm in *Figaro*, a utopian refuge from the coarse martial rhythms of the Count and Figaro. Raymond Monelle also explored the semantic dimension of topics in *The Musical Topic: Hunt, Military and Pastoral* (Bloomington: Indiana University Press, 2006), tracing three important topical traditions from the Middle Ages to the twentieth century.

Kofi Agawu, another Ratner student, initiated a semiotic strain of topic theory in *Playing with Signs: A Semiotic Interpretation of Classic Music* (Princeton: Princeton University Press, 1991), a study inspired by French and Russian structuralism. Agawu categorized topics as 'extroversive' signs, in opposition to the 'introversive' signs of musical syntax, and explored the 'play' between the two types of signs within the tonal organization of individual movements. Robert Hatten incorporated topics within a theory of musical narrative and genre in *Musical Meaning in Beethoven: Markedness, Correlation, and Interpretation* (Bloomington: Indiana University Press, 1994) and *Interpreting Musical Gestures, Topics, and Tropes: Mozart, Beethoven, Schubert* (Bloomington: Indiana University Press, 2004), introducing a theory of topical 'troping' whereby discrete topics form new compounds comparable to the literary tropes of metaphor, metonymy and irony. Stephen Rumph has focussed on the articulation of topics in *Mozart and Enlightenment Semiotics* (Berkeley: University of California Press, 2011), analysing the non-signifying 'figurae', equivalent to linguistic phonemes and distinctive features, which constitute different topics. *The Oxford Handbook of Topic Theory* (2014), edited by Danuta Mirka, contains a wealth of information on the cultural meanings, analysis and reception of topics.

---

[5] Allanbrook offered a broader view of topical representation in her 1994 Bloch lectures, published posthumously as *The Secular Commedia: Comic Mimesis in Late Eighteenth-Century Music*, eds. Mary Ann Smart and Richard Taruskin (Berkeley: University of California Press, 2014).

Mozart's importance to topic theory can hardly be overstated. His quicksilver play with contrasting styles and genres invites topical analysis, and indeed, Ratner deemed Mozart 'the greatest master at mixing and coordinating topics, often in the shortest space'.[6] The first movement of the Piano Sonata in F major K. 332 has become a *locus classicus* for topic theory, with its compact evocations of aria (bars 1–4), learned counterpoint (bars 5–8), courtly minuet (bars 9–12), hunting horns (bars 13–20) and operatic tempests (bars 22–40). Mozart's individual style arguably lends itself better to topical analysis than that of Haydn or Beethoven, who rely less upon the dramatic opposition of contrasting material than upon the sustained development of single themes. Nevertheless, W. Dean Sutcliffe has suggested that topic theory 'has been made in the image of Mozart', cautioning that his compositional practice 'has been taken to represent a more widespread practice to which the theory may not apply'.[7] Yet it could also be argued that topic theory has confined itself too narrowly to the eighteenth century, for the same manner of representation can be found in Wagnerian leitmotifs, Hollywood film cues or pop songs. Topical signification is perhaps best understood as a distinctively modern practice in which musical repertories are extracted from their social enclaves, commodified as signs and circulated within an increasingly democratized musical culture.

Galant Schemata

Mozart has found a home in music cognition studies, thanks to Robert Gjerdingen's *Music in the Galant Style* (Oxford and New York: Oxford University Press, 2007). Gjerdingen elaborated a theory of musical schemata from the 'galant' era (roughly 1720–80), a stylistic designation that is increasingly overwriting the traditional Baroque–Classical division of the eighteenth century. In psychology, schemata refer to mental patterns that allow the mind to organize sensory perception and make sense of new experiences. Gjerdingen's schemata are short contrapuntal progressions for a bass and treble voice that composers realized in a variety of ways. For instance, the Quiescenza schema consists of a tonic pedal in the bass supporting a $\hat{1}$-$\hat{7}\flat$-$\hat{6}$-$\hat{7}$-$\natural\hat{1}$ line (see the opening bars, respectively, of K. 332 and Haydn's Piano Sonata in E♭ Major Hob. XVI/52). The Italian

---

[6] Ratner, *Classic Music*, p. 27.
[7] W. Dean Sutcliffe, 'Topics in Chamber Music', in Danuta Mirka (ed.), *The Oxford Handbook of Topic Theory* (Oxford and New York: Oxford University Press, 2014), p. 119.

composers who disseminated the galant style internalized these schemata by adding voices to instructional bass lines (*partimenti*). The act of composition thus involved skilfully arranging and executing a series of stock formulae, a process that Gjerdingen compared to a figure-skating routine.

Mozart plays a central role in Gjerdingen's work. In his first book, *A Classic Turn of Phrase: Music and the Psychology of Convention* (Philadelphia: University of Pennsylvania Press, 1988), he identified the opening theme of K. 283 as the exemplar of a schema he would name the Meyer, in honour of his teacher Leonard Meyer. The Meyer consists of a $\hat{7}$-$\hat{1}$-$\hat{4}$-$\hat{3}$ melodic line supported by a $\hat{1}$-$\hat{2}$-$\hat{7}$-$\hat{1}$ bass line (in K. 283, the structural notes straddle the bar lines between bars 1–2 and 3–4). In *Music in the Galant Style*, Gjerdingen devoted an entire chapter to the first movement of Mozart's famous Piano Sonata in C major K. 545 in order to demonstrate the Prinner schema, in which a $\hat{6}$-$\hat{5}$-$\hat{4}$-$\hat{3}$ line descends in parallel tenths with a $\hat{4}$-$\hat{3}$-$\hat{2}$-$\hat{1}$ bass. In a later study, Gjerdingen showed how familiarity with the Fonte schema (a descending sequence of $V^{6/5}$-I progressions) authenticated a supposedly corrupt passage in early editions of K. 331.[8] The prominence of Mozart in Gjerdingen's work seems to echo Daniel Heartz's assessment of the composer as 'the ultimate heir and greatest genius of the galant style'.[9]

Gjerdingen's theory has important implications for the analysis and historiography of eighteenth-century music. Viewing the musical work as an assemblage of brief schemata challenges the long-range listening assumed by Schenkerian analysis. Contemporary listeners presumably listened at a more local level, enjoying the parade of formulae rather than straining to follow structural lines as they unfolded across a movement. Schema theory also challenges the image of the lonely genius, casting the eighteenth-century composer instead as a skilled artisan who stitched together common material tastefully. As Gjerdingen emphasized, the *partimento* method was designed to train court composers to compose in an accepted style. While his theory fits with the increasingly deromanticized portrait of Mozart, Beethoven scholars may be chagrined to find the same formulae not only in the composer's early music but also in such revolutionary works as the 'Eroica' Symphony.[10] Finally, Gjerdingen's analysis of the galant style has hastened the demise of the Baroque–Classical periodization of eighteenth-century

---

[8] Gjerdingen, 'Mozart's Obviously Corrupt Minuet', *Music Analysis*, 29 (2010), pp. 61–82.

[9] Daniel Heartz, *Music in European Capitals: The Galant Style, 1720–1780* (New York: Norton, 2003), p. 1008.

[10] See Vasili Byros, 'Meyer's Anvil: Revisiting the Schema Concept', *Music Analysis*, 31 (2012), pp. 273–346.

music, with its awkward 'pre-classical' gap between J. S. Bach and the
Viennese triumvirate.

Conclusion

As this survey has shown, Mozart's music has shouldered a heavy burden in
modern music theory, offering itself to a startling variety of projects.
Despite the divergent and often contradictory claims, each new theorist
has found paragons among the Köchel numbers. Mozart's amenability to
analysis is testimony to the extraordinary balance of clarity and sophistication in every facet of his music. His centrality to theory over the last
hundred years also suggests the extent to which, like Beethoven for an
earlier age, Mozart has become the mirror for modern musical thought.

CHAPTER 31

The Köchel Catalogue

Ulrich Leisinger

Many a votary of Mozart will have wondered about the letter K. (or KV in German) that seems to be inseparably tied to the number of every work of the composer. The 'K.' stands for 'Köchel', perpetuating the name of the author of the 'authoritative' catalogue of Mozart's works, first published in 1862 under the wordy title *Chronologisch-thematisches Verzeichniss sämmtlicher Tonwerke Wolfgang Amade Mozart's. Nebst Angabe der verloren gegangenen, unvollendeten, übertragenen, zweifelhaften und unterschobenen Compositionen desselben* (Chronological-Thematic Catalogue of all the Musical Works of Wolfgang Amadé Mozart. With Reference to the Lost, Incomplete, Arranged, Doubtful and Spurious Works of the Same).[1] (See Table 31.1 for editions of the catalogue published to date.) Contrary to some suppositions, the Köchel catalogue does not represent an infallible documentation of what Mozart wrote during his lifetime, requiring only minimal updating from one generation to the next in order to comply with our growing knowledge of sources and dates. Rather, like all scholarly products in the field of the humanities, it is affected by preconceptions, assumptions and a certain degree of subjectivity, even arbitrariness. To understand the merits and shortcomings of the catalogue it is necessary to bring to mind the conditions under which it was compiled for publication more than 150 years ago and to reflect on the nature of the changes that subsequent editors undertook.

Ludwig Alois Ferdinand Köchel was born in Stein an der Donau, Lower Austria, on 14 January 1800. He studied law in Vienna and soon became tutor to the four sons of Archduke Karl. After fifteen years of service he was ennobled in 1842 and granted a life-long pension that enabled him to live a life as a private scholar. Köchel had manifold interests, inter alia

---

[1] For bibliographical information on the various editions of the Köchel catalogue, see Table 31.1. Where needed, the different editions are identified by superscript numbers, for example K.[6] 173dB = K.[1–3] 183. Information on the editions is derived from the respective prefaces unless otherwise indicated; all translations are my own.

Table 31.1 *Editions of the Köchel Catalogue*

Abbreviation	Title	Edition/Editor	Place: Publisher: Year B&H = Breitkopf & Härtel
K.[1]	Chronologisch-thematisches Verzeichniss sämmtlicher Tonwerke Wolfgang Amade Mozart's. Nebst Angabe der verloren gegangenen, unvollendeten, übertragenen, zweifelhaften und unterschobenen Compositionen desselben	Ludwig Ritter von Köchel	Leipzig: B&H. 1862
K.[2]	Chronologisch-thematisches Verzeichnis sämmtlicher Tonwerke Wolfgang Amade Mozarts. Nebst Angabe der verlorengegangenen, angefangenen, übertragenen, zweifelhaften und unterschobenen Kompositionen desselben	Zweite Auflage bearbeitet und ergänzt von Paul Graf von Waldersee	Leipzig: B&H, 1905
K.[3]	Chronologisch-thematisches Verzeichnis sämmtlicher Tonwerke Wolfgang Amade Mozarts. Nebst Angabe der verlorengegangenen, angefangenen, übertragenen, zweifelhaften und unterschobenen Kompositionen	Dritte Auflage bearbeitet von Alfred Einstein	Leipzig: B&H, 1937
K.[3a]	[reprint of K.[3]]	Dritte Auflage bearbeitet von Alfred Einstein. Mit einem Supplement «Berichtigungen und Zusätze» von Alfred Einstein	Ann Arbor/MI: J.W. Edwards, 1947
K.[4], K.[5]	[unabridged reprints of K.[3]]	Vierte [Fünfte] Auflage in der Bearbeitung von Alfred Einstein	Leipzig: VEB B&H, 1958 and 1961, resp.

K. [6]	Chronologisch-thematisches Verzeichnis sämtlicher Tonwerke Wolfgang Amadé Mozarts nebst Angabe der verlorengegangenen, angefangenen, von fremder Hand bearbeiteten, zweifelhaften und unterschobenen Kompositionen	Franz Giegling, Alexander Weinmann, Gerd Sievers	Wiesbaden: B&H, 1964
K. [6a]	[unabridged reprint of K.[3]]	Sechste Auflage in der Bearbeitung von Alfred Einstein	Leipzig: VEB B&H, 1969
	[unabridged reprint of K.[3]]	Nachdruck der 3., von Alfred Einstein bearbeiteten Auflage	Leipzig: VEB B&H, 1975; further imprints 1980 and 1984, 1989
	[unabridged reprint of K.[6]]	Siebente [achte], unveränderte Auflage and further imprints (1999, 2009) as Unveränderter Nachdruck [...] der 8. Auflage 1983	Wiesbaden: B&H, 1965 and 1983

establishing remarkable botanical and geological collections. From around 1850 onwards he mainly concerned himself with the music history of Vienna. An initial impulse for a Mozart catalogue comprised the small pamphlet *In Sachen Mozart's* (On Behalf of Mozart), published by a certain Franz Lorenz in 1851, who tried to initiate an edition of the composer's works. In the following years Köchel contacted a number of experts who willingly provided him with material in their possession. Otto Jahn (1813–69) became by far his most important contact. Jahn was professor of archaeology at Leipzig and, later, Bonn universities at a time when music history was not yet taught at German universities; in his spare time, he wrote the first substantial scholarly Mozart biography, which was published in four volumes between 1856 and 1859. For his biography, Jahn studied letters and documents housed at the Mozarteum in Salzburg. Jahn also visited the André family and was granted unrestricted access to the then almost complete collection of musical autographs that had been acquired by Johann Anton André from Mozart's widow in late 1799. Between 1853 and 1859 Jahn had all the music by Mozart copied from the original sources at his own expense, creating a Mozart library at that time unequalled by any public library worldwide. Volume 1 of Jahn's Mozart biography contained as an appendix a non-thematic catalogue of Mozart's ensemble music composed before 1777. Although virtually all pieces by Mozart are addressed in the biography, however briefly, no similar surveys on Mozart's piano or vocal music or his later compositions were included in the remaining three volumes. But what may appear to represent neglect on Jahn's part is actually explained by the crossing of Jahn's and Köchel's paths. Köchel states in the preface to his catalogue, which he dedicated to Jahn, that he had shown Jahn his work when it was already well advanced but learned that Jahn had envisaged a similar project. Jahn took a step back and, from then on, supported Köchel's plan by providing a large amount of material. Köchel declared as his goal collecting all the dispersed pieces of information about Mozart, vetting and ordering them so that their relevance was apparent. He was not only concerned that the data as such was accurate but also that the sources of information were revealed, an attitude surprisingly in harmony with modern scholarly approaches.

Like Jahn, Köchel travelled extensively in order to study virtually every Mozart autograph known to be extant. The catalogue in its final form contained 626 compositions in the main body of text and an appendix of 294 numbers, comprising – as the title states – consecutively numbered lists of works believed lost or constituting fragments, arrangements and compositions of doubtful or spurious origin. For each work in the main text,

Köchel provided a number, a short title, place and date of composition, information about the autograph manuscript (serving in the first instance as verification of authenticity), details of printed editions, musical incipits and a commentary. The commentary section was largely restricted to excerpts from Jahn's biography. Despite obvious shortcomings, such pioneering work should be highly esteemed: at the appearance of the Köchel Catalogue, the first of its kind, 240 of Mozart's works had not yet been published, and Köchel also did not shy away from the expense of having all of them copied for his personal library (now in the Gesellschaft der Musikfreunde in Vienna), often making use of scores in Jahn's possession instead of the original manuscripts.

The main part of the Köchel catalogue is ordered in chronological sequence, thus reflecting the musical development of the composer. It starts with K. 1, a minuet in G (with a trio in C which is not explicitly mentioned), and ends with K. 626, the Requiem, which was incomplete at the time of Mozart's death. When compiling the catalogue Köchel relied on several precursors, including most importantly Mozart's own thematic catalogue started in 1784 and André's catalogue of those original manuscripts still in the possession of the publishing house in 1833. That Mozart's own thematic catalogue served as a basic model is witnessed by Köchel adapting the principle of notating the musical incipits on two staves, often rendering the opening bars exactly as found in Mozart's own thematic catalogue. He went beyond his model by adding the incipits of all movements and providing bar-number counts, carefully recording sources from which the incipits were taken.

On the basis of Mozart's thematic catalogue, inscriptions on the autographs and circumstantial evidence, a total of 346 out of 626 compositions could be dated securely. Köchel believed that the undated works could and should also be integrated into the chronological sequence.[2] He was aware of the fundamental difficulties of this task, stating that, in cases where no reliable information could be derived from external facts, the appearance of the autographs, the handwriting, paper, ink and so on had to be taken into account; where these were not available either, the 'innere Gehalt' (inner content) had to be evaluated in order to determine the work's chronological position. Köchel was careful not to pretend to know the exact

---

[2] On the immanent 'chronology problem' of the Köchel catalogue see also Christoph Großpietsch, 'Im chronologischen Schlepptau. Köchels Mozart-Verzeichnis von 1862 und die Folgen', in Thomas Hochradner (ed.), *Werkverzeichnis: Ordnung und Zählung als Faktoren der Rezeptionsgeschichte* (Freiburg: Rombach, 2011), pp. 167–98.

circumstances of the origins of each work; those that could not be dated with certainty followed the datable works from each year.

In certain respects, Köchel adopted the perspective of a practical musician; he was mainly interested in the 'complete compositions', for example, disregarding the numerous fragments. While it is understandable that pieces such as the Mass in C minor K. 427, the Requiem K. 626 and large-scale operatic fragments like *Zaide* K. 344, *L'oca del Cairo* K. 422 and *Lo sposo deluso* K. 430 were treated in the main body of the catalogue on the grounds that at least individual movements had been completed by Mozart, Köchel also kept completions by others in the main text. Köchel's 'musical feeling' made him reluctant to place these 'excellent and often extended beginnings, which sometimes lacked nothing but a few bars to be complete' into the appendix, where there was always a risk that they would receive less attention. But Köchel did not envisage that, over time, any fragment in the appendix could be completed by someone else.

In spite of some problematic decisions that were taken, the catalogue fulfilled its intended purpose: for the first time ever, it was possible to refer distinctly and succinctly to each individual Mozart work. A first list of addenda and corrigenda to the catalogue was published by Köchel himself in the *Allgemeine musikalische Zeitung* (1864);[3] a brief supplement appeared in 1889 with updated information about Mozart autographs, many of which were no longer held by the André family but had been sold to individual collectors and to public libraries.[4] In 1905, Paul Graf von Waldersee issued the second edition, taking into account information that had come to light during the publication of the complete edition of Mozart's works. This consisted of eliminating a few works that erroneously had been listed twice (such as K. 342, an individual movement from K. 177), those written by others and those considered to be of doubtful authenticity (for example the still-problematic Missa in G, K. 140). In addition to reporting the rediscovery of some works listed by Köchel as lost, Waldersee added eleven new numbers squeezed into the chronological list as K.² 9a, K.² 9b, K.² 25a and so on; he also enlarged the appendix by including a considerable number of fragments that had been found. Waldersee was also the first to take into account Leopold Mozart's

[3] Ludwig Ritter von Köchel, 'Nachträge und Berichtigungen zu v. Köchel's Verzeichniss der Werke Mozart's', in *Allgemeine musikalische Zeitung, Neue Folge*, vol. 2, no. 29 (20 July 1864), cols. 493–9.

[4] Anon., *Nachtrag zum chronologisch-thematischen Verzeichniss sämmtlicher Tonwerke Wolfgang Amade Mozart's* (Leipzig: Breitkof & Härtel, 1889).

'Verzeichniss alles desjenigen was dieser 12jährige Knabe seit seinem 7. Jahre componirt' of 1768,[5] summarizing its contents as K.[2] Anh. 11b.

A thorough revision of the Köchel catalogue was undertaken by Alfred Einstein (1880–1952) only in the late 1920s and 1930s. The publisher had originally contacted Bernhard Paumgartner, director of the Mozarteum in Salzburg, in 1925; Paumgartner had set up some 'Richtlinien und Grundsätze' (guidelines and principles) for the new edition. But he did not have sufficient time to devote to the project, which was then entrusted to Einstein who, already severely discriminated against as a Jew before the Nazi dictatorship, was experiencing difficulties as an independent scholar. In 1927 Einstein became a writer for the *Berliner Tageblatt*; he moved from Munich to Berlin where the Prussian State Library then housed the largest collection of Mozart autographs. The productive years in Berlin ended abruptly with the Nazi Party's 'Machtergreifung' (seizure of power); Einstein foresaw the anti-semitic pogroms and did not return to Germany after a musicological conference in Cambridge in July 1933. He spent the next years with his family in various cities in England, Switzerland, Austria and Italy before emigrating to the United States in early 1939. Einstein's work on the catalogue ended in Florence in 1936; it was published in Germany in 1937 only after major difficulties. For Einstein, the new edition was a bibliographical comprehension of 'the entire serious [body of] Mozart research'; the catalogue was meant to serve as the basis for a new or at least revised complete edition of Mozart's works.

Einstein is to be commended for a number of reasons: for example, he started virtually from scratch, re-evaluating every single piece of information in the previous editions of the catalogue. He re-examined the autograph manuscripts and added – for the first time – comprehensive information about their transmission in print. Einstein carefully examined antiquarian catalogues and was thus able not only to name the current owners of the autographs, but also to trace chains of transmission. Some manuscript copies were included too, although no clear criteria for insertion or omission were provided.

Two decisions in particular affected the catalogue. Einstein integrated the fragments, which Köchel had listed in the appendix, into the main body of the catalogue as he regarded them as first attempts that Mozart had abandoned in favour of completed works. Adopting the premise that fragments were compositions *in nuce* Einstein was able to overcome Köchel's arbitrary treatment of 'completed' fragments without having to

---

[5] MBA, vol. 1, pp. 287–90. (Not in LMF.)

banish extended fragments of major works into the appendix. Einstein also redated many compositions, mainly on stylistic grounds. In the course of these revisions, almost half of the compositions were assigned new Köchel numbers to reflect their assumed chronology. These new numbers have never really been accepted by the musical public; in the end, they were un-useful because few old numbers remained for pieces composed before 1784 that could have provided fixed points of orientation. The unfortunate circumstances under which the third edition appeared in print before actually being finished, led Einstein after he had finally settled in America to promote an annotated and slightly expanded edition in 1947, now designated K^{3a}.[6]

While the fourth and fifth editions are unchanged reprints of the third, the sixth was originally meant as a simple update of Einstein's 1937 version, including its 1947 supplement for which the rights were secured from Einstein's widow.[7] After the Second World War, the 1937 edition was out of print, the fate of almost a third of the Mozart autographs from the former Preußische Staatsbibliothek was unclear (and remained so until they were finally rediscovered in the Bibliotheka Jagiellońska in Kraków in 1977) and Breitkopf & Härtel had been divided up into two branches. The family owners established new premises in Wiesbaden (Federal Republic of Germany), while the former head office in Leipzig was closed and carried on as a nationally owned enterprise ('volkseigener Betrieb') by the communist party (German Democratic Republic). Several attempts to work on the Köchel catalogue failed. Otto Erich Deutsch, known today as the editor of the thematic catalogue of Schubert's work, had to decline for time-related reasons; Ernst Reichert, professor at the Mozarteum in Salzburg, died in 1958 after having worked on the Köchel for no more than a year. The workload was then divided between Franz Giegling, Alexander Weinmann and Gerd Sievers, the catalogue finally appearing in print in 1964. If chronological order is strictly maintained as the leading principle, each new bit of information regarding the date of a composition affects the numbering system. Later, the thorough study of Mozart's

---

[6] Concurrent projects after World War II, partly authorized and partly unauthorized, were *Der kleine Köchel. Chronologisches und systematisches Verzeichnis sämtlicher musikalischen Werke von Wolfgang Amadeus Mozart, geb. 27. Jänner 1756, gest. 5. Dezember 1791*, zusammengestellt auf Grund der dritten, von Alfred Einstein bearbeiten Auflage [...] herausgegeben von Hellmuth von Hase (Wiesbaden: Breitkopf & Härtel, 1951), and Karl Franz Müller, *W. A. Mozart. Gesamtkatalog seiner Werke: 'Köchel-Verzeichnis'* (Vienna: Kaltschmid, 1951).

[7] Most of the addenda and corrigenda had previously been published by Alfred Einstein as 'Mozartiana and Köcheliana: Supplement zur dritten Auflage von L. v. Köchel's chronologisch-thematischem Verzeichnis sämtlicher Tonwerke W. A. Mozart's' in various issues of *Music Review*, 1–6 (1940–5).

handwriting by Wolfgang Plath in the 1960s and the paper studies of Alan Tyson in the 1980s showed that many newly changed dates were still wrong; consequently, many new numbers were inappropriate.

Several decades later, the completed *Neue Mozart-Ausgabe* (NMA) has provided a plethora of new insights about sources and their transmission. Over time a number of original manuscripts have reappeared; a handful of 'lost' pieces have also been recovered, most recently (in early 2016) the *Canzonetta per la ricuperata salute di Ofelia* K.^{2} Anh. 11a/K.$^{3-6}$ 477a. And various pieces, particularly from Mozart's youth, have been publicly discussed. All these pieces need to be properly accommodated.

A new edition of the Köchel catalogue is currently being prepared by Neal A. Zaslaw at Cornell University in cooperation with the Mozarteum Foundation in Salzburg. The aim is to make the Köchel useful again for all those interested in Mozart, not just scholars. Mozart scholarship has advanced so far that Einstein's aspiration for the catalogue to serve as a compendium of all serious facts about Mozart can no longer be sustained. Rather, a selection of information is needed to guide the user. Online catalogues such as RISM (Répertoire international des sources musicales) and the Mozart bibliography at the Mozarteum Foundation can provide up-to-date information on various features in constant flux. Details about manuscripts other than the autographs is thus restricted in the printed catalogue to sources that are likely to be authorized ones; all prints directly related to the composer are listed, as are the first editions preceding the late nineteenth-century *Alte Mozart-Ausgabe*.

Strangely, none of the previous editions of the catalogue have tried to define what constitutes a Mozart work. Setting aside for a moment the problem of lost or misattributed compositions, we are confronted both by complete works (sometimes, though rarely in different versions) and by numerous incomplete ones (fragments) that are a result of a complex compositional process. There are also several bits of notated music that had already been classified as contrapuntal studies when Mozart's estate was examined around 1800. Finally, we have sketches that relate either to completed works or to no surviving composition. From the perspective of the compositional process it seems natural to follow Einstein's idea that all fragments, however short, are (incomplete) works. Sketches on the other hand do not have an independent existence but are tied to some other work. They are usually notated in private script, lacking instrument designations, often even clefs and key signatures, and are thus nearly illegible to the uninitiated. Once the work to which they are connected had been created and executed (or abandoned), their *raison d'être* was lost; consequently, most of them had probably already been discarded during Mozart's lifetime. Where they survive, it is in all likelihood because several sketches appeared on a single sheet of paper (sketch leaf) or because they were entered on empty spots of some manuscript otherwise regarded as worthy of preservation. It is necessary, however, carefully to distinguish those sketches carrying only a notated melody line from others. In certain genres, most notably arias and dance music, a melody line may already comprise the 'Anlage' (layout) of a composition and thus qualify as a fragmentary work. Given that a study in counterpoint was rarely if ever transmitted outside a pedagogical context, it may make sense to keep all these entries in a separate section and not to suggest that they were meant to be musical works for broader dissemination.

One problem that the new edition of the Köchel has not solved but circumnavigated is the question of chronological order. The term 'chronologisch' will disappear from the title page and all chronological reordering will be undone. All works as defined above will be assigned the original number under which they appeared in the main body of the catalogue.

CHAPTER 32

Mozart's Influence on Nineteenth-Century Composers

Edward Klorman

The mystique surrounding Mozart's music as essential material for an emerging composer to grapple with arose immediately after his death. A confluence of factors established Mozart's widespread and enduring influence. These include his historical position on the cusp of a period of intense interest in canon formation, which established many of his mature compositions as 'masterworks' for perennial performance and study.[1] A second factor is the variety of instrumental, operatic and sacred genres in which Mozart excelled. Moreover, generations of composers (especially those with piano backgrounds) could count Mozart among the earliest music they encountered in their formative instrumental training. And lastly, there is Mozart's uncommonly colourful biography and the efforts of his influential early biographers (notably Nissen and Jahn) to shape his image in a particular mould and to cultivate sustained interest in his life.

The present chapter surveys some nineteenth-century composers for whom Mozart's music and persona were important sources of inspiration.

Beethoven and 'Mozart's Spirit'

In 1792, on the eve of Beethoven's departure for Vienna, Count Waldstein issued the following farewell greeting: 'The Genius of Mozart is still in mourning and weeping the death of her pupil ... [But] you shall receive Mozart's spirit from Haydn's hands'. These oft-quoted words served less to *foretell* Beethoven's future reception as heir to Mozart's greatness as to help *create* that very narrative of inheritance.[2] Waldstein was not the first to

---

[1] An early expression of this attitude is in Niemetschek's biography of Mozart (*Leben des K. K. Kapellmeisters Wolfgang Gottlieb Mozart*, Prague, 1798, pp. 46–7), which compares the pleasure and value of repeated listening to Mozart's works to that of rereading Greek and Roman writings.

[2] Tia DeNora, *Beethoven and the Construction of Genius: Musical Politics in Vienna, 1792–1803* (Berkeley: University of California Press, 1995), pp. 83–9.

intimate Beethoven's place as Mozart's successor. About a decade earlier, Beethoven's teacher Christian Gottlieb Neefe described his eleven-year-old student as a *Wunderkind* of such extraordinary promise that he 'would surely become a second Wolfgang Amadeus Mozart were he to continue as he had begun'.[3]

During his Bonn period, Beethoven turned to Mozart's Sonata for piano and violin in G major, K. 379 as a model for two of his earliest chamber works: the Piano Quartet in E♭ Major, WoO 36, no. 1 (1785) and the variations from his Trio in G major for piano, flute, and bassoon, WoO 37 (1786).[4] (See Examples 32.1a and 32.1b for K. 379 and WoO 36 no. 1.) Evidence of Beethoven's 'anxiety of influence' during this period is found on a sketch leaf probably written in Bonn in 1790 (now included in the 'Kafka' Miscellany) on which Beethoven wrote a six-bar musical idea plus the following comment: 'This entire passage has been stolen from the Mozart Symphony in C minor, where the Andante in 6/8 from the … '. Beethoven's words break off mid-sentence and are followed by a four-bar version of the same material, with sharper registral extremes, that Beethoven labelled as his own ('Beethoven ipse'). Beethoven's comments are puzzling since this passage does not closely resemble any Mozart symphony. Perhaps the sketch seemed to Beethoven to be too close to Mozart's style in general or to some passage he was struggling to remember.[5]

Evidently Beethoven's task of absorbing aspects of Mozart's style, while simultaneously developing his own voice, proved challenging. When asked in

32.1a Mozart, Sonata for piano and violin in G, K. 379/i, bars 1–4 (piano part only).

[3] *Cramers Magazin der Musik* (3 March 1783). Cited in *Thayer's Life of Beethoven*, rev. and ed. Elliot Forbes (Princeton: Princeton University Press, 1967), vol. 1, p. 69.
[4] Richard Kramer, *Unfinished Music* (Oxford and New York: Oxford University Press, 2008), p. 250.
[5] Lewis Lockwood, 'Beethoven before 1800: The Mozart Legacy', *Beethoven Forum*, 3 (1994), p. 40. A similar case is found among the sketches for Beethoven's 'Eroica' Symphony. Beethoven drafted a rough version of the first movement's main theme that resembles the rondo from Mozart's Piano Concerto in B♭ major K. 595, only transposed to E♭ major and notated in augmented rhythmic values. See Lockwood, 'The Mozart Legacy', p. 41.

32.1b Beethoven, Piano Quartet in E♭ major, WoO 36, No. 1, Adagio assai, bars 1–4 (piano part only).

1798 how often he attended Mozart's operas, Beethoven reportedly replied dismissively: 'I do not know them and do not care to hear the music of others lest I forfeit some of my originality.'[6] This remark is absurd, since Beethoven had performed in three Mozart operas as a member of the court theatre orchestra in Bonn.[7] Moreover, Beethoven's first decade in Vienna saw the composition of four variation sets on themes from Mozart operas: 'Se vuol ballare', WoO 40 (1792), 'Là ci darem la mano', WoO 28 (1796), 'Ein Mädchen oder Weibchen' Op. 66 (1798) and 'Bei Männern, welche Liebe fühlen', WoO 46 (1801). Nor were such borrowings from Mozart's operas limited to Beethoven's early period, since he incorporated a parody of 'Notte e giorno faticar' as no. 22 of the 'Diabelli' Variations. Although Beethoven expressed misgivings about *Don Giovanni*'s immoral subject matter, he also wrote that the opera's 'good reception . . . gives me as much pleasure as if it were my own work'.[8] He repeatedly requested a copy of its score from Breitkopf & Härtel, along with those of other Mozart operas and the Requiem.

As Beethoven began work on his Opus 18 quartets in 1799–1800, he undertook the project of copying out (in whole or in part) study scores of two Mozart quartets, K. 387 in G and K. 464 in A. The impact of this study is most evident in Beethoven's Quartet in A, Op. 18, No. 5, which shares many characteristics with K. 464, including its key of A major, dance-like first movement, third-movement Andante variations in D major and *alla breve* finale. K. 387 served more generally as a study in the masterful interweaving of contrapuntal (fugal) and free styles that Beethoven sought to achieve throughout his quartet oeuvre. Beethoven made study copies of Mozart passages even decades later. Among the sketches of the Credo fugue

[6] This anecdote was recorded in Johann Wenzel Tomaschek's autobiography (1845). Cited in *Thayer's Life of Beethoven*, vol. 1, p. 208.
[7] Christopher Reynolds, 'Florestan Reading *Fidelio*', *Beethoven Forum*, 4 (1995), p. 136.
[8] Letter to Breitkopf & Härtel, 23 August 1811.

for his *Missa solemnis* (composed 1819–20), he wrote out and analysed the Kyrie fugue from Mozart's Requiem.[9]

Rossini and Verdi, or, *i Tedeschini*

Whilst the influence of Italian opera on Mozart's music is well known, Mozart's influence on his Italian successors is less frequently noted.[10] In 1804, Rossini's family moved to Bologna, a city that a teenage-prodigy Mozart had swept through decades earlier. As a student, Rossini devoured scores by Haydn and Mozart with such fervour as to earn the moniker 'il Tedeschino' ('the little German') from his teacher, Padre Mattei.[11]

His study of 'serious' German music was a lifelong affair. When he met Wagner in 1860, some decades after retiring from composition, Rossini discussed his ongoing study of Bach and Mozart scores. Late in life, he kept a bust of Mozart in his bedroom and described Mozart as 'the admiration of my youth, the desperation of my mature years, the consolation of my old age'.[12] Two extraordinary anecdotes are related by Louis and Pauline Viardot: when asked at a gathering which of Rossini's own operas was his favourite, Rossini thought briefly and replied, bizarrely, *Don Giovanni*; and when the Viardots – who owned the autograph of that opera and kept it in an ornate, shrine-like box – invited Rossini to view and touch the manuscript, he is said to have 'genuflect[ed] in front of the relic', declaring piously that Mozart 'is the greatest, the master of all, [since] only he had as much science as genius and as much genius as science'.[13]

Rossini's first years composing operas coincided with productions of Mozart's operas at the Teatro del Fondo (Naples) and especially at La Scala (Milan). It was during these years that Rossini developed his 'code' of operatic conventions, drawing not only from his Neapolitan predecessors Giovanni Paisiello and Domenico Cimarosa but also from Mozart, a composer he saw as transcending the Italian–German divide. Whereas

---

[9] Further details and a list of all Mozart passages copied by Beethoven appear in Bathia Churgin, 'Beethoven and Mozart's Requiem: A New Connection', *Journal of Musicology*, 5 (1987), pp. 457–77.

[10] But see Friedrich Lippmann, 'Mozart und die italienischen Komponisten des 19. Jahrhunderts', *Mozart-Jahrbuch 1980–83*, pp. 104–13.

[11] A. Azevedo, *G. Rossini: Sa vie et ses oeuvres* (Paris: Le Ménestrel, 1864), p. 43. A contemporaneous account of Rossini's views (including of Mozart's music) is relayed in Ferdinand Hiller, 'Plaudereien mit Rossini', in *Aus dem Tonleben unserer Zeit* (Leipzig: Hermann Mendelssohn, 1868), vol. 2, pp. 1–84.

[12] Philip Gossett, 'Rossini, Gioachino', in *New Grove Online*.

[13] Mark Everist, 'Enshrining Mozart: *Don Giovanni* and the Viardot Circle', *19th Century Music*, 25 (2001–2), pp. 177–8.

32.2a Rossini, *Moïse et Pharaon*, Act 2 finale, bars 73–88.

Mozart occasionally creates a special harmonic effect with sudden, chromatic-mediant shifts (as in the modulation from F major to A♭ major in 'Voi che sapete'), such modulations became Rossini's signature harmonic move.[14]

---

[14] On Rossini's chromatic-mediant relations, see William Rothstein, 'Common-Tone Tonality in Italian Romantic Opera: An Introduction', *Music Theory Online*, 14/1 (March 2008), http://www.mtosmt.org/issues/mto.08.14.1/mto.08.14.1.rothstein.html.

32.2b Mozart, Act 2 finale from *Don Giovanni*, bars 487–98 (Commendatore part only).

Specific instances of Rossini passages modelled on Mozart can be interesting fodder for speculation. Friedrich Lippmann points to the Act 2 finale of *Moïse et Pharaon*, in which Sinaide's aria is interrupted by a mysterious choir or voice delivering a message from the mother of the gods, with music that resembles the statue scene from *Don Giovanni*. (See Examples 32.2a and 32.2b.) The libretti alone suggest some links between the supernatural mother/father figures delivering solemn messages. Shared musical features include the urgent, intoning declamation, the deliberate, chromatic vocal ascent (cf. Example 32.2b) and the orchestral accompaniment with dotted rhythms and use of three trombones.[15] These resemblances may arise from the *ombra* topic common to both passages, but Rossini's deep reverence for *Don Giovanni* lends credence to this famous scene as his model.

Verdi's most Mozartian moments likewise involve *Don Giovanni*. The opening scene of *Rigoletto* – a ball involving two dance ensembles and a boastful, lecherous Duke – recalls *Don Giovanni*'s Act 1 finale.[16] Links between Verdi's final opera, *Falstaff*, and Wagner's *Die Meistersinger* are frequently noted, but echoes of *Don Giovanni* permeate it as well: the rakish, aristocratic protagonist of insatiable appetite, with his long-suffering servants; the mock-eighteenth-century minuet in the wedding scene (cf. the onstage music in both finales of *Don Giovanni*); and the final ensemble number that achieves dramatic closure in comic terms.[17]

[15] Lippmann, 'Mozart und die italienischen Komponisten des 19. Jahrhunderts', pp. 111–12.
[16] Pierluigi Petrobelli, '*Don Giovanni* in Italia: La fortuna dell'opera ed il suo influsso', *Analecta musicologica*, 18 (1978), p. 41.
[17] Emanuele Senici, 'Verdi's *Falstaff* at Italy's *Fin de siècle*', *Musical Quarterly*, 85 (2001), pp. 274–310.

Romantic Pianism: Chopin and Liszt

'Where [Beethoven] is obscure and seems lacking in unity . . . the reason is that he turns his back on eternal principles; Mozart never.' Such was Chopin's view, as recounted by the artist Eugène Delacroix.[18] If Chopin found in Bach's music an encyclopaedia of the artisanal techniques of counterpoint and fugue that he so valorized, Mozart's music may have represented these same 'eternal principles' transmuted into a more modern, fundamentally melodic-vocal style.

Yet just as Chopin managed to allude to Bach without overtly imitating his style (as in his 24 Preludes, Op. 48), what he drew from Mozart was likewise highly transformed. His most explicit homage to Mozart is surely the variations on 'Là ci darem la mano', Op. 2, which Chopin composed at the age of seventeen.[19] More subtle is the influence on Chopin's two completed piano concerti (Opp. 11 and 21), which fuse the Mozartian model with the 'brilliant' concerto style of Hummel, Field and Weber.[20] As a piano teacher, Chopin had his piano students study Bach's preludes and fugues but (for whatever reason) he taught Mozart's music rarely if ever.[21] Chopin himself performed a Mozart trio in his final public appearance at the Salle Pleyel, which otherwise consisted mainly of his own compositions,[22] and he regarded opportunities to play Mozart piano duets with Camille Pleyel as particularly revelatory experiences, perhaps partly on account of Pleyel's connection through his father to Haydn and Mozart's circle.[23]

Liszt's Mozart-related works include the Fantasy on Themes from *Figaro* and *Don Giovanni*, S. 697,[24] *Réminiscences de Don Juan*, S. 656, and various transcriptions such as the Confutatis and Lacrymosa from Mozart's Requiem, S. 550. His rival Sigismond Thalberg likewise

---

[18] Hubert Wellington (ed.), *The Journal of Eugène Delacroix*, trans. Lucy Norton (London: Phaidon Press, 1951), p. 195.

[19] By the time Chopin composed the 'Mozart' Variations in 1827, he had already been compared to Mozart for a full decade since his first published composition had appeared at the age of seven. The 'Mozart' Variations elicited a famously effusive review by Schumann.

[20] Kornel Michałowski and Jim Samson. 'Chopin, Fryderyk Francieszek' in *Grove Music Online*.

[21] Among Chopin's students, only Karol Mikuli claimed to have studied Mozart in his lessons. See Jean-Jacques Eigeldinger, *Chopin: Pianist and Teacher – as Seen by His Pupils*, trans. Naomi Shohet with Krysia Osostowicz and Roy Howat, ed. Howat (Cambridge: Cambridge University Press, 1986), p. 136 n. 142.

[22] On this Salle Pleyel performance (16 February 1848), see Alfred Cortot, *In Search of Chopin*, trans. Cyril and Rena Clarke (London and New York: Peter Nevill Ltd., 1951), p. 131.

[23] Eigeldinger, *Chopin: Pianist and Teacher*, p. 136 n. 142.

[24] S. 697 remained an unfinished manuscript at the time of Liszt's death. An abridged version known as the 'Figaro' Fantasy was published by Busoni in 1912.

composed virtuoso music based on Mozart's operas and Requiem, but unique to Liszt was a profound, life-long self-identification with Mozart.[25] Liszt was already well acquainted with Mozart's keyboard music before he came to Vienna in 1822. This fourteen-month period of tutelage under Czerny and Salieri brought him in close contact with musicians connected (to varying degrees) to Mozart's milieu, and the ensuing world tour organized by Liszt's father all but retraced the Mozart family's route from sixty years earlier. Improvisations based on or transcriptions of Mozart's operas and Requiem figured prominently in Liszt's performances throughout the 1820s–1840s but actual Mozart solo-keyboard compositions did not. This probably reflects Liszt's view that such pieces were suited only for private performance[26] but also his penchant to engage with and transform other composers' works rather than execute them as written.

Mozart's centennial year (1856) heightened Liszt's apparent identification with him. Liszt published an essay on the occasion that – in a perhaps unwitting self-portrait – depicted Mozart as a visionary-but-suffering genius whose life was foreshortened by a public that dismissed his innovative music as unplayable or incomprehensible.[27] Around the same time, he sought to promote Mozart's music by leading an initiative to publish a complete edition; although Liszt was unsuccessful, Breitkopf & Härtel would undertake the same project two decades later.

The most pronounced instance of Liszt identifying as Mozart pertains to his *Evocation à la Chapelle Sixtine*, S. 461, which was conceived in relation to a famous episode from Mozart's life: the transcription from memory of Allegri's 'Miserere' after hearing it in the Sistine Chapel. In 1862, Liszt was compelled to visit the Sistine Chapel, observing in a letter that 'it seemed to me … as if I saw [Mozart], and as if he looked back at me with gentle encouragement'.[28] From this inspiration, Liszt composed the *Evocation*, which combines Allegri's 'Miserere' with Mozart's 'Ave verum corpus', thus drawing Liszt into dialogue with his genius precursor.

Tchaikovsky's Christlike Mozart

Liszt's *Evocation* clearly had resonance, since Tchaikovsky drew on it for the third movement (entitled 'Preghiera', meaning 'prayer') of his Suite

---

[25] William Wright, 'Liszt and the Mozart Connection', *Studia Musicologica*, 48 (2007), pp. 299–318.

[26] Charles Rosen, *Piano Notes: The Hidden World of the Pianist* (London: Penguin, 2002), p. 179.

[27] *Blätter für Musik, Theater und Kunst*, 7 (21 January 1856), p. 26. Cited in Wright, 'Liszt and the Mozart Connection', pp. 316–17.

[28] Wright, 'Liszt and the Mozart Connection', p. 318.

No. 4 ('Mozartiana'), Op. 61. The suite – whose other three movements are orchestrations based on Mozart piano pieces[29] – was composed in 1887 to mark the centenary of *Don Giovanni*. That anniversary held a personal meaning for Tchaikovsky, since it was his revelatory first encounter with *Don Giovanni* as a teenager that inspired him to pursue composition. Moreover, like Rossini before him, Tchaikovsky also had a quasi-religious experience while paying respects to the *Don Giovanni* autograph at Viardot's 'shrine' in 1886.[30] A series of diary entries from that year describe Mozart as the 'musical Christ', as divine musical beauty in human form and inspiring love (as contrasted with Beethoven, who inspired awe). 'The more one learns Mozart', wrote Tchaikovsky in the margins of his copy of Jahn's Mozart biography, 'the more one loves him! Ideal of Artist and Man!!!'[31]

Tchaikovsky's most telling discussion of Mozart's music comes from an 1878 letter to his patron Nadezhda von Meck, who was a Mozart sceptic:

> I don't just like Mozart – I idolise him! ... Just as in his life he was to the very end a carefree child, so his music lacks the deep personal sadness which is felt so powerfully and mightily in Beethoven. Yet this did not prevent him from creating an impersonally tragic character, the most powerful, the most amazing human type ever portrayed in music ... Donna Anna in *Don Giovanni*.[32]

Tchaikovsky's letter proceeded to praise Mozart's chamber music for its charm, textural purity and part-writing, singling out the Adagio of Mozart's Quintet in G Minor, K. 516 for its beautiful expression of 'the feeling of resigned and hopeless grief'. He described Mozart's jolly temperament, pure soul and ease as a composer who (supposedly) never required drafts: 'The purity of his soul was untarnished ... [and] all this can be heard in his music, which is by its very nature conciliating, enlightening, and tender'. He recommended that she read Jahn's biography, which was no doubt the source of Tchaikovsky's own (mis)conceptions about Mozart as a person.[33] These remarks articulate a number of

---

[29] The sources of the four movements are as follows: (1) Little Gigue in G Major, K. 574, (2) Minuet in D Major, K. 355, (3) Liszt's *Evocation* (only the part based on Mozart's 'Ave verum corpus'), and (4) Variations on 'Unser dummer Pöbel meint', K. 455.

[30] Tchaikovsky described the manuscript with the Russian word 'svyatïnya', which denotes holy objects and relics. Mark Everist, 'Enshrining Mozart', pp. 176–7.

[31] Cited in Marina Ritzarev, *Tchaikovsky's Pathétique and Russian Culture* (London and New York: Routledge, 2014), pp. 19–20.

[32] Letter to Nadezhda von Meck, 16 March 1878. Cited in David Schroeder, *Experiencing Tchaikovsky: A Listener's Companion* (London: Rowan & Littlefield, 2015), pp. 40–1.

[33] Schroeder, *Experiencing Tchaikovsky*, pp. 40–1.

qualities Tchaikovsky admired both in Mozart's music and in his imagined personal character. On the one hand, he highlights certain moments of profound emotive expression, thus linking Mozart's music to Tchaikovsky's own aesthetics, but he also points to a certain breeziness and absence of suffering in Mozart's life (and therefore his music) that contrasted sharply with Tchaikovsky's own personal experience.

Conclusion

It is notable that *Don Giovanni* and the Requiem are the two Mozart works that most captured the imagination of his nineteenth-century successors. The former was compelling for its expressive intensity, the latter for its connection to Mozart's 'mysterious' early death (as depicted dramatically in Rimsky-Korsakov's *Mozart and Salieri*, after Pushkin).[34] These composers evidently constructed a Mozart to suit their particular aesthetic and creative purposes.

To nineteenth-century composers who identified as romantic artists, Mozart the 'craftsman-composer' may have represented a simpler time. Brahms articulated this tension between these conceptions of composition in a letter to his publisher:

> [C]omposing cannot be turned out like spinning or sewing. Some respected colleagues (Bach, Mozart, Schubert) have spoilt the world terribly. But if we can't imitate them in the beauty of their writing, we should certainly beware of seeking to match the speed of their writing . . . Many factors combine to make writing harder for us (my contemporaries), and especially for me.[35]

Perhaps it was this version of Mozart – for whom composing seemed to remain easy even when life presented obstacles – to which the next generations of composers turned for inspiration.

---

[34] Mozart's Requiem was performed at the funerals of many composers, among them Beethoven, Berlioz, Chopin, Dussek, Haydn, Paisiello, Rossini and Weber. For more on nineteenth-century reception of Mozart's Requiem, see Simon P. Keefe, *Mozart's Requiem: Reception, Work, Completion* (Cambridge: Cambridge University Press, 2012), chapters 1–3.

[35] Letter to Fritz Simrock, February 1870. Cited in Imogen Fellinger, 'Brahms's View of Mozart', in Robert Pascall (ed.), *Brahms: Biographical, Documentary, and Analytical Studies* (Cambridge: Cambridge University Press, 1983), p. 56.

CHAPTER 33

Mythmaking

Adeline Mueller

The mythography of Mozart began when he was six years old. It was then that Leopold took Wolfgang and his sister Nannerl to the courts at Munich and Vienna, launching their careers as child prodigies. Before they reached Vienna, Leopold wrote back home that 'my children, the boy especially, fill everyone with amazement. Count Herberstein has gone on to Vienna and will spread in advance a sensational report about them'.[1] The 'sensational report' was probably no exaggeration: whatever other myths we may cast off or cling on to about Mozart, most continue to agree that he and Nannerl more than lived up to the accounts of their abilities. Nevertheless, this was the first of many instances where Leopold helped to construct a publicity machine that would enable the family to maximize the profit from their expensive, dangerous and professionally fraught journeys. Ironically, it was Mozart's preternatural talent that gave rise to the first rumours that he could not possibly be capable of the things he was reported to do. Such suspicions were often recounted (and may even have been amplified) by Leopold as he choreographed Wolfgang's strange hybrid early career between court servant and free agent.[2]

Just a few short months later, the first encomium to Mozart appeared in print: a poem signed 'Puffendorf', distributed at a Christmas Day concert given by Mozart at the Vienna residence of Count Collalto. The poem began with lines of Ovid and deemed Mozart 'the smallest [and] the greatest player', concluding 'I only hope that your body can endure your soul's strength, / And does not, like the Lübeck child, go too early to the grave'.[3] The 'Lübeck child' to whom the poet referred – a prodigy of languages named Christian Heinrich Heineken (1721–5) for whom Georg Philipp Telemann penned two elegies – was thought to have died prematurely due

---

[1] MBA, vol. 1, p. 49; LMF, p. 1 (3 October 1762).
[2] See for example Leopold Mozart's letter of 30 January 1768 in MBA, vol. 1, pp. 254–8; LMF, pp. 80–3.
[3] In MDL, p. 20; MDB, pp. 18–19 (my translation).

to overexertion of mind and spirit.[4] The first myth about Mozart, then, was a venerable one, going back to child saints in the Middle Ages (and arguably Christ himself, the first *Wunderkind*): that the early flame would burn out before its time. This myth and its counterpart, that of the adult Mozart as a perpetual man-child, worked together in a reciprocally deterministic fashion, beginning with Friedrich Schlichtegroll's 1791 *Nekrolog* (first published in 1793).[5] As Ruth Halliwell reports, the seeds of these intertwined myths were first sown by Nannerl and Albert von Mölk, in their responses to Schlichtegroll's questionnaire. But one might also attribute it to an accidental privileging of evidence: Schlichtegroll's main sources for the *Nekrolog* were Nannerl and Johann Andreas Schachtner, both of whom knew Mozart best before his move to Vienna; so naturally the stories skewed towards Mozart's precocious youth.[6] 'By the time [the anecdotes] were first subjected to sceptical scrutiny (by Otto Jahn in the 1850s)', Halliwell writes, 'it was too late, because they had found their way into several other biographies and were too well established to be unwritten'.[7]

Alongside this pair of biographical myths, child-man and man-child, we might identify a family or cluster of critical myths that arose in the 1780s, to do with the artificiality or difficulty of Mozart's music. These epithets appear at least as far back as his first great independent success, *Die Entführung aus dem Serail* (1782), as encapsulated in the apocryphal critique attributed to Emperor Joseph ('Too many notes').[8] Criticism of Mozart's music as 'artificial' and 'difficult' would continue to echo in Mozart reception through the first decades after his death. In fact, these misrepresentations were only dislodged by another set of terms, equally inadequate and misleading: 'simple', 'natural' and 'light'. The process of 'rebranding' Mozart from difficult to delightful began with the earliest posthumous publications and complete works editions, for which the

---

[4] I discuss the multiple comparisons that were made between Mozart and intellectual prodigies like Heineken and Jean Philippe Baratier (1721–40) in chapter 1 of my book, *Mozart and the Mediation of Childhood* (Chicago: University of Chicago Press, forthcoming).

[5] This biographical tradition has been traced in Peter Kivy, 'Child Mozart as Aesthetic Symbol', *Journal of the History of Ideas*, 28/2 (1967), pp. 249–58; Gloria Flaherty, 'Mozart and the Mythologization of Genius', *Studies in Eighteenth-Century Culture*, 18 (1988), pp. 289–309; and Peter Pesic, 'The Child and the Daemon: Mozart and Deep Play', *19th Century Music*, 25/2–3 (2001–2), pp. 91–107 among others.

[6] Ruth Halliwell, *The Mozart Family: Four Lives in a Social Context* (Oxford: Clarendon Press, 1998), pp. 582–83.

[7] Halliwell, *The Mozart Family*, pp. 602–3.

[8] This remark's earliest appearances include Thomas Busby, 'Anecdotes of Eminent Persons: Life of Mozart', *Walpoliana*, 9 (December 1798), p. 447; and Théophile Frédéric Winckler, *Notice biographique sur Jean-Chrysostome-Wolfgang-Théophile Mozart* (Paris: Fuchs, 1801), p. 34.

'rhetoric of easiness' was necessary for the successful marketing of music for the domestic market.[9] And it continues to this day in countless deceptive 'beginner' keyboard anthologies and 'Mozart for Baby' albums.

A third set of myths has to do with the circumstances surrounding the commission and composition of the Requiem and Mozart's supposed 'early' death (not in fact unusually early, given life expectancy averages in Europe before 1800). The gothic fantasy of the Requiem as a kind of curse or prophecy was enshrined in print in Franz Xaver Niemetschek's 1798 biography, likely encouraged by Mozart's widow Constanze, and later amplified by her second husband, Georg Nikolaus von Nissen, in the monumental patchwork biography that appeared thirty years later under his name.[10] As Simon P. Keefe writes, 'For so many in the nineteenth century, the Requiem *had* to be heard biographically', and its status as the exemplar of the 'fact-fiction continuum' attending on Mozart biography is revealed in biographical fictions like the plays *Mozart and Salieri* (Alexander Pushkin, 1830) and *Amadeus* (Peter Shaffer, 1979).[11] The Requiem legends were the locus of what William Stafford calls 'the demonic genius narrative' that dominated nineteenth-century Mozart mythography, from E.T.A. Hoffmann and George Bernard Shaw to Søren Kierkegaard and Pauline Viardot.[12]

To this day, mythmaking is an integral part of Mozart reception, in scholarly and popular biographies, in monuments, anniversaries, festivals and kitsch.[13] Alongside this process is an equally enticing, and ultimately equally elusive, effort to scrub away the accretions of previous generations

---

[9] Matthew Head, *Sovereign Feminine: Music and Gender in Eighteenth-Century Germany* (Berkeley: University of California Press, 2013), pp. 52–9. For more on the posthumous 'rebranding' of Mozart as accessible and child-friendly, see chapter 6 of my *Mozart and the Mediation of Childhood* (Chicago: University of Chicago Press, forthcoming).

[10] William Stafford, 'The Evolution of Mozartian Biography', in Simon P. Keefe (ed.), *The Cambridge Companion to Mozart* (Cambridge: Cambridge University Press, 2003), p. 202.

[11] Simon P. Keefe, *Mozart's Requiem: Reception, Work, Completion* (Cambridge: Cambridge University Press, 2012), pp. 14–41 (quotations at pp. 21, 40).

[12] Stafford, 'Mozartian Biography', p. 209. See also Mark Everist, *Mozart's Ghosts: Haunting the Halls of Musical Culture* (Oxford: Oxford University Press, 2012), chapter 6, 'Enshrining Mozart: *Don Giovanni* and the Viardot Circle', and chapter 8, 'Speaking with the Supernatural: E.T.A. Hoffmann, George Bernard Shaw, and *Die Oper aller Opern*'.

[13] In addition to scholarship already cited, see Alexander Hyatt King, *Mozart in Retrospect* (3rd edition, London: Oxford University Press, 1970); Hans Lenneberg, *Witnesses and Scholars: Studies in Musical Biography* (New York: Gordon and Breach, 1988); Gernot Gruber, *Mozart and Posterity*, trans. R. S. Furness (London: Quartet Books, 1991); John Stone, 'Reception', in H. C. Robbins Landon (ed.), *The Mozart Compendium: A Guide to Mozart's Life and Music* (New York: Schirmer Books, 1990), pp. 386–401; Roye Wates, *Mozart: An Introduction to the Music, the Man, and the Myths* (Milwaukee, WI: Amadeus Press, 2010); Eric Martin Usner, '"The Condition of Mozart": Mozart Year 2006 and the New Vienna', *Ethnomusicology Forum*, 20/3 (2011), pp. 413–42; and Adeline Mueller, '*Mozart22*: A DVD Review Portfolio – Introduction', *Opera Quarterly*, 29/1 (2013), pp. 41–5.

to reveal the 'true' Mozart. As Mark Everist and others have noted, the very idea that the 'myths can be cleared away and the reality revealed' is itself a myth.[14] If we were to hazard an origin point for this fourth mythical field, it might well be Niemetschek's 1798 biography, with its audacious subtitle, 'nach Originalquellen'. The faith in an incomplete and often murky, yet abundant and candid, corpus of primary sources permeates Mozart historiography, and it underpins the very projects of the Köchel catalogue and Mozart-Ausgaben, even as their editors embrace the flexibility and ephemerality of so many of Mozart's works.

Our most tenacious myths about Mozart claim for him a transcendence and edificatory value surpassing nearly all other composers. In his famous 1989 essay, 'Mozart and the Ethnomusicological Study of Western Culture', Bruno Nettl uses Mozart to deconstruct 'the concept of the master composer'. Yet even Nettl confesses in the essay's 'coda' that 'when I hear Mozart's works, I am inclined to think that there is really only one composer'.[15] Scott Burnham is decidedly more careful in his book *Mozart's Grace*, but he still hears a 'childlike yet knowing' quality in Mozart's music, 'an ever renewable embrace of innocence' in 'those emergent passages that seem to lift off from the prevailing musical discourse, like a visitation of altered consciousness'. The succession of verbs with which Burnham's book draws to a close is telling: 'Mozart teaches us', 'Mozart meets us', 'Mozart helps us'.[16] Burnham, like many of us, is unwilling to wholly surrender the idea of Mozart as an agent of edification and solace.

In our increasingly global, postcolonial age, other myths chafe, whether they be the universality of Viennese Classicism, Austrian cultural hegemony or Western cultural imperialism itself. As Annie Yen-Ling Liu points out, in the 1979 documentary *From Mao to Mozart: Isaac Stern in China*, Stern vigorously denied any relevance of economic history to an understanding of Mozart, claiming his genius as a (the?) key to China's spiritual recovery from the Cultural Revolution.[17] Melanie Lowe has traced the

---

[14] Everist, *Mozart's Ghosts*, p. 15; original quote from William Stafford, *The Mozart Myths: A Critical Reassessment* (Stanford: Stanford University Press, 1991), pp. 267–8. See also Simon P. Keefe: 'priorities on the part of biographers – however fastidiously these issues are researched – [. . .] tell us as much (or nearly as much) about the author writing the book as they do about Mozart'. Keefe, 'Mozart, (Johann Chrysostom) Wolfgang Amadeus, H. Biographies', in Cliff Eisen and Keefe (eds.), *The Cambridge Mozart Encyclopedia* (Cambridge: Cambridge University Press, 2006), p. 339.

[15] Bruno Nettl, 'Mozart and the Ethnomusicological Study of Western Culture (an essay in four movements)', *Yearbook for Traditional Music*, 21 (1989), pp. 3, 15. Nettl dedicated the essay to his father, the Mozart scholar Paul Nettl.

[16] Scott Burnham, *Mozart's Grace* (Princeton: Princeton University Press, 2013), pp. 165, 166, 168.

[17] Annie Yen-Ling Liu, 'Mozart, Modernization, and the Fading of the Cultural Revolution in China', paper delivered at the Seventh Biennial Meeting of the Mozart Society of America, 'Mozart and Modernity', University of Western Ontario, 21 October 2017. See also Cornelia Szabó-Knotik, 'Calafati, Sou-Chong, Lang Lang, and Li Wei: Two Hundred Years of "the Chinese" in Austrian

appeal of Mozart in popular culture as 'a musical sign for elite characters, behaviors, and situations'.[18] Erik Levi has shown how the Nazis managed to claim Mozart as an icon for German imperialism.[19] The perceived missionary function of Mozart has been elaborated and debunked in contexts as disparate as refugee camps and prisons.[20] And the deconstruction of Mozart's Orientalism is now a well-established category of Mozart scholarship.[21] Recent productions of Mozart operas outside the European-American tradition show an increasing interest in confronting these issues in creative reception as well as in scholarship.[22] Already in the 1920 manifesto for the Salzburg Festival, Mozart was marshalled as a figure representing a cultural crossroads.[23] Now he stands on the cusp of new ways of thinking about music history.

Were this essay to be updated in fifty or a hundred years, new families of myths would no doubt have emerged and receded. For each age has its own needs and desires for which myths provide some illusion of an answer.

Music, Drama, and Film', in Hon-Lun Yang and Michael Saffle (eds.), *China and the West: Music, Representation, and Reception* (Ann Arbor: University of Michigan Press, 2017), especially pp. 76–9.

[18] Melanie Lowe, *Pleasure and Meaning in the Classical Symphony* (Bloomington: Indiana University Press), p. 177.

[19] Erik Levi, *Mozart and the Nazis: How the Third Reich Abused a Cultural Icon* (New Haven, CT: Yale University Press, 2010).

[20] See Rachel Beckles Willson, 'Music Teachers as Missionaries: Understanding Europe's Recent Dispatches to Ramallah', in Laudan Nooshin (ed.), *The Ethnomusicology of Western Art Music* (London: Routledge, 2014), especially p. 30; and Pierpaolo Polzonetti, 'Don Giovanni Goes to Prison: Teaching Opera Behind Bars', *MusicologyNow* (16 February 2016), and ensuing comments on this and other blogs.

[21] See for instance Mary Hunter, 'The *Alla Turca* Style in the Late Eighteenth Century: Race and Gender in the Symphony and the Seraglio', in Jonathan Bellman (ed.), *The Exotic in Western Music* (Boston: Northeastern University Press, 1998), pp. 43–73; Matthew Head, *Orientalism, Masquerade and Mozart's Turkish Music* (London: Royal Musical Association, 2000); Malcolm S. Cole, 'Monostatos and His "Sister": Racial Stereotype in *Die Zauberflöte* and Its Sequel', *Opera Quarterly*, 21/1 (2005), pp. 2–26; and Nasser Al-Taee, *Representations of the Orient in Western Music: Violence and Sensuality* (Farnham, Surrey: Ashgate, 2010), pp. 123–60.

[22] See for instance Sheila Boniface Davies and J. Q. Davies, '"So Take This Magic Flute and Blow. It Will Protect Us As We Go": *Impempe Yomlingo* (2007–11) and South Africa's Ongoing Transition' [on an adaptation of *Die Zauberflöte* by Isango Portobello, dir. Mark Dornford-May, Cape Town, South Africa, 2007], *Opera Quarterly*, 28/1–2 (2012), pp. 54–71; Gia Kourlas, 'Mozart Tale with Accent of Cambodia' [on *Pamina Devi: A Cambodian Magic Flute*, Khmer Arts Ensemble of Phnom Penh, dir. Sophiline Cheam Shapiro, 2006)], *New York Times* (11 October 2007); Robert McQueen et al., 'West Coast First Peoples and *The Magic Flute*: Tracing the Journey of a Cross-Cultural Collaboration', in Pamela Karantonis and Dylan Robinson (eds.), *Opera Indigene: Re/presenting First Nations and Indigenous Cultures* (Farnham, Surrey: Ashgate, 2011) [on Coast Salish-inspired production of *Die Zauberflöte*, produced in consultation with the First Peoples' Cultural Council, dir. Robert McQueen, 2013]; *The Abduction from the Seraglio* (Ankara State Opera, Turkey, dir. Yekta Kara, 2014); and the forthcoming 'Mozart at Angkor: A Cambodian *Magic Flute*', produced in collaboration with Amrita Performing Arts (dir. Stefano Vizioli, 2019).

[23] 'Das Salzburger Land ist das Herz vom Herzen Europas. [. . .] Mozart ist der Ausdruck von alledem.' Hugo von Hofmannsthal, 'Die Salzburger Festspiele' (1919), in Jeanne Benay (ed.), *L'Autriche 1918–1938: Recueil de textes civilisationnels* (Rouen: University of Rouen, 1999), p. 83.

Nettl asks: if the great masters 'are the deities, is their character explained by myths widely told if not rationally believed? Can one gain important insights into musical culture from the reading of myths?'[24] This observation brings to mind a single-reel film made in 1909 by Gaumont Studios in Paris, *La mort de Mozart* (The Death of Mozart; dir. Étienne Arnaud and Louis Feuillade). Reels of the film survive in the National Library of Australia and the Library of Congress, while the George Eastman House owns a set of disintegrating nitrate clippings from the film.[25] The central episode of the short film has Mozart lying on his deathbed, inspired to continue composing the Requiem after a violin student of his (perhaps intended to represent Franz Xaver Süssmayr) plays him excerpts from *Le nozze di Figaro, Don Giovanni* and *Die Zauberflöte*. As the violinist plays, a scene from each of the three operas appears in the upper left corner of the screen, a film-within-a-film that is watched both by us and by the rapt, dying Mozart. His operatic visions are incomplete, yet tantalizingly vivid, perhaps even more so to a twenty-first-century viewer observing the deterioration of the artefact itself.[26] Rather than presume to break the cycle of mythmaking, perhaps we can and need only continue to pursue the vanishing truths behind the fragments that survive.

---

[24] Nettl, 'Mozart and the Ethnomusicological Study of Western Culture', p. 6.
[25] See Keefe, *Mozart's Requiem*, pp. 36–7; and Jürg Stenzl, 'Mozarts Filmdébut als Endspiel: *La Mort de Mozart* (1909)', *Musick & Ästhetik*, 21/82 (2017), pp. 39–50.
[26] One thinks of Bill Morrison's haunting experimental collage of found nitrate film clippings, *Decasia: A Portrait of Decay* (2002). See Hannah Lewis, '*Decasia* as Audiovisual Elegy', *Journal of Musicological Research*, 37/3 (2018), pp. 189–208.

CHAPTER 34

Editing Mozart

Rupert Ridgewell

It is surely no exaggeration to say that Mozart's music has been published and disseminated in print to a greater extent than any other composer in the last 250 years. From the very first editions of his music, which appeared in Paris and London in 1764 and 1765, to the latest popular and scholarly publications, Mozart has been a mainstay of the global music publishing industry. While there is no way accurately to estimate the total number of editions that have appeared, the records for musical scores featuring Wolfgang Amadeus Mozart as 'author' in the WorldCat database provide a useful starting point, amounting to around 75,000 at the time of writing, covering everything from pedagogical editions and popular arrangements for various combinations of instrument, to complete scholarly editions.[1] All of these publications were edited, to a greater or lesser degree, in the sense that someone was responsible for rendering the details of Mozart's notation in a form ready for engraving, typesetting and printing, albeit with varying levels of diligence and scholarly acuity.

The range of strategies pursued in the editing of Mozart's music at any particular time or place was largely dependent on four factors: the accessibility of primary sources, especially his autograph manuscripts, and the choices made about their relative priority or importance; the way in which editors have evaluated and interpreted those sources, deploying scholarly techniques and editorial philosophies that have developed over time and which were themselves culturally conditioned; the changing nature of publishing practice, which was itself dependent on shifting taste, commercial imperatives and technical innovation; and the development of musical instruments and tastes in performance practice. Thus the history of editing Mozart's music embraces not only different approaches to the text but also issues of technological and social change, as well as wider thought about the

---

[1] https://www.worldcat.org/. This total admittedly includes many duplicate entries for the same editions, reflecting multiple holding locations.

nature of the work itself. The way in which these factors played out over time not only shaped the texts of the editions that were presented to the public but was also a key ingredient in influencing how Mozart's music was perceived and disseminated.

Early Editions

One of the many reasons why Mozart's music remains open to different editorial approaches is the fact that he did not, in common with the majority of composers of his era, edit his own music for publication in editions that might have become regarded as authoritative. To be sure, some of the first editions published during Mozart's lifetime undoubtedly appeared with his tacit or explicit sanction, especially those in Vienna under the imprint of the publishers Artaria, Hoffmeister and Torricella, but the concept of an 'authorized' edition was itself not fully recognized at that time. In theory, the medium of print presented composers with the opportunity to exert greater control over the texts of their works than the trade in music copying could ever allow. In these circumstances the printed text might capture a later stage in the composer's thinking than the autograph manuscript, especially if the publisher offered the facility to read and correct proof copies. But given the almost complete absence of evidence concerning Mozart's dealings with publishers (see Chapter 18 on publishing in this volume), his involvement in the publication process and attitude towards print is difficult to assess with any certainty. There also remains considerable doubt as to the extent to which the editions appearing in Mozart's lifetime were consciously edited even by their respective publishers, many of whom probably exerted relatively little control over the (often freelance) engravers who were responsible for preparing the pewter plates from which the editions were printed.

Given this apparent lack of control, it is perhaps not surprising that many of these editions from Mozart's lifetime exhibit what appear to be obvious errors and inconsistencies. Robert Riggs, for example, points to the different ways in which the keyboard and violin parts are articulated in Artaria's edition of the violin sonatas Opus 2 (Vienna, 1781), where 'the violin part has strokes throughout, but the piano part has a mixture of dots and strokes, even for the same motives that had strokes in the violin part'.[2] Modern editors have therefore tended to approach these texts with

---

[2] Riggs, 'Mozart's Notation of Staccato Articulation: A New Appraisal', *Journal of Musicology*, 15/2 (1997), pp. 230–77, at 270.

a healthy degree of scepticism, even if in some cases they offer alternative readings that may reflect authorial revision or at least authentic contemporary practice. Notable examples of such readings have been identified in Artaria's editions of the Fantasy in C minor K. 475 and the six 'Haydn' string quartets.[3] In other cases, early editions have to be the principal source in the absence of an autograph manuscript or other authentic source: notable examples include the 'Linz' Symphony K. 425, the Piano Sonata in C major K. 545, the Divertimento in E♭ major for string trio K. 563, the Piano Concerto in B♭ major K. 595 and the Clarinet Concerto K. 622.

The early reception of Mozart's music was undoubtedly influenced and propagated by the nature of these editions, and they continued to exert influence well into the nineteenth century through reprints either by the original publishers or by successor firms. This activity, however, reflected commercial expedience rather than any exalted view of the value of these editions as sources that were contemporaneous with the composer himself. At the same time, the early nineteenth century also saw increased competition between publishers attempting to claim ownership of Mozart's legacy and thereby capture a larger share of the burgeoning market for his music by issuing editions that asserted authority based either on supposed completeness or on declarations of privileged access to original sources. This was part of a larger trend to canonize Mozart's music in accordance with the biographical trope that started to emerge around 1800, in which the composer was portrayed as a romantic hero, transcending the social and economic constraints of his time to produce music of enduring value and individuality.

Between 1798 and 1806, the firm of Breitkopf & Härtel published an *Oeuvres complettes* in seventeen volumes based partly on manuscripts obtained from Constanze and Mozart's sister, Nannerl. It was not, in fact, complete even in terms of the music that was available at that time but nevertheless reflects a commercial strategy to preserve and monumentalize Mozart's output in print. In 1800 the firm of Johann Anton André started producing editions that were marked on their title pages 'Édition

---

[3] Cliff Eisen and Christopher Wintle, 'Mozart's C minor Fantasy, K. 475: An Editorial "Problem" and its Analytical and Critical Consequences', *Journal of the Royal Musical Association*, 124 (1999), pp. 26–52; Wolf-Dieter Seiffert, 'Mozart's "Haydn" Quartets: An Evaluation of the Autographs and First Edition, with Particular Attention to mm. 125–42 of the Finale of K. 378', in Cliff Eisen (ed.), *Mozart Studies 2* (Oxford: Clarendon Press, 1997), pp. 175–200; and Simon P. Keefe, 'Composing, Performing and Publishing: Mozart's "Haydn" Quartets', in Keefe (ed.), *Mozart Studies 2* (Cambridge: Cambridge University Press, 2015), pp. 140–67.

faite d'après la partition en manuscrit' or 'Édition faite d'après le manuscrit original de l'auteur', or some such formulation. This was highly unusual at a time when printed music usually appeared with no indication about the sources employed. The basis for this statement was André's acquisition in 1799 of a large portion of Mozart's musical legacy from Constanze, who had gathered up manuscripts retained by the composer or his family after his death. A total of 446 works by Mozart appeared under the firm's imprint in 369 editions, encompassing much of the chamber music Mozart composed in Vienna between 1781 and 1791, as well as solo piano music, symphonies, concertos and divertimentos; of these works, 124 were identified as being produced 'from the manuscript'.[4] Comparisons with the autograph sources show that André's editorial approach was usually faithful with regard to basic notation (pitches and note values) but rather less consistent in the treatment of articulation, phrasing or the positioning of dynamic markings, among other aspects of the musical text. In some cases, André also appears to have consulted other printed or manuscript sources at his disposal or used his own editorial discretion to deviate from the autograph texts where considered necessary.

Complete Editions

The two major complete editions of Mozart's works published in the nineteenth century and second half of the twentieth century represented major advances in knowledge and technique in their respective eras. Despite the chronological gap between them, they each embodied surprisingly similar objectives, even if the manner of their execution was different in several important respects.

The intended aim of Breitkopf & Hartel's *Kritisch durchgesehene Gesammtausgabe* (now commonly known as the *Alte Mozart-Ausgabe*, or AMA), published between 1877 and 1883 – with supplements appearing until 1910 – was to reproduce Mozart's notation faithfully with no arbitrary editorial intervention.[5] This approach represented something of a backlash against the many practical and pedagogical editions that had proliferated since the 1820s, often with an overlay of fingering, phrasing and dynamic markings reflecting the tastes and preferences of individual scholars,

---

[4] Birgit Grün, 'Johann Anton Andrés Editionspraxis der Mozartschen Werke', in Jürgen Eichenauer (ed.), *Johann Anton André (1775–1842) und der Mozart-Nachlass: Ein Notenschatz in Offenbach am Main* (Weimar: Verlag und Datenbank für Geisteswissenschaften, 2006), p. 69.

[5] *Wolfgang Amadeus Mozarts Werke – Kritisch Durchgesehene Gesammtausgabe* (Leipzig: Breitkopf & Hartel, 1877–83).

teachers and performers.[6] The AMA also coincided with the early development of music criticism as a discipline in its own right, in which the study of Mozart and his music was an important strand. The autograph manuscripts were therefore regarded as something approaching holy writ by editors of the AMA, including such figures as Johannes Brahms and Joseph Joachim, even if in practice there was little editorial consistency between different parts of the series, or even within individual editions, despite the stated aims of the endeavour. The AMA therefore represented a major step forwards in bringing together Mozart's known output in supposedly authentic texts, but from an editorial perspective it did not live up to its own scholarly aspirations and was 'inevitably biased by contemporaneous notions of notation and performance'.[7] In cases where Mozart's autograph itself was not available for consultation, somewhat arbitrary decisions were often made about the priority of sources and their evaluation: the AMA edition of the Divertimento K. 563, for example, was apparently based on an edition published by Heckel in Mannheim around 1860, which was itself derived from an André edition of 1805.[8] Misgivings about the editorial standards applied in the AMA emerged even before the series was completed, but its influence was nevertheless felt throughout the twentieth century, as either the editions themselves or new editions based on them were widely used in performance and for study.

Fifty-three years in the making, the *Neue Mozart-Ausgabe* (NMA) also aimed to cover the entirety of Mozart's creative output, employing the most up-to-date scholarly techniques to create editions that would reproduce, in the words of the editor Wolfgang Rehm, 'the unadulterated wishes of the composer' – an objective not dissimilar to that of the AMA.[9] The level of scientific engagement was, however, substantially higher than in any previous edition, each volume being furnished with an exhaustive critical commentary and a detailed evaluation of sources. It may seem, therefore, that the task of editing Mozart's music has been accomplished,

---

[6] Robin Stowell, 'Mozart's "Viennese" Sonatas for Keyboard and Violin According to Ferdinand David: A Survey of Editorial and Violin Performance Practices', in Martin Harlow (ed.), *Mozart's Chamber Music with Keyboard* (Cambridge: Cambridge University Press, 2012), pp. 69–103.

[7] Christina A. Georgiou, 'The Historical Editing of Mozart's Piano Sonatas in the Nineteenth Century: Context, Practice and Implications', *Mozart-Jahrbuch 2013* (Kassel: Bärenreiter, 2014), p. 179.

[8] Wolf-Dieter Seiffert, 'Mozarts Streichtrio KV 563: eine Quellen- und Textkritische Erörterung', *Mozart-Jahrbuch 1998* (Kassel: Bärenreiter, 1999), pp. 53–83.

[9] *Wolfgang Amadeus Mozart. Neue Ausgabe sämtlicher Werke* (Kassel: Bärenreiter, 1955–2008). Wolfgang Rehm, 'Collected Editions', in H. C. Robbins Landon (ed.), *The Mozart Compendium: A Guide to Mozart's Life and Music* (London: Thames and Hudson, 1990), pp. 426–7.

but like any work of such magnitude compiled over such a lengthy period of time, the NMA was not immune to shifts in scholarly opinion, commercial imperatives, or the vagaries of source availability.

The belated rediscovery in 1980 of a substantial number of Mozart's manuscripts that were shipped by the Nazis from Berlin to Kraków during the Second World War, for example, rendered obsolete some of the editions that had already appeared, including the Symphony No. 38 in D major K. 504 ('Prague'), the Piano Concerto in Bb major K. 595 and *Die Zauberflöte*.[10] The initial reluctance of the Internationale Stiftung Mozarteum to issue entirely new editions of these works reflected the commercial realities of scholarly publishing in the 1980s and 1990s and the subscription model adopted by Bärenreiter, the NMA's publisher.[11]

The NMA also grew up alongside some very significant advances in the study of Mozart sources since 1945, notably Alan Tyson's work on the paper types found in the autographs, Wolfgang Plath's studies of Mozart's handwriting and Ulrich Konrad's assessments of the sketches and drafts, all of which have resulted in the redating of several works and a greater understanding of Mozart's compositional process.[12] More detailed scholarly attention accorded to the description and evaluation of contemporary manuscript copies and first editions, in the work of Dexter Edge, Gertraut Haberkamp and others,[13] also tends to challenge the general editorial stance adopted by the NMA, which places any surviving autograph manuscripts at the top of the hierarchy of sources to be evaluated and advocates caution about variant readings found elsewhere. Seemingly intractable problems also remain, such as the issue of Mozart's expressive intentions in relation to the notation of dots and strokes – which varies significantly in his manuscripts – or the sometimes inexact notation of slurs and phrasing, not to mention particular difficulties associated with works such as the Requiem, in which the legitimacy of the posthumous completion by Franz Xaver Süssmayr has been the subject of ongoing dispute. Increased attention has also been directed towards related extra-musical issues, such as the editorial strategies to adopt in relation to the texts of Mozart's vocal music.

---

[10] This cache of manuscripts is now held by the Biblioteka Jagiellońska in Kraków.

[11] Cliff Eisen, 'The Old and New Mozart Editions', *Early Music*, 19 (1991), pp. 513–32.

[12] See Alan Tyson, *Mozart: Studies of the Autograph Scores* (Cambridge, MA: Harvard University Press, 1987); Wolfgang Plath, *Mozart-Schriften: ausgewählte Aufsätze*, ed. Marianne Danckwardt (Kassel: Bärenreiter, 1991); Ulrich Konrad, *Mozarts Schaffensweise: Studien zu den Werkautographen, Skizzen und Entwürfen* (Göttingen: Vandenhoeck & Ruprecht, 1992).

[13] Gertraut Haberkamp, *Die Erstdrucke der Werke von Wolfgang Amadeus Mozart* (Tutzing: Schneider, 1986); Dexter Edge, 'Mozart's Viennese Copyists' (PhD thesis, University of Southern California, 2000).

Rehm's confidence in the ability of the editor to capture Mozart's intentions sounds especially ambitious in light of more recent questioning of the very notion that a composer's wishes are ever absolute. This applies especially in the case of Mozart, for whom the concept of the work was rather more closely tied to the act of performance than might be understood today. Much scholarly debate in recent years has accordingly revolved around the notion that the business of notating music was for Mozart more closely entwined with performance than the desire to set down a *Fassung letzter Hand* or the ideal representation of his conception of the work with a view to posterity. Instead, much more latitude was expected of the eighteenth-century performer in interpreting and embellishing the musical text, to the extent that some scholars today approach Mozart's manuscripts as fluid documents arising from, or guiding, the act of performance rather than as immutable texts.[14]

If this realignment of understanding vis-à-vis the original musical sources suggests a new direction in the editing of Mozart's music, the prospects for future work are greatly enhanced by the flexibility inherent in online publication. Not only are many more original sources now available for study by the widest possible audience via digitized surrogates, technical developments also now make it possible to issue hybrid editions that overlay multiple readings or sources or automatically link the musical notation with sound recordings. The NMA itself was made freely available in digitized format from the end of 2005, while the focus of activity for the Internationale Stiftung Mozarteum has since shifted to the development of the *Digitalen Mozart-Edition*, which promises to harness emerging technical capabilities, such as the Music Encoding Initiative (MEI), to realize an interactive and flexible platform for delivering the musical texts to the user. New digital editions of selected works are also planned in order keep abreast of developments in Mozart scholarship, whilst retaining the original NMA editions as 'reference texts'.[15]

At a fundamental level, editing Mozart involves negotiating the gulf between our understanding of the 'work' and its manifestation in musical sources that inevitably reflect the tastes and practices of an era distant from our own. The multiplicity of approaches made possible by the combination of shifts in editorial philosophy and technological progress brings to

---

[14] The degree to which Mozart's compositional processes were influenced by the opportunities and vicissitudes of performance in his Vienna years is explored in Simon P. Keefe, *Mozart in Vienna: The Final Decade* (Cambridge: Cambridge University Press, 2017).

[15] http://dme.mozarteum.at. For an introduction to the project, see Ulrich Leisinger, 'Methoden und Ziele der Digitalen Mozart-Edition', *Mozart-Jahrbuch 2013* (Kassel: Bärenreiter, 2014), pp. 43–63.

the fore the element of subjectivity that comes into play when confronting that gulf. It also implies some level of transfer in decision-making from the editor to the performer or reader in navigating the proliferation of editions and variant readings. Mozart's music is not unique in being exposed to this shifting landscape, but its continuing agency in society and the notational complexities that underpin its immense expressive range mean that the impact has the potential to be felt more widely than in the case of almost any other composer.

CHAPTER 35

Mozart on Record

John Irving

Commercially, Mozart is a winner. There are so many recordings of Mozart's music that it would be easy to fill this chapter with a simple A-Z listing of a (probably quite small) selection. His music appears in boxed sets, in reissues, on period instruments, in compilations associated with states of mind ('Mozart Mindfulness', 'Relaxing Mozart Masterworks'), as tokens of taste to be displayed on social occasions to one's friends ('Essential Mozart Classics'), as benchmark recordings by a renowned interpreter, and as rites of passage for up-and-coming new stars. Mozart on Record has a habit of squeezing into every nook and cranny of our lives and across the procession of different recording technologies that have graced the last 125 years or so, including piano roll, shellac, vinyl, cassette, CD and digital download. As a subject of study, its vast scope cannot be fully accommodated in a brief chapter.

I propose to treat Mozart on Record as a phenomenon, addressing some of its characteristic qualities, and especially some of the ways in which it has mediated our responses to Mozart's music across several generations. Undoubtedly, Mozart on Record has had, and continues to have, cultural, economic and social impact. That Mozart's music is more widely available now to a larger public than at any time in its history is as a consequence of recordings (and to developments in the modes of distribution of those recordings). This is surely welcome news, as that facility also carries the potential for the cultural enrichment of many lives through great music – a positive consequence of Mozart on Record. That it depends, like any other musical genre, on a distribution model in which the music is commodified has significant consequences for our contextualization of Mozart, including the ways in which we appreciate and engage with him. It forces an admission that, these days, we actually 'use' Mozart's music for various purposes. Before the age of recording, and indeed in parallel with earlier analogue recording technologies such as LPs and cassettes throughout much of the twentieth century, we already 'used' Mozart's music (more, or less consciously) in our social encounters. Examples included going to a recital of Mozart piano works or an opera production for pleasure, entertainment or edification (in other words, a good night out); belonging to regional Gramophone Societies, at which one could spend an evening alongside other Mozart aficionados learning about different recordings of a favourite Mozart symphony or opera, perhaps guided by an invited expert from BBC radio; buying an LP of Mozart piano concertos played by (for example) Clifford Curzon, Friedrich Gulda or Murray Perahia in order to display critically acclaimed readings on our shelves as tokens of our finely tuned tastes; and later on purchasing CDs of this same repertory on period instruments that strip away all 'romantic varnish' to present the music cleanly, generally at a quicker tempo and 'authentically' on instruments of Mozart's time, exactly how he heard and/or 'intended' it – the last of these fictions a runaway commercial success, albeit a social practice easily (and rightly) ridiculed. But we perhaps did not think of such things as social utility functions, as social causes, leaving social traces that, in turn, produced social meanings. In this digital age, however, Mozart on Record behaves differently, in a much more overtly utilitarian fashion. For example, I could pay a small amount of money to an online music store to download to my iPhone a single track of, say, the finale from the 'Jupiter' Symphony K. 551 conducted by Karl Böhm. Having engaged in this transaction, I could utilize this digital information in various ways:

- I might add it to a playlist that I listen to as background music through my headphones while shopping, for instance, or (worse still) settling the bill at a self-service checkout afterwards, while simultaneously talking to my stockbroker.
- I might use it at the gym, as a component of an exercise routine (for example to pace myself on a running machine and, in particular, to 'wind down' at the end of that routine in time with the massive rallentando that Böhm injects at the end of the movement).
- I might find it convenient to be able to listen to this track at a time, and/ or in a place of my choosing, for some purpose or other – for instance, if I were writing a comparative review of performances of the 'Jupiter' for a magazine or radio programme, or perhaps a book chapter.
- I might listen to it simply for pleasure.

And so on.

These may all be perfectly reasonable situations in which to listen to Mozart (though the imaginary 'supermarket checkout Mozart' may be just a touch ostentatious). My broader point is that Mozart on Record belongs within a landscape of technological facility and commercial transaction conspiring in ways never before imagined to place Mozart's music into more and more situations for which it was never intended. During the nineteenth century, much of his instrumental music (and some of his sacred music too) steadily departed from the original domestic, salon and ecclesiastical environments whence it came for that bastion of civic pride and social responsibility, the concert hall. Newly served by virtuosos parading their prestidigitations on a continental scale in Paris, Berlin, Leipzig, Vienna, London, Amsterdam, Moscow, Madrid (etc.) and by mammoth orchestras and choral societies, Mozart's piano works, symphonies, concertos, masses and Requiem became social rituals, publicly performed in such grand spaces as Leipzig's Gewandhaus and Amsterdam's Concertgebouw. This practice played a significant role in retrospectively defining generic boundaries that, while sensible enough then as analogies to the craze for classification that was also expressed in the galleries of public museums and in factory production lines, would likely have seemed artificial to the composer just a few generations earlier.

By contrast, early recordings at the end of the nineteenth and beginning of the twentieth centuries recaptured the 'domestic' Mozart for the home listener. Their mechanical means of reproduction, while cumbersome indeed compared to today's miniature digital devices, were designed for listening in more intimate surroundings than the concert hall and on a scale more compatible with what Mozart himself had experienced. A certain mental dedication was required to listen to a 78rpm shellac disc that needed turning over every four minutes (or, later, a 33rpm vinyl LP), especially when the equipment was hand-wound (before electric-powering was introduced): the disc had to be cleaned and re-cleaned to avoid annoying pops and squeaks; the diamond-tipped record needle had to be maintained in good condition and replaced every so often; the bulky speaker (later, speakers – once stereo arrived) had to be suitably positioned. In short, your listening experience was one for which you really felt you had prepared and which would be rewarded by enjoyment of, say, Böhm's reading of the 'Jupiter' Symphony. Above all, listening to LPs of Mozart (perhaps this is still true of CDs) was often a social experience, a domestic, not civic, ritual that took place with family or friends. In the main, this is because the equipment was a relatively expensive family investment, one that looked like a piece of furniture and which occupied pride of place in a family living space. Enjoyment of Mozart on LP, cassette or CD had to be a social activity, a specific listening appointment negotiated by agreement, and fitted in amongst other family activities that might also utilize that same living-room space. By contrast, the instant availability of Böhm's recording of the 'Jupiter' finale after a deft click on a touch-screen device happens in isolation (often, indeed, while multi-tasking), no longer a shared cultural or social experience nor necessarily in the home but instead, on a peripatetic basis, perhaps on a bus or train or plane; in an academic office or library space; or in a coffee shop (or supermarket). This consequence of Mozart on Record has jolted Mozart appreciation as radically as did the nineteenth-century concert hall (though in the opposite direction). Has the gain in listening facility been accompanied by a corresponding gain in enjoyment? Mozart on Record might even have approached something close to the nihilistic in such circumstances. Whatever our view, we must surely agree that the very identity of a listening experience has become a horizon of expecta-tion for us today, in a way that it never was before.

Mozart on Record involves an encounter between two artificial media: musical notation and recordings. Both are practices. The first exhibits through symbols on a page the stuff of musical imagination in a form capable, but only to a degree, of reproduction. That capacity for reproduc-tion is imperfect because the codes through which musical notation might be understood, and which enable reproducibility at all, change their mean-ing – sometimes radically   across time and place. The slur is one example: in modern parlance, it no longer connotes a diminuendo (which is what it meant to Mozart's father). Notational symbols also operate differently depending on the particular instrument that attempts to sound them: for instance, there are types of separation between notes, perhaps indicated by some kind of staccato sign, that simply cannot mechanically be produced in the same way on different instruments and which appear in the context of a dialogue in which the same notated event is passed between those instruments. Sonic reality is thus capable of only imperfect visual expres-sion and its artificiality becomes all the more pronounced as we commit it to disc.

The second practice – recording – is likewise artificial. The fundamental thing that it is not is a performance. It includes some, at least, of the following characteristics:

• The performer(s) will have engaged deeply with the notated score over a protracted time period, mentally and physically embodying its impli-cations in ways mediated by that player's (or singer's) individual appre-ciation of the musical idiom represented in that score – leading to a coherent 'reading' or 'interpretation' of the work as represented in its notation.

- Having reached this extremely refined state of preparation, the performer(s) will enter into the recording environment, liaise with a recording producer and a sound engineer (sometimes these two roles are fulfilled by one and the same person) and in this collaborative context (and always under extreme time pressure) establish certain parameters, including the quality of sound desired in the recording space; the relative balance between different instruments involved; a range of musical factors, many of which need continual attention during the recording capture (which might last two or three days) and which call for an effective working relationship between the performer(s) and the producer – who hears from a perspective that no player can and on whose judgment much depends.

- These things agreed, the music is played before an array of microphones – a peculiar soulless 'audience' on stilts from which one receives neither empathy nor feedback as a performer; and it is played again and again, covering tiny imperfections in a variety of ways and from a variety of artificial starting-points so that there is a workable reservoir of material ('takes') from which the editing might subsequently commence.

- The editing of that large reservoir of recorded material is normally done not initially by the performer(s) but by the producer/sound engineer, based on detailed notes made at the recording sessions; this is creative work but is not that of the performer(s). Input from the performer(s) comes later in the process and is normally based on listening back to the 'first edit', from which state various, frequently minute, artistic nuances and refinements desired by the performer(s) are agreed upon (retrieved from other 'takes' whose qualities were carefully logged at the time), leading to a finished product representing a collaborative act that, while containing performed material, is nothing like a performance.

This, or something close to it, is what comprises Mozart on Record: something performed, but in a sense also 'pre-formed'. Technologies may differ over time: for instance, edits are no longer spliced together on tape but assembled digitally, and performers no longer have to get everything absolutely perfect in a single take in a situation which was once something far closer to actual performing (for instance on a shellac 78rpm disc or a piano roll). But the practice that leads to Mozart on Record still bears the trace of one artificial medium (recording) standing on the shoulders of another (notation).

Among the important social productions of meaning of Mozart on Record is an expectation engendered in the listener of absolute perfection, meaning absolute fidelity to the letter of the score. And here, several other artificial levels intrude. One of these touches on live performance and is quite bizarre: audiences frequently expect that performers whose recordings they own will perform perfectly in a real-time situation – despite all the radically different circumstances of a live performance as compared to a recording – and they are disappointed when this inevitably fails to happen. Mozart on Record in this respect carries potentially negative consequences for performance (and performers) because it warps the listener's expectations, turning their attendance at a concert performance into a more judgmental experience. A second, even more bizarre outcome is that of the concert-goer who is disappointed because the performer does not play the Mozart sonata (say) in the same way as they do on the CD! (I know at least one fellow performer who was berated after a recital by a CD collector on exactly these grounds.)

To a degree, then, Mozart on Record has led to a mutation in the qualities of the listener, viz.:

- the listener who attends a live performance of a work by Mozart as a community act (being an audience member), the serendipity of which is in and of itself appealing – essential, indeed – and who accepts the difference between this unique expressive act and a recording;
- the listener whose primary musical experience occurs in isolation (through headphones, for instance) and is an experience of an artificially constructed benchmark of perfection, guaranteed to be faithful to the notated score;
- the listener who, albeit unconsciously, mediates their experience through the lens of recorded perfection identically reproduced each and every time and who risks never being satisfied by a 'live' performance of the work.

Those for whom Mozart on Record equates to, and carries assurance and authority precisely because of, the reproducibility of an identical, note-perfect account every time are accessing Mozart in a way that differs radically from the composer's own view of his music. The very aspiration to capture Mozart on Record amounts to something of a departure from his own more flexible understanding of the relation of notation to performance. While Mozart's scores are quite carefully notated in respect of performance indications, there are many aspects of his known improvisational practice that lie beyond his notated texts and that his scores were simply never designed to capture. (This aspect is discussed in Chapter 26, 'Instrumental Performance Practice'.) The gulf already sketched between Mozart in performance and Mozart on Record is therefore further complicated by an extra variable: what Mozart wrote down and what additional (un-notated) expressive parameters his scores might suggest within his own documented performance practice are two different things. This situates Mozart on Record even more out on a limb, highlighting the tension between his own variable practice and the innate character of recordings that they are *identically reproducible accounts of something*. The (preposterous) notion that performer X's recording of a particular work by Mozart is the 'definitive account' relies upon that work having, as a prior condition, a definitive form of which such an account might be captured on record. And Mozart does not really conform to this condition.

For the recording artist sensitive to Mozart's particular situation, a creative tension can be exploited. For instance, in a recent recording of Mozart chamber works with Ensemble DeNOTE (2016), I faced the question of whether I should embellish reprises of the rondo theme in the finale of the G minor Piano Quartet K. 478 (from bar 135 [upbeat] to bar 143, and from bar 321 [termination of trill] to bar 329). In performance, I would do so without hesitation, building a progressively more elaborate melodic narrative through each of these points, treating them as moments of active recalibration rather than passive consolidation. This way, each return simultaneously offers a new perspective, stating the same thing differently or in a different tone of voice (the analogy of speech or conversation being deliberate here and fundamental to my understanding of Mozart's performance practice). But what should happen, I thought, in the context of the faithfully reproducible recording? My elaborations – departing in a performance progressively further and further from the melodic starting point, rather like Mozart's right-hand parts in his variations sets – might not sound so fresh after a dozen hearings on CD, let alone fifty. And surely, the point of improvised embellishments is that they sound fresh? So, should I have refrained from this historical performance practice altogether on the recording? Other performers (including those I greatly respect) choose in their recordings to play the notes on the page without extemporary additions precisely because their efforts may soon appear stale on account of the medium's fundamental quality of reproducibility. (Repeats can, after all, be differently played in terms of phrasing, texture balance, dynamic shadings and articulations.) Should I have allowed Mozart on Record to override, or at least curtail, my historical performance sense? Should I have represented Mozart only partially in the recording, using a copy of a Walter five-octave Viennese action instrument of a type familiar to Mozart and his original audiences, yet denying an essential performance practice in which he himself engaged habitually? Should I, in other words, have given Mozart on Record hegemony over Mozart in Performance? (Ultimately, I did not.)

Further Reading

Only a small proportion of the vast secondary literature on Mozart in context is given below. In addition to reference works, bibliographical items are listed in sections corresponding to the five sections of the book: 'Personality, Work, Worldview'; 'Towns, Cities, Countries'; 'Career Contexts and Environments'; 'Performers and Performance'; and 'Reception and Legacy'. Many items listed in one category will also be relevant to another; on occasion, when especially applicable, an individual item is listed in two categories. Readers are encouraged to survey these guidelines for further reading in their entirety when pursuing specific interests. The reference works will be useful for all – or almost all – types of contextual study.

Reference Works

Anderson, Emily (ed. and trans.). *The Letters of Mozart and his Family*. 3rd edition, London: Macmillan, 1985. (LMF)

Bauer, Wilhelm, Otto Erich Deutsch and Joseph Eibl (eds.). *Mozart: Briefe und Aufzeichnungen, Gesamtausgabe*. 7 vols. Kassel: Bärenreiter, 1962–75. (MBA)

Clive, Peter. *Mozart and His Circle: A Biographical Dictionary*. New Haven, CT: Yale University Press, 1993.

Deutsch, Otto Erich. *Mozart: Die Dokumente seines Lebens*. Kassel, Bärenreiter, 1961 (MDL). Trans. Eric Blom, Peter Branscombe and Jeremy Noble as *Mozart: A Documentary Biography*. 3rd edition, London: Simon & Schuster, 1990. (MDB)

Edge, Dexter and David Black. *Mozart: New Documents*. https://sites.google.com/site/mozartdocuments/home

Eisen, Cliff. *New Mozart Documents: A Supplement to O. E. Deutsch's Documentary Biography*. Stanford, CA: Stanford University Press, 1991. (NMD)

Eisen, Cliff (ed.), *Wolfgang Amadeus Mozart: A Life in Letters*. Trans. Stewart Spencer. London: Penguin, 2006.

Eisen, Cliff and Simon P. Keefe (eds.). *The Cambridge Mozart Encyclopedia*. Cambridge: Cambridge University Press, 2006.

Halliwell, Ruth. *The Mozart Family: Four Lives in a Social Context.* Oxford: Clarendon Press, 1998.

Heartz, Daniel. *Haydn, Mozart and the Viennese School, 1740–1780.* New York: Norton, 1995.

Mozart, Haydn and Early Beethoven, 1781–1802. New York: Norton, 2009.

Music in European Capitals: The Galant Style, 1720–1780. New York: Norton 2003.

Keefe, Simon P. *Mozart in Vienna: The Final Decade.* Cambridge: Cambridge University Press, 2017.

Landon, H. C. Robbins (ed.). *The Mozart Compendium.* London: Thames & Hudson, 1990.

Link, Dorothea. *The National Court Theatre in Mozart's Vienna.* Oxford: Clarendon Press, 1998.

Marshall, Robert L. (ed.). *Mozart Speaks: Views on Music, Musicians and the World.* New York: Schirmer, 1991.

Mozart, Wolfgang Amadeus. *Neue Ausgabe sämtlicher Werke.* Kassel: Bärenreiter, 1955–2007. (NMA) Available at Digital Mozart Edition: http://dme .mozarteum.at

Rosen, Charles. *The Classical Style: Haydn, Mozart, Beethoven.* New York: Norton, 1971 (expanded edition, New York: Norton, 1997).

Sadie, Stanley. *Mozart: The Early Years 1756–1781.* Oxford: Oxford University Press, 2006.

Spaethling, Robert (ed. and trans.). *Mozart's Letters, Mozart's Life.* New York: Norton, 2000.

Till, Nicholas. *Mozart and the Enlightenment: Truth, Virtue and Beauty in Mozart's Operas.* New York: Norton, 1993.

Zaslaw, Neal and William Cowdery (eds.). *The Compleat Mozart.* New York: Norton, 1990.

Personality, Work, Worldview

[Chapters 1–8]

Angermüller, Rudolph (ed.). *Joachim Ferdinand von Schidenhofen – Ein Freund der Mozarts.* Bad Honnef: K.H. Bock, 2006.

Arthur, John. 'Some Chronological Problems in Mozart: The Contribution of Ink Studies'. In Stanley Sadie (ed.), *Wolfgang Amadè Mozart: Essays on His Life and Music.* Oxford: Clarendon Press, 1996, pp. 35–52.

Black, David. 'Mozart and the Practice of Sacred Music, 1781–91'. PhD thesis, Harvard University, 2007.

Brown, Bruce Alan. 'In Defense of Josepha Duschek (and Mozart): Patronage, Friendship, and Evidence'. In Kathryn Libin (ed.), *Mozart in Prague: Essays on Performance, Patronage, Sources, and Reception*. Prague: Czech Academy of Sciences, 2016, pp. 155–74.

Edge, Dexter. 'Mozart's Viennese Copyists'. PhD thesis, University of Southern California, 2001.

Jacob, Margaret C. *Living the Enlightenment: Freemasonry and Politics in Eighteenth-Century Europe*. New York and Oxford: Oxford University Press, 1991.

Heartz, Daniel. 'Thomas Attwood's Lessons in Composition with Mozart'. *Proceedings of the Royal Musical Association*, 100 (1973–4), pp. 175–83.

Keefe, Simon P. *Mozart's Piano Concertos: Dramatic Dialogue in the Age of Enlightenment*. Woodbridge and Rochester, NY: Boydell Press, 2001.

Konrad, Ulrich. *Mozart's Schaffensweise. Studien zu den Werkautographen, Skizzen und Entwürfen*. Göttingen: Vandenhoeck & Ruprecht, 1992.

'Mozart the Letter Writer and His Language'. Trans. William Buchanan. In Simon P. Keefe (ed.), *Mozart Studies 2*. Cambridge: Cambridge University Press, 2015, pp. 1–22.

Landon, H. C. Robbins. *Mozart and the Masons: New Light on the Lodge 'Crowned Hope'*. London: Thames and Hudson, 1982.

Leisinger, Ulrich. 'Die Fragmente Mozarts als kompositorisches und aufführungspraktisches Problem'. In Joachim Brügge (ed.), *Sowohl Mozart als auch ... Salzburger Jubiläumstagung der Rezeptions- und Interpretationsforschung (2016)*. Freiburg: Rombach, 2017, pp. 284–304.

Leopold, Silke. 'Mozarts künstlerisches Selbstverständnis zwischen Anpassung und Autonomie'. In Leopold (ed.), *Mozart Handbuch*. Kassel: Bärenreiter, and Stuttgart: Metzler, 2005, pp. 16–20.

Mozart, Wolfgang Amadeus. *Eigenhändiges Werkverzeichnis Faksimile, British Library Stefan Zweig MS 63*. Kassel: Bärenreiter, 1991.

Plath, Wolfgang. 'Beiträge zur Mozart-Autographie II: Schriftchronologie 1770–1780'. *Mozart-Jahrbuch 1976/77*, pp. 131–73.

Mozart-Schriften: ausgewählte Aufsätze. Ed. Marianne Danckwardt. Kässel: Bärenreiter, 1991.

Schroeder, David P. 'Mozart and Late Eighteenth-Century Aesthetics'. In Simon P. Keefe (ed.), *The Cambridge Companion to Mozart*. Cambridge: Cambridge University Press, 2003, pp. 48–58.

Mozart in Revolt: Strategies of Resistance, Mischief and Deception. New Haven, CT: Yale University Press, 1999.

Thompson, Katharine. *The Masonic Thread in Mozart*. London: Lawrence and Wishart, 1977.

Tyson, Alan. *Mozart: Studies of the Autograph Scores*. Cambridge, MA: Harvard University Press, 1987.

'Proposed New Dates for Many Works and Fragments Written by Mozart from March 1781 to December 1791'. In Cliff Eisen (ed.), *Mozart Studies*. Oxford: Clarendon Press, 1991, pp. 213–26.

Towns, Cities, Countries

[Chapters 9–15]

Beales, Derek. *Joseph II, Volume II: Against the World, 1780–1790*. Cambridge: Cambridge University Press, 2009.

'Mozart and the Habsburgs'. In *Enlightenment and Reform in Eighteenth-Century Europe*. London: I.B. Tauris, 2005, pp. 90–116.

Braunbehrens, Volkmar. *Mozart in Vienna: 1781–1791*. Trans. Timothy Bell. New York: Grove Weidenfeld, 1986.

Burney, Charles. *The Present State of Music in Germany, The Netherlands, and United Provinces*. 2 vols. London, 1775.

Colley, Linda. *Britons: Forging the Nation 1707–1837*. New Haven, CT: Yale University Press, 2009.

Corneilson, Paul and Eugene K. Wolf. 'Newly Identified Manuscripts of Operas and Related Works from Mannheim'. *Journal of the American Musicological Society*, 47 (1994), pp. 244–74.

Eisen, Cliff (ed.). *Orchestral Music in Salzburg 1750–1780*. Madison, WI: A-R Editions, 1994.

Keefe, Simon P. 'Mozart "Stuck in Music" in Paris (1778): Towards a New Biographical Paradigm'. In Keefe (ed.), *Mozart Studies 2*. Cambridge: Cambridge University Press, 2015, pp. 23–54.

Landon, H. C. Robbins. *Mozart and Vienna*. London: Thames and Hudson, 1991.

Link, Dorothea. 'Mozart's Appointment to the Viennese Court'. In Dorothea Link and Judith Nagley (eds.), *Words about Mozart: Essays in Honour of Stanley Sadie*. Woodbridge and Rochester, NY: Boydell Press, 2005, pp. 153–78.

Maitland, William. *The History and Survey of London: From its Foundation by the Romans to the Present Time*. London, 1756.

McVeigh, Simon. *Concert Life in London from Mozart to Haydn*. Cambridge: Cambridge University Press, 1993.

Morrow, Mary Sue. *Concert Life in Haydn's Vienna: Aspects of a Developing Musical and Social Institution*. Stuyvesant, NY: Pendragon, 1989.

Pelker, Bärbel. 'The Palatine Court in Mannheim'. In Samantha Owens et al. (eds.), *Music at German Courts, 1715–1760: Changing Artistic Priorities*. Woodbridge and Rochester, NY: Boydell Press, 2011, pp. 131–64.

Rawson, Robert G. *Bohemian Baroque: Czech Musical Culture and Style, 1600–1750*. Woodbridge and Rochester, NY: Boydell Press, 2013.

Reitzenstein, Baron Carl von. *Reise nach Wien*. Hof, 1795.

Rice, John A. *Empress Marie Therese and Music at the Viennese Court, 1792–1807*. Cambridge: Cambridge University Press, 2003.

'Vienna under Joseph II and Leopold II'. In Neal Zaslaw (ed.), *The Classical Era*. London: Macmillan, 1989, pp. 126–65.

Riesbeck, Johann Kaspar. *Briefe eines reisenden Franzosen über Deutschland an seinen Bruder zu Paris*. Zurich, 1784.

Robins, Brian. *Catch and Glee Culture in Eighteenth-Century England*. Woodbridge and Rochester, NY: Boydell & Brewer, 2006.

Schmid, Manfred Hermann. *Mozart in Salzburg: Ein Ort für sein Talent*. Salzburg: Anton Pustet, 2006.

Templeton, Hannah. 'The Mozarts in London: Exploring the Family's Professional, Social and Intellectual Networks in 1764–1765'. PhD thesis, King's College London, 2016.

Wolf, Eugene K. 'The Mannheim Court'. In Neal Zaslaw (ed.), *The Classical Era*. London: Macmillan, 1989, pp. 213–39.

Woodfield, Ian. 'New Light on the Mozarts' London Visit: A Private Concert with Manzuoli'. *Music & Letters*, 76/2 (1995), pp. 187–208.

Performing Operas for Mozart: Impresarios, Singers and Troupes. Cambridge: Cambridge University Press, 2012.

Career Contexts and Environments

[Chapters 16–20]

Alwis, Lisa de (trans. and ed.). *Anti-Da Ponte*. Malden, MA: Mozart Society of America, 2015.

Bauer, Günther G. *Mozart: Geld, Ruhm und Ehre*. Bad Honnef: K.H. Bock, 2009.

Baumol, William J. and Hilda Baumol. 'On the Economics of Musical Composition in Mozart's Vienna'. In James M. Morris (ed.), *On Mozart*. Cambridge: Cambridge University Press, 1994, pp. 72–101.

Beales, Derek. *Joseph II, Volume I: In the Shadow of Maria Theresa, 1741–1780*. Cambridge: Cambridge University Press, 1987.

Joseph II, Volume II: Against the World, 1780–1790. Cambridge: Cambridge University Press, 2009.

'Mozart and the Habsburgs'. In *Enlightenment and Reform in Eighteenth-Century Europe*. London: I.B. Tauris, 2005, pp. 90–116.

Black, David. 'Mozart's Association with the Tonkünstler-Societät'. In Simon P. Keefe (ed.), *Mozart Studies 2*. Cambridge: Cambridge University Press, 2015, pp. 55–75.

Buch, David J. *Magic Flutes and Enchanted Forests: The Supernatural in Eighteenth-Century Musical Theater*. Chicago: University of Chicago Press, 2008.

Da Ponte, Lorenzo. *Memoirs*. New York: New York Review of Books, 2000.

DeNora, Tia. *Beethoven and the Construction of Genius: Musical Politics in Vienna, 1792–1803*. Berkeley and Los Angeles: University of California Press, 1998.

Edge, Dexter. 'Mozart's Fee for "Così fan tutte"'. *Journal of the Royal Musical Association*, 116/2 (1991), pp. 211–35.

Geffray, Geneviève (ed.). *Marie Anne Mozart 'meine tag ordnungen'*. Bad Honnef: K.H. Bock, 1998.

Haberkamp, Getraut. *Die Erstdrucke der Werke von Wolfgang Amadeus Mozart*. 2 vols. Tutzing: Hans Schneider, 1986.

Hintermaier, Ernst. 'Die Salzburger Hofkapelle von 1700 bis 1806. Organisation und Personal'. PhD thesis, University of Salzburg, 1972.

Hunter, Mary. *The Culture of Opera Buffa in Mozart's Vienna: A Poetics of Entertainment*. Princeton: Princeton University Press, 1999.

Keefe, Simon P. 'Composing, Performing and Publishing: Mozart's "Haydn" Quartets'. In Keefe (ed.), *Mozart Studies 2*. Cambridge: Cambridge University Press, 2015, pp. 140–67.

Link, Dorothea. 'Mozart's Appointment to the Viennese Court'. In Dorothea Link and Judith Nagley (eds.), *Words about Mozart: Essays in Honour of Stanley Sadie*. Woodbridge: Boydell Press, 2005, pp. 153–78.

Moore, Julia. 'Mozart in the Market-Place'. *Journal of the Royal Musical Association*, 114/1 (1989), pp. 18–42.

Morrow, Mary Sue. *Concert Life in Haydn's Vienna: Aspects of a Developing Musical and Social Institution*. Stuyvesant, NY: Pendragon, 1989.

Neff, Teresa M. 'Baron van Swieten and Late Eighteenth-Century Viennese Music Culture'. PhD thesis, Boston University, 1998.

Olleson, Edward. 'Gottfried van Swieten: Patron of Haydn and Mozart'. *Proceedings of the Royal Musical Association*, 89 (1962–3), pp. 63–74.

Rice, John A. *Antonio Salieri and Viennese Opera*. Chicago: University of Chicago Press, 1998.

    Mozart on the Stage. Cambridge: Cambridge University Press, 2009.

Ridgewell, Rupert. 'A Newly Identified Viennese Mozart Edition'. In Simon P. Keefe (ed.), *Mozart Studies 2*. Cambridge: Cambridge University Press, pp. 106–39.

    'Biographical Myth and the Publication of Mozart's Piano Quartets'. *Journal of the Royal Musical Association*, 135/1 (2010), pp. 41–114.

'Inside a Viennese *Kunsthandlung*: Artaria in 1784'. In Emily Green and Catherine Mayes (eds.), *Consuming Music: Individuals, Institutions, Communities, 1730–1830*. Woodbridge and Rochester, NY: University of Rochester Press, 2017, pp. 29–61.

Seiffert, Wolf-Dieter. 'Mozart's "Haydn" Quartets: An Evaluation of the Autographs and First Edition, with Particular Attention to mm. 125–42 of the Finale of K. 378'. In Cliff Eisen (ed.), *Mozart Studies 2*. Oxford: Clarendon Press, 1997, pp. 175–200.

Steptoe, Andrew. 'Mozart and Poverty: A Re-examination of the Evidence'. *Musical Times*, 125 (1984), pp. 196–201.

The Mozart-Da Ponte Operas: The Cultural and Musical Background to 'Le nozze di Figaro', 'Don Giovanni' and 'Così fan tutte'. Oxford: Clarendon Press, 1991.

Yates, W. E. *Theatre in Vienna: A Critical History, 1776–1995*. Cambridge: Cambridge University Press, 1996.

Weinmann, Alexander. *Die Wiener Verlagswerke von Franz Anton Hoffmeister*. Vienna: Universal Edition, 1964.

Wolff, Christoph. *Mozart at the Gateway to His Fortune: Serving the Emperor, 1788–1791*. New York: Norton, 2012.

Performers and Performance

[Chapters 21–27]

Albrechtsberger, Johann Georg. *Gründliche Anweisung zur Composition*. Leipzig: Breitkopf, 1790.

Ammerer, Gerhard and Rudolph Angermüller (eds.). *Salzburger Mozart Lexikon*. Bad Honnef: K.H. Bock, 2005.

Bach, Carl Philipp Emanuel. *Versuch über die wahre Art das Clavier zu spielen* (1753). Trans. William J. Mitchell as *Essay on the True Art of Playing Keyboard Instruments*. New York: Norton, 1949.

Badura-Skoda, Eva and Paul Badura-Skoda. *Interpreting Mozart: The Performance of His Piano Pieces and Other Compositions*. 2nd edition, New York and London: Routledge, 2008.

Bauman, Thomas. 'Mozart Belmonte'. *Early Music*, 19 (1991), pp. 556–63.

Beicken, Suzanne J. (ed. and trans.). *Treatise on Vocal Performance and Ornamentation by Joseph Adam Hiller* (1780). Cambridge: Cambridge University Press, 2001.

Brown, Clive. *Classical and Romantic Performing Practice, 1750–1900*. Oxford: Oxford University Press, 1999.

Chew, Geoffrey. 'The Public and Private Affairs of Josepha Duschek: A Reinterpretation of Mozart's *Bella mia fiamma, addio* KV 528'. *Early Music*, 40 (2012), pp. 639–57.

Corneilson, Paul. '"aber nach geendigter Oper mit Vergnügen": Mozart's Arias for Mme Duschek'. In Kathryn Libin (ed.), *Mozart in Prague: Essays on Performance, Patronage, Sources, and Reception*. Prague: Czech Academy of Sciences, 2016, pp. 175–200.

'An Intimate Vocal Portrait of Dorothea Wendling: Mozart's Concert Aria K. 295a'. *Mozart-Jahrbuch 2000*, pp. 29–45.

The Autobiography of Ludwig Fischer: Mozart's First Osmin. 2nd edition, Malden, MA: Mozart Society of America, 2016.

'Mozart's Ilia and Elettra: New Perspectives on *Idomeneo*'. In Theodor Göllner and Stephan Hörner (eds.), *Mozarts Idomeneo und die Musik in München zur Zeit Karl Theodors*. Munich: Bayerischen Akademie der Wissenschaften, 2001, pp. 97–113.

Edge, Dexter. 'Mozart's Viennese Orchestras'. *Early Music*, 20/1 (1992), pp. 63–88.

Eisen, Cliff. 'The Primacy of Performance: Text, Act and Continuo in Mozart's Piano Concertos'. In Dorothea Link and Judith Nagley (eds.), *Words About Mozart: Essays in Honour of Stanley Sadie*. Woodbridge: Boydell Press, 2005, pp. 107–19.

Harlow, Martin. 'The Clarinet in Works of Franz Xaver Süssmayr: Anton Stadler and the Mozartian Example'. *Acta Mozartiana*, 57/2 (December 2010), pp. 147–65.

Herttrich, Ernst. 'Eine neue, wichtige Quelle zu Mozarts Streichquintetten KV 515 und 516'. In Paul Mai (ed.), *Im Dienst der Quellen zur Musik: Festschrift Gertraut Haberkamp zum 65. Geburtstag*. Tutzing: Hans Schneider, 2002, pp. 435–45.

Hunter, Mary. '"To Play as if from the Soul of the Composer": The Idea of the Performer in Early Romantic Aesthetics'. *Journal of the American Musicological Society*, 58/2 (2005), pp. 357–98.

Keefe, Simon P. 'Wolfgang Amadeus Mozart the Child Performer-Composer: New Musical-Biographical Perspectives on the Early Years to 1766'. In Gary E. McPherson (ed.), *Musical Prodigies: Interpretations from Psychology, Education, Musicology, and Ethnomusicology*. New York: Oxford University Press, 2016, pp. 550–75.

Klorman, Edward. *Mozart's Music of Friends: Social Interplay in the Chamber Works*. Cambridge: Cambridge University Press, 2016.

Lawson, Colin. *Mozart: Clarinet Concerto*. Cambridge: Cambridge University Press, 1996.

Link, Dorothea (ed.). *Arias for Francesco Benucci, Mozart's First Figaro and Guglielmo*. Middleton, WI: A-R Editions, 2004.

Arias for Nancy Storace, Mozart's First Susanna. Middleton, WI: A-R Editions, 2002.

Arias for Stefano Mandini, Mozart's First Count Almaviva. Middleton, WI: A-R Editions, 2015.

Arias for Vincenzo Calvesi, Mozart's First Ferrando. Middleton, WI: A-R Editions 2011.

Maunder, Richard. 'Viennese String-Instrument Makers, 1700–1800', *Galpin Society Journal,* 52 (1999), pp. 27–51.

'Viennese Wind-Instrument Makers'. *Galpin Society Journal,* 51 (1998), pp. 170–91.

Mozart, Leopold. *Versuch einer gründlichen Violinschule, entworfen und mit 4. Kupfertafeln sammt einer Tabelle versehen* (Augsburg, 1756). Trans. Editha Knocker as *A Treatise on the Fundamental Principles of Violin Playing.* London: Oxford University Press, 1948.

Neumann, Frederick. *Ornamentation and Improvisation in Mozart.* Princeton, NJ: Princeton University Press, 1986.

Pryer, Anthony. 'Mozart's Operatic Audition. The Milan Concert, 12 March 1770: A Reappraisal and Revision'. *Eighteenth-Century Music,* 1 (2004), pp. 265–88.

Quantz, Johann Joachim. *Versuch einer Anweisung die Flöte traversiere zu spielen.* Berlin: Johann Friedrich Voß, 1752. Trans. Edward R. Reilly as *On Playing the Flute.* New York: Schirmer, 1966.

Rice, John A. 'Antonio Baglioni, Mozart First Don Ottavio and Tito, in Italy and Prague'. In Milada Jonášová and Tomislav Volek (eds.), *Böhmische Aspekte des Lebens und des Werkes von W.A. Mozart.* Prague: Akademie der Wissenschaften der Tschechischen Republik, 2011, pp. 295–322.

'Mozart and His Singers: The Case of Maria Marchetti Fantozzi, the First Vitellia'. *Opera Quarterly,* 11 (1995), pp. 31–52.

'Mozart as Soprano'. *Mozart-Jahrbuch 2006,* pp. 345–53.

Mozart on the Stage. Cambridge: Cambridge University Press, 2009.

Riggs, Robert. 'Mozart's Notation of Staccato Articulation: A New Appraisal'. *Journal of Musicology,* 15/2 (1997), pp. 230–77.

Rosenblum, Sandra P. *Performance Practices in Classic Piano Music: Their Principles and Applications.* Indianapolis: Indiana University Press, 1988.

Schmid, Manfred Hermann. 'Mozart, Hasse und Raaff: Die Mannheimer Arie KV 295 "Se al labbro mio non credi"'. *Mozart-Studien,* 14. Tutzing: Hans Schneider, 2005, pp. 101–37.

Todd, R. Larry and Peter Williams (eds.). *Perspectives on Mozart Performance.* Cambridge: Cambridge University Press, 1991.

Toft, Robert. *Bel Canto: A Performer's Guide.* Oxford: Oxford University Press, 2013.

Türk, Daniel Gottlob. *Klavierschule* (1789). Trans. Raymond H. Haggh as *School of Clavier Playing*. Lincoln: University of Nebraska Press, 1982.

Volek, Tomislav. 'Josepha Duschek und Salzburg: Zur Arie "Ah, lo previdi" KV 272 und ihrem Kontext'. *Mozart-Studien*, 14. Tutzing: Hans Scheider, 2005, pp. 85–100.

Woodfield, Ian. *Performing Operas for Mozart: Impresarios, Singers and Troupes*. Cambridge: Cambridge University Press, 2012.

Wignall, Harrison. 'Guglielmo d'Ettore: Mozart's First Mitridate'. *Opera Quarterly*, 10 (1994), pp. 93–112.

Reception and Legacy

[Chapters 28–35]

Abert, Hermann. *W. A. Mozart* (1919–1921). Trans. Stewart Spencer, ed. Cliff Eisen. New Haven, CT and London: Yale University Press, 2007.

Agawu, V. Kofi. *Playing with Signs: A Semiotic Interpretation of Classic Music*, Princeton: Princeton University Press, 1991.

Allanbrook, Wye Jamison. *Rhythmic Gesture in Mozart: 'Le nozze di Figaro' and 'Don Giovanni'*. Chicago: University of Chicago Press, 1983.

Arnold, Ignaz Ferdinand. *Mozarts Geist*. Erfurt: Henningschen Buchhandlung, 1803.

Brendel, Franz *Geschichte der Musik in Italien, Deutschland und Frankreich*. Leipzig: Hinze, 1852.

Burnham, Scott. *Mozart's Grace*. Princeton: Princeton University Press, 2013.

Caplin, William E. *Classical Form: A Theory of Formal Functions for the Instrumental Music of Haydn, Mozart and Beethoven*. New York: Oxford University Press, 1998.

Charlton, David (ed.). *E.T.A Hoffmann's Musical Writings:* Kreisleriana, The Poet and the Composer*, Music Criticism*. Trans. Martyn Clarke. Cambridge: Cambridge University Press, 1989.

Churgin, Bathia. 'Beethoven and Mozart's Requiem: A New Connection'. *Journal of Musicology*, 5 (1987), pp. 457–77.

Daverio, John. 'Mozart in the Nineteenth Century'. In Simon P. Keefe (ed.), *The Cambridge Companion to Mozart*. Cambridge: Cambridge University Press, 2003, pp. 171–84.

Edge, Dexter. 'Mozart's Reception in Vienna, 1787–1791'. In Stanley Sadie (ed.), *Wolfgang Amadè Mozart: Essays on his Life and his Music*. Oxford: Clarendon Press, 1996, pp. 66–117.

Einstein, Alfred. *Mozart: His Character, His Work* (1945). Trans. Arthur Mendel and Nathan Broder. London: Panther Arts, 1971.

Eisen, Cliff. 'The Old and New Mozart Editions'. *Early Music*, 19 (1991), pp. 513–32.

Eisen, Cliff and Christopher Wintle. 'Mozart's C minor Fantasy, K. 475: An Editorial "Problem" and its Analytical and Critical Consequences'. *Journal of the Royal Musical Association*, 124 (1999), pp. 26–52.

Everist, Mark. *Mozart's Ghosts: Haunting the Halls of Musical Culture*. Oxford: Oxford University Press, 2012.

Fellinger, Imogen. 'Brahms's View of Mozart'. In Robert Pascall (ed.), *Brahms: Biographical, Documentary, and Analytical Studies*. Cambridge: Cambridge University Press, 1983, pp. 41–57.

Georgiou, Christina A. 'The Historical Editing of Mozart's Piano Sonatas in the Nineteenth Century: Context, Practice and Implications'. *Mozart-Jahrbuch 2013*, pp. 175–96.

Gjerdingen, Robert. *Music in the Galant Style*. Oxford and New York: Oxford University Press, 2007.

Großpietsch, Christoph. 'Im chronologischen Schlepptau. Köchels Mozart-Verzeichnis von 1862 und die Folgen'. In Thomas Hochradner (ed.), *Werkverzeichnis: Ordnung und Zählung als Faktoren der Rezeptionsgeschichte*. Freiburg: Rombach, 2011, pp. 167–98.

Gruber, Gernot. *Mozart and Posterity*. Trans. R. S. Furness. London: Quartet Books, 1991.

Gutman, Robert W. *Mozart: A Cultural Biography*. New York: Harcourt, 1999.

Jahn, Otto. *Life of Mozart* (1856). Trans. Pauline Townsend. 3 vols. London: Cooper Square Publishers, 1970.

Hepokoski, James and Warren Darcy. *Elements of Sonata Theory: Norms, Types, and Deformations in the Late-Eighteenth-Century Sonata*. New York: Oxford University 2006.

Hildesheimer, Wolfgang. *Mozart* (1977). Trans. Marion Faber. New York: Vintage, 1983.

Hughes, Rosemary (ed.). *A Mozart Pilgrimage Being the Travel Diaries of Vincent & Mary Novello in the Year 1829*. Transcribed and compiled by Nerina Medici di Marignano. London: Novello, 1955.

Hyatt King, Alexander. *Mozart in Retrospect*. 3rd edition, London: Oxford University Press, 1970.

Keefe, Simon P. 'Composing, Performing and Publishing: Mozart's "Haydn" Quartets'. In Keefe (ed.), *Mozart Studies 2*. Cambridge: Cambridge University Press, 2015, pp. 140–67.

Mozart's Requiem: Reception, Work, Completion. Cambridge: Cambridge University Press, 2012.

Kierkegaard, Søren. *Either/Or: A Fragment of Life*. Trans. Alastair Hannay, ed. Victor Eremita. London: Penguin, 1992.

Knepler, Georg. *Wolfgang Amadé Mozart* (1991). Trans. J. Bradford Robinson. Cambridge: Cambridge University Press, 1994.

Köchel, Ludwig von. *Chronologisch-thematisches Verzeichnis sämtlicher Tonwerke Wolfgang Amadé Mozarts.* Ed. Franz Giegling, Alexander Weinmann and Gerd Sievers. 6th edition, Leipzig: Breitkopf und Härtel, 1964.

Küster, Konrad. *Mozart: A Musical Biography.* Trans. Mary Whittall. Oxford: Clarendon Press, 1996.

Leisinger, Ulrich. 'Methoden und Ziele der Digitalen Mozart-Edition'. *Mozart-Jahrbuch 2013*, pp. 43–63.

Lerdahl, Fred and Ray Jackendoff. *A Generative Theory of Tonal Music.* Cambridge, MA: The MIT Press, 1983.

Levi, Erik. *Mozart and the Nazis: How the Third Reich Abused a Cultural Icon.* New Haven, CT: Yale University Press, 2010.

Lockwood, Lewis. 'Beethoven before 1800: The Mozart Legacy'. *Beethoven Forum*, 3 (1994), pp. 39–52.

Mirka, Danuta. *The Oxford Handbook of Topic Theory.* Oxford: Oxford University Press, 2014.

Monelle, Raymond. *The Musical Topic: Hunt, Military and Pastoral.* Bloomington: Indiana University Press, 2006.

Mueller, Adeline. *Mozart and the Mediation of Childhood.* Chicago: University of Chicago Press, forthcoming.

Nettl, Bruno. 'Mozart and the Ethnomusicological Study of Western Culture (an Essay in Four Movements)', *Yearbook for Traditional Music*, 21 (1989), pp. 1–16.

Niemetschek, Franz Xaver. *Lebensbeschreibung des K. K. Kapellmeisters Wolfgang Amadeus Mozart, aus Originalquellen.* Prague: Herrlischen Buchhandlung, 1798. Trans. Helen Mautner as *Life of Mozart.* London: Hyman, 1956.

Nissen, Georg Nikolaus. *Biographie W. A. Mozart's.* Leipzig: Breitkopf & Härtel, 1828.

Oulibicheff, Alexandre (Alexander Ulïbïshev). *Nouvelle Biographie de Mozart.* 3 vols. Moscow: Auguste Semen, 1843.

Ratner, Leonard G. *Classic Music: Expression, Form, and Style.* New York, Schirmer, 1980.

Réti, Rudolf. *The Thematic Process in Music.* New York: Macmillan, 1951.

Rosen, Charles. *Piano Notes: The Hidden World of the Pianist.* London: Penguin, 2002.

Rumph, Stephen. *Mozart and Enlightenment Semiotics.* Berkeley and Los Angeles: University of California Press, 2011.

Saint-Foix, Georges de and Théodore de Wyzewa. *W.-A. Mozart: sa vie musicale and son oeuvre.* 5 vols. Paris: Desclée de Brouwer, 1912–1946.

Schenker, Heinrich. *The Masterwork in Music* (1926). Ed. and trans. William Drabkin. Mineola, NY: Dover Publications, 2014.

Schlichtegroll, Friedrich. 'Johannes Chrysostomos Wolfgang Gottlieb Mozart'. In *Nekrolog aus das Jahr 1791*. Gotha, 1793, pp. 82–112.

Solomon, Maynard. *Mozart: A Life*. New York: HarperCollins, 1995.

Solomon, Maynard. 'The Rochlitz Anecdotes: Issues of Authenticity in Early Mozart Biography'. In Cliff Eisen (ed.), *Mozart Studies*. Oxford: Clarendon Press, 1991, pp. 1–59. Reprinted in Simon P. Keefe (ed.), *Mozart*. Farnham and Burlington, VT: Ashgate Publishing, 2015, pp. 91–149.

Stafford, William. 'The Evolution of Mozartian Biography'. In Simon P. Keefe (ed.), *The Cambridge Companion to Mozart*. Cambridge: Cambridge University Press, 2003, pp. 200–11.

The Mozart Myths: A Critical Reassessment. Stanford, CA: Stanford University Press, 1991.

Usner, Eric Martin. '"The Condition of Mozart": Mozart Year 2006 and the New Vienna'. *Ethnomusicology Forum*, 20/3 (2011), pp. 413–42.

Wates, Roye. *Mozart: An Introduction to the Music, the Man, and the Myths*. Milwaukee, WI: Amadeus Press, 2010.

Woodfield, Ian. *Cabals and Satires: Mozart's Comic Operas in Vienna*. Oxford: Oxford University Press, forthcoming.

Wright, William. 'Liszt and the Mozart Connection'. *Studia Musicologica*, 48 (2007), pp. 299–318.

Index of Mozart's Works by Köchel Number

318

Index of Mozart's Works by Genre

General Index

324

CPSIA information can be obtained
at www.ICGtesting.com
Printed in the USA
LVHW012047191119
637879LV00016B/758